[redacted]

2010 U.S. POCKET STAMP CATALOGUE

EDITOR....James E. Kloetzel
ASSOCIATE EDITOR....William A. Jones
ASSISTANT EDITOR/NEW ISSUES & VALUING....Martin J. Frankevicz
ASSISTANT EDITOR....Charles Snee
VALUING ANALYST....Steven R. Myers
DESIGN MANAGER....Teresa M. Wenrick
GRAPHIC DESIGNER....Jennifer Lenhart
IMAGE COORDINATOR....Beth Brown
ADVERTISING....Angela Nolte
CIRCULATION/PRODUCT PROMOTION MANAGER....Tim Wagner
VICE PRESIDENT/EDITORIAL & PRODUCTION....Steve Collins
PRESIDENT....Bill Fay

Scott Publishing Co.

911 Vandemark Road, Sidney, Ohio 45365-0828

A division of AMOS PRESS INC., publishers of
Scott Stamp Monthly, Linn's Stamp News, Coin World,
and *Coin World's Coin Values*

CONTENTS

COPYRIGHT NOTE

Permission is hereby given for the use of material in this book and covered by copyright if:

(a) The material is used in advertising matter, circulars or price lists for the purpose of offering stamps for sale or purchase at the prices listed therein; and

(b) Such use is incidental to the business of buying and selling stamps and is limited in scope and length, i.e., it does not cover a substantial portion of the total number of stamps issued by any country or of any special category of stamps of any country; and

(c) Such material is not used as part of any catalogue, stamp album or computerized or other system based upon the Scott catalogue numbers, or in any updated valuations of stamps not offered for sale or purchase; and

(d) Such use is for editorial purposes in publications in the form of articles or commentary, except for computer software or the serialization of books in such publications, for which separate written permission is required.

Any use of the material in this book which does not satisfy all the foregoing conditions is forbidden in any form unless permission in each instance is given in writing by the copyright owner.

TRADEMARK NOTICE

The terms SCOTT, SCOTT'S, SCOTT CATALOGUE NUMBERING SYSTEM, SCOTT CATALOGUE NUMBER, SCOTT NUMBER and abbreviations thereof, are trademarks of Scott Publishing Co., used to identify its publications and its copyrighted system for identifying and classifying postage stamps for dealers and collectors. These trademarks are to be used only with the prior consent of Scott Publishing Co.

ISBN: 0-89487-457-4

AN OVERVIEW OF THE WORLD'S MOST POPULAR HOBBY

A fascinating hobby, an engrossing avocation and a universal pastime, stamp collecting is pursued by millions. Young and old, and from all walks of life, stamp collectors are involved in the indoor sport known as "the paper chase."

It was more than 160 years ago that Rowland Hill's far-reaching postal reforms became a reality and the world's first adhesive postage stamp, the Penny Black, was placed on sale at post offices in Great Britain. Not long after, a hobby was born that has continued to grow since.

Although there were only four stamps issued in England from 1840-47, the Penny Black, two types of the 2-penny blue and the 1-penny red, there were people who saved them. One story relates that a woman covered a wall in a room of her home with copies of the Penny Black.

As country after country began to issue postage stamps, the fraternity of stamp collectors flourished. Today, collectors number in the millions, while the number of stamp-issuing entities has exceeded 650.

The hobby of stamp collecting may take many forms. There are those people who collect the stamps of a single country. Others collect a single issue, such as the U.S. Transportation coils. Others specialize in but a single stamp, with all its nuances and variations. Some collectors save one type of postage stamp, such as airmails, commemoratives or other types. Another type of collection would consist only of covers (envelopes) bearing a stamp with a postmark from the first day of that stamp's issue.

Most popular, however, is collecting by country, especially one's own country. This catalogue is designed to aid in forming just such a collection. It lists the postage stamps of the United States and is a simplified edition of information found in Volume I of the *Scott Standard Postage Stamp Catalogue.*

Catalogue Information

The number (1616) in the first column of the example below is the stamp's identifying Scott number. Each stamp issued by the United States has a unique Scott number. Each illustration shows the Scott number beneath. In cases where two or more Scott numbers share a common design, the illustration will show the first Scott number that shows that design. Notes in the text will guide the user to find the correct design of subsequent Scott numbers showing the same design. This will be done by information in the header notes for the stamp or set, or by showing the design type by Scott number in parenthesis after its description (e.g., (1590) following the Scott 1616 listing.) Following in the same line are the denomination of the stamp, its color or other description along with the color of the paper (in italic type) if other than white, and the catalogue value both unused and used.

Scott Number	Denomination	Descrip.	Design, Type	Color	Color of the Stamp Paper	Unused Value	Used Value
1616	9c	Capitol	(1590)	slate grn	gray	.20	.20

Catalogue value

Scott Catalogue value is a retail value; what you could expect to pay for a sound stamp in a grade of Very Fine. The value listed is a reference that reflects recent actual dealer selling prices.

Dealer retail price lists, public auction results, published prices in advertising and individual solicitation of retail prices from dealers, collectors and specialty organizations have been used in establishing the values found in this catalogue.

Use this catalogue as a guide in your own buying and selling. The actual price you pay for a stamp may be higher or lower than the catalogue value because of one or more of the following factors: the grade and condition of the actual stamp; the amount of personal service a dealer offers: increased interest in the country or topic represented by the stamp or set; whether an item is a "loss leader," part of a special sale, or is otherwise being sold for a short period of time at a lower price; or if at a public auction you are able to obtain an item inexpensively because of little interest in the item at that time.

The Scott Catalogue values stamps on the basis of the cost of purchasing them individually. You will find packets, mixtures and collections where the unit cost of the material will be substantially less than the total catalogue value of the component stamps.

Values for pre-1890 unused issues are for stamps with approximately half or more of their original gum. Later issues are assumed to have full original gum.

Unused stamps are valued in never hinged condition beginning with Nos. 772, C19, E17, FA1, J88, O127 and RW1. No. 485 also is valued never hinged.

Grade

A stamp's grade and condition are crucial to its value. Values quoted in this catalogue are for stamps graded at Very Fine, and with no faults. The accompanying illustrations show an example of a Very Fine grade between the grades immediately below and above it: Fine to Very Fine and Extremely Fine.

FINE to VERY FINE stamps may be somewhat off center on one side, or slightly off center on two sides. Imperforate stamps will have two margins at least normal size and the design will not touch the edge. *Early issues may be printed in such a way that the design is naturally very close to the edges.* Used stamps will not have a cancellation that detracts from the design.

VERY FINE stamps may be slightly off center on one side, but the design will be well clear of the edge. The stamp will present a nice, balanced appearance. Imperforate stamps will have three normal-sized margins. *However, early perforated issues may be printed in such a way that the perforations may touch the design on one or more sides.* Used stamps will have light or otherwise neat cancellations. This is the grade used to establish Scott Catalgoue values.

EXTREMELY FINE stamps are close to being perfectly centered. Imperforate stamps will have even margins that are larger than normal. Even the earliest perforated issues will have perforations clear of the design on all sides.

1898 TRANS-MISSISSIPPIS

1908-20 WASHINGTON-FRANKLINS

Fine-Very Fine →

SCOTT CATALOGUES VALUE STAMPS IN THIS GRADE

Very Fine →

Extremely Fine →

Scott Publishing Co. recognizes that there is no formal, enforced grading scheme for postage stamps, and that the final price you pay for a stamp or obtain for a stamp you are selling will be determined by individual agreement at the time of the transaction.

Condition

The definitions given with the illustrations describe *grade*, which is centering and, for used stamps, cancellation. *Condition* refers to the soundness of the stamp; that is, faults, repairs and other factors influencing price.

Copies of a stamp that are of a lesser grade or condition trade at lower prices. Those of exceptional quality often command higher than catalogue prices.

Factors that can increase the value of a stamp include exceptionally wide margins, particularly fresh color, the presence of selvage (sheet margin), and plate or die varieties. Unusual cancels on used stamps (particularly those of the 19th century) can greatly enhance their value as well.

Factors other than faults that decrease the value of a stamp include loss of original gum or regumming, hinge remnants, foreign objects adhering to gum, natural inclusions, straight edges, or notations applied by collectors or dealers.

Faults include a missing piece, tear, clipped perforation, pin or other hole, surface scuff, thin spot, crease, toning, oxidation or other form of color changeling, short or pulled perforation, stains or such man-made changes as reperforations or the chemical removal or lightening of a cancellation.

Forming a collection

Methods of collecting stamps are many and varied. A person may begin by attempting to gather a single specimen of every face-different stamp issued by a country. An extension of that approach is to include the different types of each stamp, such as perforation varieties, watermark varieties, different printings and color changes. The stamps may be collected on cover (envelope) complete with postal markings, thus showing postal rates, types of cancellations and other postal information.

Collections also may be limited to types of stamps. The stamps issued by most countries are divided into such categories as regular postage (made up of definitives and commemoratives), airmail stamps, special delivery stamps, postage due stamps and others. Any of those groups may provide the basis for a good collection.

Definitive stamps are those regular issues used on most mail sent out on a daily basis. They are normally issued in extended sets, sometimes over a period of years. The sets feature a rising series of face values that allows a mailer to meet any current postal rate. Definitive stamps may be printed in huge quantities and are often kept in service by the Postal Service for long periods of time.

Commemorative stamps meet another need. They are primarily issued to celebrate an important event, honor a famous person or promote a special project or cause. Such stamps are issued on a limited basis for a limited time. They are usually more colorful and are often of a larger size than definitives.

Although few airmail stamps are currently issued by the United States, they continue to remain very popular among collectors. Just as with regular issues, airmail stamps are subject to several types of collecting. In addition to amassing the actual stamps, airmail enthusiasts pursue first-flight covers, airport dedication covers and even crash covers.

Not as popular, but still collected as units, are special delivery and postage due stamps. Special delivery stamps ensured speedier delivery of a letter once it reached its destination post office through normal postal means. Postage due stamps were used when a letter or parcel did not carry enough postage to pay for its delivery, subjecting the recipient to a fee to make up the difference. The United States no longer issues postage due stamps.

The resurrection in 1983 of Official Mail stamps-those used only by departments and offices of the federal government-has also brought about a resurgence of interest in them by stamp collectors. Originally issued between 1873 and 1911, Official Mail stamps were obsolete until recently. To be legally used, they must be on cards, envelopes or parcels that bear the return address of a federal office or facility.

"Topical" collecting is becoming more and more popular. Here the paramount attraction to the collector is the subject depicted on the stamp. The topics or themes from which to choose are virtually unlimited, other than by your own imagination. Animals, flowers, music, ships, birds and famous people on stamps make interesting collections. The degree of specializations is limitless, leading to such topics as graduates of a specific college or university, types of aircraft or the work of a specific artist.

There are several ways to obtain topical information, one of which is through the "By Topic" section of the *Scott Stamp Monthly*. "By Topic" is a regular feature of the magazine that divides the stamps of the world into more than 100 topical areas.

The album

To be displayed at their best, stamps should be properly housed. A quality album not only achieves this, but gives protection from dirt, loss and damage. When choosing an album, consider these three points: Is it within your means, does it meet your special interests and is it the best you can afford?

The Scott *Pony Express* and *Minuteman* albums are ideal companions to this Catalogue. Scott also publishes the National Album series for United States stamps, for a more complete collection.

Looseleaf albums are recommended for all collectors beyond the novice level. Not only do looseleaf albums allow for expansion of a collection, but the pages may be removed for mounting stamps as well as for display. A special advantage of a looseleaf album is that in many cases it may be kept current with supplements published annually on matching pages. All Scott albums noted are looseleaf and are supplemented annually.

Mounts and hinges

Mounts and hinges specially manufactured for collectors are used to affix stamps to album pages. Most stamp mounts are pre-gummed, clear plastic containers that hold a stamp safely and may be affixed to an album page with minimum effort. They are available in sizes to fit any stamp, block or even complete envelopes. Mounts are particularly important with unused stamps when there is a desire to not disturb the gum.

Although the mount is important, so is the venerable hinge. Innumerable stamps have been ruined beyond redemption by being glued to an album page. Hinges are inexpensive and effective. Use only peelable hinges. These may be removed from a stamp or album page without leaving an unsightly mark or causing damage to either.

Hinges are perfect for less-expensive stamps, used stamps and stamps that previously have been hinged. The use of stamp hinges is simple. Merely fold back, adhesive side out, about a quarter of the hinge (if it is not pre-folded). Lightly moisten the shorter side and affix it near the top of the back of the stamp. Then, holding the stamp with a pair of tongs, moisten the longer side of the hinge and place it (with stamp attached) in its proper place on the album page.

Stamp tongs

As previously noted, stamp tongs are a simple but important accessory and should always be used when handling a stamp. Fingers can easily damage or soil a stamp. Tongs cost little and will quickly pay for themselves. They come in a variety of styles. Beginners should start with tongs having a blunt or rounded tip. Those with sharp ends may inadvertently cause damage to a stamp. With just a little practice you will find tongs easier to work with than using your fingers...and your stamps will be better for it.

Magnifying glass

A good magnifying glass for scrutinizing stamps in detail is another useful philatelic tool. It allows you to see variations in stamps that may otherwise be invisible to the naked eye. Also, a magnifying glass makes minute parts of a stamp design large enough to see well. Your first glass should be a least 5- to 10-power magnification, with edge-to-edge clarity. Stronger magnifications are available and may also be useful.

Perforation gauge and watermark detector

Although many stamps appear to be alike, they are not. Even though the design may be the same and the color identical, there are at least two other areas where differences occur, and where specialized devices are needed for such identification. These are perforation measurement and watermark detection. A ruler that measures in millimeters is also useful.

The perforation gauge, printed on plastic, cardboard or metal, contains a graded scale that enables you to measure the number of perforation "teeth" in two centimeters. To determine the perforation measurement, place the stamp on the gauge and move the former along the scale until the points on one entry of the scale align perfectly with the teeth of the stamp's perforations. A stamp may have different perforations horizontally and vertically.

Watermarks are a bit more difficult to detect. They are letters or designs impressed into the paper at the time of manufacture. A watermark may occasionally be seen by holding a stamp up to the light, but a watermark detector is often necessary. The simplest of the many types of detectors available consists of a small black tray (glass or hard plastic). The stamp is placed face down in the tray and watermark detection fluid is poured over it. If there is a watermark, or a part of one, it should become visible when the stamp becomes soaked with the fluid.

There are a number of other liquids that over the years have been recommended for use to detect watermarks. The currently available fluids made specifically for that purpose are the safest for the stamp and the collector. We do not recommend anything other than such watermark detection fluids for that use.

Where to get accessories

Your local stamp dealer probably stocks a variety of stamp albums and accessories. Check the Yellow Pages under "Stamps for Collectors." Scott Publishing Co. also has a variety of albums and accessories available for sale. Call 1-800-572-6885 for a Scott Product Guide.

Benjamin Franklin
1
3

George Washington
2
4

Reproductions. The letters R.W.H. & E. at the bottom of each stamp are less distinct on the reproductions than on the originals.

5c. On the originals the left side of the white shift frill touches the oval on a level with the top of the "F" of "Five." On the reproductions it touches the oval about on a level with the top of the figure "5."

10c. On the reproductions, line of coat at left points to right tip of "X" and line of coat at right points to center of "S" of CENTS. On the originals, line of coat points to "T" of TEN and between "T" and "S" of CENTS. On the reproductions the eyes have a sleepy look, the line of the mouth is straighter, and in the curl of hair near the left cheek is a strong black dot, while the originals have only a faint one.

Franklin
5

5

ONE CENT.

Type I. Has complete curved lines outside the labels with "U.S. Postage" and "One Cent." The scrolls below the lower label are turned under, forming little balls. The ornaments at top are substantially complete.

Type Ib. Same as I but balls below the bottom label are not so clear. The plume-like scrolls at bottom are not complete.

6

Type Ia. Same as I at bottom but top ornaments and outer line at top are partly cut away.

Type Ic. Same as Ia, but bottom right plume and ball ornament incomplete. Bottom left plume complete or nearly complete.

7

Type II. Same as type I at top, but the little balls of the bottom scrolls and the bottoms of the lower plume ornaments are missing. The side ornaments are substantially complete.

8

Type III. The top and bottom curved lines outside the labels are broken in the middle. The side ornaments are complete.

Type IIIa. Similar to type III with the outer line broken at top or bottom but not both.

9

Type IV. Similar to type II, but with the curved lines outside the labels recut at top or bottom or both.

Prices for types I and III are for stamps showing the marked characteristics plainly. Copies of type I showing the balls indistinctly and of type III with the lines only slightly broken, sell for much lower prices.

UNITED STATES

Scott No.	Description	Unused Value	Used Value
1847, Imperf.			
1	5c Benjamin Franklin, red brown	6,750.	550.00
	Pen cancel		300.00
a.	5c dark brown	8,750.	775.00
b.	5c orange brown	10,000.	1,100.
c.	5c red orange	*25,000.*	*9,500.*
d.	5c brown orange	—	1,300.
e.	Double impression		—
2	10c George Washington, black	*35,000.*	1,250.
	Pen cancel		750.00
a.	Diagonal half used as 5c on cover		*13,000.*
b.	Vert. half used as 5c on cover		*35,000.*
c.	Horiz. half used as 5c on cover		—
1875, Reproductions, Bluish Paper Without Gum, Imperf.			
3	5c Franklin (1), red brown	750.00	
4	10c Washington (2), black	900.00	
1851-57, Imperf.			
5	1c Franklin, blue, type I	*225,000.*	*85,000.*
5A	1c Franklin (5), blue, type Ib	*32,500.*	*10,000.*
6	1c Franklin (5), blue, type Ia	*45,000.*	*13,000.*
b.	Type Ic	*7,000.*	*3,000.*
7	1c Franklin (5), blue, type II	1,100.	170.00
8	1c Franklin (5), blue, type III	*25,000.*	3,500.
8A	1c Franklin (5), blue, type IIIa	6,000.	1,200.
9	1c Franklin (5), blue, IV	800.00	130.00
a.	Printed on both sides, reverse inverted		—
10	3c Washington, orange brown, type I.	3,750.	200.00
10A	3c Washington, orange brown, type II.	3,500.	150.00
b.	Printed on both sides		*20,000.*
11	3c Washington (10), dull red, type I...	275.00	15.00
11A	3c Washington (10A), dull red, type II	275.00	15.00
c.	Vert. half used as 1c on cover		*5,000.*

Washington
10

Thomas Jefferson
12

Type I

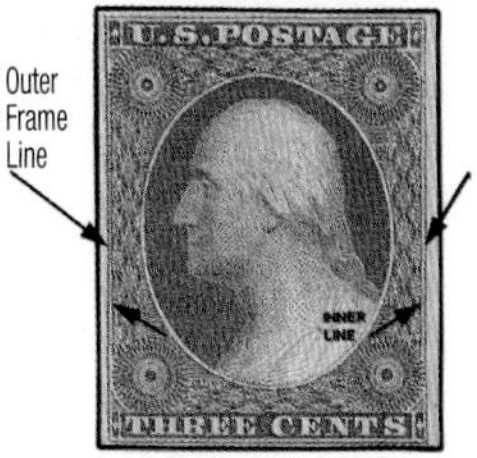

Type II

Top, the 1851 3¢ stamp with outer frame lines only on all four sides, type I. Bottom, the 3¢ stamp with outer frame lines and recut inner lines, type II.

12

FIVE CENTS.

Type I. There are projections on all four sides.

13

13

TEN CENTS.

Type I. The "shells" at the lower corners are practically complete. The outer line below the label is very nearly complete. The outer lines are broken above the middle of the top label and the "X" in each upper corner.

14

Type II. The design is complete at the top. The outer line at the bottom is broken in the middle. The shells are partly cut away.

15

Type III. The outer lines are broken above the top label and the "X" numerals. The outer line at the bottom and the shells are partly cut away, as in Type II.

16

Type IV. The outer lines have been recut at top or bottom or both.

Types I, II, III, and IV have complete ornaments at the sides of the stamps and three pearls at each outer edge of the bottom panel.

17

Franklin
24

ONE CENT.
Type V. Similar to type III of 1851-56 but with side ornaments partly cut away.

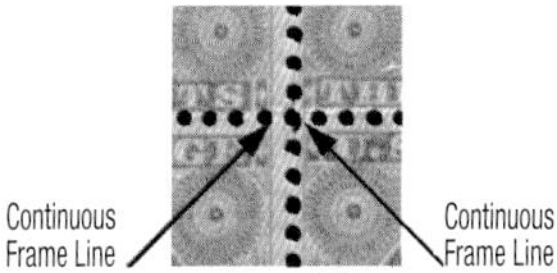

Type III

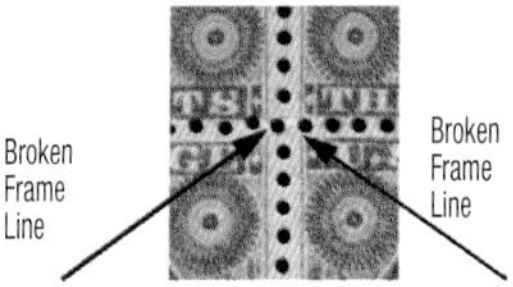

Type IV

THREE CENTS.
Types III & IV. Top, the perforated 1857 3¢ stamp with top and bottom frame lines removed and with continuous side frame lines (type III, No. 26). Bottom, the perforated 3¢ stamp with side frame lines broken between stamps (type IV, No. 26A).

30

30

FIVE CENTS.
Type II. The projections at top and bottom are partly cut away.

35
(Two typical examples).

TEN CENTS.
Type V. The side ornaments are slightly cut away. Usually only one pearl remains at each end of the lower label but some copies show two or three pearls at the right side. At the bottom the outer line is complete and the shells nearly so. The outer lines at top are complete except over the right "X."

TWELVE CENTS.
Plate I. Outer frame lines complete.
Plate III. Outer frame lines noticeably uneven or broken, sometimes partly missing.

37

38

39

63

63

1c. A dash appears under the tip of the ornament at right of the numeral in upper left corner.

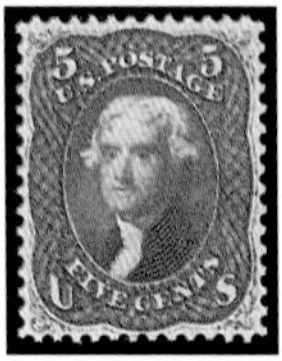

67

67

5c. A leaflet appears on the foliated ornaments at each corner.

64

64

3c. Ornaments at corners end in a small ball.

68

62B

68

10c. A heavy curved line has been cut below the stars and an outer line added to the ornaments above them.

HOW TO USE THIS BOOK

In cases where two or more Scott numbers share a common design, the illustration shows the first Scott number that bears that design. Subsequent Scott numbers showing the same design will have the first Scott number in parentheses following the description to guide the user to the correct design.

Scott No.	Description	Unused Value	Used Value	/ / / / / /
d.	Diagonal half used as 1c on cover		*5,000.*	☐☐☐☐☐
e.	Double impression		*5,000.*	☐☐☐☐☐
12	5c Thomas Jefferson, red brown, type I	*30,000.*	825.00	☐☐☐☐☐
13	10c Washington, green, type I	*18,000.*	950.00	☐☐☐☐☐
14	10c Washington (13), green, type II	5,000.	200.00	☐☐☐☐☐
15	10c Washington (13), green, type III	5,000.	200.00	☐☐☐☐☐
16	10c Washington (13), green, type IV	*35,000.*	1,700.	☐☐☐☐☐
17	12c Washington, black	6,250.	300.00	☐☐☐☐☐
a.	Diagonal half used as 6c on cover		*2,750.*	☐☐☐☐☐
b.	Vert. half used as 6c on cover		*8,500.*	☐☐☐☐☐
c.	Printed on both sides		*30,000.*	☐☐☐☐☐
1857-61, Perf. 15½				
18	1c Franklin (5), blue, type I	2,250.	700.00	☐☐☐☐☐
19	1c Franklin (5), blue, type Ia	*40,000.*	*11,500.*	☐☐☐☐☐
b.	Type Ic	*4,500.*	*2,250.*	☐☐☐☐☐
20	1c Franklin (5), blue, type II	1,100.	300.00	☐☐☐☐☐
21	1c Franklin (5), blue, type III	*17,500.*	2,750.	☐☐☐☐☐
22	1c Franklin (5), blue, type IIIa	2,600.	550.00	☐☐☐☐☐
b.	Horiz. pair, imperf. btwn.		*5,000.*	☐☐☐☐☐
23	1c Franklin (5), blue, type IV	10,000.	950.00	☐☐☐☐☐
24	1c Franklin (5), blue, type V	150.00	45.00	☐☐☐☐☐
b.	Laid paper		2,500.	☐☐☐☐☐
25	3c Washington (10), rose, type I	2,750.	125.00	☐☐☐☐☐
25A	3c Washington (10A), rose, type II	5,250.	550.00	☐☐☐☐☐
b.	Vert. pair, imperf. horiz.		*10,000.*	☐☐☐☐☐
26	3c Washington, dull red, type III	65.00	9.00	☐☐☐☐☐
b.	Horiz. pair, imperf. vert., type II	*4,000.*	—	☐☐☐☐☐
c.	Vert. pair, imperf. horiz., type II		*13,000.*	☐☐☐☐☐
d.	Horiz. pair, imperf. btwn., type II		—	☐☐☐☐☐
e.	Double impression, type II		*2,500.*	☐☐☐☐☐
26A	3c Washington, dull red, type IV	550.00	125.00	☐☐☐☐☐
f.	As "a," horiz. strip of 3, imperf. vert., on cover		*14,500.*	☐☐☐☐☐
27	5c Jefferson (12), brick red, type I	*80,000.*	1,800.	☐☐☐☐☐
28	5c Jefferson (12), red brown, type I	*60,000.*	1,300.	☐☐☐☐☐
b.	bright red brown	*70,000.*	2,000.	☐☐☐☐☐
28A	5c Jefferson (12), Indian red, type I	*175,000.*	3,750.	☐☐☐☐☐
29	5c Jefferson (12), brown, type I	5,000.	425.00	☐☐☐☐☐
30	5c Jefferson, orange brown, type II	1,350.	1,400.	☐☐☐☐☐
30A	5c Jefferson (30), brown, type II	2,200.	300.00	☐☐☐☐☐
b.	Printed on both sides		*55,000.*	☐☐☐☐☐
31	10c Washington (13), green, type I	*30,000.*	1,350.	☐☐☐☐☐
32	10c green, type II	6,250.	275.00	☐☐☐☐☐
33	10c green, type III	6,250.	275.00	☐☐☐☐☐

Scott No.	Description	Unused Value	Used Value
34	10c green, type IV	*50,000.*	2,500.
35	10c green, type V	250.00	65.00
36	12c black, plate I	1,900.	375.00
a.	Diagonal half used as 6c on cover (I)		*17,500.*
c.	Horiz. pair, imperf. between (I)		*12,500.*
36B	12c black, plate III	825.00	350.00
37	24c gray lilac	1,600.	400.00
a.	24c gray	1,600.	400.00
38	30c orange	2,400.	500.00
39	90c blue	3,500.	*10,000.*
1875, Reprints, Without Gum, Perf. 12			
40	1c bright blue (5)	*600.00*	
41	3c scarlet (10)	*3,000.*	
42	5c orange brown (30)	*1,300.*	
43	10c blue green (13)	*2,750.*	
44	12c greenish black (17)	*3,000.*	
45	24c black violet (37)	*3,000.*	
46	30c yellow orange (38)	*3,000.*	
47	90c deep blue (39)	*4,500.*	
1861			
62B	10c Washington, dark green (68)	*8,000.*	1,600.
1861-62			
63	1c blue	325.00	50.00
a.	1c ultramarine	*2,500.*	650.00
b.	1c dark blue	800.00	400.00
c.	Laid paper	*10,000.*	*7,500.*
d.	Vert. pair, imperf. horiz.		—
e.	Printed on both sides	—	*65,000.*
64	3c pink	*14,000.*	1,000.
a.	3c pigeon blood pink	*50,000.*	*5,000.*
b.	3c rose pink	600.00	160.00
65	3c rose	125.00	3.00
b.	Laid paper	—	750.00
d.	Vert. pair, imperf. horiz.	*15,000.*	*1,500.*
e.	Printed on both sides	*40,000.*	*5,000.*
f.	Double impression		*7,500.*
67	5c buff	*27,500.*	1,200.
a.	5c brown yellow	*30,000.*	1,300.
b.	5c olive yellow	—	3,500.
68	10c Washington, yellow green	1,200.	62.50
a.	10c dark green	1,450.	85.00
b.	Vert. pair, imperf. horiz.		*3,500.*
69	12c Washington, black	2,000.	120.00
70	24c Washington, red lilac	3,000.	300.00
a.	24c brown lilac	3,250.	300.00
b.	24c steel blue	*16,500.*	900.00
c.	24c violet, thin paper	*35,000.*	2,200.

Scott No.	Description	Unused Value	Used Value	/ / / / / /
d.	24c pale gray violet, thin paper	25,000.	2,400.	
71	30c Franklin, orange	2,600.	200.00	
a.	Printed on both sides		—	
72	90c Washington, blue	3,250.	600.00	
a.	90c pale blue	3,250.	650.00	
b.	90c dark blue	4,000.	800.00	
1861-66				
73	2c Andrew Jackson, black	375.00	70.00	
a.	Diagonal half used as 1c as part of 3c rate on cover.		1,500.	
b.	Diagonal half used alone as 1c on cover		*3,000.*	
c.	Horiz. half used as 1c as part of 3c rate on cover		*3,500.*	
d.	Vert. half used as 1c as part of 3c rate on cover		2,000.	
e.	Vert. half used alone as 1c on cover		4,000.	
f.	Printed on both sides		*18,500.*	
g.	Laid paper	—	*12,500.*	
75	5c Jefferson (67), red brown	5,750.	600.00	
76	5c Jefferson (67), brown	1,600.	150.00	
a.	5c dark brown	2,250.	350.00	
b.	Laid paper		—	
77	15c Abraham Lincoln, black	4,500.	225.00	
78	24c Washington (70), lilac	2,750.	350.00	
a.	24c grayish lilac	2,900.	300.00	
b.	24c gray	2,900.	300.00	
c.	24c blackish violet	*100,000.*	*17,500.*	
d.	Printed on both sides		*50,000.*	
1867, Perf. 12, Grill With Points Up				
A. Grill Covering The Entire Stamp				
79	3c Washington (64), rose	8,500.	1,750.	
b.	Printed on both sides		—	
80	5c Jefferson (67), brown		*250,000.*	
a.	5c dark brown		*250,000.*	
81	30c Franklin (71), orange		*200,000.*	
B. Grill About 18 x 15mm (22 by 18 points)				
82	3c Washington (64), rose		*1,000,000.*	
Grill With Points Down				
C. Grill About 13 x 16mm (16 to 17 by 18 to 21 points)				
83	3c Washington (64), rose	6,250.	1,200.	
D. Grill About 12 x 14mm (15 by 17 to 18 points)				
84	2c Jackson (73)	*16,000.*	4,500.	
85	3c Washington (64), rose	6,500.	1,250.	
Z. Grill About 11 x 14mm (13 to 14 by 17 to 18 points)				
85A	1c Franklin (63), blue		*3,000,000.*	
85B	2c Jackson (73)	17,500.	1,500.	
85C	3c Washington (64), rose	*25,000.*	3,750.	

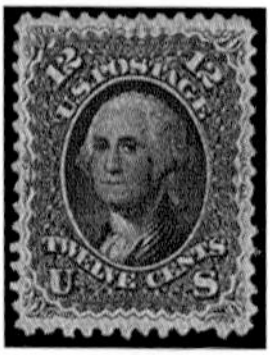

69

12c. Ovals and scrolls have been added to the corners.

70

71

72

Grill

72

90c. Parallel lines form an angle above the ribbon with "U.S. Postage;" between these lines a row of dashes has been added and a point of color to the apex of the lower pair.

73

77

112

113

114

115

116

117

118

120

121

122

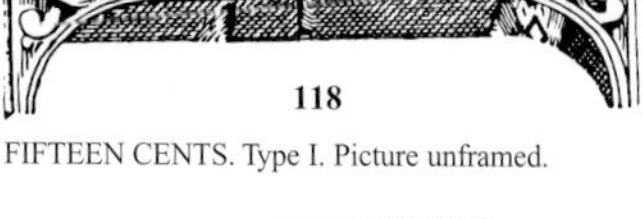

118

FIFTEEN CENTS. Type I. Picture unframed.

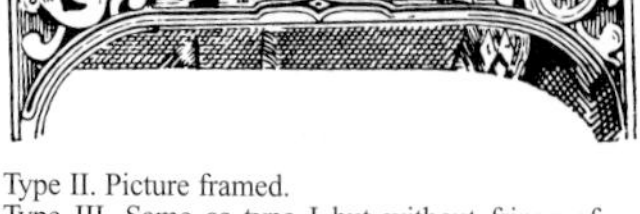

Type II. Picture framed.
Type III. Same as type I but without fringe of brown shading lines around central vignette.

Scott No.	Description	Unused Value	Used Value	/ / / / / /
85D	10c Washington (68), green		*650,000.*	
85E	12c Washington (69)	*17,500.*	2,500.	
85F	15c Lincoln (77)		*2,000,000.*	
E. Grill About 11 x 13mm (14 by 15 to 17 points)				
86	1c Franklin (63), blue	3,500.	575.00	
a.	1c dull blue	3,500.	550.00	
87	2c Jackson (73)	1,750.	225.00	
a.	Half used as 1c on cover, diagonal or vert.		*2,000.*	
88	3c Washington (64), rose	1,000.	30.00	
a.	3c lake red	1,250.	60.00	
89	10c Washington (68), green	5,500.	350.00	
90	12c Washington (69)	5,050.	425.00	
91	15c Lincoln (77)	13,500.	750.00	
F. Grill About 9 x 13mm (11 to 12 by 15 to 17 points)				
92	1c Franklin (63), blue	3,250.	575.00	
a.	1c pale blue	2,275.	525.00	
93	2c Jackson (73)	500.00	60.00	
a.	Vert. half used as 1c as part of 3c rate on cover		*1,250.*	
b.	Diagonal half used as 1c as part of 3c rate on cover		*1,250.*	
c.	Horiz. half used alone as 1c on cover		*2,500.*	
d.	Diagonal half used alone as 1c on cover		*2,500.*	
94	3c Washington (64), red	375.00	10.00	
a.	3c rose	375.00	10.00	
c.	Vert. pair, imperf. horiz	*15,000.*		
d.	Printed on both sides	*9,000.*		
95	5c Jefferson (67), brown	3,750.	1,000.	
a.	5c dark brown	4,750.	1,400.	
96	10c Washington (68), yellow green	3,000.	290.00	
a.	10c dark green	3,500.	350.00	
97	12c Washington (69)	3,250.	325.00	
98	15c Lincoln (77)	4,500.	400.00	
99	24c Washington (70), gray lilac	9,0000.	1,500.	
100	30c Franklin (71), orange	8,500.	1,000.	
101	90c Washington (72), blue	14,500.	2,400.	
1875, Reprints, Without Grill, White Crackly Gum, Hard White Paper, Perf. 12				
102	1c Franklin (63), blue	*900.00*	*1,250.*	
103	2c Jackson (73)	*4,750.*	*10,000.*	
104	3c Washington (64), brown red	*4,750.*	*15,000.*	
105	5c Jefferson (67), brown	*3,250.*	*7,500.*	
106	10c Washington (68), green	*4,000.*	*25,000.*	
107	12c Washington (69)	*4,750.*	*12,500.*	
108	15c Lincoln (77)	*5,250.*	*19,000.*	
109	24c Washington (70), deep violet	*6,500.*	*19,000.*	

134

138

135

139

136

140

137

141

Scott No.	Description	Unused Value	Used Value	/ / / / / /
110	30c Franklin (71), brownish orange	*22,500.*	*17,500.*	☐☐☐☐☐
111	90c Washington (72), blue	*7,250.*	*225,000.*	☐☐☐☐☐
1869, Perf. 12				
G. Grill Measuring 9½ x 9mm				
112	1c Franklin, buff	750.00	175.00	☐☐☐☐☐
b.	Without grill	*20,000.*		☐☐☐☐☐
113	2c Pony Express, brown	700.00	100.00	☐☐☐☐☐
b.	Without grill	*7,500.*		☐☐☐☐☐
c.	Half used as 1c on cover, diagonal, vert. or horiz.		*6,000.*	☐☐☐☐☐
d.	Printed on both sides		*9,000.*	☐☐☐☐☐
114	3c Locomotive, ultramarine	275.00	20.00	☐☐☐☐☐
a.	Without grill	*12,500.*		☐☐☐☐☐
b.	Vert. one third used as 1c on cover		—	☐☐☐☐☐
c.	Vert. two thirds used as 2c on cover		*5,000.*	☐☐☐☐☐
d.	Double impression		*11,000.*	☐☐☐☐☐
e.	Printed on both sides		*55,000.*	☐☐☐☐☐
115	6c Washington, ultramarine	2,750.	250.00	☐☐☐☐☐
b.	Vert. half used as 3c on cover		*50,000.*	☐☐☐☐☐
116	10c Shield & Eagle, yellow	2,250.	150.00	☐☐☐☐☐
117	12c Ship, green	2,250.	160.00	☐☐☐☐☐
118	15c Landing of Columbus, brown & blue, Type I	10,000.	750.00	☐☐☐☐☐
a.	Without grill	*13,000.*		☐☐☐☐☐
119	15c Landing of Columbus (118), type II	3,500.	275.00	☐☐☐☐☐
b.	Center inverted	*1,250,000.*	*20,000.*	☐☐☐☐☐
c.	Center double, one inverted		*80,000.*	☐☐☐☐☐
120	24c Declaration of Independence, grn & vio	9,000.	775.00	☐☐☐☐☐
a.	Without grill	*15,000.*		☐☐☐☐☐
b.	Center inverted	*750,000.*	*32,500.*	☐☐☐☐☐
121	30c Shield, Eagle & Flags, blue & car .	7,000.	550.00	☐☐☐☐☐
a.	Without grill	*12,000.*		☐☐☐☐☐
b.	Flags inverted	*1,000,000.*	*110,000.*	☐☐☐☐☐
122	90c Lincoln, carmine & black	13,000.	2,500.	☐☐☐☐☐
a.	Without grill	*25,000.*		☐☐☐☐☐
1875, Re-issues, Without Grill, Hard White Paper				
123	1c Franklin (112), buff	600.00	400.00	☐☐☐☐☐
124	2c Pony Express (113)	700.00	875.00	☐☐☐☐☐
125	3c Locomotive (114), blue	5,500.	*27,500.*	☐☐☐☐☐
126	6c Washington (115), blue	2,000.	*2,750.*	☐☐☐☐☐
127	10c Shield & Eagle (116)	2,000.	2,000.	☐☐☐☐☐
128	12c Ship (117)	2,750.	3,250.	☐☐☐☐☐
129	15c Landing of Columbus (118), type III	1,650.	1,300.	☐☐☐☐☐
a.	Imperf. horiz., single	*6,250.*	*7,000.*	☐☐☐☐☐
130	24c Declaration of Independence (120)	2,500.	1,750.	☐☐☐☐☐
131	30c Shield, Eagle & Flags (121)	3,000.	3,000.	☐☐☐☐☐
132	90c Lincoln (122), carmine and black .	4,500.	*6,500.*	☐☐☐☐☐

156

1c. In pearl at left of numeral "1" is a small crescent.

157

2c. Under the scroll at the left of "U.S." there is a small diagonal line. This mark seldom shows clearly. The stamp, No. 157, can be distinguished by its color.

158

3c. The under part of the upper tail of the left ribbon is heavily shaded.

159

6c. The first four vertical lines of the shading in the lower part of the left ribbon have been strengthened.

160

7c. Two small semi-circles are drawn around the ends of the lines which outline the ball in the lower right hand corner.

161

10c. There is a small semi-circle in the scroll at the right end of the upper label.

142

143

144

Scott No.	Description	Unused Value	Used Value	/ / / / / /
1880, Soft Porous Paper				
133	1c Franklin (112), buff, with gum	350.00	*400.00*	
a.	1c brown orange, without gum	225.00	*350.00*	
1870-71, Perf. 12, With Grill				
134	1c Franklin, ultramarine	2,250.	210.00	
135	1c Jackson, red brown	1,100.	90.00	
a.	Diagonal half used as 1c on cover.		—	
b.	Vert. half used as 1c on cover		—	
136	3c Washington, green	675.00	32.50	
137	6c Lincoln, carmine	5,250.	575.00	
a.	Pair, one without grill		—	
138	7c Edwin M. Stanton, vermilion	4,500.	575.00	
139	10c Jefferson, brown	7,000.	850.00	
140	12c Henry Clay, dull violet	*27,500.*	3,750.	
141	15c Daniel Webster, orange	8,000.	1,500.	
142	24c Gen. Winfield Scott, purple	—	*7,500.*	
143	30c Alexander Hamilton, black	20,000.	4,000.	
144	90c Commodore O. H. Perry, carmine.	25,000.	2,750.	
1870-71, Perf. 12, Without Grill				
145	1c Franklin (134), ultramarine	750.00	25.00	
146	2c Jackson (135), red brown	350.00	20.00	
a.	Diagonal half used as 1c on cover.		*700.00*	
b.	Vert. half used as 1c on cover		*800.00*	
c.	Horiz. half used as 1c on cover		*800.00*	
d.	Double impression	9,000.		
147	3c Washington (136), green	275.00	2.00	
a.	Printed on both sides		*15,000.*	
b.	Double impression		*40,000.*	
148	6c Lincoln (137), carmine	1,100.	37.50	
a.	Vert. half used as 3c on cover		*3,500*	
b.	Double impression		*1,500*	
149	7c Stanton (138), vermilion	1,100.	100.00	
150	10c Jefferson (139), brown	2,000.	35.00	
151	12c Clay (140), dull violet	2,750.	220.00	
152	15c Webster (141), bright orange	3,000.	220.00	
a.	Double impression		*6,000.*	
153	24c Scott (142), purple	2,000.	230.00	
154	30c Hamilton (143), black	7,500.	300.00	
155	90c Perry (144), carmine	5,500.	350.00	
1873, Perf. 12				
156	1c Franklin (134), ultramarine	275.00	6.00	
e.	With grill	*2,000.*		
f.	Imperf., pair	—	*1,500.*	
157	2c Jackson (135), brown	400.00	25.00	
c.	With grill	*1,850.*	*750.00*	
d.	Double impression	—	5,000.	
e.	Vert. half used as 1c on cover		—	
158	3c Washington (136), green	130.00	1.00	

173

12c. The balls of the figure "2" are crescent shaped.

174

15c. In the lower part of the triangle in the upper left corner two lines have been made heavier forming a "V". This mark can be found on some of the Continental and American (1879) printings, but not all stamps show it.

Secret marks were added to the dies of the 24c, 30c and 90c but new plates were not made from them. The various printings of these stamps can be distinguished only by the shades and paper.

179

205

206

1c. The vertical lines in the upper part of the stamp have been so deepened that the background often appears to be solid. Lines of shading have been added to the upper arabesques.

207

3c. The shading at the sides of the central oval appears only about one-half the previous width. A short horizontal dash has been cut about 1 mm below the "TS" of "CENTS."

208

6c. On the original stamps four vertical lines can be counted from the edge of the panel to the outside of the stamp. On the re-engraved stamps there are but three lines in the same place.

209

10c. On the original stamps there are five vertical lines between the left side of the oval and the edge of the shield. There are only four lines on the re-engraved stamps. In the lower part of the latter, also, the horizontal lines of the background have been strengthened.

210

211

212

Scott No.	Description	Unused Value	Used Value	/ / / / / /
e.	With grill	*500.00*		
h.	Horiz. pair, imperf. vert.		—	
i.	Horiz. pair, imperf. btwn.		*1,300.*	
j.	Double impression		*10,000.*	
k.	Printed on both sides		*15,000.*	
159	6c Lincoln (137), dull pink	425.00	20.00	
a.	Diagonal half used as 3c on cover		*4,000.*	
b.	With grill	*1,800.*		
160	7c Stanton (138), orange vermilion	1,400.	90.00	
a.	With grill	*3,500.*		
161	10c Jefferson (139), brown	1,250.	25.00	
c.	With grill	*3,750.*		
d.	Horiz. pair, imperf. btwn.		*2,750.*	
162	12c Clay (140), blackish violet	2,500.	140.00	
a.	With grill	*5,500.*		
163	15c Webster (141), yellow orange	2,750.	160.00	
a.	With grill	*5,750.*		
164	24c Scott (142), purple, vertically ribbed paper		*357,500.*	
165	30c Hamilton (143), gray blk	3,250.	140.00	
c.	With grill	*22,500.*		
166	90c Perry(144), rose car	2,400.	300.00	
1875, Re-issues, Without Gum, Hard White Paper, Perf. 12				
167	1c Franklin (134), ultramarine	*20,000.*		
168	2c Jackson (135), dark brown	*10,000.*		
169	3c Washington (136), blue green	*25,000.*	—	
170	6c Lincoln (137), dull rose	*24,000.*		
171	7c Stanton (138), reddish vermilion	*6,250.*		
172	10c Jefferson (139), pale brown	*23,000.*		
173	12c Clay (140), dark violet	*8,000.*		
174	15c Webster (141), bright orange	*23,000.*		
175	24c Scott (142), dull purple	*5,500.*	*22,500.*	
176	30c Hamilton (143), greenish black	*19,000.*		
177	90c Perry (144), violet carmine	*30,000.*		
Yellowish Wove Paper, Perf. 12				
178	2c Jackson (135), vermilion	390.00	15.00	
b.	Half used as 1c on cover		*750.00*	
c.	With grill	900.00	2,750.	
179	5c Zachary Taylor, blue	750.00	25.00	
c.	With grill	4,500.		
Re-issues, Without Gum, Hard White Paper, Perf. 12				
180	2c Jackson (135), carmine vermilion	*85,000.*		
181	2c Taylor (179), bright blue	*500,000.*		
1879, Perf. 12, Soft Paper				
182	1c Franklin (134), dark ultramarine	300.00	6.00	
183	2c Jackson (135), vermilion	110.00	5.00	
a.	Double impression	—	*5,500.*	

219

219D

221

222

223

224

225

226

227

228

229

230

231

232

233

234

235

236

237

238

Scott No.	Description	Unused Value	Used Value
b.	Half used as 1c on cover		750.00
184	3c Washington (136), green	95.00	1.00
b.	Double impression		*5,500*
185	5c Taylor (179), blue	475.00	17.50
186	6c Lincoln (137), pink	950.00	32.50
187	10c Jefferson (138), brown	3,500.	37.50
188	10c Jefferson (138), brown w/secret mk.	2,000.	32.50
189	15c Webster (141), red orange	275.00	27.50
190	30c Hamilton (143), full black	950.00	100.00
191	90c Perry (144), carmine	2,250.	375.00
1880, Special Printing, Without Gum, Soft Porous Paper, Perf. 12			
192	1c Franklin (134), dark ultramarine	*75,000.*	
193	2c Jackson (135), black brown	*27,500.*	
194	3c Washington (136), blue green	*125,000.*	
195	6c Lincoln (137), dull rose	*100,000.*	
196	7c Stanton (138), scarlet vermilion	*10,000.*	
197	10c Jefferson (139), deep brown	*55,000.*	
198	12c Clay (140), blackish purple	*15,000.*	
199	15c Webster (141), orange	*50,000.*	
200	24c Scott (142), dark violet	*14,000.*	
201	30c Hamilton (143), greenish black	*35,000.*	
202	90c Perry (144), dull carmine	*45,000.*	
203	30c Jackson (135), scarlet vermilion	*140,000.*	
204	90c Taylor (179), deep blue	*350,000.*	
1882, Perf. 12			
205	5c James Garfield, yellow brown	275.00	12.00
Special Printing, Soft Porous Paper, Without Gum			
205C	5c Garfield (205), gray brown	*85,000.*	
1881-82, Perf. 12			
206	1c Franklin (134), gray blue	80.00	1.00
207	3c Washington (136), blue green	85.00	.80
c.	Double impression		—
208	6c Lincoln (137), rose	800.00	110.00
a.	6c brown red	600.00	175.00
209	10c Jefferson (139), brown	175.00	6.00
b.	10c black brown	3,000.	350.00
c.	Double impression		—
1883, Perf. 12			
210	2c Washington, red brown	42.50	.75
211	4c Jackson, blue green	300.00	27.50
Special Printing, Soft Porous Paper, Without Gum			
211B	2c Washington (210), pale red brown, with gum	375.00	—
c.	Horiz. pair, imperf. btwn.	*2,000.*	—
211D	4c Jackson (211), dp blue grn, w/o gum	*80,000.*	
1887, Perf. 12			
212	1c Franklin, ultramarine	100.00	2.50

239

240

241

242

243

244

245

246

247

248

253

254

255

256

257

258

259

260

261

262

263

Scott No.	Description	Unused Value	Used Value
213	2c Washington (210), green	45.00	.60
b.	Printed on both sides		—
214	3c Washington (136), vermilion	65.00	67.50
1888, Perf. 12			
215	4c Jackson (211), carmine	225.00	27.50
216	5c Garfield (205), indigo	250.00	17.50
217	30c Hamilton (143), orange brown	375.00	130.00
218	90c Perry (144), purple	1,000.	275.00
1890-93, Perf. 12			
219	1c Franklin, dull blue	25.00	.75
219D	2c Washington, lake	220.00	5.50
220	2c Washington (219D), carmine	22.50	.70
a.	Cap on left "2"	140.00	11.00
c.	Cap on both "2s"	625.00	32.50
221	3c Jackson, purple	75.00	9.00
222	4c Lincoln, dark brown	100.00	4.50
223	5c U. S. Grant, chocolate	80.00	4.50
224	6c Garfield, brown red	75.00	25.00
225	8c William T. Sherman, lilac	60.00	17.00
226	10c Webster, green	190.00	4.25
227	15c Clay, indigo	250.00	27.50
228	30c Jefferson, black	400.00	42.50
229	90c Perry, orange	550.00	160.00
1893, Perf. 12			
230	1c Columbian Exposition, deep blue	16.00	.40
231	2c Columbian Exposition, brown violet	16.00	.30
232	3c Columbian Exposition, green	45.00	17.50
233	4c Columbian Exposition, ultra	65.00	9.00
a.	4c Columbian Exposition, blue (error)	*19,000.*	*16,500.*
234	5c Columbian Exposition, chocolate	70.00	9.50
235	6c Columbian Exposition, purple	65.00	25.00
a.	6c Columbian Exposition, red violet	65.00	25.00
236	8c Columbian Exposition, magenta	60.00	12.00
237	10c Columbian Exposition, black brown	110.00	9.00
238	15c Columbian Exposition, dark green	225.00	82.50
239	30c Columbian Exposition, orange brown	240.00	100.00
240	50c Columbian Exposition, slate blue	500.00	200.00
241	$1 Columbian Exposition, salmon	1,100.	700.00
242	$2 Columbian Exposition, brown red	1,150.	700.00
243	$3 Columbian Exposition, yellow green	1,600.	1,000.
a.	$3 Columbian Exposition, olive green	1,600.	1,000.
244	$4 Columbian Exposition, crimson lake	2,250.	1,300.
a.	$4 Columbian Exposition, rose carmine	2,250.	1,300.
245	$5 Columbian Exposition, black	2,700.	1,500.
1894, Perf. 12, Unwatermarked			
246	1c Franklin (247), ultramarine	30.00	7.00
247	1c Franklin, blue	65.00	4.00

Wmk. 190-"USPS" in Single-lined Capitals

Wmk. 191-Double-lined "USPS" in Capitals

Triangle A (Type I)

Triangle B (Type II)

TWO CENTS.

Type I. The horizontal lines of the ground work run across the triangle and are of the same thickness within it as without.

Type II. The horizontal lines cross the triangle but are thinner within it than without.

Triangle C (Type III & IV

Type IV design

Type III. The horizontal lines do not cross the double frame lines of the triangle. The lines within the triangle are thin, as in type II.

Type IV. Same triangle C as type III, but other design differences including, (1) re-cutting and lengthening of hairline, (2) shaded toga button, (3) strengthening of lines on sleeve, (4) additional dots on ear, (5) "T" of "TWO" straight at right, (6) background lines extend into white oval opposite "U" of "UNITED".

ONE DOLLAR

Type I

Type I. The circles enclosing "$1" are broken where they meet the curved line below "One Dollar." The fifteen left vertical rows of impressions from plate 76 are Type I, the balance being Type II.

Type II

Type II. The circles are complete.

TEN CENTS

Type I

Type I. Tips of foliate ornaments do not impinge on white curved line below "TEN CENTS."

Type II

Type II. Tips of ornaments break curved line below "E" of "TEN" and "T" of "CENTS."

Scott No.	Description	Unused Value	Used Value	/ / / / / /
248	2c Washington, pink, type I	27.50	9.00	☐☐☐☐☐
a.	Vert. pair, imperf. horiz.	*5,500.*		☐☐☐☐☐
249	2c Washington (248), carmine lake, type I	150.00	7.00	☐☐☐☐☐
a.	Double impression		—	☐☐☐☐☐
250	2c Washington (248), carmine, type I	27.50	3.00	☐☐☐☐☐
a.	2c rose, type I	27.50	20.00	☐☐☐☐☐
b.	2c scarlet, type I	27.50	22.50	☐☐☐☐☐
d.	Horiz, pair, imperf. btwn.	*2,000.*		☐☐☐☐☐
251	2c Washington (248), carmine, type II	350.00	14.00	☐☐☐☐☐
a.	2c scarlet, type II	350.00	11.00	☐☐☐☐☐
252	2c Washington (248), carmine, type III	120.00	14.00	☐☐☐☐☐
a.	2c scarlet, type III	120.00	14.00	☐☐☐☐☐
b.	Horiz. pair, imperf. vert.	*5,000.*		☐☐☐☐☐
c.	Horiz. pair, imperf. btwn.	*5,500.*		☐☐☐☐☐
253	3c Jackson, purple	110.00	13.00	☐☐☐☐☐
254	4c Lincoln, dark brown	175.00	9.00	☐☐☐☐☐
255	5c Grant, chocolate	110.00	9.00	☐☐☐☐☐
c.	Vert. pair, imperf. horiz.	*4,000.*		☐☐☐☐☐
256	6c Garfield, dull brown	160.00	30.00	☐☐☐☐☐
a.	Vert. pair, imperf. horiz.	*2,000.*		☐☐☐☐☐
257	8c Sherman, violet brown	175.00	22.50	☐☐☐☐☐
258	10c Webster, dark green	325.00	19.00	☐☐☐☐☐
259	15c Clay, dark blue	325.00	70.00	☐☐☐☐☐
260	50c Jefferson, orange	525.00	160.00	☐☐☐☐☐
261	$1 Perry, black, type I	1,050.	375.00	☐☐☐☐☐
261A	$1 Perry (261), type II	2,200.	850.00	☐☐☐☐☐
262	$2 James Madison, bright blue	2,750.	1,300.	☐☐☐☐☐
263	$5 John Marshall, dark green	4,500.	2,900.	☐☐☐☐☐
1895, Watermark 191, Perf. 12				
264	1c Franklin (247), blue	6.00	.60	☐☐☐☐☐
265	2c Washington (248), carmine, type I	27.50	3.50	☐☐☐☐☐
266	2c Washington (248), carmine, type II	32.50	5.50	☐☐☐☐☐
267	2c Washington (248), carmine, type III	5.50	.50	☐☐☐☐☐
a.	2c pink, type III	20.00	2.25	☐☐☐☐☐
b.	2c vermilion, type III.	*50.00*	10.00	☐☐☐☐☐
c.	2c rose carmine, type III	—	—	☐☐☐☐☐
268	3c Jackson (253), purple	37.50	2.25	☐☐☐☐☐
269	4c Lincoln (254), dark brown	45.00	3.50	☐☐☐☐☐
270	5c Grant (255), chocolate	35.00	3.50	☐☐☐☐☐
271	6c Garfield (256), dull brown	120.00	8.50	☐☐☐☐☐
a.	Wmkd. USIR	*15,000.*	*12,500.*	☐☐☐☐☐
272	8c Sherman (257), violet brown	70.00	2.75	☐☐☐☐☐
a.	Wmkd. USIR	*6,000.*	1,000.	☐☐☐☐☐
273	10c Webster (258), dark green	95.00	2.25	☐☐☐☐☐
274	15c Clay (259), dark blue	225.00	17.50	☐☐☐☐☐
275	50c Jefferson (260), orange	275.00	40.00	☐☐☐☐☐
a.	50c Jefferson (260), red orange	325.00	47.50	☐☐☐☐☐
276	$1 Perry (261), black, type I	650.00	110.00	☐☐☐☐☐

Scott No.	Description	Unused Value	Used Value	/ / / / /
276A	$1 Perry (261), black, type II	1,350.	225.00	☐☐☐☐☐
277	$2 Madison (262), bright blue	1,000.	*450.00*	☐☐☐☐☐
a.	$2 dark blue	1,000.	*450.00*	☐☐☐☐☐
278	$5 Marshall (263), dark green	2,250.	650.00	☐☐☐☐☐
1897-1903, Watermark 191, Perf. 12				
279	1c Franklin (247), deep green	9.00	.50	☐☐☐☐☐
279B	2c Washington (248), red, type IV	9.00	.40	☐☐☐☐☐
c.	2c rose carmine, type IV	300.00	200.00	☐☐☐☐☐
d.	2c orange red, type IV	11.50	.55	☐☐☐☐☐
f.	2c carmine, type IV	10.00	.50	☐☐☐☐☐
g.	2c pink, type IV	50.00	1.75	☐☐☐☐☐
h.	2c vermilion, type IV	11.00	.55	☐☐☐☐☐
i.	2c brown orange, type IV	*150.00*	*15.00*	☐☐☐☐☐
j.	Booklet pane of 6 horiz. watermark	500.00	*1,250.*	☐☐☐☐☐
k.	Booklet pane of 6 vert. watermark	500.00	*1,250.*	☐☐☐☐☐
280	4c Lincoln (254), rose brown	27.50	3.50	☐☐☐☐☐
a.	4c lilac brown	27.50	3.50	☐☐☐☐☐
b.	4c orange brown	27.50	3.50	☐☐☐☐☐
281	5c Grant (255), dark blue	32.50	2.25	☐☐☐☐☐
282	6c Garfield (256), lake	45.00	6.50	☐☐☐☐☐
a.	6c purple lake	70.00	15.00	☐☐☐☐☐
282C	10c Webster (258), brown, type I	190.00	6.50	☐☐☐☐☐
283	10c Webster (258), orange brown, type II, horiz. watermark	150.00	5.50	☐☐☐☐☐
a.	Type II, vert. watermark	*225.00*	*11.00*	☐☐☐☐☐
284	15c Clay (259), olive green	160.00	13.00	☐☐☐☐☐
285	1c Trans-Mississippi Expo	25.00	7.00	☐☐☐☐☐
286	2c Trans-Mississippi Expo	25.00	2.75	☐☐☐☐☐
287	4c Trans-Mississippi Expo	120.00	27.50	☐☐☐☐☐
288	5c Trans-Mississippi Expo	120.00	25.00	☐☐☐☐☐
289	8c Trans-Mississippi Expo	175.00	50.00	☐☐☐☐☐
a.	Vert. pair, imperf. horiz	*27,500.*		☐☐☐☐☐
290	10c Trans-Mississippi Expo	160.00	35.00	☐☐☐☐☐
291	50c Trans-Mississippi Expo	650.00	210.00	☐☐☐☐☐
292	$1 Trans-Mississippi Expo	1,100.	*650.00*	☐☐☐☐☐
293	$2 Trans-Mississippi Expo	1,900.	*1,050.*	☐☐☐☐☐
1901, Watermark 191, Perf. 12				
294	1c Pan-American Exposition	17.50	3.00	☐☐☐☐☐
a.	Center inverted	*12,500.*	*16,500.*	☐☐☐☐☐
295	2c Pan-American Exposition	16.50	1.00	☐☐☐☐☐
a.	Center inverted	*55,000.*	*60,000.*	☐☐☐☐☐
296	4c Pan-American Exposition	75.00	19.00	☐☐☐☐☐
a.	Center inverted	*70,000.*		☐☐☐☐☐
297	5c Pan-American Exposition	80.00	18.50	☐☐☐☐☐
298	8c Pan-American Exposition	100.00	55.00	☐☐☐☐☐
299	10c Pan-American Exposition	130.00	32.50	☐☐☐☐☐
1902-03, Watermark 191, Perf. 12				
300	1c Franklin	12.00	.25	☐☐☐☐☐

285

286

287

288

289

290

291

292

293

294

295

296

297

298

299

Scott No.	Description	Unused Value	Used Value
b.	Booklet pane of 6	600.00	*12,500.*
301	2c Washington	16.00	.50
c.	Booklet pane of 6	500.00	*4,500.*
302	3c Jackson	55.00	4.00
303	4c Grant	60.00	2.50
304	5c Lincoln	60.00	2.25
305	6c Garfield	60.00	5.75
306	8c Martha Washington	40.00	3.50
307	10c Webster	60.00	3.25
308	13c Benjamin Harrison	40.00	11.00
309	15c Clay	200.00	14.00
310	50c Jefferson	425.00	35.00
311	$1 David G. Farragut	700.00	90.00
312	$2 Madison	1,000.	250.00
313	$5 Marshall, dark green	2,500.	800.00
1906-08, Imperf.			
314	1c Franklin (300)	16.00	18.00
314A	4c Grant (303), brown	*90,000.*	*50,000.*
315	5c Lincoln (304), blue	200.00	*1,250.*
1908, Coil Stamps, Perf. 12 Horizontally			
316	1c Franklin (300)	*70,000.*	—
317	5c Lincoln (304)	*6,000.*	—
Perf. 12 Vertically			
318	1c Franklin (300)	*6,000.*	—
1903, Watermark 191, Perf. 12			
319	2c Washington, carmine, type I	6.00	.25
a.	2c lake, type I	—	—
b.	2c carmine rose, type I	10.00	.40
c.	2c scarlet, type I	10.00	.30
d.	Vert. pair, imperf. horiz.	*7,500.*	
e.	Vert. pair, imperf. btwn.	2,500.	
f.	2c lake, type II	10.00	.30
g.	Booklet pane of 6, carmine, type I	125.00	*550.00*
h.	As "g," type II	900.00	
i.	2c carmine, type II	75.00	*50.00*
j.	2c carmine rose, type II	70.00	1.75
k.	2c scarlet, type II	70.00	.65
n.	As "g," carmine rose, type I	250.00	*650.00*
p.	As "g," scarlet, type I	185.00	*575.00*
q.	As "g," lake, type II	300.00	*750.00*
1906, Imperf.			
320	2c Washington (319), carmine, type I	16.00	*19.00*
a.	2c lake, type II	45.00	50.00
b.	2c scarlet, type I	18.50	15.00
c.	2c carmine rose, type I	60.00	42.50
d.	2c carmine, type II	*120.00*	*250.00*

300

301

302

303

304

305

306

307

308

309

310

311

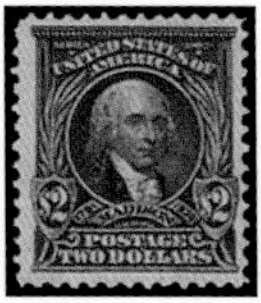
312

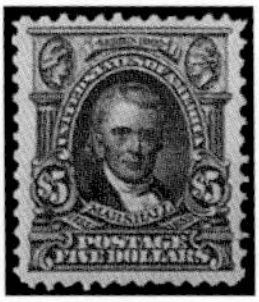
313

319

Type I

Type II

Type I. Leaf next to left "2" penetrates the border.
Type II. Strong line forming border left of leaf.

323

324

325

326

327

Scott No.	Description	Unused Value	Used Value	/ / / / / /
1908, Coil Stamps, Perf. 12 Horizontally				
321	2c Washington (319), car., type I, pair	*450,000.*	—	☐☐☐☐☐
Perf. 12 Vertically				
322	2c Washington (319), car., type II	*7,000.*	—	☐☐☐☐☐
1904, Watermark 191, Perf. 12				
323	1c Louisiana Purchase	25.00	5.00	☐☐☐☐☐
324	2c Louisiana Purchase	25.00	2.00	☐☐☐☐☐
a.	Vert. pair, imperf. horiz.................	*17,500.*		☐☐☐☐☐
325	3c Louisiana Purchase	75.00	30.00	☐☐☐☐☐
326	5c Louisiana Purchase	80.00	25.00	☐☐☐☐☐
327	10c Louisiana Purchase	145.00	30.00	☐☐☐☐☐
1907, Watermark 191, Perf. 12				
328	1c Jamestown Exposition	25.00	5.00	☐☐☐☐☐
329	2c Jamestown Exposition	30.00	4.50	☐☐☐☐☐
a.	2c carmine lake	—		☐☐☐☐☐
330	5c Jamestown Exposition	130.00	32.50	☐☐☐☐☐
1908-09, Watermark 191, Perf. 12				
331	1c Franklin, green	6.75	.40	☐☐☐☐☐
a.	Booklet pane of 6	160.00	*450.00*	☐☐☐☐☐
332	2c Washington, carmine	6.25	.35	☐☐☐☐☐
a.	Booklet pane of 6	135.00	*400.00*	☐☐☐☐☐
b.	2c lake	—		☐☐☐☐☐
333	3c Washington, deep violet, type I	30.00	3.00	☐☐☐☐☐
334	4c Washington (333), orange brown ..	37.50	1.50	☐☐☐☐☐
335	5c Washington (333), blue	50.00	2.50	☐☐☐☐☐
336	6c Washington (333), red orange	65.00	6.50	☐☐☐☐☐
337	8c Washington (333), olive green	45.00	3.00	☐☐☐☐☐
338	10c Washington (333), yellow	67.50	2.00	☐☐☐☐☐
339	13c Washington (333), blue green	37.50	19.00	☐☐☐☐☐
340	15c Washington (333), pale ultramarine	65.00	6.50	☐☐☐☐☐
341	50c Washington (333), violet	300.00	20.00	☐☐☐☐☐
342	$1 Washington (333), violet brown	500.00	100.00	☐☐☐☐☐
Imperf.				
343	1c Franklin (331)	4.00	5.50	☐☐☐☐☐
344	2c Washington (332)	4.75	3.25	☐☐☐☐☐
345	3c Washington (333), deep violet, type I	9.00	*22.50*	☐☐☐☐☐
346	4c Washington (333), orange brown ..	13.50	*25.00*	☐☐☐☐☐
347	5c Washington (333), blue	27.50	37.50	☐☐☐☐☐
1908-10, Coil Stamps, Perf. 12 Horizontally				
348	1c Franklin (331)	37.50	50.00	☐☐☐☐☐
349	2c Washington (332)	80.00	100.00	☐☐☐☐☐
350	4c Washington (333), orange brown ..	150.00	210.00	☐☐☐☐☐
351	5c Washington (333), blue	160.00	275.00	☐☐☐☐☐
Coil Stamps, Perf. 12 Vertically				
352	1c Franklin (331)	95.00	190.00	☐☐☐☐☐
353	2c Washington (332)	95.00	220.00	☐☐☐☐☐

328

329

330

Franklin
331

Washington
332

Washington
333

Franklin
414

367

370

372

397

398

399

400

TYPE I

THREE CENTS.

Type I. The top line of the toga rope is weak and the rope shading lines are thin. The fifth line from the left is missing.

The line between the lips is thin.

Used on both flat plate and rotary press printings.

Scott No.	Description	Unused Value	Used Value	/ / / / / /
354	4c Washington (333), orange brown ..	220.00	275.00	☐☐☐☐☐
355	5c Washington (333), blue..................	225.00	300.00	☐☐☐☐☐
356	10c Washington (333), yellow..............	3,250.	*4,500.*	☐☐☐☐☐
1909, Bluish paper, Perf. 12				
357	1c Franklin (331)................................	85.00	100.00	☐☐☐☐☐
358	2c Washington (332)...........................	80.00	*100.00*	☐☐☐☐☐
359	3c Washington (333), deep violet, type I	1,800.	*5,000.*	☐☐☐☐☐
360	4c Washington (333), orange brown ..	*27,500.*		☐☐☐☐☐
361	5c Washington (333), blue..................	5,750.	*15,000.*	☐☐☐☐☐
362	6c Washington (333), red orange	1,350.	*15,000.*	☐☐☐☐☐
363	8c Washington (333), olive green.......	*30,000.*		☐☐☐☐☐
364	10c Washington (333), yellow..............	1,750.	*7,000.*	☐☐☐☐☐
365	13c Washington (333), blue green........	2,750.	*2,250.*	☐☐☐☐☐
366	15c Washington (333), pale ultra	1,350.	*11,000.*	☐☐☐☐☐
1909, Watermark 191, Perf. 12				
367	2c Lincoln Memorial	500.00	2.00	☐☐☐☐☐
Imperf.				
368	2c Lincoln Memorial (367)	15.00	22.50	☐☐☐☐☐
Bluish paper				
369	2c Lincoln Memorial (367)	180.00	*275.00*	☐☐☐☐☐
Perf. 12				
370	2c Alaska-Yukon-Pacific Exposition .	7.50	2.25	☐☐☐☐☐
Imperf.				
371	2c Alaska-Yukon-Pacific Exposition (370)	17.50	24.00	☐☐☐☐☐
Perf. 12				
372	2c Hudson-Fulton	10.00	4.75	☐☐☐☐☐
Imperf.				
373	2c Hudson-Fulton (372).....................	20.00	27.50	☐☐☐☐☐
1910-11, Watermark 190, Perf. 12				
374	1c Franklin (331)................................	6.50	.25	☐☐☐☐☐
a.	Booklet pane of 6..........................	225.00	*300.00*	☐☐☐☐☐
375	2c Washington (332)...........................	6.50	.25	☐☐☐☐☐
a.	Booklet pane of 6...........................	125.00	*200.00*	☐☐☐☐☐
b.	2c lake...	*900.00*		☐☐☐☐☐
c.	Double impression	*600.00*		☐☐☐☐☐
376	3c Washington (333), deep violet, type I	20.00	2.00	☐☐☐☐☐
377	4c Washington (333), brown..............	30.00	1.00	☐☐☐☐☐
378	5c Washington (333), blue..................	30.00	.75	☐☐☐☐☐
379	6c Washington (333), red orange	35.00	1.00	☐☐☐☐☐
380	8c Washington (333), olive green.......	100.00	15.00	☐☐☐☐☐
381	10c Washington (333), yellow..............	95.00	6.00	☐☐☐☐☐
382	15c Washington (333), pale ultra	250.00	19.00	☐☐☐☐☐
1910, Imperf.				
383	1c Franklin (331)................................	2.00	2.25	☐☐☐☐☐
384	2c Washington (332)...........................	3.25	2.75	☐☐☐☐☐

TYPE I

TWO CENTS.

Type I. There is one shading line in the first curve of the ribbon above the left "2" and one in the second curve of the ribbon above the right "2."

The button of the toga has a faint outline.

The top line of the toga rope, from the button to the front of the throat, is also very faint.

The shading lines at the face terminate in front of the ear with little or no joining, to form a lock of hair.

Used on both flat and rotary press printings.

TYPE Ia

TWO CENTS.

Type Ia. Design characteristics similar to type I except that all lines of design are stronger.

The toga button, toga rope and rope shading lines are heavy. The latter characteristics are those of type II, which, however, occur only on impressions from rotary plates.

Used only on flat plates 10208 and 10209.

TYPE II

TWO CENTS.

Type II. Shading lines in ribbons as on type I.

The toga button, rope, and shading lines are heavy.

The shading lines of the face at the lock of hair end in a strong vertical curved line.

Used on rotary press printings only.

TYPE III

TWO CENTS.

Type III. Two lines of shading in the curves of the ribbons.

Other characteristics similar to type II.

Used on rotary press printings only.

Scott No.	Description	Unused Value	Used Value	/ / / / / /
1910, Coil Stamps, Perf. 12 Horizontally				
385	1c Franklin (331)................................	45.00	45.00	□□□□□
386	2c Washington (332)..........................	110.00	100.00	□□□□□
1910-11, Coil Stamps, Perf. 12 Vertically				
387	1c Franklin (331)................................	200.00	140.00	□□□□□
388	2c Washington (332)..........................	1,400.	2,250.	□□□□□
389	3c Washington (333), deep violet, type I	*110,000.*	*11,000.*	□□□□□
1910, Perf. 8½ Horizontally				
390	1c Franklin (331)................................	5.00	*14.00*	□□□□□
391	2c Washington (332)..........................	42.50	50.00	□□□□□
1910-13, Perf. 8½ Vertically				
392	1c Franklin (331)................................	30.00	55.00	□□□□□
393	2c Washington (332)..........................	47.50	45.00	□□□□□
394	3c Washington (333), deep violet, type I	60.00	67.50	□□□□□
395	4c Washington (333), brown...............	62.50	70.00	□□□□□
396	5c Washington (333), blue..................	60.00	67.50	□□□□□
1913, Watermark 190, Perf. 12				
397	1c Panama-Pacific Exposition...........	16.50	2.00	□□□□□
398	2c Panama-Pacific Exposition...........	18.00	1.00	□□□□□
a.	2c carmine lake..................................	*1,500.*		□□□□□
b.	2c lake	*5,000.*		□□□□□
399	5c Panama-Pacific Exposition...........	70.00	10.00	□□□□□
400	10c Panama-Pacific Expo., orange yellow	120.00	22.50	□□□□□
400A	10c Panama-Pacific Expo. (400), orange	200.00	20.00	□□□□□
1914-15, Perf. 10				
401	1c Panama-Pacific Expo. (397)..........	25.00	7.00	□□□□□
402	2c Panama-Pacific Expo. (398)..........	70.00	2.75	□□□□□
403	5c Panama-Pacific Expo. (399)..........	160.00	20.00	□□□□□
404	10c Panama-Pacific Expo. (400), orange	750.00	70.00	□□□□□
1912-14, Watermark 190, Perf. 12				
405	1c Washington (333), green...............	6.50	.25	□□□□□
a.	Vert. pair, imperf. horiz.................	*2,000.*	—	□□□□□
b.	Booklet pane of 6..........................	65.00	*75.00*	□□□□□
406	2c Washington (333), carmine, type I	6.50	.25	□□□□□
a.	Booklet pane of 6..........................	65.00	*90.00*	□□□□□
b.	Double impression	—		□□□□□
c.	2c lake, type I................................	*2,000.*	*2,750.*	□□□□□
407	7c Washington (333), black...............	70.00	14.00	□□□□□
1912, Imperf.				
408	1c Washington (333), green...............	1.00	1.00	□□□□□
409	2c Washington (333), carmine, type I	1.20	1.20	□□□□□
Coil Stamps, Perf. 8½ Horizontally				
410	1c Washington (333), green...............	6.00	12.50	□□□□□
411	2c Washington (333), carmine, type I	10.00	15.00	□□□□□
Coil Stamps, Perf. 8½ Vertically				
412	1c Washington (333), green...............	25.00	25.00	□□□□□
413	2c Washington (333), carmine, type I	55.00	25.00	□□□□□

TYPE II

THREE CENTS.

Type II. The top line of the toga rope is strong and the rope shading lines are heavy and complete.

The line between the lips is heavy.

Used on both flat plate and rotary press printings.

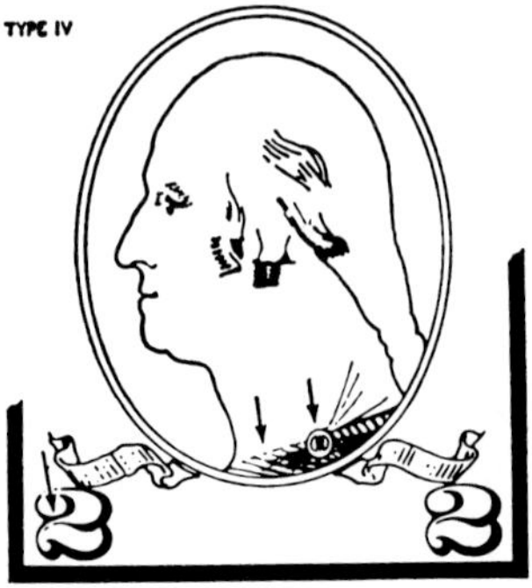

TYPE IV

TWO CENTS.

Type IV. Top line of the toga rope is broken. Shading lines in toga button are so arranged that the curving of the first and last form “ ID.”

Line of color in left “2” is very thin and usually broken.

Used on offset printings only.

TYPE V

TWO CENTS.

Type V. Top line of toga is complete.

Five vertical shading lines in toga button.

Line of color in left “2” is very thin and usually broken.

Shading dots on the nose and lip are as indicated on the diagram.

Used on offset printings only.

TYPE Va

TWO CENTS.

Type Va. Characteristics same as type V, except in shading dots of nose. Third row from bottom has 4 dots instead of 6. Overall height of type Va is 1/3 mm. less than type V.

Used on offset printings only.

Scott No.	Description	Unused Value	Used Value
1912-14, Watermark 190, Perf. 12			
414	8c Franklin, pale olive green	40.00	2.00
415	9c Franklin (414), salmon red	50.00	14.00
416	10c Franklin (414), orange yellow	40.00	.80
a.	10c brown yellow	*1,250.*	—
417	12c Franklin (414), claret brown	45.00	5.00
418	15c Franklin (414), gray	80.00	4.50
419	20c Franklin (414), ultra	180.00	19.00
420	30c Franklin (414), orange red	110.00	19.00
421	50c Franklin (414), violet	400.00	30.00
1912, Watermark 191, Perf. 12			
422	50c Franklin (414), violet	240.00	22.50
423	$1 Franklin (414), violet brown	500.00	75.00
1914, Watermark 190, Perf. 12 x 10			
423A	1c Washington (333), green	*20,000.*	*10,000.*
423B	2c Washington (333), rose red, type 1	*175,000.*	*32,500.*
423C	5c Washington (333), blue		*37,500.*
1914, Watermark 190, Perf. 10 x 12			
423D	1c Washington (333), green		*20,000.*
423E	2c Washington (333), rose red, type 1.		—
1914-15, Watermark 190, Perf. 10			
424	1c Washington (333), green	2.50	.20
c.	Vert. pair, imperf. horiz.	*2,800.*	*2,500.*
d.	Booklet pane of 6	5.25	*7.50*
e.	As "d.," imperf.	*2,000.*	
f.	Vert. pair, imperf. between and with straight edge at top	*9,000.*	
425	2c Washington (333), rose red, type I	2.30	.20
e.	Booklet pane of 6	17.50	*25.00*
426	3c Washington (333), deep violet, type I	14.00	1.50
427	4c Washington (333), brown	32.50	1.00
428	5c Washington (333), blue	32.50	1.00
429	6c Washington (333), red orange	45.00	2.00
430	7c Washington (333), black	90.00	5.00
431	8c Franklin (414), pale olive green	35.00	3.00
a.	Double impression	—	
432	9c Franklin (414), salmon red	45.00	9.00
433	10c Franklin (414), orange yellow	45.00	1.00
434	11c Franklin (414), dark green	22.50	8.50
435	12c Franklin (414), claret brown	25.00	6.00
a.	12c Franklin (414), copper red	30.00	7.00
437	15c Franklin (414), gray	125.00	7.25
438	20c Franklin (414), ultramarine	200.00	6.00
439	30c Franklin (414), orange red	240.00	17.50
440	50c Franklin (414), violet	525.00	17.50
1914, Coil Stamps, Perf. 10 Horizontally			
441	1c Washington (333), green	1.00	*1.50*

TYPE VI

TWO CENTS.

Type VI. General characteristics same as type V, except that line of color in left "2" is very heavy.

Used on offset printings only.

TYPE VII

TWO CENTS.

Type VII. Line of color in left "2" is invariably continuous, clearly defined, and heavier than in type V or Va, but not as heavy as in type VI.

Additional vertical row of dots has been added to the upper lip.

Numerous additional dots have been added to hair on top of head.

Used on offset printings only.

TYPE III

THREE CENTS.

Type III. The top line of the toga rope is strong but the fifth shading line is missing as in type I.

Center shading line of the toga button consists of two dashes with a central dot.

The "P" and "O" of "POSTAGE" are separated by a line of color.

The frame line at the bottom of the vignette is complete.

Used on offset printings only.

TYPE IV

THREE CENTS.

Type IV. Shading lines of toga rope are complete.

Second and fourth shading lines in toga button are broken in the middle and the third line is continuous with a dot in the center.

"P" and "O" of "POSTAGE" are joined.

Frame line at bottom of vignette is broken.

Used on offset printings only.

Scott No.	Description	Unused Value	Used Value	/ / / / / /
442	2c Washington (333), carmine, type I	10.00	*45.00*	☐☐☐☐☐
Coil Stamps, Perf. 10 Vertically				
443	1c Washington (333), green................	30.00	45.00	☐☐☐☐☐
444	2c Washington (333), carmine, type I	50.00	35.00	☐☐☐☐☐
a.	2c lake..		*1,250.*	☐☐☐☐☐
445	3c Washington (333), violet, type I....	250.00	250.00	☐☐☐☐☐
446	4c Washington (333), brown...............	140.00	150.00	☐☐☐☐☐
447	5c Washington (333), blue..................	50.00	115.00	☐☐☐☐☐
1914-16, Coil Stamps, Perf. 10 Horizontally, Rotary Press Printing				
448	1c Washington (333), green................	7.50	17.50	☐☐☐☐☐
449	2c Washington (333), red, type I	2,750.	650.00	☐☐☐☐☐
450	2c Washington (333), carmine, type III	12.50	22.50	☐☐☐☐☐
1914-16, Coil Stamps, Perf. 10 Vertically, Rotary Press Printing				
452	1c Washington (333), green................	10.00	*17.50*	☐☐☐☐☐
453	2c Washington (333), car rose, type I	150.00	17.50	☐☐☐☐☐
454	2c Washington (333), red, type II.......	75.00	22.50	☐☐☐☐☐
455	2c Washington (333), carmine, type III	8.50	3.50	☐☐☐☐☐
456	3c Washington (333), violet, type I....	250.00	170.00	☐☐☐☐☐
457	4c Washington (333), brown...............	25.00	30.00	☐☐☐☐☐
458	5c Washington (333), blue..................	30.00	30.00	☐☐☐☐☐
1914, Coil Stamp, Imperf., Rotary Press Printing				
459	2c Washington (333), carmine, type I	175.00	*1,300.*	☐☐☐☐☐
1915, Watermark 191, Perf. 10				
460	$1 Franklin (414), violet black	775.00	150.00	☐☐☐☐☐
1915, Watermark 190, Perf. 11				
461	2c Washington (333), pale car red, type I	140.00	*360.00*	☐☐☐☐☐
1916-17, Perf. 10, Unwatermarked				
462	1c Washington (333), green................	7.00	.35	☐☐☐☐☐
a.	Booklet pane of 6..........................	9.50	*12.50*	☐☐☐☐☐
463	2c Washington (333), carmine, type I	4.50	.40	☐☐☐☐☐
a.	Booklet pane of 6..........................	110.00	*110.00*	☐☐☐☐☐
464	3c Washington (333), violet, type I....	70.00	19.00	☐☐☐☐☐
465	4c Washington (333), orange brown ..	40.00	2.50	☐☐☐☐☐
466	5c Washington (333), blue..................	70.00	2.50	☐☐☐☐☐
467	5c Washington (333), car (error in plate of 2c)................................	475.00	*850.00*	☐☐☐☐☐
468	6c Washington (333), red orange	85.00	9.00	☐☐☐☐☐
469	7c Washington (333), black................	120.00	15.00	☐☐☐☐☐
470	8c Franklin (414), olive green	55.00	8.00	☐☐☐☐☐
471	9c Franklin (414), salmon red	55.00	18.50	☐☐☐☐☐
472	10c Franklin (414), orange yellow	100.00	2.50	☐☐☐☐☐
473	11c Franklin (414), dark green............	40.00	18.50	☐☐☐☐☐
474	12c Franklin (414), claret brown..........	50.00	7.50	☐☐☐☐☐
475	15c Franklin (414), gray	180.00	16.00	☐☐☐☐☐
476	20c Franklin (414), light ultramarine...	225.00	17.50	☐☐☐☐☐
476A	30c Franklin (414), orange red............	*3,250.*		☐☐☐☐☐

Scott No.	Description	Unused Value	Used Value	/ / / / / /
477	50c Franklin (414), light violet	1,000.	80.00	☐☐☐☐☐
478	$1 Franklin (414), violet black	700.00	25.00	☐☐☐☐☐
479	$2 Madison (312), dark blue	225.00	42.50	☐☐☐☐☐
480	$5 Marshall (313), light green	180.00	40.00	☐☐☐☐☐
Imperf.				
481	1c Washington (333), green	.95	.95	☐☐☐☐☐
482	2c Washington (333), carmine, type I	1.30	1.30	☐☐☐☐☐
482A	2c Washington (333), deep rose, type Ia	—	*65,000.*	☐☐☐☐☐
483	3c Washington (333), violet, type I	10.00	10.00	☐☐☐☐☐
484	3c Washington (333), violet, type II	8.00	8.00	☐☐☐☐☐
485	5c Washington (333), carmine (error in plate of 2c)	*12,000.*		☐☐☐☐☐
1916-18, Coil Stamps, Perf. 10 Horizontally, Rotary Press Printing				
486	1c Washington (333), green	.85	.85	☐☐☐☐☐
487	2c Washington (333), carmine, type II	12.50	14.00	☐☐☐☐☐
488	2c Washington (333), carmine, type III	3.00	*5.00*	☐☐☐☐☐
489	3c Washington (333), violet, type I	4.50	2.25	☐☐☐☐☐
1916-22, Coil Stamps, Perf.10 Vertically				
490	1c Washington (333), green	.50	*.60*	☐☐☐☐☐
491	2c Washington (333), carmine, type II	2,500.	750.00	☐☐☐☐☐
492	2c Washington (333), carmine, type III	9.00	1.00	☐☐☐☐☐
493	3c Washington (333), violet, type I	14.00	4.50	☐☐☐☐☐
494	3c Washington (333), violet, type II	10.00	2.50	☐☐☐☐☐
495	4c Washington (333), orange brown	10.00	7.00	☐☐☐☐☐
496	5c Washington (333), blue	3.25	2.50	☐☐☐☐☐
497	10c Franklin (414), orange yellow	19.00	17.50	☐☐☐☐☐
Types of 1912-14 Issue				
1917-19, Perf. 11				
498	1c Washington (333), green	.35	.25	☐☐☐☐☐
a.	Vert. pair, imperf. horiz.	900.00		☐☐☐☐☐
b.	Horiz. pair, imperf. btwn.	575.00		☐☐☐☐☐
c.	Vert. pair, imperf. btwn.	*700.00*	—	☐☐☐☐☐
d.	Double impression	250.00	*4,000.*	☐☐☐☐☐
e.	Booklet pane of 6	2.50	*2.00*	☐☐☐☐☐
f.	Booklet pane of 30	*1,150.*		☐☐☐☐☐
g.	Perf. 10 at top or bottom	*15,000.*	*45,000.*	☐☐☐☐☐
499	2c Washington (333), rose, type I	.35	.25	☐☐☐☐☐
a.	Vert. pair, imperf. horiz.	600.00		☐☐☐☐☐
b.	Horiz. pair, imperf. vert.	*375.00*	*225.00*	☐☐☐☐☐
c.	Vert. pair, imperf. btwn.	*1,000.*	*300.00*	☐☐☐☐☐
e.	Booklet pane of 6	4.00	*2.50*	☐☐☐☐☐
f.	Booklet pane of 30	*28,000.*		☐☐☐☐☐
g.	Double impression	200.00	—	☐☐☐☐☐
h.	2c lake	500.00	350.00	☐☐☐☐☐
500	2c Washington (333), deep rose, type Ia	250.00	240.00	☐☐☐☐☐
501	3c Washington (333), light violet, type I	10.00	.40	☐☐☐☐☐
b.	Booklet pane of 6	75.00	*60.00*	☐☐☐☐☐

Scott No.	Description	Unused Value	Used Value	/ / / / / /
c.	Vert. pair, imperf. horiz.	*2,500.*		
d.	Double impression	*3,500.*	*3,500.*	
502	3c Washington (333), dark violet, type II	13.00	.75	
b.	Booklet pane of 6	60.00	*55.00*	
c.	Vert. pair, imperf. horiz.	*1,400.*	750.00	
d.	Double impression	850.00	750.00	
e.	Perf. 10 at top or bottom	*15,000.*	*12,500.*	
503	4c Washington (333), brown	9.00	.40	
b.	Double impression	–		
504	5c Washington (333), blue	8.00	.35	
a.	Horiz. pair, imperf. btwn.	*20,000.*	—	
b.	Double impression	2,000.	*900.00*	
505	5c Washington (333), rose (error in plate of 2c)	300.00	*550.00*	
506	6c Washington (333), red orange	12.00	.40	
a..	Perf. 10 at top or bottom	*5,000.*	*9,000.*	
507	7c Washington (333), black	26.00	1.25	
a.	Perf. 10 at top	*20,000.*		
508	8c Franklin (414), olive bister	12.00	.65	
b.	Vert. pair, imperf. btwn.	—	—	
c.	Perf at 10 at top or bottom		*15,000.*	
509	9c Franklin (414), salmon red	12.00	1.75	
a.	Perf. 10 at top or bottom	*4,250.*	*7,000.*	
510	10c Franklin (414), orange yellow	16.00	.25	
a.	10c brown yellow	*1,500.*		
511	11c Franklin (414), light green	9.00	2.50	
a.	Perf. 10 at top or bottom	*5,000.*	*4,500.*	
512	12c Franklin (414), claret brown	8.00	.40	
a.	12c brown carmine	9.00	.50	
b.	Perf. 10 at top or bottom	*17,500.*	*10,000.*	
513	13c Franklin (414), apple green	10.00	6.00	
514	15c Franklin (414), gray	35.00	1.50	
a.	Perf. 10 at bottom		*10,000.*	
515	20c Franklin (414), light ultramarine	42.50	.45	
b.	Vert. pair, imperf. btwn.	2,000.	*1,750.*	
c.	Double impression	*1,250.*		
d.	Perf. at top or bottom	—	*15,000.*	
516	30c Franklin (414), orange red	35.00	1.50	
a.	Perf. at top or bottom	*20,000.*	*7,500.*	
b.	Double impression		—	
517	50c Franklin (414), red violet	55.00	.75	
b.	Vert. pair, imperf. btwn. & at bottom		*6,000.*	
c.	Perf. 10 at top or bottom		*10,000.*	
518	$1 Franklin (414), violet brown	40.00	1.50	
b.	$1 deep brown	*1,900.*	*1,250.*	

1917-19, Watermark 191

Scott No.	Description	Unused Value	Used Value	/ / / / / /
519	2c Washington (332)	400.00	*1,750.*	

Scott No.	Description	Unused Value	Used Value
1918, Perf. 11, Unwatermarked			
523	$2 Franklin, orange red & black	550.00	250.00
524	$5 Franklin (523), deep green & black	175.00	35.00
1918-20, Perf. 11, Offset Printing			
525	1c Washington (333), gray green	2.50	.90
a.	1c dark green	6.00	1.75
c.	Horiz. pair, imperf. btwn.	100.00	*700.00*
d.	Double impression	40.00	—
526	2c Washington (333), carmine, type IV	25.00	4.00
527	2c Washington (333), carmine, type V	18.00	1.25
a.	Double impression	75.00	—
b.	Vert. pair, imperf. horiz.	*850.00*	
c.	Horiz. pair, imperf. vert.	*1,000.*	—
528	2c Washington (333), carmine, type Va	9.00	.40
c.	Double impression	55.00	
g.	Vert. pair, imperf. btwn.	*3,500.*	
528A	2c Washington (333), carmine, type VI	47.50	2.00
d.	Double impression	180.00	—
f.	Vert. pair, imperf. horiz.	—	
h.	Vert. pair, imperf. btwn.	*1,000.*	
528B	2c Washington (333), carmine, type VII	20.00	.75
e.	Double impression	77.50	*400.00*
529	3c Washington (333), violet, type III	3.50	.50
a.	Double impression	45.00	—
b.	Printed on both sides	*2,500.*	
530	3c Washington (333), purple, type IV	2.00	.30
a.	Double impression	35.00	—
b.	Printed on both sides	*350.00*	
c.	Triple impression	*1,750.*	—
Imperf.			
531	1c Washington (333), green	10.00	12.00
532	2c Washington (333), car rose, type IV	32.50	35.00
533	2c Washington (333), carmine, type V	90.00	95.00
534	2c Washington (333), carmine, type Va	12.00	9.00
534A	2c Washington (333), carmine, type VI	37.50	32.50
534B	2c Washington (333), carmine, type VII	1,750.	1,250.
535	3c Washington (333), violet, type IV	8.00	5.00
a.	Double impression	95.00	—
Perf. 12½			
536	1c Washington (333), gray green	20.00	*27.50*
a.	Horiz. pair, imperf. vert.	*1,250.*	
1919, Perf. 11, Flat Plate Printing			
537	3c Victory, violet	10.00	3.25
a.	3c deep red violet	*1,250.*	*2,250.*
b.	3c light reddish violet	125.00	45.00
c.	3c red violet	150.00	55.00

Scott No.		Description	Unused Value	Used Value
1919, Perf. 11 x 10, Rotary Press Printings, Size: 19½ to 20mm wide by 22 to 22¼ mm high				
538	1c	Washington (333), green	10.00	9.00
a.		Vert. pair, imperf. horiz	50.00	*100.00*
539	2c	Washington (333), car rose, type II	2,750.	*5,500.*
540	2c	Washington (333), car rose, type III	12.00	9.50
a.		Vert. pair, imperf. horiz	50.00	*100.00*
b.		Horiz. pair, imperf. vert.	*1,750.*	
541	3c	Washington (333), violet, type II	40.00	32.50
1920, Perf. 10 x 11, Size: 19 x 22½-22¾ mm				
542	1c	Washington (333), green	12.50	1.50
1921, Perf. 10, Size: 19 x 22½ mm				
543	1c	Washington (333), green	.70	.40
a.		Horiz. pair, imperf. btwn.	*2,750.*	
1922, Perf. 11, Size: 19 x 22½ mm				
544	1c	Washington (333), green	*22,500.*	*3,750.*
1921, Perf. 11, Size: 19½-20x22mm				
545	1c	Washington (333), green	180.00	210.00
546	2c	Washington (333), car rose, type III	110.00	*190.00*
1920, Perf. 11				
547	$2	Franklin (523), carmine & black	130.00	40.00
a.		$2 lake & black	190.00	40.00
548	1c	Pilgrim Tercentenary	4.50	2.25
549	2c	Pilgrim Tercentenary	5.75	1.60
550	5c	Pilgrim Tercentenary	40.00	14.00
1922-25, Perf. 11				
551	½c	Nathan Hale, olive brown	.25	.20
552	1c	Franklin, deep green	1.50	.20
a.		Booklet pane of 6	7.50	*4.00*
553	1½c	Warren G. Harding, yellow brown	2.30	.20
554	2c	Washington, carmine	1.40	.20
a.		Horiz. pair, imperf. vert.	*275.00*	
b.		Vert. pair, imperf. horiz	*4,000.*	
c.		Booklet pane of 6	7.00	*3.00*
d.		Perf. 10 at top or bottom	*7,000.*	*5,500.*
555	3c	Lincoln, violet	16.00	1.25
556	4c	Martha Washington, yellow brown	18.00	.50
a.		Vert. pair, imperf. horiz	*10,500.*	
b.		Perf. 10 at 10 top or bottom	*3,500.*	*25,000.*
557	5c	Theodore Roosevelt, dark blue	18.00	.30
a.		Imperf., pair	*2,000.*	
b.		Horiz. pair, imperf. vert.	—	
c.		Perf. 10 at top or bottom	—	*11,000.*

523

537

548

549

550

551

552

553

554

555

556

557

558

559

560

561

562

563

564

565

566

Scott No.	Description	Unused Value	Used Value
558	6c Garfield, red orange	35.00	1.00
559	7c William McKinley, black	8.00	.75
560	8c Grant, olive green	45.00	1.00
561	9c Jefferson, rose	13.00	1.25
562	10c James Monroe, orange	16.00	.35
a.	Vert. pair, imperf. horiz.	*2,250.*	
b.	Imperf., pair	*2,500.*	
c.	Perf. 10 at top or bottom	*25,000.*	*20,000.*
563	11c Rutherford B. Hayes, light blue	1.50	.60
a.	11c light bluish green	1.50	.60
d.	Imperf., pair		*20,000.*
564	12c Grover Cleveland, brown violet	5.50	.35
a.	Horiz. pair, imperf. vert.	*1,750.*	
565	14c American Indian, blue	4.75	.90
566	15c Statue of Liberty, gray	18.00	.30
567	20c Golden Gate, carmine rose	18.00	.30
a.	Horiz. pair, imperf. vert.	*2,000.*	
568	25c Niagara Falls, yellow green	17.50	.75
b.	Vert. pair, imperf. horiz.	*2,500.*	
c.	Perf. 10 at one side	*5,000.*	*11,000.*
569	30c American Buffalo, olive brown	27.50	.60
570	50c Arlington Amphitheater, lilac	35.00	.40
571	$1 Lincoln Memorial, violet black	37.50	.65
572	$2 U.S. Capitol, deep blue	65.00	9.00
573	$5 "America," carmine & blue	85.00	15.00
a.	$5 carmine lake & dark blue	175.00	20.00

1923-25, Imperf.

Scott No.	Description	Unused Value	Used Value
575	1c Franklin (552), green	5.00	5.00
576	1½c Harding (553), yellow brown	1.25	1.50
577	2c Washington (554), carmine	1.30	1.25
a.	2c carmine lake	—	

Rotary Press Printings, Perf. 11 x 10, Size: 19¾ x 22¼ mm

Scott No.	Description	Unused Value	Used Value
578	1c Franklin (552), green	85.00	*160.00*
579	2c Washington (554), carmine	80.00	*140.00*

Perf. 10

Scott No.	Description	Unused Value	Used Value
581	1c Franklin (552), green	10.00	.75
582	1½c Harding (553), brown	6.00	.65
583	2c Washington (554), carmine	3.00	.30
a.	Booklet pane of 6	95.00	*150.00*
584	3c Lincoln (555), violet	27.50	3.00
585	4c Martha Washington (556)	18.00	.65
586	5c Theodore Roosevelt (557), blue	18.00	.40
a.	Horiz. pair, imperf. vertically		*8,000.*
587	6c Garfield (558), red orange	9.25	.60
588	7c McKinley (559)	12.50	6.25
589	8c Grant (560)	27.50	4.50
590	9c Jefferson (561), rose	6.00	2.50
591	10c Monroe (562), orange	50.00	.50

567

568

569

570

571

572

573

610

Type I.

Type I.

Type II.

Type II.

Type I–No heavy hair lines at top center of head. Outline of left acanthus scroll generally faint at top and toward base at left side.

Type II–The heavy hair lines at top center of head; two being outstanding in the white area. Outline of left acanthus scroll very strong and clearly defined at top (under left edge of lettered panel) and at lower curve (above and to the left of numeral oval). Type II is found only on Nos. 599a and 634A.

614

615

616

Scott No.	Description	Unused Value	Used Value	/ / / / / /
Perf. 11				
594	1c Franklin (552), green	*16,000.*	11,000.	☐☐☐☐☐
595	2c Washington (554), carmine	275.00	*375.00*	☐☐☐☐☐
596	1c Franklin (552), green		*130,000.*	☐☐☐☐☐

Nos. 578-579, 594-595 were made from coil waste of Nos. 597 and 599 and measure approx. $19^3/_4$ x $22^1/_4$ mm. No 596 was made from rotary press sheet waste and measures approx. $19^1/_4$ x $22^1/_2$ mm.

Scott No.	Description	Unused Value	Used Value	/ / / / / /
1923-29, Coil Stamps, Perf. 10 Vertically, Rotary Press Printing				
597	1c Franklin (552), green	.30	.20	☐☐☐☐☐
598	1½c Harding (553), brown	.90	.20	☐☐☐☐☐
599	2c Washington (554), carmine, type I	.35	.20	☐☐☐☐☐
b.	2c carmine lake, type I	*175.00*		☐☐☐☐☐
599A	2c Washington (554), carmine, type II	105.00	17.50	☐☐☐☐☐
600	3c Lincoln (555), violet	6.25	.20	☐☐☐☐☐
601	4c Martha Washington (556)	3.75	.35	☐☐☐☐☐
602	5c Theodore Roosevelt (557), dark blue	1.75	.20	☐☐☐☐☐
603	10c Monroe (562), orange	3.50	.20	☐☐☐☐☐
Perf. 10 Horizontally				
604	1c Franklin (552), green	.40	.20	☐☐☐☐☐
605	1½c Harding (553), yellow brown	.40	.20	☐☐☐☐☐
606	2c Washington (554), carmine	.40	.20	☐☐☐☐☐
a.	2c carmine lake, type I	*75.00*		☐☐☐☐☐
1923, Perf. 11, Flat Plate Printing, Size: 19¼ x 22¼ mm				
610	2c Harding Memorial, black	.55	.25	☐☐☐☐☐
a.	Horiz. pair, imperf. vert.	*1,750.*		☐☐☐☐☐
Imperf.				
611	2c Harding Memorial (610)	4.75	4.00	☐☐☐☐☐
1923, Perf. 10, Rotary Press Printing, Size: 19¼ x 22½ mm				
612	2c Harding Memorial (610)	16.00	1.75	☐☐☐☐☐
1923, Perf. 11				
613	2c Harding Memorial (610)		*45,000.*	☐☐☐☐☐
1924-26, Perf. 11				
614	1c Huguenot-Walloon Tercentenary	2.25	*3.25*	☐☐☐☐☐
615	2c Huguenot-Walloon Tercentenary	4.50	2.25	☐☐☐☐☐
616	5c Huguenot-Walloon Tercentenary	18.00	13.00	☐☐☐☐☐
617	1c Lexington-Concord	2.10	2.50	☐☐☐☐☐
618	2c Lexington-Concord	3.90	4.00	☐☐☐☐☐
619	5c Lexington-Concord	17.00	13.00	☐☐☐☐☐
620	2c Norse-American	3.50	3.00	☐☐☐☐☐
621	5c Norse-American	11.00	11.00	☐☐☐☐☐
622	13c Benjamin Harrison, green	11.00	.75	☐☐☐☐☐
623	17c Woodrow Wilson, black	12.00	.30	☐☐☐☐☐
1926, Perf. 11				
627	2c Sesquicentennial Exposition	2.50	.50	☐☐☐☐☐
628	5c Ericsson Memorial	5.50	3.25	☐☐☐☐☐

617

618

619

620

621

622

623

627

628

629

643

644

645

Scott No.	Description	Unused Value	Used Value
629	2c Battle of White Plains	1.90	1.70
a.	Vert. pair, imperf. btwn.	—	
630	2c Battle of White Plains (629), sht of 25	375.00	450.00

1926, Imperf., Rotary Press Printings

Scott No.	Description	Unused Value	Used Value
631	1½c Harding (553), yellow brown	2.00	1.70

1926-34, Perf. 11x 10½

Scott No.	Description	Unused Value	Used Value
632	1c Franklin (552), green	.25	.20
a.	Booklet pane of 6	5.00	4.00
b.	Vert. pair, imperf. btwn.	*3,250.*	—
c.	Horiz. pair, imperf btwn.	*5,000.*	
633	1½c Harding (553), yellow brown	1.70	.20
634	2c Washington (554), carmine, type I	.20	.20
b.	2c carmine lake	225.00	—
c.	Horiz. pair, imperf. btwn.	*7,000.*	
d.	Booklet pane of 6	1.50	*1.50*
e.	As "d", carmine lake	*625.00*	
f.	2c lake, on cover		—
634A	2c Washington (554), carmine, type II	325.00	13.50
635	3c Lincoln (555), violet	.50	.20
a.	3c bright violet	.20	.20
636	4c Martha Washington (556)	1.90	.20
637	5c Theodore Roosevelt (557), dark blue	1.90	.20
638	6c Garfield (558), red orange	2.00	.20
639	7c McKinley (559)	2.00	.20
a.	Vert. pair, imperf. btwn.	325.00	250.00
640	8c Grant (560)	2.00	.20
641	9c Jefferson (561), orange red	1.90	.20
642	10c Monroe (562), orange	3.25	.20

1927, Perf. 11

Scott No.	Description	Unused Value	Used Value
643	2c Vermont Sesquicentennial	1.20	.80
644	2c Burgoyne Campaign	3.10	2.10

1928, Perf. 11

Scott No.	Description	Unused Value	Used Value
645	2c Valley Forge	.95	.50
a.	2c lake	—	

1928, Perf. 11 x 10½, Rotary Press Printing

Scott No.	Description	Unused Value	Used Value
646	2c Battle of Monmouth (Molly Pitcher), ovptd. on Washington	1.00	1.00
a.	"Pitcher" only	*500.00*	
647	2c Hawaii Sesquicentennial, ovptd. on Washington, carmine	4.00	4.00
648	5c Hawaii Sesquicentennial, ovptd. on T. Roosevelt, dark blue	11.00	12.50

1928, Perf. 11

Scott No.	Description	Unused Value	Used Value
649	2c Aeronautics Conference	1.10	.80
650	5c Aeronautics Conference	4.50	3.25

No. 634 Overprinted **MOLLY PITCHER**

Scott 646

No. 634 and 637 Overprinted **HAWAII 1778 - 1928**

Scott 647-648

649

650

Nos. 632-634, 635-642 Overprinted **Kans.**

Scott 658-668

651

Nos. 632-634, 635-642 Overprinted **Nebr.**

Scott 669-679

654

657

680

681

682

683

684

685

688

Scott No.	Description	Unused Value	Used Value	/ / / / / /
1929, Perf. 11				
651	2c George Rogers Clark	.70	.50	☐☐☐☐☐
1929, Perf. 11 x 10½, Rotary Press Printing				
653	½c Hale (551), olive brown	.25	.20	☐☐☐☐☐
1929, Perf. 11				
654	2c Electric Light	.60	.65	☐☐☐☐☐
a.	2c lake	—		☐☐☐☐☐
Perf. 11 x 10½, Rotary Press Printing				
655	2c Electric Light (654)	.55	.20	☐☐☐☐☐
Coil Stamp (Rotary Press), Perf. 10 Vertically				
656	2c Electric Light (654)	11.00	1.75	☐☐☐☐☐
1929, Perf. 11				
657	2c Sullivan Expedition	.60	.60	☐☐☐☐☐
a.	2c lake	325.00	300.00	☐☐☐☐☐
1929, Perf. 11 x 10½, Rotary Press Printing, Overprinted				
658	1c Kans. ovpt., on Franklin, green	2.50	2.00	☐☐☐☐☐
a.	Vert. pair, one without ovpt.	*375.00*		☐☐☐☐☐
659	1½c Kans. ovpt., on Harding, brown	3.10	2.90	☐☐☐☐☐
a.	Vert. pair, one without ovpt.	*425.00*		☐☐☐☐☐
660	2c Kans. ovpt., on Washington, carmine	4.00	1.00	☐☐☐☐☐
661	3c Kans. ovpt., on Lincoln, violet	18.50	15.00	☐☐☐☐☐
a.	Vert. pair, one without ovpt.	*525.00*		☐☐☐☐☐
662	4c Kans. ovpt., on Martha Washington	18.50	9.00	☐☐☐☐☐
a.	Vert. pair, one without ovpt.	*500.00*		☐☐☐☐☐
663	5c Kans. ovpt., on T. Roosevelt, dp blue	12.00	9.75	☐☐☐☐☐
664	6c Kans. ovpt., on Garfield, red orange	27.50	18.00	☐☐☐☐☐
665	7c Kans. ovpt., on McKinley	27.50	27.50	☐☐☐☐☐
a.	Vert. pair, one without ovpt.	—		☐☐☐☐☐
666	8c Kans. ovpt., on Grant	90.00	70.00	☐☐☐☐☐
667	9c Kans. ovpt., on Jefferson, light rose	13.00	11.50	☐☐☐☐☐
668	10c Kans. ovpt., on Monroe, orange yel	22.00	12.50	☐☐☐☐☐
669	1c Nebr. ovpt., on Franklin, green	3.25	2.25	☐☐☐☐☐
a.	Vert. pair, one without ovpt.	—		☐☐☐☐☐
670	1½c Nebr. ovpt., on Harding, brown	3.00	2.50	☐☐☐☐☐
671	2c Nebr. ovpt., on Washington, carmine	3.00	1.30	☐☐☐☐☐
672	3c Nebr. ovpt., on Lincoln, violet	12.00	12.00	☐☐☐☐☐
a.	Vert. pair, one without ovpt.	*500.00*		☐☐☐☐☐
673	4c Nebr. ovpt., on Martha Washington	17.50	15.00	☐☐☐☐☐
674	5c Nebr. ovpt., on T. Roosevelt, dp blue	16.00	15.00	☐☐☐☐☐
675	6c Nebr. ovpt., on Garfield, red orange	37.50	24.00	☐☐☐☐☐
676	7c Nebr. ovpt., on McKinley	21.00	18.00	☐☐☐☐☐
677	8c Nebr. ovpt., on Grant	32.50	25.00	☐☐☐☐☐
678	9c Nebr. ovpt., on Jefferson, light rose	35.00	27.50	☐☐☐☐☐
a.	Vert. pair, one without ovpt.	*750.00*		☐☐☐☐☐
679	10c Nebr. ovpt., on Monroe, orange yel	115.00	22.50	☐☐☐☐☐

689

690

692

693

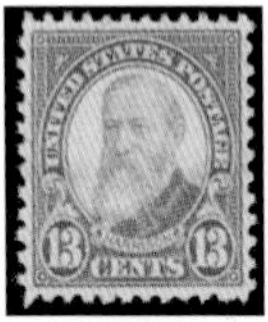

694

695

696

697

698

699

700

701

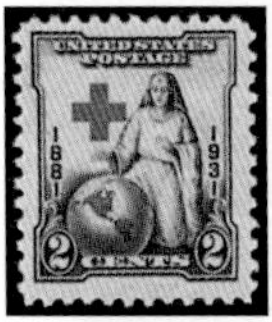

702

703

704

705

706

707

708

709

710

711

712

713

Scott No.		Description	Unused Value	Used Value	/ / / / / /
1929, Perf. 11					
680	2c	Battle of Fallen Timbers	.70	.70	
681	2c	Ohio River Canalization	.60	.60	
a.	2c	lake		—	
1930, Perf. 11					
682	2c	Massachusetts Bay Colony	.50	.50	
683	2c	Carolina-Charleston	1.05	1.05	
1930, Perf. 11x10½, Rotary Press Printing					
684	1½c	Harding, brown	.40	.20	
685	4c	William H. Taft, brown	.80	.25	
Coil Stamps, Perf. 10 Vertically					
686	1½c	Harding (684), brown	1.75	.20	
687	4c	Taft (685), brown	3.00	.45	
1930, Perf. 11					
688	2c	Battle of Braddock's Field	.90	.85	
689	2c	Von Steuben	.50	.50	
a.		Imperf., pair	*2,750.*		
1931, Perf. 11					
690	2c	Pulaski	.30	.25	
1931, Perf. 11x10½, Rotary Press Printing					
692	11c	Hayes (563)	2.50	.25	
693	12c	Cleveland (564)	5.00	.20	
694	13c	Benjamin Harrison (622), yellow green	2.25	.25	
695	14c	American Indian (565), dark blue	4.00	.45	
696	15c	Statue of Liberty (566)	7.75	.25	
Perf. 10½ x11					
697	17c	Wilson (623)	4.75	.25	
698	20c	Golden Gate (567)	7.75	.25	
699	25c	Niagara Falls (568), blue green	8.00	.25	
700	30c	American Buffalo (569), brown	13.00	.25	
701	50c	Arlington Amphitheater (570)	30.00	.25	
1931, Perf. 11, Flat Plate					
702	2c	Red Cross	.20	.20	
a.		Red cross missing (from a foldover)	*40,000.*		
703	2c	Yorktown, carmine rose & black	.35	.25	
a.	2c	lake & black	4.50	.75	
b.	2c	dark lake & black	*400.00*		
c.		Horiz. pair, imperf. vert	*5,000.*		
1932, Perf. 11x10½, Rotary Press Printings					
704	1/2c	Washington Bicentennial, olive brown	.25	.20	
705	1c	Washington Bicentennial, green	.25	.20	
706	1½c	Washington Bicentennial, brown	.45	.20	
707	2c	Washington Bicentennial, car rose	.30	.20	
708	3c	Washington Bicentennial, deep violet	.55	.20	
709	4c	Washington Bicentennial, light brown	.40	.20	
710	5c	Washington Bicentennial, blue	1.50	.20	

714

715

716

717

718

719

720

723

724

725

726

727

728

729

732

733

734

736

737

739

740

741

742

Scott No.		Description	Unused Value	Used Value
711	6c	Washington Bicentennial, red orange	3.00	.20
712	7c	Washington Bicentennial, black....	.50	.20
713	8c	Washington Bicentennial, olive bister	2.75	.50
714	9c	Washington Bicentennial, pale red.....	2.25	.20
715	10c	Washington Bicentennial, orange yel.	10.00	.20
Perf. 11				
716	2c	Olympic Winter Games, carmine rose	.40	.20
a.		2c lake	—	
Perf. 11x10½, Rotary Press Printing				
717	2c	Arbor Day	.25	.20
Perf. 11x10½				
718	3c	Olympic Games	1.50	.20
719	5c	Olympic Games	2.25	.20
720	3c	Washington, deep violet	.20	.20
b.		Booklet pane of 6	35.00	*12.50*
c.		Vert. pair, imperf. btwn.	*700.00*	*1,350.*
Coil Stamps, Perf. 10 Vertically, Rotary Press Printing				
721	3c	Washington (720)	2.75	.20
Perf. 10 Horizontally				
722	3c	Washington (720)	1.50	.35
Perf. 10 Vertically				
723	6c	Garfield (558), deep orange..........	11.00	.30
1932-33, Perf. 11				
724	3c	William Penn	.45	.20
a.		Vert. pair, imperf. horiz.	—	
725	3c	Daniel Webster..............................	.45	.25
726	3c	Georgia Bicentennial....................	.45	.20
1933, Perf. 10½x11, Rotary Press Printing				
727	3c	Peace of 1783...............................	.20	.20
728	1c	Century of Progress, yellow green	.20	.20
729	3c	Century of Progress, violet...........	.25	.20
1933, Imperf., Flat Plate Printing				
730		American Phil. Society, Sheet of 25	27.50	27.50
a.	1c	Single stamp, Century of Progress (728)	.75	.50
731		American Phil. Society, Sheet of 25	25.00	25.00
a.	3c	Single stamp, Century of Progress (729)	.65	.50
1933, Perforated				
732	3c	National Recovery Act	.20	.20
733	3c	Byrd Antarctic	.50	.50
734	5c	Kosciuszko...................................	.55	.25
a.		Horiz. pair, imperf. vert................	*2,250.*	
1934, Imperf.				
735	3c	National Stamp Exhibition, Sheet of 6	12.00	10.00
a.		Single stamp, Byrd Antarctic	1.90	1.65

743

744

745

747

746

748

749

752

753

754

755

772

773

774

775

Scott No.		Description	Unused Value	Used Value	/ / / / / /
Perf. 11					
736	3c	Maryland Tercentenary	.25	.20	
a.		Horiz. pair, imperf. btwn.	7,000.		
Perf. 11x10½					
737	3c	Mothers of America	.20	.20	
Perf. 11					
738	3c	Mothers of America (737)	.20	.20	
739	3c	Wisconsin Tercentenary	.25	.20	
a.		Vert. pair, imperf. horiz.	*350.00*		
b.		Horiz. pair, imperf. vert.	*500.00*		
740	1c	National Parks - Yosemite	.25	.20	
a.		Vert. pair, imperf. horiz., with gum	*1,500.*		
741	2c	National Parks - Grand Canyon	.25	.20	
a.		Vert. pair, imperf. horiz., with gum	*575.00*		
b.		Horiz. pair, imperf. vert., with gum	*550.00*		
742	3c	National Parks - Mt. Rainier	.35	.20	
a.		Vert. pair, imperf. horiz., with gum	*700.00*		
743	4c	National Parks - Mesa Verde	.45	.40	
a.		Vert. pair, imperf. horiz., with gum	*1,000.*		
744	5c	National Parks - Yellowstone	.75	.65	
a.		Horiz. pair, imperf. vert., with gum	*600.00*		
745	6c	National Parks - Crater Lake	1.10	.85	
746	7c	National Parks - Acadia	.75	.75	
a.		Horiz. pair, imperf. vert., with gum	*600.00*		
747	8c	National Parks - Zion	1.60	1.50	
748	9c	National Parks - Glacier	1.50	.65	
749	10c	National Parks - Great Smoky Mountains	3.00	1.25	
Imperf.					
750		American Philatelic Society, sheet of 6	30.00	27.50	
a.	3c	Single stamp, National Parks (742)	3.75	3.25	
751		Trans-Mississippi Phil. Exhib, sheet of 6	12.50	12.50	
a.	1c	Single stamp, National Parks (740)	2.00	1.60	
1935, Perf. 10½x11, Rotary Press Printing					
752	3c	Peace of 1783 Issue (727)	.25	.20	
Perf. 11, Flat Plate Printing					
753	3c	Byrd Antarctic (733)	.50	.45	

No. 753 is similar to No. 733. Positive identification is by blocks or pairs showing guide lines between stamps. These lines between stamps are found only on No. 753.

Scott No.		Description	Unused Value	Used Value	/ / / / / /
Imperf.					
754	3c	Mothers of America (737).............	.60	.60	☐☐☐☐☐
755	3c	Wisconsin Tercentenary (739).......	.60	.60	☐☐☐☐☐
756	1c	National Parks - Yosemite (740) ...	.20	.20	☐☐☐☐☐
757	2c	National Parks - Grand Canyon (741)	.25	.25	☐☐☐☐☐
758	3c	National Parks - Mt. Rainier (742)	.50	.45	☐☐☐☐☐
759	4c	National Parks - Mesa Verde (743)	.95	.95	☐☐☐☐☐
760	5c	National Parks - Yellowstone (744)	1.50	1.40	☐☐☐☐☐
761	6c	National Parks - Crater Lake (745)	2.25	2.25	☐☐☐☐☐
762	7c	National Parks - Acadia (746).......	1.50	1.40	☐☐☐☐☐
763	8c	National Parks - Zion (747)	1.80	1.50	☐☐☐☐☐
764	9c	National Parks - Glacier (748)......	1.90	1.75	☐☐☐☐☐
765	10c	National Parks - Great Smoky Mountains (749)..........................	3.75	3.50	☐☐☐☐☐
766		American Phil. Society, Pane of 25	25.00	25.00	☐☐☐☐☐
a.	1c	Single stamp, Century of Progress (728)	.70	.50	☐☐☐☐☐
767		American Phil. Society, Pane of 25	23.50	23.50	☐☐☐☐☐
a.	3c	Single stamp, Century of Progress (729)	.60	.50	☐☐☐☐☐
768		National Stamp Exhibition, Pane of 6	20.00	15.00	☐☐☐☐☐
a.	3c	Single stamp, Byrd Antarctic (733)	2.80	2.40	☐☐☐☐☐
769		Trans-Mississippi Phil. Exhib, Pane of 6	12.50	11.00	☐☐☐☐☐
a.	1c	Single stamp - Yosemite (740)	1.85	1.80	☐☐☐☐☐
770		American Phil. Society, Pane of 6	30.00	24.00	☐☐☐☐☐
a.	3c	Single stamp, Mt. Rainier - (742).	3.25	3.10	☐☐☐☐☐
771	16c	Air Post Special Delivery (CE1)...	2.60	2.60	☐☐☐☐☐

Nos. 766-770 were issued in sheets of 9 panes of 25 stamps each. Single items from these sheets are identical with other varieties, 766 and 730, 766a and 730a, 767 and 731, 767a and 731a, 768 and 735, 768a and 735a, 769 and 756, 770 and 758. Positive identification is by blocks or pairs showing wide gutters between stamps. These wide gutters occurs only on Nos. 766-770 and measure, horizontally, 13mm on Nos. 766-767, 16mm on No. 768, and 23mm on Nos. 769-770.

Scott No.		Description	Unused Value	Used Value	/ / / / / /
1935, Perf. 11x10½, 11					
772	3c	Connecticut Tercentenary.............	.30	.20	☐☐☐☐☐
773	3c	California Pacific Exposition........	.30	.20	☐☐☐☐☐
774	3c	Boulder Dam	.30	.20	☐☐☐☐☐
775	3c	Michigan Centenary	.30	.20	☐☐☐☐☐
1936					
776	3c	Texas Centennial............................	.30	.20	☐☐☐☐☐
777	3c	Rhode Island Tercentenary...........	.35	.20	☐☐☐☐☐
778		3rd Intl. Phil. Exhib., Sht. of 4, imperf.	1.75	1.25	☐☐☐☐☐
a.	3c	Connecticut Tercentenary (772)....	.40	.30	☐☐☐☐☐
b.	3c	California Pacific Exposition (773)	.40	.30	☐☐☐☐☐
c.	3c	Michigan Centennial (775)	.40	.30	☐☐☐☐☐
d.	3c	Texas Centennial (776).................	.40	.30	☐☐☐☐☐
782	3c	Arkansas Centennial......................	.30	.20	☐☐☐☐☐
783	3c	Oregon Territory	.25	.20	☐☐☐☐☐
784	3c	Susan B. Anthony	.25	.20	☐☐☐☐☐

Scott No.	Description	Unused Value	Used Value	/ / / / / /
1936-37				
785	1c Army - Washington & Greene	.25	.20	☐☐☐☐☐
786	2c Army - A. Jackson & Scott	.25	.20	☐☐☐☐☐
787	3c Army - Sherman, Grant & Sheridan	.35	.20	☐☐☐☐☐
788	4c Army - Lee & "Stonewall" Jackson	.55	.20	☐☐☐☐☐
789	5c Army - West Point	.65	.25	☐☐☐☐☐
790	1c Navy - Jones & Barry	.25	.20	☐☐☐☐☐
791	2c Navy - Decatur & MacDonough	.25	.20	☐☐☐☐☐
792	3c Navy - Farragut & Porter	.35	.20	☐☐☐☐☐
793	4c Navy - Sampson, Dewey & Schley	.55	.20	☐☐☐☐☐
794	5c Navy - Academy Seal & Cadets	.65	.25	☐☐☐☐☐
1937				
795	3c Ordinance of 1787	.30	.20	☐☐☐☐☐
796	5c Virginia Dare	.35	.20	☐☐☐☐☐
797	10c Society of Philatelic Americans, blue green, imperf	.60	.40	☐☐☐☐☐
798	3c Constitution Sesquicentennial	.35	.20	☐☐☐☐☐
799	3c Hawaii	.35	.20	☐☐☐☐☐
800	3c Alaska	.35	.20	☐☐☐☐☐
801	3c Puerto Rico	.35	.20	☐☐☐☐☐
802	3c Virgin Islands	.35	.20	☐☐☐☐☐
1938-54, Perf. 11x10½, 11				
803	½c Benjamin Franklin	.20	.20	☐☐☐☐☐
804	1c George Washington	.25	.20	☐☐☐☐☐
b.	Booklet pane of 6	2.00	.50	☐☐☐☐☐
805	1½c Martha Washington	.20	.20	☐☐☐☐☐
b.	Horiz. pair, imperf. btwn.	125.00	20.00	☐☐☐☐☐
806	2c John Adams	.25	.20	☐☐☐☐☐
b.	Booklet pane of 6	5.50	1.00	☐☐☐☐☐
807	3c Thomas Jefferson	.25	.20	☐☐☐☐☐
a.	Booklet pane of 6	8.50	*2.00*	☐☐☐☐☐
b.	Horiz. pair, imperf. btwn.	*1,750.*	—	☐☐☐☐☐
c.	Imperf., pair	*2,750.*		☐☐☐☐☐
808	4c James Madison	.75	.20	☐☐☐☐☐
809	4½c White House	.30	.20	☐☐☐☐☐
810	5c James Monroe	.35	.20	☐☐☐☐☐
811	6c John Quincy Adams	.40	.20	☐☐☐☐☐
812	7c Andrew Jackson	.40	.20	☐☐☐☐☐
813	8c Martin Van Buren	.40	.20	☐☐☐☐☐
814	9c William Henry Harrison	.40	.20	☐☐☐☐☐
815	10c John Tyler	.40	.20	☐☐☐☐☐
816	11c James Knox Polk	.75	.20	☐☐☐☐☐
817	12c Zachary Taylor	1.00	.20	☐☐☐☐☐
818	13c Millard Fillmore	1.30	.20	☐☐☐☐☐
819	14c Franklin Pierce	1.00	.20	☐☐☐☐☐
820	15c James Buchanan	.70	.20	☐☐☐☐☐
821	16c Abraham Lincoln	3.00	.25	☐☐☐☐☐
822	17c Andrew Johnson	1.00	.20	☐☐☐☐☐

776

777

782

783

784

785

786

787

788

789

790

791

HOW TO USE THIS BOOK

The number in the first column is its Scott number or identifying number. Following that is the denomination of the stamp and its color or description. Finally, the values, unused and used, are shown.

792

793

796

794

795

799

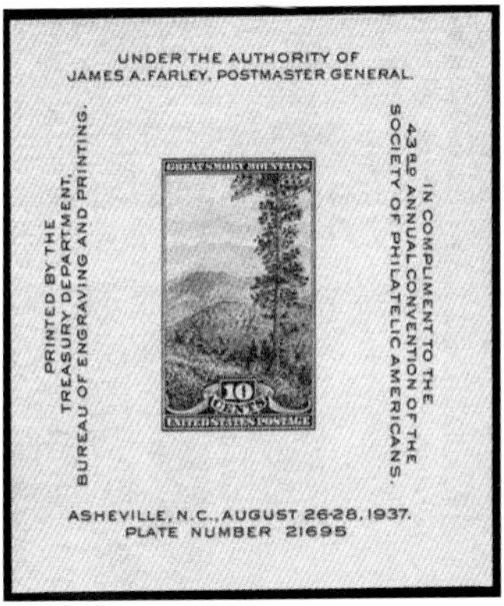

797

798

800

801

802

803

804

805

806

807

808

809

810

811

812

813

814

815

816

817

818

819

820

821

822

823

824

825

826

827

828

829

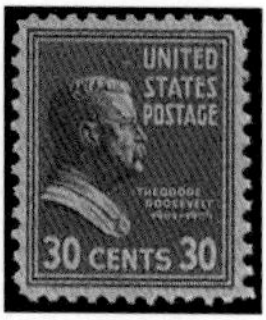

830

Scott No.		Description	Unused Value	Used Value
823	18c	Ulysses S. Grant	2.25	.20
824	19c	Rutherford B. Hayes	1.30	.35
825	20c	James A. Garfield	1.00	.20
826	21c	Chester Arthur	1.30	.20
827	22c	Grover Cleveland	1.20	.40
828	24c	Benjamin Harrison	3.50	.20
829	25c	William McKinley	1.00	.20
830	30c	Theodore Roosevelt, deep ultramarine	4.00	.20
a.	30c	blue	15.00	—
b.	30c	deep blue	240.00	—
831	50c	William Howard Taft	5.00	.20
832	$1	Woodrow Wilson, purple & black	7.00	.20
a.		Vert. pair, imperf. horiz.	*1,500.*	
b.		Wmkd. USIR	150.00	65.00
c.	$1	red violet & black	6.00	.20
d.		As "c," vert. pair, imperf. horiz.	*1,250.*	
e.		Vert. pair, imperf. btwn.	*2,750.*	
f.		As "c," vert. pair, imperf. btwn.	*8,500.*	
833	$2	Warren G. Harding	17.50	3.75
834	$5	Calvin Coolidge, carmine and black	85.00	3.00
a.	$5	red brown & black	*3,000.*	*7,000.*
1938				
835	3c	Constitution Ratification	.45	.20
836	3c	Swedish-Finnish Tercentenary	.35	.20
837	3c	Northwest Territory Sesquicentennial	.30	.20
838	3c	Iowa Territory Centennial	.35	.20
1939, Coil Stamps, Perf. 10 Vertically				
839	1c	George Washington (804)	.30	.20
840	1½c	Martha Washington (805)	.30	.20
841	2c	John Adams (806)	.40	.20
842	3c	Thomas Jefferson (807)	.50	.20
843	4c	James Madison (808)	7.50	.40
844	4½c	White House (809)	.70	.40
845	5c	James Monroe (810)	5.00	.35
846	6c	John Quincy Adams (811)	1.10	.20
847	10c	John Tyler (815)	11.00	1.00
Perf. 10 Horizontally				
848	1c	George Washington (804)	.85	.20
849	1½c	Martha Washington (805)	1.25	.30
850	2c	John Adams (806)	2.50	.40
851	3c	Thomas Jefferson (807)	2.50	.40
1939				
852	3c	Golden Gate Intl. Exposition	.30	.20
853	3c	New York World's Fair	.30	.20
854	3c	Washington Inauguration	.55	.20
855	3c	Baseball Centennial	1.75	.20
856	3c	Panama Canal	.35	.20

831

832

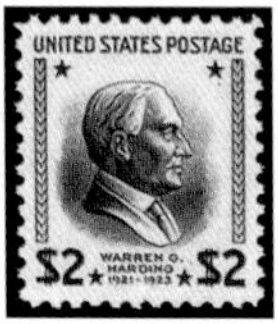

833

834

835

836

837

838

852

853

854

855

856

857

858

Scott No.	Description	Unused Value	Used Value	/ / / / / /
857	3c Printing Tercentenary	.25	.20	
858	3c 50th Anniversary of Statehood	.35	.20	
1940				
859	1c Washington Irving	.20	.20	
860	2c James Fenimore Cooper	.20	.20	
861	3c Ralph Waldo Emerson	.25	.20	
862	5c Louise May Alcott	.35	.20	
863	10c Samuel L. Clemens	1.75	1.20	
864	1c Henry Wadsworth Longfellow	.20	.20	
865	2c John Greenleaf Whittier	.20	.20	
866	3c James Russell Lowell	.25	.20	
867	5c Walt Whitman	.50	.20	
868	10c James Whitcomb Riley	1.75	1.25	
869	1c Horace Mann	.20	.20	
870	2c Mark Hopkins	.20	.20	
871	3c Charles W. Eliot	.25	.20	
872	5c Frances E. Willard	.50	.20	
873	10c Booker T. Washington	2.25	1.10	
874	1c John James Audubon	.20	.20	
875	2c Dr. Crawford W. Long	.20	.20	
876	3c Luther Burbank	.25	.20	
877	5c Dr. Walter Reed	.35	.20	
878	10c Jane Addams	1.50	.85	
879	1c Stephen Collins Foster	.20	.20	
880	2c John Philip Sousa	.20	.20	
881	3c Victor Herbert	.25	.20	
882	5c Edward A. MacDowell	.50	.20	
883	10c Ethelbert Nevin	3.75	1.35	
884	1c Gilbert Charles Stuart	.20	.20	
885	2c James A. McNeill Whistler	.20	.20	
886	3c Augustus Saint-Gaudens	.30	.20	
887	5c Daniel Chester French	.50	.20	
888	10c Frederic Remington	1.75	1.25	
889	1c Eli Whitney	.25	.20	
890	2c Samuel F.B. Morse	.30	.20	
891	3c Cyrus Hall McCormick	.30	.20	
892	5c Elias Howe	1.10	.30	
893	10c Alexander Graham Bell	11.00	2.00	
894	3c Pony Express	.50	.20	
895	3c Pan American Union	.30	.20	
896	3c Idaho Statehood	.35	.20	
897	3c Wyoming Statehood	.30	.20	
898	3c Coronado Expedition	.25	.20	
899	1c National Defense	.20	.20	
a.	Vert. pair, imperf. btwn.	*600.00*	—	
b.	Horiz. pair, imperf. btwn.	35.00	—	
900	2c National Defense	.20	.20	
a.	Horiz. pair, imperf. btwn.	37.50	—	

859

860

861

862

863

864

865

866

867

868

869

870

871

872

873

874

875

876

877

878

879

880

881

882

883

884

885

886

887

888

889

890

891

892

893

894

895

896

897

898

899

900

901

905

907

902

903

904

Scott No.	Description	Unused Value	Used Value	/ / / / / /
901	3c National Defense	.20	.20	□□□□□
a.	Horiz. pair, imperf. btwn.	22.50	—	□□□□□
902	3c Thirteenth Amendment	.30	.20	□□□□□
1941				
903	3c Vermont Statehood	.45	.20	□□□□□
1942				
904	3c Kentucky Statehood	.30	.20	□□□□□
905	3c Win the War, violet	.20	.20	□□□□□
b.	3c reddish violet	*750.00*	*500.00*	□□□□□
906	5c Chinese Resistance	1.40	.20	□□□□□
1943				
907	2c Allied Nations	.20	.20	□□□□□
908	1c Four Freedoms	.20	.20	□□□□□
1943-44, Nos. 910-921 like No. 909				
909	5c Poland	.25	.20	□□□□□
a.	Double impression of "Poland"	—		□□□□□
b.	Double impression of black flag color and red "Poland"	—		□□□□□
910	5c Czechoslovakia	.25	.20	□□□□□
a.	Double impression of "Czecholovakia"	—		□□□□□
911	5c Norway	.25	.20	□□□□□
a.	Double impression of "Norway"	—		□□□□□
912	5c Luxembourg	.25	.20	□□□□□
a.	Double impression of "Luxembourg"	—		□□□□□
913	5c Netherlands	.25	.20	□□□□□
c.	Double impression of black	—		□□□□□
914	5c Belgium	.20	.20	□□□□□
a.	Double impression of "Belgium".	—		□□□□□
915	5c France	.25	.20	□□□□□
916	5c Greece	.50	.25	□□□□□
917	5c Yugoslavia	.40	.20	□□□□□
b.	Double impression of black.	—		□□□□□
918	5c Albania	.25	.20	□□□□□
a.	Double impression of "Albania"	—		□□□□□
919	5c Austria	.30	.20	□□□□□
a.	Double impression of "Austria".	—		□□□□□
c.	Double impression of black	—		□□□□□
920	5c Denmark, blue violet, red & black	.30	.20	□□□□□
b.	5c blue violet, red & gray	.30	.20	□□□□□
921	5c Korea reverse printing of flag colors (light blue over gray)	.25	.20	□□□□□
a.	Double impression of "Korea"	—		□□□□□

906

908

909

922

923

924

925

926

927

928

929

930

931

932

933

934

935

936

937

938

939

940

941

942

943

944

945

946

947

948

949

950

951

952

953

954

955

956

957

958

959

960

961

962

963

964

965

966

967

968

969

970

971

972

Scott No.	Description	Unused Value	Used Value	/ / / / / /
1944				
922	3c Transcontinental Railroad	.25	.20	☐☐☐☐☐
923	3c Steamship	.20	.20	☐☐☐☐☐
924	3c Telegraph	.20	.20	☐☐☐☐☐
925	3c Philippines	.20	.20	☐☐☐☐☐
926	3c Motion Pictures	.20	.20	☐☐☐☐☐
1945				
927	3c Florida Statehood	.20	.20	☐☐☐☐☐
928	5c United Nations Conference	.20	.20	☐☐☐☐☐
929	3c Iwo Jima (Marines)	.30	.20	☐☐☐☐☐
1945-46				
930	1c Franklin D. Roosevelt	.20	.20	☐☐☐☐☐
931	2c Franklin D. Roosevelt	.20	.20	☐☐☐☐☐
932	3c Franklin D. Roosevelt	.20	.20	☐☐☐☐☐
933	5c Franklin D. Roosevelt	.20	.20	☐☐☐☐☐
1945				
934	3c Army	.20	.20	☐☐☐☐☐
935	3c Navy	.20	.20	☐☐☐☐☐
936	3c Coast Guard	.20	.20	☐☐☐☐☐
937	3c Alfred E. Smith	.20	.20	☐☐☐☐☐
938	3c Texas Statehood	.20	.20	☐☐☐☐☐
1946				
939	3c Merchant Marine	.20	.20	☐☐☐☐☐
940	3c Veterans of World War II	.20	.20	☐☐☐☐☐
941	3c Tennessee Statehood	.20	.20	☐☐☐☐☐
942	3c Iowa Statehood	.20	.20	☐☐☐☐☐
943	3c Smithsonian Institution	.20	.20	☐☐☐☐☐
944	3c Kearny Expedition	.20	.20	☐☐☐☐☐
1947				
945	3c Thomas A. Edison	.20	.20	☐☐☐☐☐
946	3c Joseph Pulitzer	.20	.20	☐☐☐☐☐
947	3c Postage Stamp Centenary	.20	.20	☐☐☐☐☐
948	CIPEX, Sheet of 2, imperf	.55	.45	☐☐☐☐☐
a.	5c Franklin (1), blue	.20	.20	☐☐☐☐☐
b.	10c Washington (2), brown orange	.25	.25	☐☐☐☐☐
949	3c Doctors	.20	.20	☐☐☐☐☐
950	3c Utah	.20	.20	☐☐☐☐☐
951	3c U.S. Frigate *Constitution*	.20	.20	☐☐☐☐☐
952	3c Everglades National Park	.20	.20	☐☐☐☐☐
1948				
953	3c George Washington Carver	.20	.20	☐☐☐☐☐
954	3c California Gold	.20	.20	☐☐☐☐☐
955	3c Mississippi Territory	.20	.20	☐☐☐☐☐
956	3c Four Chaplains	.20	.20	☐☐☐☐☐
957	3c Wisconsin Statehood	.20	.20	☐☐☐☐☐
958	5c Swedish Pioneers	.20	.20	☐☐☐☐☐

973

974

975

976

977

978

979

980

981

982

983

989

984

985

986

987

988

Scott No.	Description	Unused Value	Used Value	/ / / / / /
959	3c Progress of Women	.20	.20	☐☐☐☐☐
960	3c William Allen White	.20	.20	☐☐☐☐☐
961	3c U.S.-Canada Friendship	.20	.20	☐☐☐☐☐
962	3c Francis Scott Key	.20	.20	☐☐☐☐☐
963	3c Salute to Youth	.20	.20	☐☐☐☐☐
964	3c Oregon Territory	.20	.20	☐☐☐☐☐
965	3c Harlan F. Stone	.20	.20	☐☐☐☐☐
966	3c Palomar Mountain Observatory	.20	.20	☐☐☐☐☐
a.	Vert. pair, imperf. btwn.	*350.00*		☐☐☐☐☐
967	3c Clara Barton	.20	.20	☐☐☐☐☐
968	3c Poultry Industry	.20	.20	☐☐☐☐☐
969	3c Gold Star Mothers	.20	.20	☐☐☐☐☐
970	3c Fort Kearny	.20	.20	☐☐☐☐☐
971	3c Volunteer Firemen	.20	.20	☐☐☐☐☐
972	3c Indian Centennial	.20	.20	☐☐☐☐☐
973	3c Rough Riders	.20	.20	☐☐☐☐☐
974	3c Juliette Low	.20	.20	☐☐☐☐☐
975	3c Will Rogers	.20	.20	☐☐☐☐☐
976	3c Fort Bliss	.20	.20	☐☐☐☐☐
977	3c Moina Michael	.20	.20	☐☐☐☐☐
978	3c Gettysburg Address	.20	.20	☐☐☐☐☐
979	3c American Turners	.20	.20	☐☐☐☐☐
980	3c Joel Chandler Harris	.20	.20	☐☐☐☐☐
1949				
981	3c Minnesota Territory	.20	.20	☐☐☐☐☐
982	3c Washington and Lee University	.20	.20	☐☐☐☐☐
983	3c Puerto Rico Election	.20	.20	☐☐☐☐☐
984	3c Annapolis Tercentenary	.20	.20	☐☐☐☐☐
985	3c Grand Army of the Republic	.20	.20	☐☐☐☐☐
986	3c Edgar Allan Poe	.20	.20	☐☐☐☐☐
1950				
987	3c American Bankers Association	.20	.20	☐☐☐☐☐
988	3c Samuel Gompers	.20	.20	☐☐☐☐☐
989	3c Statue of Freedom	.20	.20	☐☐☐☐☐
990	3c White House	.20	.20	☐☐☐☐☐
991	3c Supreme Court	.20	.20	☐☐☐☐☐
992	3c U.S. Capitol	.20	.20	☐☐☐☐☐
993	3c Railroad Engineers	.20	.20	☐☐☐☐☐
994	3c Kansas City, Missouri	.20	.20	☐☐☐☐☐
995	3c Boy Scouts	.20	.20	☐☐☐☐☐
996	3c Indiana Territory	.20	.20	☐☐☐☐☐
997	3c California Statehood	.20	.20	☐☐☐☐☐
1951				
998	3c United Confederate Veterans	.20	.20	☐☐☐☐☐
999	3c Nevada Centennial	.20	.20	☐☐☐☐☐
1000	3c Landing of Cadillac	.20	.20	☐☐☐☐☐
1001	3c Colorado Statehood	.20	.20	☐☐☐☐☐

990

991

992

993

994

995

996

997

998

999

1000

1001

1002

1003

1004

1005

1006

1007

1008

1009

1010

1011

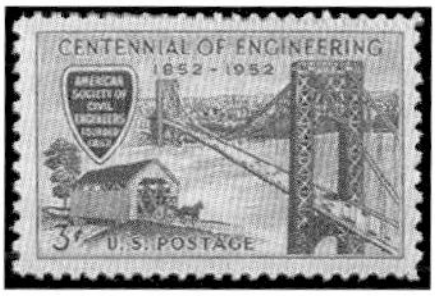

1012

1013

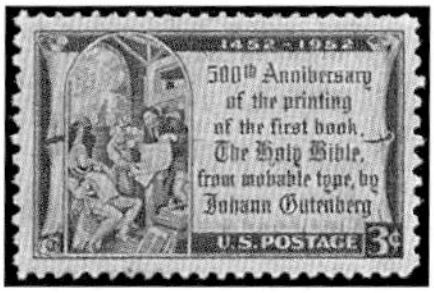

1014

1015

1016

1017

1018

1019

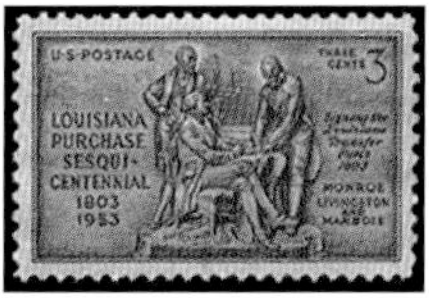

1020

1021

1022

1023

1024

1025

1026

1027

1028

1029

1030

1031

1031A

1032

1033

1034

1035

1036

1037

1038

1039

1040

1041

1042

1042A

1043

1044

Scott No.	Description	Unused Value	Used Value	/ / / / / /
1002	3c American Chemical Society	.20	.20	□□□□□
1003	3c Battle of Brooklyn	.20	.20	□□□□□
1952				
1004	3c Betsy Ross	.20	.20	□□□□□
1005	3c 4-H Clubs	.20	.20	□□□□□
1006	3c B. & O. Railroad	.20	.20	□□□□□
1007	3c American Automobile Association	.20	.20	□□□□□
1008	3c NATO	.20	.20	□□□□□
1009	3c Grand Coulee Dam	.20	.20	□□□□□
1010	3c Lafayette	.20	.20	□□□□□
1011	3c Mt. Rushmore	.20	.20	□□□□□
1012	3c Engineering	.20	.20	□□□□□
1013	3c Service Women	.20	.20	□□□□□
1014	3c Gutenberg Bible	.20	.20	□□□□□
1015	3c Newspaper Boys	.20	.20	□□□□□
1016	3c Red Cross	.20	.20	□□□□□
1953				
1017	3c National Guard	.20	.20	□□□□□
1018	3c Ohio Statehood	.20	.20	□□□□□
1019	3c Washington Territory	.20	.20	□□□□□
1020	3c Louisiana Purchase	.20	.20	□□□□□
1021	5c Opening of Japan	.20	.20	□□□□□
1022	3c American Bar Association	.20	.20	□□□□□
1023	3c Sagamore Hill	.20	.20	□□□□□
1024	3c Future Farmers of America	.20	.20	□□□□□
1025	3c Trucking Industry	.20	.20	□□□□□
1026	3c General George S. Patton, Jr.	.20	.20	□□□□□
1027	3c New York City	.20	.20	□□□□□
1028	3c Gadsden Purchase	.20	.20	□□□□□
1954				
1029	3c Columbia University	.20	.20	□□□□□
1954-68, Perf. 11x10½, 10½ x11, 11				
1030	½c Benjamin Franklin	.20	.20	□□□□□
1031	1c George Washington	.20	.20	□□□□□
1031A	1¼c Palace of the Governors	.20	.20	□□□□□
1032	1½c Mount Vernon	.20	.20	□□□□□
1033	2c Thomas Jefferson	.20	.20	□□□□□
1034	2½c Bunker Hill Monument	.20	.20	□□□□□
1035	3c Statue of Liberty, untagged	.20	.20	□□□□□
a.	Booklet pane of 6	4.00	*1.25*	□□□□□
b.	Tagged	.35	.25	□□□□□
c.	Imperf. pair	*1,750.*		□□□□□
d.	Horiz. pair, imperf. btwn.	—		□□□□□
g.	As "a," vert. imperf. btwn.	—		□□□□□
1036	4c Abraham Lincoln, untagged	.20	.20	□□□□□
a.	Booklet pane of 6	2.75	1.25	□□□□□
b.	Tagged	.65	.40	□□□□□

1044A

1045

1046

1047

1048

1049

1050

1051

1052

1053

1060

1061

1062

1063

1064

1065

1066

1067

Scott No.		Description	Unused Value	Used Value	/ / / / / /
d.		As "a," vert. imperf. horiz.	—		
e.		Horiz. pair, imperf btwn.	*3,500.*		
1037	4½c	Hermitage	.20	.20	
1038	5c	James Monroe	.20	.20	
1039	6c	Theodore Roosevelt	.25	.20	
b.		Imper., pair	*23,000.*		
1040	7c	Woodrow Wilson	.20	.20	
a.	7c	Dark rose carmine	.20	.20	
1041	8c	Statue of Liberty, 22.7 mm high	.25	.20	
a.		Double impression of carmine	*575.00*		
1041B	8c	Statue of Liberty(1041), 2.9 mm high	.40	.20	
1042	8c	Statue of Liberty	.20	.20	
1042A	8c	General John J. Pershing	.20	.20	
1043	9c	Alamo	.30	.20	
a.	9c	Dark rose lilac	.30	.20	
1044	10c	Independence Hall, untagged	.30	.20	
b.	10c	Dark rose lake	.25	.20	
d.		Tagged	2.00	1.00	
1044A	11c	Statue of Liberty, untagged	.30	.20	
c.		Tagged	2.50	1.60	
1045	12c	Benjamin Harrison, untagged	.35	.20	
a.		Tagged	.35	.20	
1046	15c	John Jay, untagged	.60	.20	
a.		Tagged	1.10	.80	
1047	20c	Monticello	.50	.20	
a.	20c	Deep bright ultramarine	.50	.20	
1048	25c	Paul Revere	1.10	.75	
1049	30c	Robert E. Lee	1.00	.20	
a.	30c	Intense black	1.20	.75	
1050	40c	John Marshall	1.50	.20	
1051	50c	Susan B. Anthony	1.50	.20	
1052	$1	Patrick Henry	4.50	.20	
1053	$5	Alexander Hamilton	57.50	6.75	

1954-73, Perf. 10 Vertically, Horizontally (1¼c, 4½c)

Scott No.		Description	Unused Value	Used Value	/ / / / / /
1054	1c	George Washington (1031)	.20	.20	
b.		Imperf., pair	*2,500.*	—	
1054A	1¼c	Palace of the Governors (1031A)	.20	.20	
c.		Imperf. pair	—		
1055	2c	Thomas Jefferson (1033), untagged	.35	.20	
a.		Tagged	.20	.20	
b.		Imperf. pair, untagged (Bureau precanceled)		*425.00*	
c.		As "a," imperf. pair, tagged	*550.00*		
1056	2½c	Bunker Hill Monument (1034)	.30	.25	
1057	3c	Statue of Liberty (1035), untagged	.35	.20	
a.		Imperf., pair	*1,750.*	800.00	

1068

1069

1070

1071

1072

1074

1073

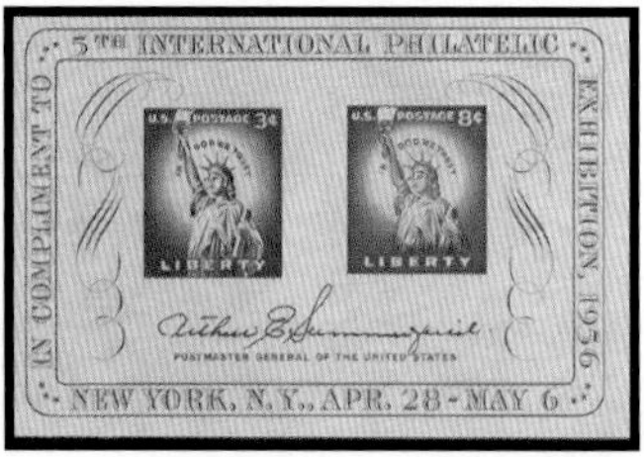

1075

1076

1077

1078

1079

1080

1081

Scott No.		Description	Unused Value	Used Value	/ / / / / /
b.		Tagged	1.00	.50	☐☐☐☐☐
1058	4c	Abraham Lincoln (1036)	.50	.20	☐☐☐☐☐
a.		Imperf., pair	75.00	70.00	☐☐☐☐☐
1059	4½c	Hermitage (1037)	1.50	1.00	☐☐☐☐☐
1059A	25c	Paul Revere (1048), untagged	.50	.30	☐☐☐☐☐
b.		Tagged	.80	.20	☐☐☐☐☐
d.		Imperf., pair	30.00		☐☐☐☐☐
1954					
1060	3c	Nebraska Territory	.20	.20	☐☐☐☐☐
1061	3c	Kansas Territory	.20	.20	☐☐☐☐☐
1062	3c	George Eastman	.20	.20	☐☐☐☐☐
1063	3c	Lewis and Clark Expedition	.20	.20	☐☐☐☐☐
1955					
1064	3c	Pennsylvania Academy of the Fine Arts	.20	.20	☐☐☐☐☐
1065	3c	Land Grant Colleges	.20	.20	☐☐☐☐☐
1066	8c	Rotary International	.25	.20	☐☐☐☐☐
1067	3c	Armed Forces Reserve	.20	.20	☐☐☐☐☐
1068	3c	New Hampshire	.20	.20	☐☐☐☐☐
1069	3c	Soo Locks	.20	.20	☐☐☐☐☐
1070	3c	Atoms for Peace	.20	.20	☐☐☐☐☐
1071	3c	Fort Ticonderoga	.20	.20	☐☐☐☐☐
1072	3c	Andrew W. Mellon	.20	.20	☐☐☐☐☐
1956					
1073	3c	Benjamin Franklin	.20	.20	☐☐☐☐☐
1074	3c	Booker T. Washington	.20	.20	☐☐☐☐☐
1075		FIPEX, Sheet of 2, imperf.	1.80	1.50	☐☐☐☐☐
a.	3c	Statue of Liberty (1035)	.80	.60	☐☐☐☐☐
b.	8c	Statue of Liberty (1041)	.90	.75	☐☐☐☐☐
1076	3c	FIPEX	.20	.20	☐☐☐☐☐
1077	3c	Wildlife Conservation, Wild Turkey	.20	.20	☐☐☐☐☐
1078	3c	Wildlife Conserv., Pronghorn Antelope	.20	.20	☐☐☐☐☐
1079	3c	Wildlife Conservation, King Salmon	.20	.20	☐☐☐☐☐
1080	3c	Pure Food and Drug Laws	.20	.20	☐☐☐☐☐
1081	3c	Wheatland	.20	.20	☐☐☐☐☐
1082	3c	Labor Day	.20	.20	☐☐☐☐☐
1083	3c	Nassau Hall	.20	.20	☐☐☐☐☐
1084	3c	Devils Tower	.20	.20	☐☐☐☐☐
1085	3c	Children	.20	.20	☐☐☐☐☐
1957					
1086	3c	Alexander Hamilton	.20	.20	☐☐☐☐☐
1087	3c	Polio	.20	.20	☐☐☐☐☐
1088	3c	Coast and Geodetic Survey	.20	.20	☐☐☐☐☐
1089	3c	Architects	.20	.20	☐☐☐☐☐

1082

1083

1084

1087

1085

1086

1088

1089

1090

1091

1092

1093

1094

1095

1096

1097

1098

1099

1100

1109

1104

1105

1106

1107

1108

1110

1112

1113

1115

1114

1116

1117

1119

1120

1121

1122

1123

1124

1125

1127

1128

1129

1130

1131

1132

1133

1135

1134

1136

1138

Scott No.	Description	Unused Value	Used Value	/ / / / / /
1090	3c Steel Industry	.20	.20	☐☐☐☐☐
1091	3c International Naval Review	.20	.20	☐☐☐☐☐
1092	3c Oklahoma Statehood	.20	.20	☐☐☐☐☐
1093	3c School Teachers	.20	.20	☐☐☐☐☐
1094	4c 48-Star Flag	.20	.20	☐☐☐☐☐
1095	3c Shipbuilding	.20	.20	☐☐☐☐☐
1096	8c Ramon Magsaysay	.20	.20	☐☐☐☐☐
1097	3c Lafayette Bicentenary	.20	.20	☐☐☐☐☐
1098	3c Wildlife Conserv., Whooping Cranes	.20	.20	☐☐☐☐☐
1099	3c Religious Freedom	.20	.20	☐☐☐☐☐
1958				
1100	3c Gardening and Horticulture	.20	.20	☐☐☐☐☐
1104	3c Brussels Exhibition	.20	.20	☐☐☐☐☐
1105	3c James Monroe	.20	.20	☐☐☐☐☐
1106	3c Minnesota Statehood	.20	.20	☐☐☐☐☐
1107	3c Geophysical Year	.20	.20	☐☐☐☐☐
1108	3c Gunston Hall	.20	.20	☐☐☐☐☐
1109	3c Mackinac Bridge	.20	.20	☐☐☐☐☐
1110	4c Simon Bolivar, olive bister	.20	.20	☐☐☐☐☐
1111	8c Bolivar (1110), carmine, ultra & ocher	.20	.20	☐☐☐☐☐
1112	4c Atlantic Cable	.20	.20	☐☐☐☐☐
1958-59				
1113	1c Lincoln	.20	.20	☐☐☐☐☐
1114	3c Lincoln Bust	.20	.20	☐☐☐☐☐
1115	4c Lincoln-Douglas Debates	.20	.20	☐☐☐☐☐
1116	4c Lincoln Statue	.20	.20	☐☐☐☐☐
1958				
1117	4c Lajos Kossuth, green	.20	.20	☐☐☐☐☐
1118	8c Kossuth (1117), carmine, ultra & ocher	.20	.20	☐☐☐☐☐
1119	4c Freedom of Press	.20	.20	☐☐☐☐☐
1120	4c Overland Mail	.20	.20	☐☐☐☐☐
1121	4c Noah Webster	.20	.20	☐☐☐☐☐
1122	4c Forest Conservation	.20	.20	☐☐☐☐☐
1123	4c Fort Duquesne	.20	.20	☐☐☐☐☐
1959				
1124	4c Oregon Statehood	.25	.20	☐☐☐☐☐
1125	4c Jose de San Martin	.20	.20	☐☐☐☐☐
a.	Horiz. pair, imperf. btwn.	*1,000.*		☐☐☐☐☐
1126	8c San Martin (1125), car., ultra & ocher	.20	.20	☐☐☐☐☐
1127	4c NATO	.20	.20	☐☐☐☐☐
1128	4c Arctic Explorations	.20	.20	☐☐☐☐☐
1129	8c World Peace through World Trade	.20	.20	☐☐☐☐☐
1130	4c Silver Centennial	.20	.20	☐☐☐☐☐
1131	4c St. Lawrence Seaway	.20	.20	☐☐☐☐☐

1139

1140

1141

1142

1143

1144

1145

1146

1147

1149

1150

1152

1151

1154

1153

1155

Scott No.		Description	Unused Value	Used Value
1132	4c	49-Star Flag	.20	.20
1133	4c	Soil Conservation	.20	.20
1134	4c	Petroleum Industry	.20	.20
1135	4c	Dental Health	.20	.20
1136	4c	Ernst Reuter, gray	.20	.20
1137	8c	Reuter (1136), carmine, ultra & ocher	.20	.20
a.		Ocher missing (from extaneous paper)	*3,500.*	
b.		Ultramarine missing (from extaneous paper)	*4,250.*	
c.		Ocher & ultramarine missing (from extaneous paper)	*4,500.*	
d.		All colors missing (from extaneous paper)	*2,500.*	
1138	4c	Dr. Ephraim McDowell	.20	.20
a.		Vert. pair, imperf. btwn.	*400.00*	
b.		Vert. pair, imperf. horiz.	*275.00*	
1960-61				
1139	4c	Credo - Washington	.20	.20
1140	4c	Credo - Franklin	.20	.20
1141	4c	Credo - Jefferson	.20	.20
1142	4c	Credo - Key	.20	.20
1143	4c	Credo - Lincoln	.20	.20
1144	4c	Credo - Henry	.20	.20
1960				
1145	4c	Boy Scout Jubilee	.20	.20
1146	4c	Olympic Winter Games	.20	.20
1147	4c	Thomas G. Masaryk, blue	.20	.20
a.		Vert. pair, imperf. btwn.	*2,750.*	
1148	8c	Masaryk (1147), carmine, ultra & ocher	.20	.20
a.		Horiz. pair, imperf. btwn.	—	
1149	4c	World Refugee Year	.20	.20
1150	4c	Water Conservation	.20	.20
a.		Brown orange missing (from extraneous paper)	*2,250.*	
1151	4c	SEATO	.20	.20
a.		Vert. pair, imperf. btwn.	*140.00*	
1152	4c	American Woman	.20	.20
1153	4c	50-Star Flag	.20	.20
1154	4c	Pony Express	.20	.20
1155	4c	Employ the Handicapped	.20	.20
1156	4c	World Forestry Congress	.20	.20
1157	4c	Mexican Independence	.20	.20
1158	4c	U.S.-Japan Treaty	.20	.20
1159	4c	Ignacy Jan Paderewski, blue	.20	.20
1160	8c	Paderewski (1159), car., ultra & ocher	.20	.20
1161	4c	Robert A. Taft	.20	.20

1156

1157

1158

1159

1161

1162

1163

1164

1165

1167

1168

1170

1171

1172

1173

1174

1176

1177

1178

1179

1180

1181

1183

1184

1185

1191

1182

1186

1187

1193

1188

1189

1190

1192

1195

1196

1202

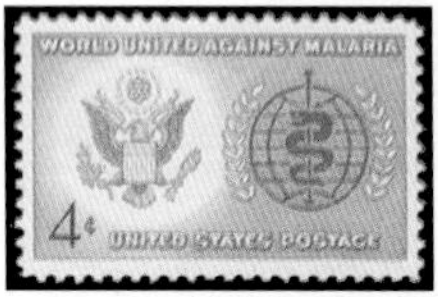

1194

1197

1198

1199

1200

1201

1203

1206

1207

1205

1208

1209

1213

1230

1232

1233

Scott No.	Description	Unused Value	Used Value	/ / / / / /
1162	4c Wheels of Freedom	.20	.20	☐☐☐☐☐
1163	4c Boys' Clubs of America	.20	.20	☐☐☐☐☐
1164	4c First Automated Post Office	.20	.20	☐☐☐☐☐
1165	4c Gustaf Mannerheim, blue	.20	.20	☐☐☐☐☐
1166	8c Mannerheim (1165), car., ultra & ocher	.20	.20	☐☐☐☐☐
1167	4c Camp Fire Girls	.20	.20	☐☐☐☐☐
1168	4c Giuseppe Garibaldi, green	.20	.20	☐☐☐☐☐
1169	8c Garibaldi (1168), carmine, ultra & ocher	.20	.20	☐☐☐☐☐
1170	4c Senator Walter F. George	.20	.20	☐☐☐☐☐
1171	4c Andrew Carnegie	.20	.20	☐☐☐☐☐
1172	4c John Foster Dulles	.20	.20	☐☐☐☐☐
1173	4c Echo I	.20	.20	☐☐☐☐☐
1961				
1174	4c Mahatma Gandhi, red orange	.20	.20	☐☐☐☐☐
1175	8c Gandhi (1174), carmine, ultra & ocher	.20	.20	☐☐☐☐☐
1176	4c Range Conservation	.20	.20	☐☐☐☐☐
1177	4c Horace Greeley	.20	.20	☐☐☐☐☐
1961-65				
1178	4c Firing on Fort Sumter	.25	.20	☐☐☐☐☐
1179	4c Battle of Shiloh	.20	.20	☐☐☐☐☐
1180	5c Battle of Gettysburg	.20	.20	☐☐☐☐☐
1181	5c Battle of the Wilderness	.20	.20	☐☐☐☐☐
1182	5c Surrender at Appomattox	.35	.20	☐☐☐☐☐
a.	Horiz. pair, imperf. vert.	*4,500.*		☐☐☐☐☐
1961				
1183	4c Kansas Statehood	.20	.20	☐☐☐☐☐
1184	4c Senator George W. Norris	.20	.20	☐☐☐☐☐
1185	4c Naval Aviation	.20	.20	☐☐☐☐☐
1186	4c Workmen's Compensation	.20	.20	☐☐☐☐☐
1187	4c Frederic Remington	.20	.20	☐☐☐☐☐
1188	4c Republic of China	.20	.20	☐☐☐☐☐
1189	4c Naismith - Basketball	.20	.20	☐☐☐☐☐
1190	4c Nursing	.20	.20	☐☐☐☐☐
1962				
1191	4c New Mexico Statehood	.20	.20	☐☐☐☐☐
1192	4c Arizona Statehood	.20	.20	☐☐☐☐☐
1193	4c Project Mercury	.20	.20	☐☐☐☐☐
1194	4c Malaria Eradication	.20	.20	☐☐☐☐☐
1195	4c Charles Evans Hughes	.20	.20	☐☐☐☐☐
1196	4c Seattle World's Fair	.20	.20	☐☐☐☐☐
1197	4c Louisiana Statehood	.20	.20	☐☐☐☐☐
1198	4c Homestead Act	.20	.20	☐☐☐☐☐
1199	4c Girl Scouts	.20	.20	☐☐☐☐☐
1200	4c Senator Brien McMahon	.20	.20	☐☐☐☐☐
1201	4c Apprenticeship	.20	.20	☐☐☐☐☐
1202	4c Sam Rayburn	.20	.20	☐☐☐☐☐
1203	4c Dag Hammarskjold, blk, brn and yel	.20	.20	☐☐☐☐☐

1234

1235

1238

1236

1237

1239

1240

1241

1242

1245

1243

1244

1246

1247

1248

1249

1250

Scott No.		Description	Unused Value	Used Value	/ / / / / /
1204	4c	Hammarskjold (1203), (yel inverted)	.20	.20	
1205	4c	Christmas	.20	.20	
1206	4c	Higher Education	.20	.20	
1207	4c	Winslow Homer	.20	.20	
a.		Horiz. pair, imperf. btwn. and at right	*6,750.*		
1963-66					
1208	5c	Flag, untagged	.20	.20	
a.		Tagged	.20	.20	
b.		Horiz. pair, imperf. btwn.	*1,500.*		
1962-66, Perf. 11 x 10½					
1209	1c	Andrew Jackson, untagged	.20	.20	
a.		Tagged	.20	.20	
1213	5c	George Washington, untagged	.20	.20	
a.		Booklet pane 5 + label	3.00	*2.00*	
b.		Tagged	.50	.20	
c.		As "a," tagged	2.25	*1.50*	
d.		Horiz. pair, imperf. btwn	*1,500.*		
Coil Stamps, Perf. 10 Vertically					
1225	1c	Jackson (1209), untagged	.20	.20	
a.		Tagged	.20	.20	
1229	5c	Washington (1213), untagged	1.50	.20	
a.		Tagged	1.80	.20	
b.		Imperf., pair	*325.00*		
1963					
1230	5c	Carolina Charter	.20	.20	
1231	5c	Food for Peace	.20	.20	
1232	5c	West Virginia Statehood	.20	.20	
1233	5c	Emancipation Proclamation	.20	.20	
1234	5c	Alliance for Progress	.20	.20	
1235	5c	Cordell Hull	.20	.20	
1236	5c	Eleanor Roosevelt	.20	.20	
1237	5c	Science	.20	.20	
1238	5c	City Mail Delivery	.20	.20	
1239	5c	Red Cross Centenary	.20	.20	
1240	5c	Christmas, untagged	.20	.20	
a.		Tagged	.65	.50	
b.		Horiz. pair, imperf. btwn	7,750.		
c.		Red missing (from perf. shift)	—		
1241	5c	John James Audubon	.25	.20	
1964					
1242	5c	Sam Houston	.25	.20	
1243	5c	Charles M. Russell	.20	.20	
1244	5c	New York World's Fair	.20	.20	
1245	5c	John Muir	.20	.20	
1246	5c	John F. Kennedy	.20	.20	
1247	5c	New Jersey Tercentenary	.20	.20	

1251

1252

1253

1254-1257

1258

1259

1260

1262

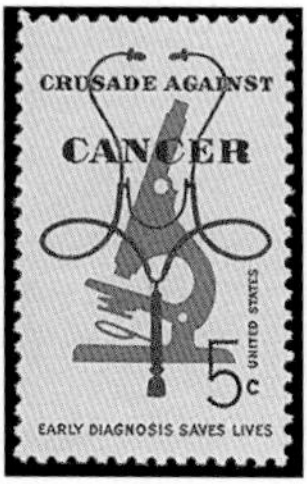

1263

1264

1261

1265

1266

Scott No.		Description	Unused Value	Used Value
1248	5c	Nevada Statehood	.25	.20
1249	5c	Register and Vote	.20	.20
1250	5c	William Shakespeare	.20	.20
1251	5c	Doctors Mayo	.20	.20
1252	5c	American Music	.20	.20
a.		Blue omitted	*800.00*	
b.		Blue missing (from perf. shift)	—	
1253	5c	Homemakers	.20	..20
1254	5c	Christmas - Holly, untagged	.25	.20
a.		Tagged	.65	.50
b.		Printed on gummed side	—	
1255	5c	Christmas - Mistletoe, untagged	.25	.20
a.		Tagged	.65	.50
1256	5c	Christmas - Poinsettia, untagged	.25	.20
a.		Tagged	.65	.50
1257	5c	Christmas - Conifer, untagged	.25	.20
a.		Tagged	.65	.50
b.		Block of 4, #1254-1257	1.00	1.00
c.		Block of 4, #1254a-1257a	3.00	2.25
1258	5c	Verrazano-Narrows Bridge	.20	.20
1259	5c	Fine Arts	.20	.20
1260	5c	Amateur Radio	.20	.20

1965

Scott No.		Description	Unused Value	Used Value
1261	5c	Battle of New Orleans	.20	.20
1262	5c	Physical Fitness - Sokol	.20	.20
1263	5c	Crusade against Cancer	.20	.20
1264	5c	Winston Churchill	.20	.20
1265	5c	Magna Carta	.20	.20
1266	5c	International Cooperation Year	.20	.20
1267	5c	Salvation Army	.20	.20
1268	5c	Dante Alighieri	.20	.20
1269	5c	Herbert Hoover	.20	.20
1270	5c	Robert Fulton	.20	.20
1271	5c	Florida Settlement	.20	.20
a.		Yellow omitted	*250.00*	
1272	5c	Traffic Safety	.20	.20
1273	5c	John Singleton Copley	.20	.20
1274	11c	Intl. Telecommunication Union	.35	.20
1275	5c	Adlai Stevenson	.20	.20
1276	5c	Christmas, untagged	.20	.20
a.		Tagged	.75	.25

1965-78, Perf. 11 x 10½, 10½ x11

Scott No.		Description	Unused Value	Used Value
1278	1c	Thomas Jefferson, tagged	.20	.20
a.		Booklet pane of 8	1.00	*.75*
b.		Booklet pane of 4 + 2 labels	.80	*.60*
c.		Untagged (Bureau precanceled)	6.25	1.25
1279	1¼c	Albert Gallatin	.20	.20
1280	2c	Frank Lloyd Wright, tagged	.20	.20

1267

1268

1269

1271

1270

1272

1273

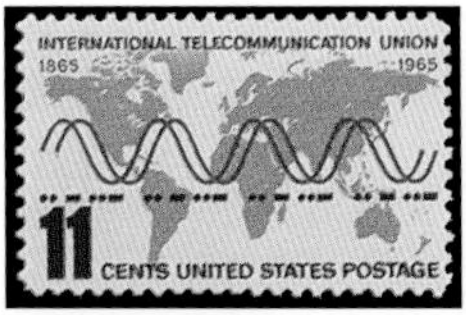

1274

1275

1276

1278

1279

1280

1281

1282

1283

1283B
Redrawn

1284

1285

Scott No.		Description	Unused Value	Used Value
a.		Booklet pane of 5 + label	1.25	.80
b.		Untagged (Bureau precanceled)	1.35	.40
c.		Booklet pane of 6	1.00	*.75*
1281	3c	Francis Parkman, tagged	.20	.20
a.		Untagged (Bureau precanceled)	3.00	.75
1282	4c	Abraham Lincoln, untagged	.20	.20
a.		Tagged	.20	.20
1283	5c	Washington, untagged	.20	.20
a.		Tagged	.20	.20
1283B	5c	Washington, redrawn, tagged	.20	.20
d.		Untagged (Bureau precanceled)	12.50	1.00
1284	6c	Franklin D. Roosevelt, untagged	.20	.20
a.		Tagged	.20	.20
b.		Booklet pane of 8	1.50	1.00
c.		Booklet pane of 5 + label	1.50	1.00
d.		Horiz. pair, imperf. between	*2,400.*	
1285	8c	Albert Einstein, untagged	.20	.20
a.		Tagged	.20	.20
1286	10c	Andrew Jackson, tagged	.20	.20
b.		Untagged (Bureau precanceled)	57.50	1.75
1286A	12c	Henry Ford, tagged	.25	.20
c.		Untagged (Bureau precanceled)	4.75	1.00
1287	13c	John F. Kennedy, tagged	.30	.20
a.		Untagged (Bureau precanceled)	6.00	1.00
1288	15c	Oliver Wendell Holmes, magenta, tagged	.30	.20
a.		Untagged (Bureau precanceled)	.75	.75
d.		Type II	.55	.20

Type II: The necktie does not touch coat at bottom.

Perf. 10

Scott No.		Description	Unused Value	Used Value
1288B	15c	Holmes (1288), magenta, (from bklt. pane)	.35	.20
c.		Booklet pane of 8	2.80	*1.75*
e.		As "c," vert. imperf. btwn.	*1,750.*	

Perf. 11 x 10½, 10½ x 11

Scott No.		Description	Unused Value	Used Value
1289	20c	George C. Marshall, deep olive, untagged	.40	.20
a.		Tagged	.40	.20
b.	20c	black olive, tagged	.50	.20
1290	25c	Frederick Douglass, rose lake untagged	.55	.20
a.		Tagged	.45	.20
b.	25c	magenta	*25.00*	—
1291	30c	John Dewey, untagged	.65	.20
a.		Tagged	.50	.20
1292	40c	Thomas Paine, untagged	.80	.20
a.		Tagged	.65	.20

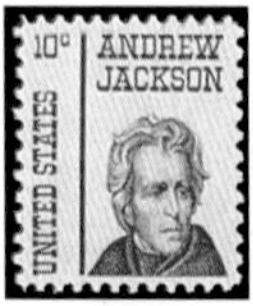

1286

1286A

1287

1288

1289

1290

1291

1292

1293

1294

1295

1305

1306

1307

1308

1309

1310

1311

1312

1313

Scott No.		Description	Unused Value	Used Value	/ / / / / /
1293	50c	Lucy Stone, untagged	1.00	.20	□□□□□
a.		Tagged	.80	.20	□□□□□
1294	$1	Eugene O'Neill, untagged	2.25	.20	□□□□□
a.		Tagged	1.65	.20	□□□□□
1295	$5	John Bassett Moore, untagged	10.00	2.25	□□□□□
a.		Tagged	8.50	2.00	□□□□□
1966-81, Coil Stamps, Tagged, Perf. 10 Horizontally					
1297	3c	Francis Parkman (1281)	.20	.20	□□□□□
a.		Imperf., pair	*22.50*		□□□□□
b.		Untagged (Bureau precanceled)	.40	.25	□□□□□
c.		As "b," imperf. pair	*6.00*	—	□□□□□
1298	6c	Franklin D. Roosevelt (1284)	.20	.20	□□□□□
a.		Imperf., pair	*1,750.*		□□□□□
Tagged Perf. 10 Vertically					
1299	1c	Thomas Jefferson (1278)	.20	.20	□□□□□
a.		Untagged (Bureau precanceled)	8.00	1.75	□□□□□
b.		Imperf., pair	*22.50*	—	□□□□□
1303	4c	Abraham Lincoln (1282)	.20	.20	□□□□□
a.		Untagged (Bureau precanceled)	8.75	.75	□□□□□
b.		Imperf., pair	*700.00*		□□□□□
1304	5c	George Washington (1283)	.20	.20	□□□□□
a.		Untagged (Bureau precanceled)	6.50	.65	□□□□□
b.		Imperf., pair	*125.00*		□□□□□
e.		As "a," imperf. pair	*275.00*		□□□□□
1304C	5c	Washington, redrawn (1283B)	.20	.20	□□□□□
d.		Imperf., pair	*475.00*		□□□□□
1305	6c	Franklin D. Roosevelt	.20	.20	□□□□□
a.		Imperf., pair	*60.00*		□□□□□
b.		Untagged (Bureau precanceled)	20.00	1.00	□□□□□
1305E	15c	Oliver Wendell Holmes (1288), type I	.25	.20	□□□□□
f.		Untagged (Bureau precanceled)	32.50	—	□□□□□
g.		Imperf., pair	*20.00*		□□□□□
h.		Pair, imperf. btwn.	*150.00*		□□□□□
i.		Type II	1.50	.20	□□□□□
j.		Imperf., pair, type II	*65.00*		□□□□□
1305C	$1	Eugene O'Neill (1294)	2.75	.40	□□□□□
d.		Imperf., pair	*1,750.*		□□□□□
1966					
1306	5c	Migratory Bird Treaty	.20	.20	□□□□□
1307	5c	Humane Treatment of Animals	.20	.20	□□□□□
1308	5c	Indiana Statehood	.20	.20	□□□□□
1309	5c	American Circus	.20	.20	□□□□□
1310	5c	SIPEX	.20	.20	□□□□□
1311	5c	SIPEX Souvenir Sheet, imperf.	.20	.20	□□□□□
1312	5c	Bill of Rights	.20	.20	□□□□□
1313	5c	Polish Millennium	.20	.20	□□□□□

1315

1317

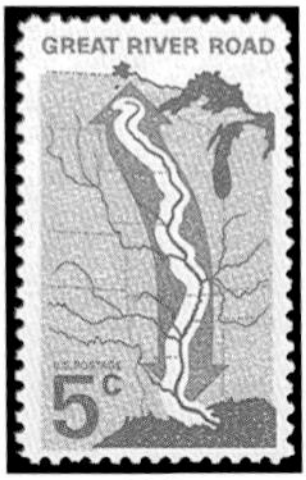

1319

1320

1314

1316

1318

1321

1322

1324

1325

1326

1328

1323

1327

1329

1330

Scott No.	Description	Unused Value	Used Value	/ / / / / /
1314	5c National Park Service, untagged..	.20	.20	☐☐☐☐☐
a.	Tagged..	.35	.35	☐☐☐☐☐
1315	5c Marine Corps Reserve, untagged.	.20	.20	☐☐☐☐☐
a.	Tagged..	.40	.20	☐☐☐☐☐
b.	missing (from extraneous paper)..	*16,000.*		☐☐☐☐☐
1316	5c Women's Clubs, untagged	.20	.20	☐☐☐☐☐
a.	Tagged..	.40	.20	☐☐☐☐☐
1317	5c Johnny Appleseed, untagged	.20	.20	☐☐☐☐☐
a.	Tagged..	.40	.20	☐☐☐☐☐
1318	5c Beautification of America, untagged	.20	.20	☐☐☐☐☐
a.	Tagged..	.40	.20	☐☐☐☐☐
1319	5c Great River Road, untagged	.20	.20	☐☐☐☐☐
a.	Tagged..	.40	.20	☐☐☐☐☐
1320	5c Savings Bond, untagged	.20	.20	☐☐☐☐☐
a.	Tagged..	.40	.20	☐☐☐☐☐
b.	missing (from extraneous paper)..	*4,500.*		☐☐☐☐☐
c.	missing (from extraneous paper)..	*5,500.*		☐☐☐☐☐
1321	5c Christmas, untagged	.20	.20	☐☐☐☐☐
a.	Tagged..	.40	.20	☐☐☐☐☐
1322	5c Mary Cassatt, untagged	.20	.20	☐☐☐☐☐
a.	Tagged..	.40	.25	☐☐☐☐☐
1967				
1323	5c National Grange...........................	.20	.20	☐☐☐☐☐
1324	5c Canada Centenary.........................	.20	.20	☐☐☐☐☐
1325	5c Erie Canal	.20	.20	☐☐☐☐☐
1326	5c Search for Peace	.20	.20	☐☐☐☐☐
1327	5c Henry David Thoreau	.20	.20	☐☐☐☐☐
1328	5c Nebraska Statehood.....................	.20	.20	☐☐☐☐☐
1329	5c Voice of America	.20	.20	☐☐☐☐☐
1330	5c Davy Crockett..............................	.20	.20	☐☐☐☐☐
a.	Vert. pair, imperf. btwn.	*7,000.*		☐☐☐☐☐
b.	Green (engr.) missing (from a foldover)	—		☐☐☐☐☐
c.	Black & green (engr.) missing (from a foldover)...........	—		☐☐☐☐☐
1331	5c Astronaut	.50	.20	☐☐☐☐☐
1332	5c Gemini 4 Capsule	.50	.20	☐☐☐☐☐
b.	Pair, #1331-1332...........................	1.10	*1.25*	☐☐☐☐☐
1333	5c Urban Planning............................	.20	.20	☐☐☐☐☐
1334	5c Finnish Independence..................	.20	.20	☐☐☐☐☐
1335	5c Thomas Eakins	.20	.20	☐☐☐☐☐
1336	5c Christmas.....................................	.20	.20	☐☐☐☐☐
1337	5c Mississippi Statehood..................	.20	.20	☐☐☐☐☐
1968-71, Perf. 11				
1338	6c Flag	.20	.20	☐☐☐☐☐
k.	Vert. pair, imperf. btwn.	*325.00*	*175.00*	☐☐☐☐☐
s.	Red missing (from a foldover)	—		☐☐☐☐☐

1331-1332

1333

1334

1336

1339

1335

1337

1338

1341

1342

1340

1343

1344

Scott No.		Description	Unused Value	Used Value
Coil Stamp, Perf. 10 Vertically				
1338A	6c	Flag (1338)	.20	.20
b.		Imperf., pair	*400.00*	
Perf. 11x10½				
1338D	6c	Flag (1338)	.20	.20
e.		Horiz. pair, imperf. btwn.	*125.00*	
1338F	8c	Flag (1338), red denomination	.20	.20
i.		Vert. pair, imperf.	35.00	
j.		Horiz. pair, imperf. btwn.	45.00	
p.		Slate green omitted	*325.00*	
t.		Horiz. pair, imperf. vertically	—	
Coil Stamp, Perf. 10 Vertically				
1338G	8c	Flag (1338), red denomination	.30	.20
h.		Imperf., pair	*45.00*	
1968				
1339	6c	Illinois Statehood	.20	.20
1340	6c	HemisFair '68	.20	.20
a.		White omitted	*925.00*	
1341	$1	Airlift	2.00	1.25
1342	6c	Support our Youth	.20	.20
1343	6c	Law and Order	.20	.20
1344	6c	Register and Vote	.20	.20
1345	6c	Fort Moultrie Flag	.40	.25
1346	6c	Fort McHenry Flag	.40	.25
1347	6c	Washington's Cruisers Flag	.30	.25
1348	6c	Bennington Flag	.30	.25
1349	6c	Rhode Island Flag	.30	.25
1350	6c	First Stars and Stripes	.30	.25
1351	6c	Bunker Hill Flag	.30	.25
1352	6c	Grand Union Flag	.30	.25
1353	6c	Philadelphia Light Horse Flag	.30	.25
1354	6c	First Navy Jack	.30	.25
a.		Strip of 10, #1345-1354	3.25	*3.25*
c.		As "a," imperf.	*4,500.*	
1355	6c	Walt Disney	.40	.20
a.		Ocher (Walt Disney, 6c, etc.) omitted	*400.00*	—
b.		Vert. pair, imperf. horiz.	*575.00*	
c.		Imperf., pair	*425.00*	
d.		Black omitted	*1,850.*	
e.		Horiz. pair, imperf. btwn.	*3,500.*	
f.		Blue omitted	*1,850.*	
1356	6c	Father Marquette	.20	.20
1357	6c	Daniel Boone	.20	.20
1358	6c	Arkansas River Navigation	.20	.20
1359	6c	Leif Erikson	.20	.20
1360	6c	Cherokee Strip	.20	.20

1345

1346

1347

1348

1349

1350

1351

1352

1353

1354

1356

1357

1358

1355

1359

1361

1363

1360

1362

1364

1365-1368

1369

1370

1371

1373

1372

1374

1375

1376-1379

1380

1381

1382

1383

1384

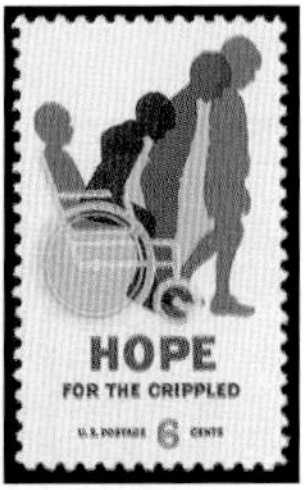

1385

1387-1390

1386

1391

1392

Scott No.	Description	Unused Value	Used Value	/ / / / / /
1361	6c John Trumbull	.20	.20	
b.	missing (from a foldover)	*11,000.*	—	
1362	6c Waterfowl Conservation	.20	.20	
a.	Vert. pair, imperf. btwn.	*275.00*	—	
b.	Red & dark blue omitted	*475.00*		
c.	Red omitted		*1,750.*	
1363	6c Christmas, tagged	.20	.20	
a.	Untagged	.20	.20	
b.	Imperf., pair, tagged	*175.00*		
c.	Light yellow omitted	*50.00*	—	
d.	Imperf., pair, untagged	*250.00*		
1364	6c Chief Joseph	.20	.20	
1969				
1365	6c Beautification - Cities	.25	.20	
1366	6c Beautification - Parks	.25	.20	
1367	6c Beautification - Highways	.25	.20	
1368	6c Beautification - Streets	.25	.20	
a.	Block of 4, #1365-1368	1.00	*1.25*	
1369	6c American Legion	.20	.20	
1370	6c Grandma Moses	.20	.20	
a.	Horiz. pair, imperf. btwn.	*165.00*	—	
b.	Black and Prussian blue omitted	*575.00*		
1371	6c Apollo 8	.20	.20	
1372	6c W.C. Handy	.20	.20	
1373	6c California Settlement	.20	.20	
b.	Red (engr.) missing (from perf. shift)	10.00		
1374	6c John Wesley Powell	.20	.20	
1375	6c Alabama Statehood	.20	.20	
1376	6c Douglas Fir	.35	.20	
1377	6c Lady's Slipper	.35	.20	
1378	6c Ocotillo	.35	.20	
1379	6c Franklinia	.35	.20	
a.	Block of 4, #1376-1379	1.50	*1.75*	
1380	6c Dartmouth College Case	.20	.20	
1381	6c Professional Baseball	.55	.20	
a.	Black (1869-1969, United States, 6c, Professional Baseball) omitted	*800.00*		
1382	6c Intercollegiate Football	.20	.20	
a.	Vert. pair, imperf. horizontally	—		
1383	6c Dwight D. Eisenhower	.20	.20	
1384	6c Christmas	.20	.20	
	Precanceled	.50	.20	
b.	Imperf., pair	*800.00*		
c.	Light green omitted	*25.00*		
d.	Lt green, red & yellow omitted	*700.00*	—	
e.	Yellow omitted	*2,000.*		
g.	Red & yellow omitted	*2,750.*		
h.	Light green & yellow omitted	—		
i.	Light green & red omitted	—		

1393

1393D

1394

1396

1397

1398

1399

1400

1405

1406

1407

1408

1409

1410-1413

Scott No.		Description	Unused Value	Used Value
j.		Vert. pair, top stamp Baltimore precancel, bottom stamp precancel missing	—	
k.		Baltimore precancel printed on gum side	—	
1385	6c	Hope for the Crippled	.20	.20
1386	6c	William M. Harnett	.20	.20
1970				
1387	6c	American Bald Eagle	.20	.20
1388	6c	African Elephant Herd	.20	.20
1389	6c	Haida Ceremonial Canoe	.20	.20
1390	6c	Age of Reptiles	.20	.20
a.		Block of 4, #1387-1390	.55	.60
1391	6c	Maine Statehood	.20	.20
1392	6c	Wildlife Conservation	.20	.20
1970-74, Tagged, Perf. 11x10½ , 10½ x11, 11 (#1394)				
1393	6c	Dwight D. Eisenhower, untagged	.20	.20
a.		Booklet pane of 8	1.50	.75
b.		Booklet pane of 5 + label	1.50	.75
c.		Untagged (Bureau precanceled)	12.75	3.00
1393D	7c	Benjamin Franklin, tagged	.20	.20
e.		Untagged (Bureau precanceled)	4.25	1.00
1394	8c	Eisenhower	.20	.20
b.		missing (from perf. shift).	*175.00*	
c.		missing (from perf. shift).	—	
1395	8c	Eisenhower (1393), deep claret (from bklt. pane)	.20	.20
a.		Booklet pane of 8	1.80	1.25
b.		Booklet pane of 6	1.25	1.10
c.		Booklet pane of 4 + 2 labels	1.65	1.00
d.		Booklet pane of 7 + label	1.90	1.10
e.		Vert. pair, imperf btwn.	*800.00*	
1396	8c	Postal Service Emblem	.20	.20
1397	14c	Fiorello LaGuardia, tagged	.25	.20
a.		Untagged (Bureau precanceled)	*140.00*	17.50
1398	16c	Ernie Pyle, tagged	.35	.20
a.		Untagged (Bureau precanceled)	22.50	5.00
1399	18c	Dr. Elizabeth Blackwell	.35	.20
1400	21c	Amadeo P. Giannini	.40	.20
Coil Stamps, Perf. 10 Vertically				
1401	6c	Eisenhower (1393), dk bl gray, tagged	.20	.20
a.		Untagged (Bureau precanceled)	19.50	3.00
b.		Imperf., pair	*1,750.*	
1402	8c	Eisenhower (1393), dp claret, tagged	.20	.20
a.		Imperf., pair	37.50	
b.		Untagged (Bureau precanceled)	6.75	.75
c.		Pair, imperf. btwn.	*6,250.*	
1970				
1405	6c	Edgar Lee Masters	.20	.20
1406	6c	Woman Suffrage	.20	.20

1415-1418

1414

1419

1420

1421-1422

1423

1424

1425

1426

Scott No.	Description	Unused Value	Used Value	/ / / / / /
1407	6c South Carolina	.20	.20	
1408	6c Stone Mountain Memorial	.20	.20	
1409	6c Fort Snelling	.20	.20	
1410	6c Save Our Soil	.25	.20	
1411	6c Save Our Cities	.25	.20	
1412	6c Save Our Water	.25	.20	
1413	6c Save Our Air	.25	.20	
a.	Block of 4, #1410-1413	1.10	*1.25*	
1414	6c Christmas - Religious	.20	.20	
a.	Precanceled	.20	.20	
b.	Black omitted	*450.00*		
c.	As "a," blue omitted	*1,450.*		
1415	6c Christmas - Locomotive	.30	.20	
a.	Precanceled	.75	.20	
b.	Black omitted	*2,500.*		
1416	6c Christmas - Toy Horse	.30	.20	
a.	Precanceled	.75	.20	
b.	Black omitted	*2,500.*		
c.	Imperf., pair (#1416, 1418)		*2,500.*	
1417	6c Christmas - Tricycle	.30	.20	
a.	Precanceled	.75	.20	
b.	Black omitted	*2,500.*		
1418	6c Christmas - Doll Carriage	.30	.20	
a.	Precanceled	.75	..20	
b.	Block of 4, #1415-1418	1.25	*1.40*	
c.	As "b," precanceled	3.25	*3.50*	
d.	Black omitted	*2,500.*		
e.	As "b," black omitted.	*10,000.*		
1419	6c United Nations	.20	.20	
1420	6c Landing of the Pilgrims	.20	.20	
a.	Orange & yellow omitted	*625.00*		
1421	6c Disabled American Veterans	.20	.20	
1422	6c Servicemen	.20	.20	
a.	Pair, #1421-1422	.30	.30	
1971				
1423	6c Wool Industry	.20	.20	
b.	Teal blue ("United States") missing (from a color misregistration)	*350.00*		
1424	6c General Douglas MacArthur	.20	.20	
a.	Red missing (from perf. shift)	—		
c.	Blue missing (from perf. shift)	—		
1425	6c Blood Donors	.20	.20	
1426	8c Missouri Statehood	.20	.20	
1427	8c Trout	.20	.20	
a.	red omitted		*1,250.*	
b.	Green (engr.) omitted.	—		
1428	8c Alligator	.20	.20	
1429	8c Polar Bear	.20	.20	
1430	8c California Condor	.20	.20	

1427-1430

1431 1432 1433

1434-1435

1436 1437 1438 1439

Scott No.		Description	Unused Value	Used Value
a.		Block of 4, #1427-1430	.80	*.90*
b.		As "a," lt grn & dk grn omitted from #1427-1428	*4,500.*	
c.		As "a," red omitted from #1427, 1429-1430	*3,500.*	
1431	8c	Antarctic Treaty	.20	.20
b.		Both colors missing (from extraneous paper)	*500.00*	
1432	8c	Bicentennial Emblem	.20	.20
a.		Gray & black missing (from extraneous paper)	*500.00*	
b.		Gray ("U.S. Postage 8c") missing (from extraneous paper)	*750.00*	
1433	8c	John Sloan	.20	.20
b.		Red engr. ("John Sloan" and "8") missing (from a color misregistration)	*950.00*	
1434	8c	Lunar Module	.20	.20
1435	8c	Lunar Rover	.20	.20
b.		Pair, #1434-1435	.40	.45
d.		As "b," blue & red (litho.) omitted	*1,00.*	
1436	8c	Emily Dickinson	.20	.20
a.		Black & olive (engr.) omitted	*525.00*	
b.		Pale rose missing (from extraneous paper)	*6,000.*	
c.		Red omitted	—	
1437	8c	San Juan	.20	.20
1438	8c	Prevent Drug Abuse	.20	.20
1439	8c	CARE	.20	.20
a.		Black omitted	*1,750.*	
1440	8c	Decatur House	.20	.20
1441	8c	Whaler Charles W. Morgan	.20	.20
1442	8c	Cable Car	.20	.20
1443	8c	San Xavier del Bac Mission	.20	.20
a.		Block of 4, #1440-1443	.75	*.85*
b.		As "a," black brown omitted	*1,250.*	
c.		As "a," ocher omitted	*3,000.*	
1444	8c	Christmas - Religious	.20	.20
a.		Gold omitted	*400.00*	
1445	8c	Christmas - Partridge	.20	.20

1972

Scott No.		Description	Unused Value	Used Value
1446	8c	Sidney Lanier	.20	.20
1447	8c	Peace Corps	.20	.20
1448	2c	Cape Hatteras - Ship	.20	.20
1449	2c	Cape Hatteras - Lighthouse	.20	.20
1450	2c	Cape Hatteras - Three Gulls	.20	.20
1451	2c	Cape Hatteras - Dunes	.20	.20
a.		Block of 4, #1448-1451	.25	*.30*
b.		As "a," black (litho.) omitted	*1,400.*	
1452	6c	Wolf Trap Farm	.20	.20

1440-1443

1444

1445

1446

1447

1452

1454

1448-1451

1453

1455

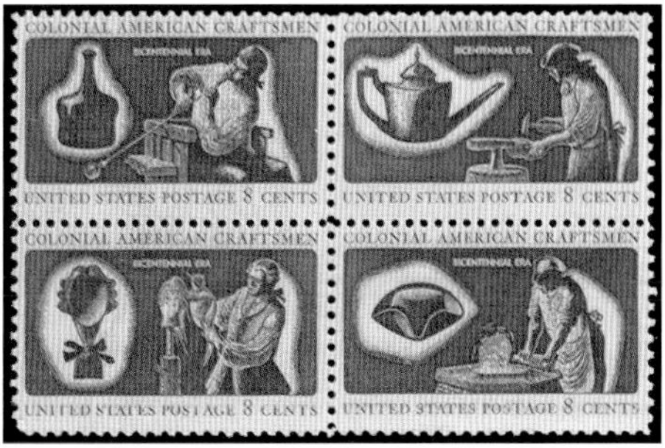

1456-1459

1460

1461

1462

1463

1464-1467

1468

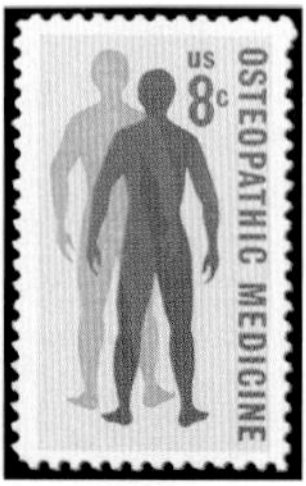

1469

1470

1471

1472

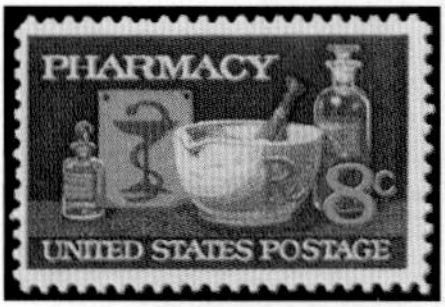

1473

1474

1475

1476

1477

1478

1479

Scott No.		Description	Unused Value	Used Value
1453	8c	Yellowstone	.20	.20
1454	15c	Mt. McKinley	.30	.20
b.		Yellow omitted	*3,500.*	
1455	8c	Family Planning	.20	.20
a.		Yellow omitted	*400.00*	
c.		Dark brown missing (from foldover)	*9,000.*	
1456	8c	Glass Blower	.20	.20
1457	8c	Silversmith	.20	.20
1458	8c	Wigmaker	.20	.20
1459	8c	Hatter	.20	.20
a.		Block of 4, #1456-1459	.65	*.75*
1460	6c	Olympics - Bicycling	.20	.20
1461	8c	Olympics - Bobsledding	.20	.20
1462	15c	Olympics - Running	.30	.20
1463	8c	Parent Teacher Association	.20	.20
1464	8c	Fur Seal	.25	.20
1465	8c	Cardinal	.25	.20
1466	8c	Brown Pelican	.25	.20
1467	8c	Bighorn Sheep	.25	.20
a.		Block of 4, #1464-1467	1.00	*.75*
b.		As "a," brown omitted	*3,750.*	
c.		As "a," green & blue omitted	*3,750.*	
d.		As "a," red & brown omitted	*4,000.*	
1468	8c	Mail Order Business	.20	.20
1469	8c	Osteopathic Medicine	.20	.20
1470	8c	Tom Sawyer	.20	.20
a.		Horiz. pair, imperf. btwn.	*7,500.*	
b.		Red & black (engr.) omitted	*1,250.*	
c.		Yellow & tan (litho.) omitted	*1,750.*	
1471	8c	Christmas - Religious	.20	.20
a.		Pink omitted	*120.00*	
b.		Black omitted	*3,250.*	
1472	8c	Christmas - Santa Claus	.20	.20
1473	8c	Pharmacy	.20	.20
a.		Blue & orange omitted	*675.00*	
b.		Blue omitted	*1,750.*	
c.		Orange omitted	*1,750.*	
e.		Vertical pair, imperf. horiz.	*2,100.*	
1474	8c	Stamp Collecting	.20	.20
a.		Black (litho.) omitted	*475.00*	
1973				
1475	8c	Love	.20	.20
1476	8c	Printer	.20	.20
1477	8c	Posting a Broadside	.20	.20
1478	8c	Postrider	.20	.20
a.		Red missing (from a color misregistration)	—	
1479	8c	Drummer	.20	.20
1480	8c	Boston Tea Party - upper left	.20	.20
1481	8c	Boston Tea Party - upper right	.20	.20

1480-1483

1484

1485

1486

1487

1488

1489-1493

1494-1498

1499

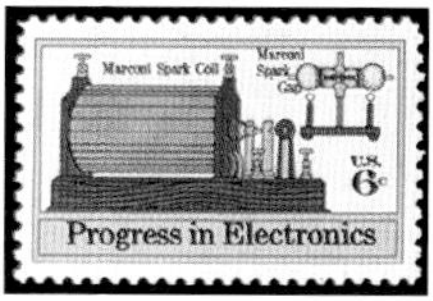

1500

1501

1502

1503

1507

1508

1504

1505

1506

1509

1510

1511

1518

1525

1526

1527

Scott No.	Description	Unused Value	Used Value
1482	8c Boston Tea Party - lower left	.20	.20
1483	8c Boston Tea Party - lower right	.20	.20
a.	Block of 4, #1480-1483	.65	*.75*
b.	As "a," black (engr.) omitted	*1,100.*	
c.	As "a," black (litho.) omitted	*1,000.*	
1484	8c George Gershwin	.20	.20
a.	Vert. pair, imperf. horiz.	*175.00*	
1485	8c Robinson Jeffers	.20	.20
a.	Vert. pair, imperf. horiz.	*200.00*	
1486	8c Henry Ossawa Tanner	.20	.20
1487	8c Willa Cather	.20	.20
a.	Vert. pair, imperf. horiz.	*225.00*	
1488	8c Nicolaus Copernicus	.20	.20
a.	Orange omitted	*775.00*	
b.	Black (engraved) omitted	*875.00*	
1489	8c Stamp Counter	.20	.20
1490	8c Mail Collection	.20	.20
1491	8c Letters on Conveyor Belt	.20	.20
1492	8c Parcel Post Sorting	.20	.20
1493	8c Mail Canceling	.20	.20
1494	8c Manual Letter Routing	.20	.20
1495	8c Electronic Letter Routing	.20	.20
1496	8c Loading Mail on Truck	.20	.20
1497	8c Mailman	.20	.20
1498	8c Rural Mail Delivery	.20	.20
a.	Strip of 10, #1489-1498	1.75	*1.90*
1499	8c Harry S Truman	.20	.20
1500	6c Spark Coil and Spark Gap	.20	.20
1501	8c Transistors	.20	.20
a.	Black (inscriptions & U.S. 8c) omitted	*350.00*	
b.	Tan (background) & lilac omitted	*850.00*	
1502	15c Microphone, Tubes and Speaker	.30	.20
a.	Black (inscriptions & U.S. 15c) omitted	*1,250.*	
1503	15c Lyndon B. Johnson	.20	.20
a.	Horiz. pair, imperf. vert.	*250.00*	
1973-74			
1504	8c Angus Cattle	.20	.20
a.	Green & red brown omitted	*750.00*	
b.	Vert. pair, imperf. between		*5,000.*
1505	10c Chautauqua	.20	.20
a.	Black (litho.) omitted		*1,750.*
1506	10c Kansas Hard Winter Wheat	.20	.20
a.	Black & blue (engr.) omitted	*650.00*	
1973			
1507	8c Christmas - Religious	.20	.20
1508	8c Christmas - Tree	.20	.20
a.	Vert. pair, imperf. btwn.	*225.00*	
1973-74, Tagged, Perf. 11x10½			
1509	10c Crossed Flags	.20	.20

1528

1529

1530-1537

Scott No.		Description	Unused Value	Used Value	/ / / / / /
a.		Horiz. pair, imperf. btwn	*40.00*	—	☐☐☐☐☐
b.		Blue omitted	*160.00*	—	☐☐☐☐☐
c.		Vert. pair, imperf.	*750.00*		☐☐☐☐☐
d.		Horiz. pair, imperf. vert.	*900.00*		☐☐☐☐☐
f.		Vert. pair, imperf. btwn.	—		☐☐☐☐☐
1510	10c	Jefferson Memorial, tagged	.20	.20	☐☐☐☐☐
a.		Untagged (Bureau precanceled)	4.00	1.00	☐☐☐☐☐
b.		Booklet pane of 5 + label	1.65	.90	☐☐☐☐☐
c.		Booklet pane of 8	1.65	1.00	☐☐☐☐☐
d.		Booklet pane of 6	5.25	1.75	☐☐☐☐☐
e.		Vert. pair, imperf. horiz.	*375.00*		☐☐☐☐☐
f.		Vert. pair, imperf. btwn.	*475.00*		☐☐☐☐☐
1511	10c	Zip Code	.20	.20	☐☐☐☐☐
a.		Yellow omitted	*45.00*		☐☐☐☐☐
Coil Stamps, Perf. 10 Vertically					
1518	6.3c	Liberty Bell, tagged	.20	.20	☐☐☐☐☐
a.		Untagged (Bureau precanceled)	.35	.20	☐☐☐☐☐
b.		Imperf., pair	*150.00*		☐☐☐☐☐
c.		As "a," imperf. pair	*80.00*		☐☐☐☐☐
1519	10c	Crossed Flags (1509)	.20	.20	☐☐☐☐☐
a.		Imperf., pair	35.00		☐☐☐☐☐
1520	10c	Jefferson Memorial (1510), tagged	.25	.20	☐☐☐☐☐
a.		Untagged (Bureau precanceled)	5.50	1.25	☐☐☐☐☐
b.		Imperf., pair	30.00		☐☐☐☐☐
1974					
1525	10c	Veterans of Foreign Wars	.20	.20	☐☐☐☐☐
b.		Blue missing (from perf. shift)	—		☐☐☐☐☐
1526	10c	Robert Frost	.20	.20	☐☐☐☐☐
1527	10c	Expo '74 World's Fair	.20	.20	☐☐☐☐☐
1528	10c	Horse Racing	.25	.20	☐☐☐☐☐
a.		Blue (Horse Racing) omitted	*800.00*		☐☐☐☐☐
b.		Red (U.S. postage 10 cents) omitted	*2,250.*		☐☐☐☐☐
1529	10c	Skylab	.20	.20	☐☐☐☐☐
a.		Vert. pair, imperf. btwn.	—		☐☐☐☐☐
c.		Vert. pair, imperf. horiz.	—		☐☐☐☐☐
1530	10c	Raphael	.20	.20	☐☐☐☐☐
1531	10c	Hokusai	.20	.20	☐☐☐☐☐
1532	10c	Peto	.20	.20	☐☐☐☐☐
1533	10c	Liotard	.20	.20	☐☐☐☐☐
1534	10c	Terborch	.20	.20	☐☐☐☐☐
1535	10c	Chardin	.20	.20	☐☐☐☐☐
1536	10c	Gainsborough	.20	.20	☐☐☐☐☐
1537	10c	Goya	.20	.20	☐☐☐☐☐
a.		Block or strip of 8, #1530-1537	1.75	1.75	☐☐☐☐☐
b.		As "a" (block), imperf. vert.	*3,500.*		☐☐☐☐☐
1538	10c	Petrified Wood	.20	.20	☐☐☐☐☐
a.		Light blue & yellow omitted	—		☐☐☐☐☐
1539	10c	Tourmaline	.20	.20	☐☐☐☐☐
a.		Light blue omitted	—		☐☐☐☐☐

1538-1541

1543-1546

1542

1547

1548

Scott No.		Description	Unused Value	Used Value
b.		Black & purple omitted	—	
1540	10c	Amethyst	.20	.20
a.		Light blue & yellow omitted	—	
1541	10c	Rhodochrosite	.20	.20
a.		Block or strip of 4, #1538-1541 ...	.80	.90
b.		As "a," lt blue & yellow omitted ..	*1,500.*	—
c.		Light blue omitted	—	
d.		Black & red omitted	—	
1542	10c	Kentucky Settlement	.20	.20
a.		Dull black (litho.) omitted	*575.00*	
b.		Green (engr. & litho.), black (engr. & litho.) & blue missing (from extraneous paper)	*3,000.*	
c.		Green (engr.) missing (from extraneous paper)	*3,750.*	
d.		Green (engr.) & black (litho) missing (from extraneous paper)	—	
f.		Blue (litho.) omitted	—	
1543	10c	Carpenter's Hall	.20	.20
1544	10c	"We ask but for peace . . ."	.20	.20
1545	10c	"Deriving their just powers . . . " .	.20	.20
1546	10c	Independence Hall	.20	.20
a.		Block of 4, #1543-1546	.80	.90
1547	10c	Energy Conservation	.20	.20
a.		Blue & orange omitted	*750.00*	
b.		Orange & green omitted	*500.00*	
c.		Green omitted	700.00	
1548	10c	Legend of Sleepy Hollow	.20	.20
1549	10c	Retarded Children	.20	.20
1550	10c	Christmas - Angel	.20	.20
1551	10c	Christmas - Currier & Ives	.20	.20
a.		Buff omitted	12.50	
1552	10c	Christmas - Dove	.20	.20
1975				
1553	10c	Benjamin West	.20	.20
1554	10c	Paul Laurence Dunbar	.20	.20
a.		Imperf., pair	*1,100.*	
1555	10c	D.W. Griffith	.20	.20
a.		Brown (engr.) omitted	*575.00*	
1556	10c	Pioneer 10	.20	.20
a.		Red & dark yellow omitted	*1,000.*	
b.		Dark blue (engr.) omitted	*675.00*	
d.		Dark yellow omitted	—	
1557	10c	Mariner 10	.20	.20
a.		Red omitted	*375.00*	—
b.		Ultra & bister omitted	*1,575.*	
d.		Red missing (from perf. shift)	*575.00*	
1558	10c	Collective Bargaining	.20	.20
1559	8c	Sybil Ludington	.20	.20

1549

1550

1553

1554

1551

1552

1555

1556

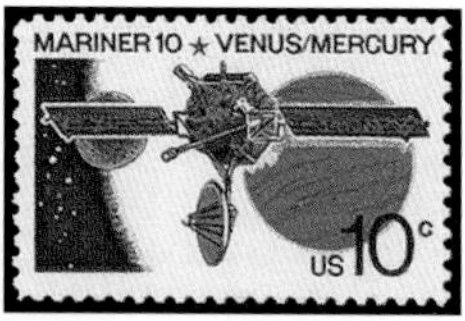

1557

1559

1560

1561

1562

Scott No.		Description	Unused Value	Used Value
a.		Back inscription omitted	*175.00*	
1560	10c	Salem Poor	.20	.20
a.		Back inscription omitted	*175.00*	
1561	10c	Haym Salomon	.20	.20
a.		Back inscription omitted	*175.00*	
b.		Red omitted	*225.00*	
1562	18c	Peter Francisco	.35	.20
1563	10c	Battle of Lexington & Concord	.20	.20
a.		Vert. pair, imperf. horiz.	*400.00*	
1564	10c	Battle of Bunker Hill	.20	.20
1565	10c	Continental Army	.20	.20
1566	10c	Continental Navy	.20	.20
1567	10c	Continental Marines	.20	.20
1568	10c	American Militia	.20	.20
a.		Block of 4, #1565-1568	.85	.90
1569	10c	Apollo and Soyuz Linked	.20	.20
1570	10c	Apollo and Soyuz Separated	.20	.20
a.		Pair, #1569-1570	.45	.40
c.		As "a," vert. pair, imperf. horiz.	*2,100.*	
d.		As "a," yellow omitted	1,000.	
1571	10c	International Women's Year	.20	.20
1572	10c	Stagecoach & Truck	.20	.20
1573	10c	Locomotives	.20	.20
1574	10c	Airplanes	.20	.20
1575	10c	Satellites	.20	.20
a.		Block of 4, #1572-1575	.85	.90
b.		As "a," red (10c) omitted	—	
1576	10c	World Peace Through Law	.20	.20
b.		Horiz. pair, imperf. vert.	*7,500.*	
1577	10c	Banking	.25	.20
1578	10c	Commerce	.25	.20
a.		Pair, #1577-1578	.50	.40
b.		As "a," brown & blue (litho.) omitted	*2,000.*	
c.		As "a," brown, blue & yellow (litho.) omitted	*2,500.*	
1579	(10c)	Christmas - Religious	.20	.20
a.		Imperf., pair	*90.00*	
1580	(10c)	Christmas Card, by Louis Prang, perf. 11	.20	.20
a.		Imperf., pair	*90.00*	
c.		Perf. 10.9	.25	.20
1580B	(10c)	Christmas Card, by Louis Prang, 1878, perf. 10.5 x 11.3 (1580)	.65	.20

1975-81, Perf. 11x10½

Scott No.		Description	Unused Value	Used Value
1581	1c	Inkwell & Quill, tagged	.20	.20
a.		Untagged (Bureau precanceled)	4.50	1.50
1582	2c	Speaker's Stand, red brn, *grnish*, tagged	.20	.20
a.		Untagged (Bureau precanceled)	4.50	1.50
b.		Cream paper	.20	.20
1584	3c	Ballot Box, tagged	.20	.20

1558

1563

1564

1565-1568

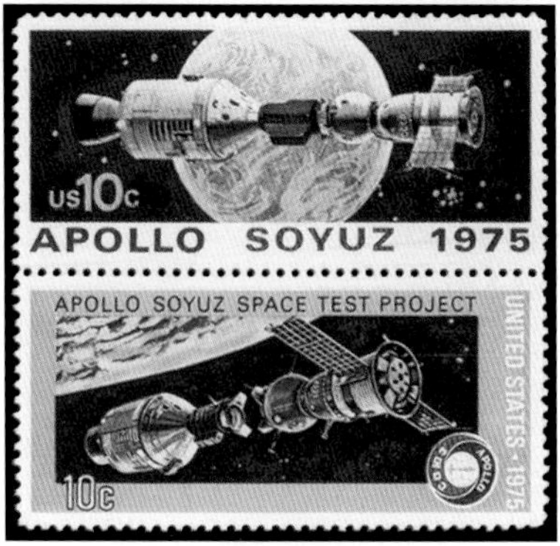

1569-1570

1571

1576

1572-1575

1577-1578

1579

1580

1581

1582

1584

1585

1591

1592

1593

1594

1595

1596

1597

1599

1603

1604

1605

1606

1608

1610

1611

1612

Scott No.		Description	Unused Value	Used Value
a.		Untagged (Bureau precanceled)	.75	.50
1585	4c	Books, tagged	.20	.20
a.		Untagged (Bureau precanceled)	1.00	.75
1590	9c	Capitol, slate green (from bklt. pane #1623a), perf. 11 x 10½	.45	.20
1590A	9c	Capitol (from bklt. pane #1623Bc), perf. 10 x 9¾ (1590)	20.00	15.00
1591	9c	Capitol, slate green, *gray*	.20	.20
a.		Untagged (Bureau precanceled)	1.75	1.00
1592	10c	Justice, tagged	.20	.20
a.		Untagged (Bureau precanceled)	9.50	5.00
1593	11c	Printing Press	.20	.20
1594	12c	Torch	.25	.20
1595	13c	Liberty Bell (from bklt. pane)	.30	.20
a.		Booklet pane of 6	2.25	1.00
b.		Booklet pane of 7 + label	2.25	1.00
c.		Booklet pane of 8	2.25	1.00
d.		Booklet pane of 5 + label	1.75	1.00
e.		Vert. pair, imperf. btwn.	*1,250.*	
g.		Horiz. pair, imperf. btwn.	—	
h.		As "a," miscut and inserted upside-down into booklet cover, imperf. below bottom stamps and with "tab" at bottom.	—	
Perf. 11				
1596	13c	Eagle & Shield	.25	.20
a.		Imperf., pair	*40.00*	—
b.		Yellow omitted	*115.00*	
1597	15c	Flag	.30	.20
a.		Vert. pair, imperf.	*17.50*	
b.		Gray omitted	*350.00*	
c.		Vert. strip of 3, imperf. btwn. & at top or bottom	*375.00*	
Perf. 11x10½				
1598	15c	Flag (1597, from bklt. pane)	.40	.20
a.		Booklet pane of 8	4.25	*.80*
1599	16c	Statue of Liberty	.35	.20
1603	24c	Old North Church, Boston	.50	.20
1604	28c	Fort Nisqually, Washington	.55	.20
1605	29c	Sandy Hook Lighthouse, N.J.	.60	.20
1606	30c	School, North Dakota	.55	.20
Perf. 11				
1608	50c	Iron "Betty" Lamp	.85	.20
a.		Black omitted	*250.00*	
b.		Vert. pair, imperf. horiz.	*1,500.*	
1610	$1	Rush Lamp & Candle Holder	2.00	.20
a.		Brown (engraved) omitted	*225.00*	
b.		Tan, orange & yellow omitted	*250.00*	
c.		Brown (engraved) inverted	*21,000.*	
1611	$2	Kerosene Lamp	3.75	.75

1613

1614

1615

1615C

1622

1623

1629-1631

1632

Scott No.		Description	Unused Value	Used Value	/ / / / / /
1612	$5	Railroad Lantern	8.50	1.75	□□□□□
Coil Stamps, Perf. 10 Vertically, Tagged					
1613	3.1c	Guitar	.20	.20	□□□□□
a.		Untagged (Bureau precanceled)	.35	.35	□□□□□
b.		Imperf., pair	*1,200.*		□□□□□
1614	7.7c	Saxhorns	.20	.20	□□□□□
a.		Untagged (Bureau precanceled)	.40	.30	□□□□□
b.		As "a," imperf., pair	*1,400.*		□□□□□
1615	7.9c	Drum	.20	.20	□□□□□
a.		Untagged (Bureau precanceled)	.40	.40	□□□□□
b.		Imperf., pair	*525.00*		□□□□□
1615C	8.4c	Piano	.20	.20	□□□□□
d.		Untagged (Bureau precanceled)	.50	.40	□□□□□
e.		As "d," pair, imperf. btwn.	45.00		□□□□□
f.		As "d," imperf., pair	15.00		□□□□□
1616	9c	Capitol (1590), slate grn, *gray*	.20	.20	□□□□□
a.		Imperf., pair	*135.00*		□□□□□
b.		Untagged (Bureau precanceled)	1.15	.75	□□□□□
c.		As "b," imperf., pair	*650.00*		□□□□□
1617	10c	Justice (1592)	.20	.20	□□□□□
a.		Untagged (Bureau precanceled)	42.50	1.35	□□□□□
b.		Imperf., pair	50.00		□□□□□
c.		As "a," imperf., pair, dull gum	*3,500.*		□□□□□
1618	13c	Liberty Bell (1595)	.25	.20	□□□□□
a.		Untagged (Bureau precanceled)	5.75	.75	□□□□□
b.		Imperf., pair	22.50		□□□□□
g.		Vertical pair, imperf. btwn.	—		□□□□□
h.		As "a," imperf., pair	—		□□□□□
1618C	15c	Flag (1597)	.75	.20	□□□□□
d.		Imperf., pair	20.00		□□□□□
e.		Pair, imperf. btwn.	*125.00*		□□□□□
f.		Gray omitted	*30.00*		□□□□□
1619	16c	Statue of Liberty (1599)	.35	.20	□□□□□
a.		Block tagging	.50	.20	□□□□□
1975-81, Perf. 11x10¾					
1622	13c	Flag, Independence Hall	.25	.20	□□□□□
a.		Horizontal pair, imperf. btwn.	*40.00*		□□□□□
b.		Vertical pair, imperf.	*375.00*		□□□□□
e.		Horiz. pair, imperf. vert.	—		□□□□□
1622C	13c	Flag, Independence Hall, perf. 11¼ (1622)	1.00	.25	□□□□□
d.		Vert. pair, imperf.	*120.00*		□□□□□
1623	13c	Flag over Capitol (from bklt. pane) perf. 11x10½	.25	.20	□□□□□
a.		Bklt. pane of 8, #1590 + 7 #1623	2.25	*1.25*	□□□□□
d.		Pair, #1590 & 1623	.70	*1.00*	□□□□□
1623B	13c	Flag over Capitol (from bklt. pane #1623Bc), perf. 10 x 9¾ (1623)	.80	.80	□□□□□
c.		Booklet pane, 1 #1590A + 7 #1623B	22.50	—	□□□□□
e.		Pair, #1590A & #1623B	18.50	18.50	□□□□□

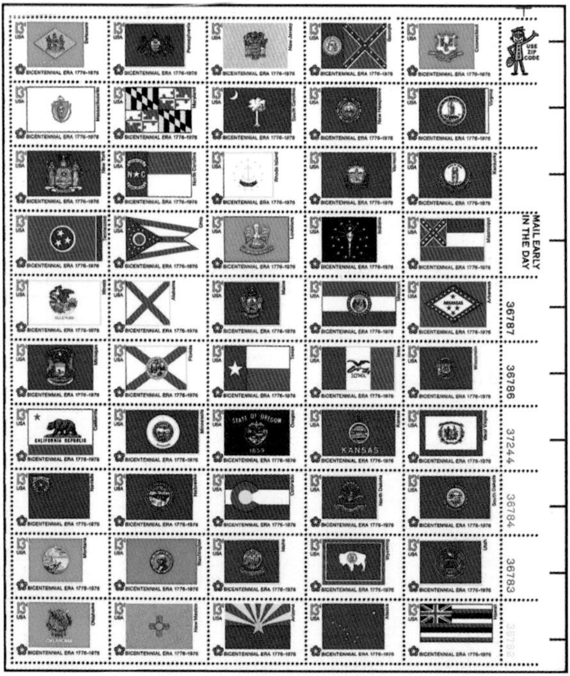

1633-1682

1683

1684

1685

Scott No.		Description	Unused Value	Used Value
Coil Stamp, Perf. 10 Vertically				
1625	13c	Flag, Independence Hall (1622)	.35	.20
a.		Imperf., pair	20.00	
1976 , Perf. 11				
1629	13c	Drummer Boy	.25	.20
1630	13c	Old Drummer	.25	.20
1631	13c	Fifer	.25	.20
a.		Strip of 3, #1629-1631	.75	.75
b.		As "a," imperf.	*800.00*	
c.		Imperf., vert. pair, #1631	*700.00*	
1632	13c	Interphil 76	.20	.20
a.		Dark blue and red (engr.) missing (from a color misregistration)	—	
b.		Red (engr.) missing (from a color misregistration)	—	
1633	13c	Delaware	.30	.25
1634	13c	Pennsylvania	.30	.25
1635	13c	New Jersey	.30	.25
1636	13c	Georgia	.30	.25
1637	13c	Connecticut	.30	.25
1638	13c	Massachusetts	.30	.25
1639	13c	Maryland	.30	.25
1640	13c	South Carolina	.30	.25
1641	13c	New Hampshire	.30	.25
1642	13c	Virginia	.30	.25
1643	13c	New York	.30	.25
1644	13c	North Carolina	.30	.25
1645	13c	Rhode Island	.30	.25
1646	13c	Vermont	.30	.25
1647	13c	Kentucky	.30	.25
1648	13c	Tennessee	.30	.25
1649	13c	Ohio	.30	.25
1650	13c	Louisiana	.30	.25
1651	13c	Indiana	.30	.25
1652	13c	Mississippi	.30	.25
1653	13c	Illinois	.30	.25
1654	13c	Alabama	.30	.25
1655	13c	Maine	.30	.25
1656	13c	Missouri	.30	.25
1657	13c	Arkansas	.30	.25
1658	13c	Michigan	.30	.25
1659	13c	Florida	.30	.25
1660	13c	Texas	.30	.25
1661	13c	Iowa	.30	.25
1662	13c	Wisconsin	.30	.25
1663	13c	California	.30	.25
1664	13c	Minnesota	.30	.25
1665	13c	Oregon	.30	.25
1666	13c	Kansas	.30	.25
1667	13c	West Virginia	.30	.25

The Surrender of Lord Cornwallis at Yorktown
From a Painting by John Trumbull

1686

The Declaration of Independence, 4 July 1776 at Philadelphia
From a Painting by John Trumbull

1687

Scott No.		Description	Unused Value	Used Value
1668	13c	Nevada	.30	.25
1669	13c	Nebraska	.30	.25
1670	13c	Colorado	.30	.25
1671	13c	North Dakota	.30	.25
1672	13c	South Dakota	.30	.25
1673	13c	Montana	.30	.25
1674	13c	Washington	.30	.25
1675	13c	Idaho	.30	.25
1676	13c	Wyoming	.30	.25
1677	13c	Utah	.30	.25
1678	13c	Oklahoma	.30	.25
1679	13c	New Mexico	.30	.25
1680	13c	Arizona	.30	.25
1681	13c	Alaska	.30	.25
1682	13c	Hawaii	.30	.25
a.		Pane of 50	17.50	15.00
1683	13c	Telephone Centennial	.25	.20
a.		Black and purple missing (from extraneous paper)	*450.00*	
b.		Red missing (from extraneous paper)	—	
c.		All colors missing (from extraneous paper)	—	
1684	13c	Commercial Aviation	.25	.20
1685	13c	Chemistry	.25	.20
1686		Surrender of Cornwallis, Sheet of 5	3.25	2.25
a.-e.	13c	Any single	.45	.40
f.		USA/13c omitted on b, c & d., imperf.	—	*1,750.*
g.		USA/13c omitted on a & e	*450.00*	—
h.		Imperf., tagging omitted		*2,250.*
i.		USA/13c omitted on b, c & d	*450.00*	
j.		USA/13c double on b	—	
k.		USA/13c omitted on c & d	*750.00*	
l.		USA/13c omitted on e	*550.00*	
m.		USA/13c omitted, imperf., tagging omitted		—
n.		As "g," imperf., tagging omitted		—
o.		USA/13c missing on a (from perf. shift)	—	
q.		USA/13c omitted on a	—	
r.		Imperf., tagged		—
1687		Declaration of Independence, Sht. of 5	4.25	3.25
a.-e.	18c	Any single	.55	.55
f.		Design & margin inscriptions omitted	*3,000.*	
g.		USA/18c omitted on a & c	*600.00*	—
h.		USA/18c omitted on b, d & e	*400.00*	
i.		USA/18c omitted on d	*425.00*	*475.00*
j.		Black omitted in design	*2,000.*	
k.		USA/18c omitted, imperf., tagging omitted	*2,000.*	
m.		USA/18c omitted on b & e	*500.00*	
n.		USA/18c omitted on b & d	*1,000.*	
p.		Imperf., tagged	*1,000.*	

1688

1689

1690

Scott No.	Description	Unused Value	Used Value
q.	USA/18c omitted on c	—	
r.	Yellow omitted	—	
s.	USA/18c missing on a, c and d (from perf. shift)	—	
1688	Washington Crossing the Delaware, Sheet of 5	5.25	4.25
a.-e. 24c	Any single	.70	.70
f.	USA/24c omitted, imperf.	*950.00*	
g.	USA/24c omitted on d & e	*450.00*	*450.00*
h.	Design & margin inscriptions omitted	*2,750.*	
i.	USA/24c omitted on a, b & c	*450.00*	*450.00*
j.	Imperf., tagging omitted	*1,500.*	
k.	USA/24c of d & e inverted	*40,000.*	
l.	As "i," imperf, tagging omitted	*3,250.*	—
n.	As No. 1688, perfs inverted	*450.00*	
1689	Washington Reviewing Army, Sheet of 5	6.25	5.25
a.-e. 31c	multi, any single	.85	.85
f.	USA/31c omitted	*1,500.*	
g.	USA/31c omitted on a & c	*375.00*	
h.	USA/31c omitted on b, d & e	*500.00*	—
i.	USA/31c omitted on e	*375.00*	
j.	Black omitted in design	*1,500.*	
k.	Imperf., tagging omitted		*1,250.*
l.	USA/31c omitted on b & d	*375.00*	
m.	USA/31c omitted on a, c & e	*750.00*	
n.	As "m," imperf., tagging omitted	—	
p.	As "h," imperf., tagging omitted		*1,250.*
q.	As "g," imperf., tagging omitted	*2,750.*	
r.	"USA/31c" omitted on d & e	*500.00*	
t.	USA/31c omitted on d	500.00	
v.	As No. 1689, perfs and tagging inverted	*10,000.*	
w.	USA/31c missing on a, b, c and d (from perf. shift)	—	
1690	13c Benjamin Franklin	.25	.20
a.	Light blue omitted	*200.00*	
1691	13c Declaration of Independence - Left	.30	.20
1692	13c Declaration of Independence - Gathered Curtains	.30	.20
1693	13c Declaration of Independence - Table	.30	.20
1694	13c Declaration of Independence - Right	.30	.20
a.	Strip of 4, #1691-1694	1.20	1.10
1695	13c Olympics - Diving	.30	.20
1696	13c Olympics - Skiing	.30	.20
1697	13c Olympics - Running	.30	.20
1698	13c Olympics - Skating	.30	.20
a.	Block of 4, #1695-1698	1.20	*1.20*
b.	As "a," imperf.	*550.00*	

1691-1694

1699

1695-1698

1700

1701

1702

1704

1705

1706-1709

1710

1711

1716

1712-1715

1717-1720

1721

1722

1725

1723-1724

1726

1727

1728

1729

1730

1731

Scott No.		Description	Unused Value	Used Value
1699	13c	Clara Maass	.25	.20
a.		Horiz. pair, imperf. vert.	*400.00*	
1700	13c	Adolph S. Ochs	.25	.20
1701	13c	Christmas - Religious	.25	.20
a.		Imperf., pair	*85.00*	
1702	13c	Christmas - "Winter Pastime"	.25	.20
a.		Imperf., pair	*85.00*	
1703	13c	Christmas - "Winter Pastime" (1702), block tagging	.25	.20
a.		Imperf., pair	*90.00*	
b.		Vert. pair, imperf. btwn.	325.00	
d.		Red omitted	*650.00*	
e.		Yellow omitted	—	
1977				
1704	13c	Washington at Princeton	.25	.20
a.		Horiz. pair, imperf. vert.	*500.00*	
b.		Black (inscriptions) missing (from perf. shift)	—	
1705	13c	Sound Recording	.25	.20
1706	13c	Zia Pot	.25	.20
1707	13c	San Ildefonso Pot	.25	.20
1708	13c	Hopi Pot	.25	.20
1709	13c	Acoma Pot	.25	.20
a.		Block or strip of 4	1.00	1.00
b.		As "a," imperf. vert.	*2,000.*	
1710	13c	Lindbergh Flight	.25	.20
a.		Imperf., pair	*825.00*	
1711	13c	Colorado Statehood	.25	.20
a.		Horiz. pair, imperf. btwn. and with natural straight edge at right	—	
b.		Horiz. pair, imperf. vert.	*750.00*	
1712	13c	Swallowtail Butterfly	.25	.20
1713	13c	Checkerspot Butterfly	.25	.20
1714	13c	Dogface Butterfly	.25	.20
1715	13c	Orange-tip Butterfly	.25	.20
a.		Block of 4, #1712-1715	1.00	1.00
b.		As "a," imperf. horiz.	*15,000.*	
1716	13c	Marquis de Lafayette	.25	.20
a.		Red missing (from perf. shift)	*200.00*	
1717	13c	Seamstress	.25	.20
1718	13c	Blacksmith	.25	.20
1719	13c	Wheelwright	.25	.20
1720	13c	Leatherworker	.25	.20
a.		Block of 4, #1717-1720	1.00	1.00
1721	13c	Peace Bridge	.25	.20
1722	13c	Battle of Oriskany	.25	.20
1723	13c	Energy Conservation	.25	.20
1724	13c	Energy Development	.25	.20
a.		Pair, #1723-1724	.50	.50

1732-1733

1745-1748

1734

1735

1738-1742

1737

1749-1752

1744

1753

Scott No.		Description	Unused Value	Used Value
1725	13c	Alta California	.25	.20
1726	13c	Articles of Confederation	.25	.20
b.		Red omitted	600.00	
c.		Red & brown omitted	400.00	
1727	13c	Talking Pictures	.25	.20
1728	13c	Surrender at Saratoga	.25	.20
1729	13c	Christmas - Washington Praying	.25	.20
a.		Imperf., pair	*65.00*	
1730	13c	Christmas - Mailbox	.25	.20
a.		Imperf., pair	*200.00*	
1978				
1731	13c	Carl Sandburg	.25	.20
a.		Brown omitted	*2,250.*	
1732	13c	Capt. James Cook - Portrait	.25	.20
1733	13c	Capt. James Cook - Ships	.25	.20
a.		Vert. pair, imperf. horiz.	—	
b.		Pair, #1732-1733	.50	.50
c.		As "a," imperf. btwn.	*4,250.*	
1978-80				
1734	13c	Indian Head Penny	.25	.20
a.		Horiz. pair, imperf. vert.	*250.00*	
1735	(15c)	"A" & Eagle, photogravure	.30	.20
a.		Imperf., pair	*85.00*	
b.		Vert. pair, imperf. horiz.	*600.00*	
c.		Perf 11.2	.35	.20
Booklet Stamps, Engraved				
1736	(15c)	"A" & Eagle (1735)	.30	.20
a.		Booklet pane of 8	2.50	*1.50*
c.		Vert. pair, imperf. between	*850.00*	
1737	15c	Roses	.30	.20
a.		Booklet pane of 8	2.50	*1.50*
b.		Imperf. pair	*450.00*	
1738	15c	Virginia Windmill	.30	.20
1739	15c	Rhode Island Windmill	.30	.20
1740	15c	Massachusetts Windmill	.30	.20
1741	15c	Illinois Windmill	.30	.20
1742	15c	Texas Windmill	.30	.20
a.		Bklt. pane, 2 each #1738-1742	3.50	3.00
b.		Strip of 5, #1738-1742	1.50	1.40
Coil Stamp, Perf. 10 Vertically				
1743	(15c)	"A" & Eagle (1735)	.30	.20
a.		Imperf., pair	75.00	
1978				
1744	13c	Harriet Tubman	.25	.20
1745	13c	Quilts - Orange Flowered Fabric	.25	.20
1746	13c	Quilts - Red & White Fabric	.25	.20
1747	13c	Quilts - Orange Striped Fabric	.25	.20
1748	13c	Quilts - Black Plaid Fabric	.25	.20
a.		Block of 4, #1745-1748	1.00	1.00

1757

1754

1755

1759

1756

1760-1763

1768

1769

1758

Scott No.		Description	Unused Value	Used Value	/ / / / / /
1749	13c	Ballet	.25	.20	
1750	13c	Dance in Theater	.25	.20	
1751	13c	Folk Dancing	.25	.20	
1752	13c	Modern Dance	.25	.20	
a.		Block of 4, #1749-1752	1.00	1.00	
1753	13c	French Alliance	.25	.20	
a.		Red missing (from a perf. shift)	—		
1754	13c	Early Cancer Detection	.25	.20	
1755	13c	Jimmie Rodgers	.25	.20	
1756	15c	George M. Cohan	.30	.20	
1757		CAPEX, block of 8	2.00	1.75	
a.	13c	Cardinal	.25	.20	
b.	13c	Mallard	.25	.20	
c.	13c	Canada goose	.25	.20	
d.	13c	Blue jay	.25	.20	
e.	13c	Moose	.25	.20	
f.	13c	Chipmunk	.25	.20	
g.	13c	Red fox	.25	.20	
h.	13c	Raccoon	.25	.20	
i.		Yellow, green, red, brown, blue, and black (litho.) omitted	*7,000.*		
j.		Strip of 4 (a.-d.), imperf. vert.	*5,000.*		
k.		Strip of 4 (e.-h.), imperf. vert.	*3,000.*		
l.		As No. 1757, 'd' and 'h' with black omitted	—		
m.		As No. 1757, 'b' with blue missing (from perf. shift)	—		
1758	15c	Photography	.30	.20	
1759	15c	Viking Missions to Mars	.30	.20	
1760	15c	Great Gray Owl	.30	.20	
1761	15c	Saw-whet Owl	.30	.20	
1762	15c	Barred Owl	.30	.20	
1763	15c	Great Horned Owl	.30	.20	
a.		Block of 4, #1760-1763	1.25	1.25	
1764	15c	Giant Sequoia	.30	.20	
1765	15c	White Pine	.30	.20	
1766	15c	White Oak	.30	.20	
1767	15c	Gray Birch	.30	.20	
a.		Block of 4, #1764-1767	1.25	1.25	
b.		As "a," imperf. horiz.	*17,500.*		
1768	15c	Christmas - Religious	.30	.20	
a.		Imperf., pair	*80.00*		
1769	15c	Christmas - Hobby Horse	.30	.20	
a.		Imperf., pair	*85.00*		
b.		Vert. pair, imperf. horiz.	*1,250.*		
1979					
1770	15c	Robert F. Kennedy	.35	.20	
1771	15c	Dr. Martin Luther King, Jr.	.40	.20	
a.		Imperf., pair	1,400.		
1772	15c	International Year of the Child	.30	.20	
1773	15c	John Steinbeck	.30	.20	

1764-1767

1770

1771

1772

1773

1774

1775-1778

Scott No.		Description	Unused Value	Used Value
1774	15c	Albert Einstein	.35	.20
1775	15c	Toleware - Straight-spouted coffeepot	.30	.20
1776	15c	Toleware - Tea Caddy	.30	.20
1777	15c	Toleware - Sugar Bowl	.30	.20
1778	15c	Toleware - Curved-spouted coffeepot	.30	.20
a.		Block of 4, #1775-1778	1.25	1.25
b.		As "a," imperf. horiz.	*3,000.*	
1779	15c	Architecture - Jefferson	.30	.20
1780	15c	Architecture - Latrobe	.30	.20
1781	15c	Architecture - Bulfinch	.30	.20
1782	15c	Architecture - Strickland	.30	.20
a.		Block of 4, #1779-1782	1.25	*1.25*
1783	5c	Persistent Trillium	.30	.20
1784	15c	Hawaiian Wild Broadbean	.30	.20
1785	15c	Contra Costa Wallflower	.30	.20
1786	15c	Antioch Dunes Evening Primrose	.30	.20
a.		Block of 4, #1783-1786	1.25	1.25
b.		As "a," imperf.	*275.00*	
1787	15c	Seeing Eye Dogs	.30	.20
a.		Imperf., pair	*375.00*	
1788	15c	Special Olympics	.30	.20
1789	15c	John Paul Jones, perf. 11x12	.30	.20
c.		Vert. pair, imperf. horiz.	*150.00*	
1789A	15c	John Paul Jones, perf. 11 (1789)	.55	.20
d.		Vert. pair, imperf horiz.	*125.00*	
1789B	15c	John Paul Jones, perf. 12 (1789)	*3,500.*	*3,500.*
1979-80				
1790	10c	Olympics - Decathlon	.20	.20
1791	15c	Olympics - Running	.30	.20
1792	15c	Olympics - Women's Swimming	.30	.20
1793	15c	Olympics - Rowing	.30	.20
1794	15c	Olympics - Equestrian	.30	.20
a.		Block of 4, #1791-1794	1.25	*1.25*
b.		As "a," imperf.	*1,400.*	
1795	15c	Olympics - Speed Skating, perf. 11¼ x 10½	.35	.20
1796	15c	Olympics - Downhill Skiing, perf. 11¼ x 10½	.35	.20
1797	15c	Olympics - Ski Jump, perf. 11¼ x 10½	.35	.20
1798	15c	Olympics - Ice Hockey, perf. 11¼ x 10½	.35	.20
b.		Block of 4, #1795-1798	1.50	1.40
1795A	15c	Olympics - Speed Skating, perf. 11 (1795)	1.10	.60
1796A	15c	Olympics - Downhill Skiing, perf. 11 (1796)	1.10	.60
1797A	15c	Olympics - Ski Jump, perf. 11 (1797)	1.10	.60
1798A	15c	Olympics - Ice Hockey, perf. 11 (1798)	1.10	.60
c.		Block of 4, #1795A-1798A (1795-1798)	4.50	3.50

1779-1782

1783-1786

1787

1788

1789

1790

1791-1794

1795-1798

1799

1800

1802

1801

1803

1804

1805

1806

1807

1809

1813

1818

1821

1822

1823

1824

1825

1826

Scott No.		Description	Unused Value	Used Value
1979				
1799	15c	Christmas - Religious	.30	.20
a.		Imperf., pair	*80.00*	
b.		Vert. pair, imperf. horiz.	*575.00*	
c.		Vert. pair, imperf. btwn.	*1,100.*	
1800	15c	Christmas - Santa Claus	.30	.20
a.		Green & yellow omitted	*500.00*	
b.		Green, yellow & tan omitted	*450.00*	
1801	15c	Will Rogers	.30	.20
a.		Imperf., pair	*175.00*	
1802	15c	Vietnam Veterans	.30	.20
1980				
1803	15c	W.C. Fields	.30	.20
a.		Imperf., pair	—	
1804	15c	Benjamin Banneker	.35	.20
a.		Horiz. pair, imperf. vert.	*400.00*	
1805	15c	Letters Preserve Memories	.30	.20
1806	15c	P.S. Write Soon, purple & multi	.30	.20
1807	15c	Letters Lift Spirits	.30	.20
1808	15c	P.S. Write Soon (1806), grn & multi	.30	.20
1809	15c	Letters Shape Opinions	.30	.20
1810	15c	P.S. Write Soon (1806), red & multi	.30	.20
a.		Vert. strip of 6, #1805-1810	1.85	*2.00*
1980-81, Coil Stamps, Perf. 10 Vertically				
1811	1c	Inkwell & Quill (1581)	.20	.20
a.		Imperf., pair	*125.00*	
1813	3.5c	Violins, tagged	.20	.20
a.		Untagged (Bureau precanceled, lines only)	.20	.20
b.		Imperf., pair	*150.00*	
1816	12c	Torch (1594), tagged	.25	.20
a.		Untagged (Bureau precanceled)	1.15	1.15
b.		Imperf., pair	*150.00*	
c.		As "a," brownish red, *reddish beige*	—	—
1981				
1818	(18c)	"B" & Eagle, photogravure	.35	.20
Booklet Stamp, Perf. 10, Engraved				
1819	(18c)	"B" & Eagle (1818)	.40	.20
		a. Booklet pane of 8	3.75	2.25
Coil Stamp, Perf. 10 Vertically				
1820	(18c)	"B" & Eagle (1818), engraved	.40	.20
a.		Imperf., pair	*125.00*	
1980				
1821	15c	Frances Perkins	.30	.20
1822	15c	Dolley Madison	.30	.20
a.		Red brown missing (from perf. shift)	—	
1823	15c	Emily Bissell	.35	.20
a.		Vert. pair, imperf. horiz.	*325.00*	
b.		All colors missing (from extraneous paper)	—	

1827-1830

1831

1832

1833

1834-1837

Scott No.		Description	Unused Value	Used Value
c.		Red missing (from foldover)	—	
1824	15c	Helen Keller, Anne Sullivan	.30	.20
1825	15c	Veterans Administration..................	.30	.20
a.		Horiz. pair, imperf. vert.	*400.00*	
1826	15c	Bernardo de Galvez.........................	.30	.20
a.		Red, brown & blue (engr.) omitted.	*625.00*	
b.		Blue, brown, red (engr.), yellow (litho.) omitted	*1,150.*	
1827	15c	Brain Coral	.30	.20
1828	15c	Elkhorn Coral..................................	.30	.20
1829	15c	Chalice Coral..................................	.30	.20
1830	15c	Finger Coral....................................	.30	.20
a.		Block of 4, #1827-1830	1.25	1.10
b.		As "a," imperf.................................	*450.00*	
c.		As "a," vert. imperf. btwn.	*2,000.*	
d.		As "a," imperf. vert.	*3,000.*	
1831	15c	Organized Labor..............................	.30	.20
a.		Imperf., pair....................................	*300.00*	
1832	15c	Edith Wharton	.30	.20
1833	15c	Education..	.30	.20
a.		Horiz. pair, imperf. vert.	*175.00*	
1834	15c	Bella Bella Mask.............................	.35	.20
1835	15c	Chilkat Tlingit Mask	.35	.20
1836	15c	Tlingit Mask....................................	.35	.20
1837	15c	Bella Coola Mask............................	.35	.20
a.		Block of 4, #1834-1837	1.50	1.25
1838	15c	Architecture - Renwick..................	.30	.20
1839	15c	Architecture - Richardson..............	.30	.20
1840	15c	Architecture - Furness....................	.30	.20
1841	15c	Architecture - Davis........................	.30	.20
a.		Block of 4, #1838-1841	1.25	*1.25*
b.		As "a," red missing on Nos. 1838, 1839 (from perf. shift)................	400.00	
1842	15c	Christmas - Religious.....................	.30	.20
a.		Imperf., pair....................................	*50.00*	
1843	15c	Christmas - Wreath & Toys............	.30	.20
a.		Imperf., pair....................................	*60.00*	
b.		Buff omitted	*22.50*	
c.		Vert. pair, imperf. horiz.	—	
d.		Horiz. pair, imperf. btwn.	*3,750.*	
1980-85				
1844	1c	Dorothea Dix..................................	.20	.20
a.		Imperf. pair....................................	*375.00*	
b.		Vert. pair, imperf. btwn. & with natural straight edge at bottom...................	*1,900.*	
e.		Vert. pair, imperf. horiz..................	—	
1845	2c	Igor Stravinsky	.20	.20
1846	3c	Henry Clay	.20	.20
1847	4c	Carl Schurz.....................................	.20	.20
1848	5c	Pearl Buck	.30	.20

1838-1841

1842

1843

1874

1875

1876-1879

HOW TO USE THIS BOOK

The number in the first column is its Scott number or identifying number. Following that is the denomination of the stamp and its color or description. Finally, the values, unused and used, are shown.

1844

1845

1846

1847

1848

1849

1850

1851

1852

1853

1854

1855

1856

1857

1858

1859

1860

1861

1862

1863

1864

1865

1866

1867

1868

1869

1890

1891

1892

1893

1895

1880-1889

HOW TO USE THIS BOOK

The number in the first column is its Scott number or identifying number. Following that is the denomination of the stamp and its color or description. Finally, the values, unused and used, are shown.

Scott No.		Description	Unused Value	Used Value
1849	6c	Walter Lippmann	.20	.20
a.		Vert. pair, imperf. btwn. & with natural straight edge at bottom	*1,750.*	
1850	7c	Abraham Baldwin	.20	.20
1851	8c	Henry Knox	.20	.20
1852	9c	Sylvanus Thayer	.20	.20
1853	10c	Richard Russell	.25	.20
b.		Vert. pair, imperf. btwn. & at bottom	*750.00*	
c.		Horiz. pair, imperf. btwn	*1,850.*	
d.		Vert. pair imperf. horiz.	—	
1854	11c	Alden Partridge	.40	.20
1855	13c	Crazy Horse	.40	.20
1856	14c	Sinclair Lewis	.30	.20
b.		Vert. pair, imperf. horiz.	*110.00*	
c.		Horiz. pair, imperf. btwn	8.00	
d.		Vert. pair, imperf. btwn.	*1,650.*	
e.		All color omitted.	—	
1857	17c	Rachel Carson	.35	.20
1858	18c	George Mason	.35	.20
1859	19c	Sequoyah	.45	.20
1860	20c	Ralph Bunche	.40	.20
1861	20c	Thomas H. Gallaudet	.50	.20
1862	20c	Harry S Truman	.40	.20
1863	22c	John James Audubon	.75	.20
d.		Vert. pair, imperf. horiz.	*1,750.*	
e.		Vert. pair, imperf. btwn.	—	
f.		Horiz. pair, imperf. btwn	*1,750.*	
1864	30c	Frank C. Laubach	.60	.20
1865	35c	Dr. Charles R. Drew	.75	.20
1866	37c	Robert Millikan	.80	.20
1867	39c	Grenville Clark	.90	.20
a.		Vert. pair, imperf. horiz.	*475.00*	
b.		Vert. pair, imperf. btwn.	*1,650.*	
1868	40c	Lillian M. Gilbreth	.90	.20
1869	50c	Chester W. Nimitz	.95	.20
1981				
1874	15c	Everett Dirksen	.30	.20
a.		All color omitted	*500.00*	
1875	15c	Whitney M. Young	.35	.20
1876	18c	Rose	.35	.20
1877	18c	Camellia	.35	.20
1878	18c	Dahlia	.35	.20
1879	18c	Lily	.35	.20
a.		Block of 4, #1876-1879	1.40	1.25
1880	18c	Bighorn	.85	.20
1881	18c	Puma	.85	.20
1882	18c	Harbor seal	.85	.20
1883	18c	American Buffalo	.85	.20
1884	18c	Brown bear	.85	.20

1897

1897A

1898

1898A

1899

1900

1901

1902

1903

1904

1905

1906

1907

1908

1909

Scott No.		Description	Unused Value	Used Value
1885	18c	Polar bear	.85	.20
1886	18c	Elk (wapiti)	.85	.20
1887	18c	Moose	.85	.20
1888	18c	White-tailed deer	.85	.20
1889	18c	Pronghorn	.85	.20
a.		Bklt. pane of 10, #1880-1889	8.50	6.00
1890	18c	Flag, Grain Field	.35	.20
a.		Imperf., pair	*80.00*	
b.		Vert. pair, imperf. horiz.	*600.00*	
c.		Vert. pair, imperf. between	—	

Coil Stamp, Perf. 10 Vertically

Scott No.		Description	Unused Value	Used Value
1891	18c	Flag, Sea Coast	.35	.20
a.		Imperf., pair	18.00	—
b.		Pair, imperf. btwn.	*1,850.*	

Booklet Stamps, Perf. 11

Scott No.		Description	Unused Value	Used Value
1892	6c	Stars (from bklt. pane)	.50	.20
1893	18c	Flag, Mountain (from bklt. pane)	.30	.20
a.		Booklet pane of 8 (2 #1892, 6 #1893)	3.00	2.50
b.		As "a," vert. imperf. btwn.	*70.00*	
c.		Pair, #1892, 1893	.90	1.00
1894	20c	Flag, Supreme Court (1895)	.40	.20
a.		Vert. pair, imperf.	30.00	
b.		Vert. pair, imperf. horiz.	*400.00*	
c.		Dark blue omitted	*70.00*	
d.		Black omitted	*275.00*	

Coil Stamp, Perf. 10 Vertically

Scott No.		Description	Unused Value	Used Value
1895	20c	Flag, Supreme Court, tagged	.40	.20
b.		Untagged (Bureau precanceled)	.50	.50
d.		Imperf., pair	8.00	—
e.		Pair, imperf. btwn.	*800.00*	
f.		Black omitted	*45.00*	
g.		Dark blue omitted	*1,350.*	
h.		Black field of stars instead of blue		—

Booklet Stamps, Perf. 11 x 10½

Scott No.		Description	Unused Value	Used Value
1896	20c	Flag, Supreme Court (1894)	.40	.20
a.		Booklet pane of 6	3.00	*2.25*
b.		Booklet pane of 10	5.25	*3.25*

1981-84, Coil Stamps, Perf. 10 Vertically

Scott No.		Description	Unused Value	Used Value
1897	1c	Omnibus	.20	.20
b.		Imperf., pair	*500.00*	
1897A	2c	Locomotive	.20	.20
c.		Imperf., pair	45.00	
1898	3c	Handcar	.20	.20
1898A	4c	Stagecoach, tagged	.20	.20
b.		Untagged (Bureau precanceled).	.20	.20
c.		As "b," imperf., pair	*675.00*	
d.		No. 1898A, imperf., pair	*700.00*	—
1899	5c	Motorcycle	.20	.20
a.		Imperf., pair	*2,750.*	

1910

1911

1912-1919

1921-1924

Scott No.		Description	Unused Value	Used Value
1900	5.2c	Sleigh, tagged	.20	.20
a.		Untagged (Bureau precanceled).	.20	.20
1901	5.9c	Bicycle, tagged	.25	.20
a.		Untagged (Bureau precanceled, lines only).	.20	.20
b.		As "a," imperf., pair	*160.00*	
1902	7.4c	Baby Buggy, tagged	.20	.20
a.		Untagged (Bureau precanceled).	.20	.20
1903	9.3c	Mail Wagon, tagged	.30	.20
a.		Untagged (Bureau precanceled, lines only).	.25	.25
b.		As "a," imperf., pair	100.00	
1904	10.9c	Hansom Cab, tagged	.30	.20
a.		Untagged (Bureau precanceled, lines only).	.30	.25
b.		As "a," imperf., pair	140.00	
1905	11c	Caboose, tagged	.30	.20
a.		Untagged	.25	.20
1906	17c	Electric Auto, tagged	.35	.20
a.		Untagged (Bureau precanceled, Presorted First Class)	.35	.35
b.		Imperf., pair	140.00	
c.		As "a," imperf., pair	*550.00*	
1907	18c	Surrey	.35	.20
a.		Imperf., pair	110.00	
1908	20c	Fire Pumper	.35	.20
a.		Imperf., pair	90.00	

1983, Booklet Stamp, Perf. 10 Vertically on 1 or 2 Sides

Scott No.		Description	Unused Value	Used Value
1909		$9.35 Eagle & Moon	20.00	15.00
a.		Booklet pane of 3	60.00	—

1981

Scott No.		Description	Unused Value	Used Value
1910	18c	American Red Cross	.35	.20
1911	18c	Savings & Loan	.35	.20
1912	18c	Moon Walk	.40	.20
1913	18c	Shuttle - Jettison of Boosters	.40	.20
1914	18c	Shuttle - Cargo Doors Open	.40	.20
1915	18c	Skylab	.40	.20
1916	18c	Pioneer 11, Saturn	.40	.20
1917	18c	Shuttle - Lifting Off	.40	.20
1918	18c	Shuttle - Landing	.40	.20
1919	18c	Space Telescope	.40	.20
a.		Block of 8, #1912-1919	3.25	3.00
b.		As "a," imperf.	*6,750.*	
c.		As "a," imperf. vert.	—	
1920	18c	Professional Management	.35	.20
1921	18c	Save Wetland Habitats	.35	.20
1922	18c	Save Grassland Habitats	.35	.20
1923	18c	Save Mountain Habitats	.35	.20
1924	18c	Save Woodland Habitats	.35	.20
a.		Block of 4, #1921-1924	1.50	1.25

1920

1925

1927

1926

1932

1933

1928-1931

1934

1941

1935

Scott No.		Description	Unused Value	Used Value	/ / / / / /
1925	18c	International Year of the Disabled ..	.35	.20	
a.		Vert. pair, imperf. horiz.	*2,500.*		
1926	18c	Edna St. Vincent Millay	.35	.20	
a.		Black (engr., inscriptions) omitted .	*275.00*	—	
1927	18c	Alcoholism	.45	.20	
a.		Imperf., pair	*375.00*		
b.		Vert. pair, imperf. horiz.	*2,400.*		
1928	18c	Architecture - White	.40	.20	
1929	18c	Architecture - Hunt	.40	.20	
1930	18c	Architecture - Maybeck	.40	.20	
1931	18c	Architecture - Sullivan	.40	.20	
a.		Block of 4, #1928-1931	1.65	1.65	
1932	18c	Babe Zaharias	.40	.20	
1933	18c	Bobby Jones	.60	.20	
1934	18c	Frederic Remington	.35	.20	
a.		Vert. pair, imperf. btwn.	*225.00*		
b.		Brown omitted	*350.00*		
1935	18c	James Hoban	.35	.20	
1936	20c	James Hoban (1935)	.35	.20	
1937	18c	Battle of Yorktown	.35	.20	
1938	18c	Battle of Virginia Capes	.35	.20	
a.		Pair, #1937-1938	.90	.75	
b.		As "a," black (engr., inscriptions) omitted	*350.00*		
1939	(20c)	Christmas - Religious	.40	.20	
a.		Imperf. pair	*100.00*		
b.		Vert. pair, imperf. horiz.	*1,000.*		
1940	(20c)	Christmas - Bear on Sled	.40	.20	
a.		Imperf., pair	*200.00*		
b.		Vert. pair, imperf. horiz.	*2,750.*		
1941	20c	John Hanson	.40	.20	
1942	20c	Barrel Cactus	.35	.20	
1943	20c	Agave	.35	.20	
1944	20c	Beavertail Cactus	.35	.20	
1945	20c	Saguaro	.35	.20	
a.		Block of 4, #1942-1945	1.50	1.25	
b.		As "a," deep brown (litho.) omitted	*4,250.*		
c.		No. 1945 imperf., vert. pair	*3,500.*		
d.		As "a," dark green & dark blue (engr.) missing (from extraneous paper)	—		
e.		As "a," dark green (engr.) missing on left stamp (from extraneous paper)	—		
1946	(20c)	"C" & Eagle	.40	.20	
b.		All color omitted	—		

Coil Stamp, Perf. 10 Vertically

1947	(20c)	"C" & Eagle (1946)	.60	.20	
a.		Imperf., pair	*950.00*		

1937-1938

1939

1940

1942-1945

1946

1948

1949

1950

1951

1952

2005

Scott No.		Description	Unused Value	Used Value	/ / / / / /
1948	(20c)	"C" & Eagle (from bklt. pane), perf. 11	.40	.20	
a.		Booklet pane of 10	4.50	3.25	
1982					
1949	20c	Bighorn, (from bklt. pane)	.55	.20	
a.		Booklet pane of 10	5.50	2.50	
b.		As "a," imperf. btwn.	*95.00*		
c.		Type II	1.40	.20	
d.		As "c," booklet pane of 10	14.00	—	
1950	20c	Franklin D. Roosevelt	.40	.20	
1951	20c	Love, perf. 11¼	.40	.20	
b.		Imperf., pair	*225.00*		
c.		Blue omitted	*200.00*		
d.		Yellow omitted	*650.00*		
e.		Purple omitted	—		
1951A	20c	Love, Perf. 11¼ x 10½ (1951)	.75	.25	
1952	20c	George Washington	.40	.20	
Perf 10½ x 11¼					
1953	20c	Alabama	.55	.30	
1954	20c	Alaska	.55	.30	
1955	20c	Arizona	.55	.30	
1956	20c	Arkansas	.55	.30	
1957	20c	California	.55	.30	
1958	20c	Colorado	.55	.30	
1959	20c	Connecticut	.55	.30	
1960	20c	Delaware	.55	.30	
1961	20c	Florida	.55	.30	
1962	20c	Georgia	.55	.30	
1963	20c	Hawaii	.55	.30	
1964	20c	Idaho	.55	.30	
1965	20c	Illinois	.55	.30	
1966	20c	Indiana	.55	.30	
1967	20c	Iowa	.55	.30	
1968	20c	Kansas	.55	.30	
1969	20c	Kentucky	.55	.30	
1970	20c	Louisiana	.55	.30	
1971	20c	Maine	.55	.30	
1972	20c	Maryland	.55	.30	
1973	20c	Massachusetts	.55	.30	
1974	20c	Michigan	.55	.30	
1975	20c	Minnesota	.55	.30	
1976	20c	Mississippi	.55	.30	
1977	20c	Missouri	.55	.30	
1978	20c	Montana	.55	.30	
1979	20c	Nebraska	.55	.30	
1980	20c	Nevada	.55	.30	
1981	20c	New Hampshire	.55	.30	
b.		Black missing (from extraneous paper)	*5,000.*		
1982	20c	New Jersey	.55	.30	

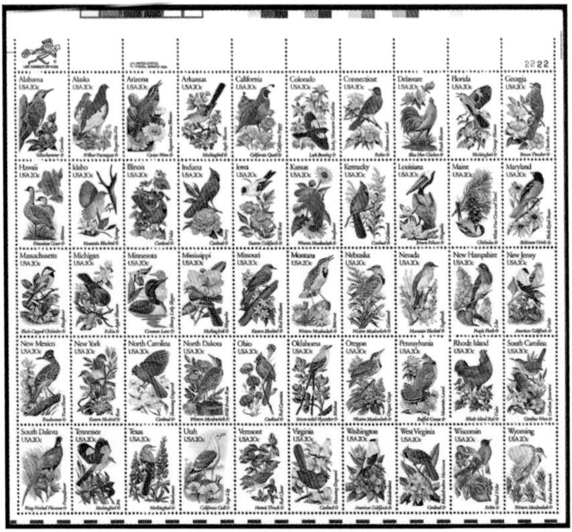

State Birds and Flowers 1953-2002, 1953A-2002A

2003

2010

2004

2006-2009

Scott No.		Description	Unused Value	Used Value
1983	20c	New Mexico	.55	.30
1984	20c	New York	.55	.30
1985	20c	North Carolina	.55	.30
1986	20c	North Dakota	.55	.30
1987	20c	Ohio	.55	.30
1988	20c	Oklahoma	.55	.30
1989	20c	Oregon	.55	.30
1990	20c	Pennsylvania	.55	.30
1991	20c	Rhode Island	.55	.30
b.		Black missing (from extraneous paper)	*5,000.*	
1992	20c	South Carolina	.55	.30
1993	20c	South Dakota	.55	.30
1994	20c	Tennessee	.55	.30
1995	20c	Texas	.55	.30
1996	20c	Utah	.55	.30
1997	20c	Vermont	.55	.30
1998	20c	Virginia	.55	.30
1999	20c	Washington	.55	.30
2000	20c	West Virginia	.55	.30
2001	20c	Wisconsin	.55	.30
b.		Black missing (from extraneous paper)	*5,000.*	
2002	20c	Wyoming	.55	.30
b.		Pane of 50, Nos. 1953-2002	27.50	20.00
d.		Pane of 50, imperf.	*27,500.*	
Perf 11¼ x 11				
1953A	20c	Alabama	.65	.30
1954A	20c	Alaska	.65	.30
1955A	20c	Arizona	.65	.30
1956A	20c	Arkansas	.65	.30
1957A	20c	California	.65	.30
1958A	20c	Colorado	.65	.30
1959A	20c	Connecticut	.65	.30
1960A	20c	Delaware	.65	.30
1961A	20c	Florida	.65	.30
1962A	20c	Georgia	.65	.30
1963A	20c	Hawaii	.65	.30
1964A	20c	Idaho	.65	.30
1965A	20c	Illinois	.65	.30
1966A	20c	Indiana	.65	.30
1967A	20c	Iowa	.65	.30
1968A	20c	Kansas	.65	.30
1969A	20c	Kentucky	.65	.30
1970A	20c	Louisiana	.65	.30
1971A	20c	Maine	.65	.30
1972A	20c	Maryland	.65	.30
1973A	20c	Massachusetts	.65	.30
1974A	20c	Michigan	.65	.30
1975A	20c	Minnesota	.65	.30
1976A	20c	Mississippi	.65	.30
1977A	20c	Missouri	.65	.30

2011

2014

2012

2013

2015

2016

2017

2018

2019-2022

Scott No.		Description	Unused Value	Used Value	/ / / / / /
1978A	20c	Montana	.65	.30	
1979A	20c	Nebraska	.65	.30	
1980A	20c	Nevada	.65	.30	
1981A	20c	New Hampshire	.65	.30	
1982A	20c	New Jersey	.65	.30	
1983A	20c	New Mexico	.65	.30	
1984A	20c	New York	.65	.30	
1985A	20c	North Carolina	.65	.30	
1986A	20c	North Dakota	.65	.30	
1987A	20c	Ohio	.65	.30	
1988A	20c	Oklahoma	.65	.30	
1989A	20c	Oregon	.65	.30	
1990A	20c	Pennsylvania	.65	.30	
1991A	20c	Rhode Island	.65	.30	
1992A	20c	South Carolina	.65	.30	
1993A	20c	South Dakota	.65	.30	
1994A	20c	Tennessee	.65	.30	
1995A	20c	Texas	.65	.30	
1996A	20c	Utah	.65	.30	
1997A	20c	Vermont	.65	.30	
1998A	20c	Virginia	.65	.30	
1999A	20c	Washington	.65	.30	
2000A	20c	West Virginia	.65	.30	
2001A	20c	Wisconsin	.65	.30	
2002A	20c	Wyoming	.65	.30	
c.		Pane of 50, Nos. 1953A-2002A	32.50	22.50	
2003	20c	U.S. - Netherlands	.40	.20	
a.		Imperf., pair	*275.00*		
2004	20c	Library of Congress	.40	.20	

Coil Stamp, Perf. 10 Vertically

Scott No.		Description	Unused Value	Used Value	/ / / / / /
2005	20c	Consumer Education	.55	.20	
a.		Imperf., pair	85.00		
2006	20c	Solar Energy	.45	.20	
2007	20c	Synthetic Fuels	.45	.20	
2008	20c	Breeder Reactor	.45	.20	
2009	20c	Fossil Fuels	.45	.20	
a.		Block of 4, #2006-2009	1.80	1.50	
2010	20c	Horatio Alger	.40	.20	
b.		Red and black omitted	—		
2011	20c	Aging Together	.40	.20	
2012	20c	The Barrymores	.40	.20	
a.		Black missing (from extraneous paper)	—		
2013	20c	Dr. Mary Walker	.40	.20	
2014	20c	International Peace Garden	.50	.20	
a.		Black & green (engr.) omitted	*225.00*		
2015	20c	America's Libraries	.40	.20	
a.		Vert. pair, imperf. horiz.	*250.00*		
c.		All colors missing (from extraneous paper)	*175.00*		

2023

2024

2025

2026

2031

2027-2030

2036

2037

HOW TO USE THIS BOOK

The number in the first column is its Scott number or identifying number. Following that is the denomination of the stamp and its color or description. Finally, the values, unused and used, are shown.

2032-2035

2039

2038

2040

2041

2042

2043

2044

2045

2046

2047

2048-2051

2052

2053

2054

2055-2058

Scott No.		Description	Unused Value	Used Value
2016	20c	Jackie Robinson	1.10	.20
2017	20c	Touro Synagogue	.45	.20
a.		Imperf., pair	*2,250.*	
2018	20c	Wolf Trap Farm Park	.40	.20
2019	20c	Architecture - Wright	.45	.20
b.		Red omitted	—	
2020	20c	Architecture - Mies van der Rohe. .	.45	.20
a.		Red omitted	—	
2021	20c	Architecture - Gropius	.45	.20
2022	20c	Architecture -Saarinen	.45	.20
a.		Block of 4, #2019-2022	2.00	1.75
2023	20c	Francis of Assisi	.40	.20
2024	20c	Ponce de Leon	.50	.20
a.		Imperf., pair	*425.00*	
b.		Vert. pair, imperf. between & at top	—	
2025	13c	Christmas - Dog & Cat	.25	.20
a.		Imperf., pair	*350.00*	
2026	20c	Christmas - Religious	.40	.20
a.		Imperf., pair	125.00	
b.		Horiz. pair, imperf. vert.	—	
c.		Vert. pair, imperf. horiz.	—	
2027	20c	Christmas - Sledding	.60	.20
2028	20c	Christmas - Snowman	.60	.20
2029	20c	Christmas - Skating	.60	.20
2030	20c	Christmas - Tree	.60	.20
a.		Block of 4, #2027-2030	2.40	1.50
b.		As "a," imperf.	*1,750.*	
c.		As "a," imperf. horiz.	*800.00*	
1983				
2031	20c	Science & Technology	.40	.20
a.		Black (engr.) omitted	*1,200.*	
2032	20c	Intrepid Balloon	.50	.20
2033	20c	Two Large Balloons	.50	.20
2034	20c	Large Balloon at Right	.50	.20
2035	20c	Explorer II Balloon	.50	.20
a.		Block of 4, #2032-2035	2.00	1.50
b.		As "a," imperf.	*3,750.*	
c.		As "a," right stamp perf. otherwise imperf.	3,750.	
2036	20c	U.S. - Sweden	.40	.20
2037	20c	Civilian Conservation Corps	.40	.20
a.		Imperf., pair	*2,750.*	
b.		Vert. pair, imperf. horiz.	—	
2038	20c	Joseph Priestley	.40	.20
2039	20c	Voluntarism	.40	.20
a.		Imperf., pair	*300.00*	
2040	20c	U.S. - Germany	.40	.20
2041	20c	Brooklyn Bridge	.40	.20
b.		All color missing (from extraneous paper)	*75.00*	

2059-2062

2063

2064

2065

2066

2071

2067-2070

2072

Scott No.		Description	Unused Value	Used Value
2042	20c	Tennessee Valley Authority	.40	.20
2043	20c	Physical Fitness	.40	.20
2044	20c	Scott Joplin	.50	.20
a.		Imperf., pair	*400.00*	
2045	20c	Medal of Honor	.55	.20
a.		Red omitted	*200.00*	
2046	20c	Babe Ruth	1.40	.20
2047	20c	Nathaniel Hawthorne	.45	.20
2048	13c	Olympics - Discus	.35	.20
2049	13c	Olympics - High Jump	.35	.20
2050	13c	Olympics - Archery	.35	.20
2051	13c	Olympics - Boxing	.35	.20
a.		Block of 4, #2048-2051	1.50	1.25
2052	20c	Treaty of Paris	.40	.20
2053	20c	Civil Service	.40	.20
2054	20c	Metropolitan Opera	.40	.20
2055	20c	Charles Steinmetz	.50	.20
2056	20c	Edwin Armstrong	.50	.20
2057	20c	Nikola Tesla	.50	.20
2058	20c	Philo T. Farnsworth	.50	.20
a.		Block of 4, #2055-2058	2.00	1.50
b.		As "a," black omitted	*325.00*	
2059	20c	Streetcar - New York	.50	.20
2060	20c	Streetcar - Alabama	.50	.20
a.		Horiz. pair, black (engr.) missing on Nos. 2059, 2060 (from extraneous paper)	—	
2061	20c	Streetcar - Arkansas	.50	.20
a.		Vert. pair, black (engr.) missing on Nos. 2059, 2061 (from extraneous paper)	—	
2062	20c	Streetcar - Louisiana	.50	.20
a.		Block of 4, #2059-2062	2.00	1.50
b.		As "a," black (engr.) omitted	*300.00*	
c.		As "a," black (engr.) omitted on #2059, 2061	—	
2063	20c	Christmas - Religious	.40	.20
2064	20c	Christmas - Santa Claus	.40	.20
a.		Imperf., pair	*125.00*	
2065	20c	Martin Luther	.40	.20
1984				
2066	20c	Alaska Statehood	.40	.20
2067	20c	Olympics - Ice Dancing	.55	.20
2068	20c	Olympics - Alpine Skiing	.55	.20
2069	20c	Olympics - Nordic Skiing	.55	.20
2070	20c	Olympics - Ice Hockey	.55	.20
a.		Block of 4, #2067-2070	2.20	1.75
2071	20c	Federal Deposit Insurance Corp.	.40	.20
2072	20c	Love	.40	.20
a.		Horiz. pair, imperf. vert.	*150.00*	
2073	20c	Carter G. Woodson	.40	.20
a.		Horiz. pair, imperf. vert.	*1,000.*	

2073

2074

2075

2076-2079

2080

2081

2086

2082-2085

2087

2088

2089

Scott No.		Description	Unused Value	Used Value
2074	20c	Soil & Water Conservation	.40	.20
2075	20c	Credit Union Act	.40	.20
2076	20c	Wild Pink Orchid	.50	.20
2077	20c	Yellow Lady's-slipper Orchid	.50	.20
2078	20c	Spreading Pogonia Orchid	.50	.20
2079	20c	Pacific Calypso Orchid	.50	.20
a.		Block of 4, #2076-2079	2.00	1.50
2080	20c	Hawaii Statehood	.40	.20
2081	20c	National Archives	.40	.20
2082	20c	Olympics - Diving	.55	.20
2083	20c	Olympics - Long Jump	.55	.20
2084	20c	Olympics - Wrestling	.55	.20
2085	20c	Olympics - Kayak	.55	.20
a.		Block of 4, #2082-2085	2.40	1.90
b.		As "a," imperf btwn. vertically	*9,500.*	
2086	20c	Louisiana World Exposition	.50	.20
2087	20c	Health Research	.40	.20
2088	20c	Douglas Fairbanks	.50	.20
b.		Horiz. pair, imperf. btwn.	—	
2089	20c	Jim Thorpe	.50	.20
2090	20c	John McCormack	.40	.20
2091	20c	St. Lawrence Seaway	.40	.20
2092	20c	Waterfowl Preservation Act	.50	.20
a.		Horiz. pair, imperf. vert.	*325.00*	
2093	20c	Roanoke Voyages	.40	.20
2094	20c	Herman Melville	.40	.20
2095	20c	Horace Moses	.45	.20
2096	20c	Smokey Bear	.40	.20
a.		Horiz. pair, imperf. btwn.	*250.00*	
b.		Vert. pair, imperf. btwn.	*200.00*	
c.		Block of 4, imperf. btwn, vert. & horiz.	*4,000.*	
d.		Horiz. pair, imperf. vert.	*1,000.*	
2097	20c	Roberto Clemente	1.40	.20
a.		Horiz. pair, imperf. vert.	*1,800.*	
2098	20c	Beagle & Boston Terrier	.50	.20
2099	20c	Chesapeake Bay Retriever & Cocker Spaniel	.50	.20
2100	20c	Alaskan Malamute & Collie	.50	.20
2101	20c	Black & Tan Coonhound & American Foxhound	.50	.20
a.		Block of 4, #2098-2101	2.00	1.90
b.		As "a," imperf. horiz.	—	
2102	20c	Crime Prevention	.40	.20
2103	20c	Hispanic Americans	.40	.20
a.		Vert. pair, imperf. horiz.	*2,000.*	
2104	20c	Family Unity	.40	.20
a.		Horiz. pair, imperf. vert.	*425.00*	
c.		Vert. pair, imperf. btwn. & at bottom	—	
d.		Horiz. pair, imperf btwn.	—	

2091

2092

2090

2093

2094

2095

2096

2097

2098-2101

Scott No.		Description	Unused Value	Used Value
2105	20c	Eleanor Roosevelt	.40	.20
2106	20c	Nation of Readers	.40	.20
2107	20c	Christmas - Religious	.40	.20
2108	20c	Christmas - Santa Claus	.40	.20
a.		Horiz. pair, imperf. vert.	*875.00*	
2109	20c	Vietnam Veterans' Memorial	.50	.20
1985				
2110	22c	Jerome Kern	.40	.20
2111	(22c)	"D" & Eagle	.60	.20
a.		Vert. pair, imperf.	35.00	
b.		Vert. pair, imperf. horiz.	*1,000.*	
Coil Stamp, Perf. 10 Vertically				
2112	(22c)	"D" & Eagle (2111)	.60	.20
a.		Imperf., pair	40.00	
2113	(22c)	"D" & Eagle (from bklt. pane)	.80	.20
a.		Booklet pane of 10	8.50	*3.00*
b.		As "a," imperf. btwn. horiz.	—	
2114	22c	Flag Over Capitol (2115)	.40	.20
a.		All color missing (from extraneous paper)	—	
Coil Stamp, Perf. 10 Vertically				
2115	22c	Flag Over Capitol	.40	.20
c.		Inscribed "T" at bottom	.50	.40
d.		Black field of stars	—	—
f.		Imperf., pair	10.00	
Booklet Stamp, Perf. 10 Horizontal on 1 or 2 Sides				
2116	22c	Flag Over Capitol	.50	.20
a.		Booklet pane of 5	2.50	1.25
Booklet Stamps, Perf. 10				
2117	22c	Frilled Dogwinkle	.40	.20
2118	22c	Reticulated Helmet	.40	.20
2119	22c	New England Neptune	.40	.20
2120	22c	Calico Scallop	.40	.20
2121	22c	Lightning Whelk	.40	.20
a.		Booklet pane of 10, 2 ea. #2117-2121	4.00	3.00
b.		As "a," violet omitted	*475.00*	
c.		As "a," vert. imperf. btwn.	*450.00*	
d.		As "a," imperf.	—	
e.		Strip of 5, #2117-2121	2.00	—
Booklet Stamp, Perf. 10 Vertically on 1 or 2 Sides				
2122	$10.75	Eagle & Half Moon, Type I	19.00	7.50
a.		Booklet pane of 3	60.00	—
b.		Type II	21.00	10.00
c.		As "b," booklet pane of 3	65.00	—

Type I has a washed out dull appearance. Denomination appears splotchy or grainy. (P#11111) Type II has brighter, more intense colors. Denomination appears smoother (P#22222).

Scott No.		Description	Unused Value	Used Value
1985-87, Coil Stamps, Perf. 10 Vertically				
2123	3.4c	School Bus, tagged	.20	.20

2102

2103

2104

2105

2106

2107

2108

2109

2110

2111

2113

2115

2116

Scott No.		Description	Unused Value	Used Value	/ / / / / /
a.		Untagged (Bureau precanceled).....	.20	.20	□□□□□
2124	4.9c	Buckboard, tagged...........................	.20	.20	□□□□□
a.		Untagged (Bureau precanceled).....	.20	.20	□□□□□
2125	5.5c	Star Route Truck, tagged................	.20	.20	□□□□□
a.		Untagged (Bureau precanceled).....	.20	.20	□□□□□
2126	6c	Tricycle, tagged..............................	.25	.20	□□□□□
a.		Untagged (Bureau precanceled).....	.20	.20	□□□□□
b.		Imperf., pair....................................	200.00		□□□□□
2127	7.1c	Tractor, tagged................................	.20	.20	□□□□□
a.		Untagged (Bureau precanceled).....	.20	.20	□□□□□
c.		As "a," black (precancel) omitted...	—		□□□□□
2128	8.3c	Ambulance, tagged..........................	.20	.20	□□□□□
a.		Untagged (Bureau precanceled).....	.20	.20	□□□□□
2129	8.5c	Tow Truck, tagged...........................	.20	.20	□□□□□
a.		Untagged (Bureau precanceled).....	.20	.20	□□□□□
2130	10.1c	Oil Wagon, tagged...........................	.55	.20	□□□□□
a.		Untagged (Bureau precanceled).....	.25	.25	□□□□□
b.		As "a," imperf. pair.........................	15.00		□□□□□
2131	11c	Stutz Bearcat..................................	.25	.20	□□□□□
2132	12c	Stanley Steamer, Type I, tagged......	.25	.20	□□□□□
a.		Type I, untagged (Bureau precanceled)	.25	.25	□□□□□
b.		Type II, untagged (Bureau precanceled)	.40	.30	□□□□□
		Type II has "Stanley Steamer 1909" 17½ mm. On Type I it is 18 mm.			
2133	12.5c	Pushcart, tagged..............................	.35	.20	□□□□□
a.		Untagged (Bureau precanceled).....	.25	.25	□□□□□
b.		As "a," imperf., pair........................	50.00		□□□□□
2134	14c	Iceboat, Type I.................................	.30	.20	□□□□□
a.		Imperf. pair......................................	90.00		□□□□□
b.		Type II...	.30	.20	□□□□□
		Type I design is 17½ mm wide, has overall tagging. Type II is 17¼ mm wide, has block tagging.			
2135	17c	Dog Sled..	.55	.20	□□□□□
a.		Imperf., pair....................................	*375.00*		□□□□□
2136	25c	Bread Wagon..................................	.45	.20	□□□□□
a.		Imperf., pair....................................	10.00		□□□□□
b.		Pair, imperf. btwn............................	*600.00*		□□□□□
1985					
2137	22c	Mary McLeod Bethune...................	.60	.20	□□□□□
2138	22c	Broadbill Decoy..............................	1.00	.20	□□□□□
2139	22c	Mallard Decoy................................	1.00	.20	□□□□□
2140	22c	Canvasback Decoy..........................	1.00	.20	□□□□□
2141	22c	Redhead Decoy...............................	1.00	.20	□□□□□
a.		Block of 4, #2138-2141..................	4.00	2.75	□□□□□
2142	22c	Winter Special Olympics................	.50	.20	□□□□□
a.		Vert. pair, imperf. horiz..................	*400.00*		□□□□□
2143	22c	Love..	.40	.20	□□□□□
a.		Imperf., pair....................................	*1,250.*		□□□□□
2144	22c	Rural Electrification Administration	.60	.20	□□□□□
a.		Vert. pair, imperf. btwn..................	—		□□□□□
2145	22c	AMERIPEX '86................................	.40	.20	□□□□□

2117-2121

2123

2124

2125

2126

2127

2128

2129

2130

2131

2132

2133

2134

2135

2122

2136

HOW TO USE THIS BOOK

The number in the first column is its Scott number or identifying number. Following that is the denomination of the stamp and its color or description. Finally, the values, unused and used, are shown.

Scott No.		Description	Unused Value	Used Value	/ / / / / /
a.		Red, black & blue omitted	*175.00*		
b.		Red & black omitted	—		
c.		Red omitted	*2,350.*		
d.		Black missing (from perf. shift)	—		
2146	22c	Abigail Adams	.40	.20	
a.		Imperf., pair	*225.00*		
2147	22c	Frederic Auguste Bartholdi	.40	.20	
Coil Stamps, Perf. 10 Vertically					
2149	18c	George Washington, tagged	.40	.20	
a.		Untagged (Bureau precanceled)	.35	.35	
b.		Imperf., pair	*825.00*		
c.		As "a," imperf., pair	*625.00*		
2150	21.1c	Envelopes, tagged	.40	.20	
a.		Untagged (Bureau precanceled)	.40	.40	
1985					
2152	22c	Korean War Veterans	.40	.20	
2153	22c	Social Security Act	.40	.20	
2154	22c	World War I Veterans	.40	.20	
a.		Red missing (from perf. shift)	*400.00*		
2155	22c	Quarter Horse	1.25	.20	
2156	22c	Morgan Horse	1.25	.20	
2157	22c	Saddlebred Horse	1.25	.20	
2158	22c	Appaloosa Horse	1.25	.20	
a.		Block of 4, #2155-2158	6.00	4.00	
2159	22c	Public Education	.45	.20	
2160	22c	YMCA Youth Camping	.70	.20	
2161	22c	Boy Scouts	.70	.20	
2162	22c	Big Brothers/Big Sisters	.70	.20	
2163	22c	Camp Fire	.70	.20	
a.		Block of 4, #2160-2163	3.00	2.25	
2164	22c	Help End Hunger	.45	.20	
2165	22c	Christmas - Religious	.40	.20	
a.		Imperf., pair	*65.00*		
2166	22c	Christmas - Poinsettias	.40	.20	
a.		Imperf., pair	*100.00*		
1986-93					
2167	22c	Arkansas Statehood	.75	.20	
a.		Vert. pair, imperf. horiz.	—		
2168	1c	Margaret Mitchell	.20	.20	
2169	2c	Mary Lyon	.20	.20	
2170	3c	Dr. Paul Dudley White	.20	.20	
2171	4c	Father Edward Flanagan	.20	.20	
a.		4c grayish violet	.20	.20	
b.		4c deep grayish blue	.20	.20	
2172	5c	Hugo L. Black	.20	.20	
2173	5c	Luis Munoz Marin, tagged	.20	.20	
a.		Untagged	.20	.20	
2175	10c	Red Cloud, lake	.20	.20	
e.		10c carmine	.40	.20	

2137

2138-2141

2142

2143

2144

2145

2146

2147

2149

2150

2152

2153

2154

2155-2158

2160-2163

2168

2169

2170

2171

2172

2173

2175

2176

2177

2178

2179

2180

2181

2182

2183

2184

2185

2186

2187

2188

2189

2190

2191

2192

2193

2194

2195

2196

Scott No.		Description	Unused Value	Used Value
f.		As "c," all color omitted	—	
2176	14c	Julia Ward Howe	.30	.20
2177	15c	Buffalo Bill Cody	.35	.20
d.		All color omitted	—	
2178	17c	Belva Ann Lockwood	.35	.20
2179	20c	Dr. Virginia Apgar, red brown	.40	.20
a.		20c orange brown	.45	.20
b.		20c bright red brown	1.00	.25
2180	21c	Chester Carlson	.45	.20
2181	23c	Mary Cassatt	.45	.20
2182	25c	Jack London, perf. 11	.50	.20
a.		Booklet pane of 10	5.00	*3.75*
d.		Horiz. pair, imperf btwn	*850.00*	
e.		As "a," all color omitted on right stamps	—	
f.		As No. 2182 (sheet stamp), vert. pair, bottom stamp all color omitted	—	
2183	28c	Sitting Bull	.65	.35
2184	29c	Earl Warren	.70	.20
2185	29c	Thomas Jefferson	.65	.20
2186	35c	Dennis Chavez	.75	.20
2187	40c	Claire Chennault, dark blue	.85	.20
2188	45c	Dr. Harvey Cushing, bright blue	1.00	.20
a.		45c blue	2.25	.20
2189	52c	Hubert H. Humphrey	1.10	.20
2190	56c	John Harvard	1.20	.20
2191	65c	H.H. 'Hap' Arnold	1.30	.20
2192	75c	Wendell Willkie	1.60	.20
2193	$1	Bernard Revel	3.00	.50
a.		All color omitted	—	
2194	$1	Johns Hopkins, intense deep blue	2.25	.50
b.		$1 deep blue	2.50	.50
d.		$1 dark blue	2.50	.50
e.		$1 blue	2.75	.60
2195	$2	William Jennings Bryan	4.25	.50
2196	$5	Bret Harte	9.00	2.50
Booklet Stamp, Perf. 10 on 2 or 3 Sides				
2197	25c	Jack London (2182)	.55	.20
a.		Booklet pane of 6	3.30	2.50
1986				
2198	22c	Handstamped Cover	.45	.20
2199	22c	Boy, Stamp Collection	.45	.20
2200	22c	No. 836 Magnified	.45	.20
2201	22c	No. 2216 on First Day Cover	.45	.20
a.		Booklet pane of 4, #2198-2201	2.00	1.75
b.		As "a," black omitted on #2198, 2201	47.50	—
c.		As "a," blue (litho.) omitted on #2198-2200	*2,250.*	
d.		As "a," buff (litho.) omitted	—	

2159

2164

2165

2166

2167

2202

2203

2204

2211

2210

2205-2209

Scott No.		Description	Unused Value	Used Value
2202	22c	Love	.55	.20
2203	22c	Sojourner Truth	.55	.20
2204	22c	Republic of Texas.	.55	.20
a.		Horiz. pair, imperf. vert.	*900.00*	
b.		Dark red omitted	*2,250.*	
c.		Dark blue omitted	*8,000.*	
2205	22c	Muskellunge	1.00	.20
2206	22c	Atlantic Cod	1.00	.20
2207	22c	Largemouth Bass	1.00	.20
2208	22c	Bluefin Tuna	1.00	.20
2209	22c	Catfish	1.00	.20
a.		Booklet pane of 5, #2205-2209	6.00	*2.75*
2210	22c	Public Hospitals	.40	.20
a.		Vert. pair, imperf. horiz.	*275.00*	
b.		Horiz. pair, imperf. vert.	*1,150.*	
2211	22c	Duke Ellington	.40	.20
a.		Vert. pair, imperf. horiz.	*750.00*	
2216		Washington-Harrison, sheet of 9	7.50	4.00
a.-i.	22c	Any single	.75	.40
j.		Blue omitted	*2,500.*	
k.		Black inscription omitted	*2,000.*	
l.		Imperf.	*10,500.*	
m.		As "k," double impression of red	—	
n.		Blue omitted on stamps 1-3, 5-6, 8, 9	—	
2217		Tyler-Grant, sheet of 9	7.50	4.00
a.-i.	22c	Any single	.75	.40
j.		Black inscription omitted	*2,500.*	
2218		Hayes-Wilson, sheet of 9	7.50	4.00
a.-i.	22c	Any single	.75	.40
j.		Brown omitted	—	
k.		Black inscription omitted	*2,500.*	
2219		Harding-Johnson, White House, sht. of 9	7.50	—
a.-i.	22c	Any single	.75	.40
j.		Blkish blue (engr.) inscription omitted on a.-b., d.-e., g.-h.	*2,500.*	
l.		Blackish blue (engr.) omitted on all stamps	—	
2220	22c	Elisha Kent Kane	.65	.20
2221	22c	Adolphus W. Greely	.65	.20
2222	22c	Vilhjalmur Stefansson	.65	.20
2223	22c	Robert E. Peary & Matthew Henson	.65	.20
a.		Block of 4, #2220-2223	2.75	2.25
b.		As "a," black omitted	*6,000.*	
c.		As "a," Nos. 2220, 2221 black (engr.) omitted	—	
d.		As "a," Nos. 2222, 2223 black (engr.) omitted	—	
2224	22c	Statue of Liberty	.40	.20

2216

2217

2218

2219

2198-2201

2220-2223

2235-2238

2225

2224

2226

2240-2243

2239

2246

Scott No.		Description	Unused Value	Used Value	/ / / / / /
a.		Scarlet omitted	—		

1986-87, Coil Stamps, Perf. 10 Vertically

2225	1c	Omnibus, tagged	.20	.20	
b.		Untagged	.20	.20	
c.		Imperf., pair	*2,000.*		
2226	2c	Locomotive, tagged	.20	.20	
a.		Untagged	.20	.20	
2228	4c	Stagecoach (1898A)	.20	.20	
b.		Imperf., pair	250.00		
2231	8.3c	Ambulance (2128), (Bureau precancel)	.65	.20	

On No. 2228 "Stagecoach 1890s" is 17 mm long, on No. 1898A 19½ mm long. On No. 2231 "Ambulance 1860s" is 18 mm long, on No. 2128 18½ mm long.

1986

2235	22c	Navajo Art - Stripes & Diamonds	.80	.20	
2236	22c	Navajo Art - 2 Diamonds Across	.80	.20	
2237	22c	Navajo Art - 5 Diamonds Across	.80	.20	
2238	22c	Navajo Art - 4 Diamonds Across	.80	.20	
a.		Block of 4, #2235-2238	3.25	2.25	
b.		As "a," black (engr.) omitted	*325.00*		
2239	22c	T.S. Eliot	.55	.20	
2240	22c	Highlander Figure	.50	.20	
2241	22c	Ship Figurehead	.50	.20	
2242	22c	Nautical Figure	.50	.20	
2243	22c	Cigar Store Indian	.50	.20	
a.		Block of 4, #2240-2243	2.00	1.50	
b.		As "a," imperf. vert.	*1,000.*		
2244	22c	Christmas - Religious	.40	.20	
a.		Imperf., pair	*600.00*		
2245	22c	Christmas - Village	.40	.20	

1987

2246	22c	Michigan Statehood	.55	.20	
2247	22c	Pan-American Games	.40	.20	
a.		Silver omitted	*1,250.*		
2248	22c	Love	.40	.20	
2249	22c	Jean Baptiste Pointe du Sable	.50	.20	
2250	22c	Enrico Caruso	.40	.20	
a.		Black (engr.) omitted	*4,500.*		
2251	22c	Girl Scouts	.40	.20	
a.		All litho. colors omitted	*2,450.*		
b.		Red & black (engr.) omitted	*1,950.*		

1987-88, Coil Stamps, Perf. 10 Vertically

2252	3c	Conestoga Wagon, tagged	.20	.20	
a.		Untagged	.20	.20	
b.		Imperf., pair	—		
2253	5c	Milk Wagon	.20	.20	
2254	5.3c	Elevator (Bureau precancel in red)	.20	.20	

2244

2245

2247

2248

2249

2250

2251

2268

2267

2269

2271

2272

2274

2270

2273

Scott No.		Description	Unused Value	Used Value
2255	7.6c	Carretta (Bureau precancel in red).	.20	.20
2256	8.4c	Wheelchair (Bureau precancel in red)	.20	.20
a.		Imperf., pair	*550.00*	
2257	10c	Canal Boat	.40	.20
e.		Imperf., pair	*1,750.*	
2258	13c	Patrol Wagon (Bureau precancel in red)	.50	.25
2259	13.2c	Coal Car (Bureau precancel in red)	.25	.25
a.		Imperf., pair	80.00	
2260	15c	Tugboat	.25	.20
c.		Imperf., pair	*650.00*	
2261	16.7c	Popcorn Wagon (Bureau precancel in blk)	.30	.30
a.		Imperf., pair	*150.00*	
2262	17.5c	Racing Car, tagged	.65	.20
a.		Untagged	.50	.30
b.		Imperf., pair	*2,250.*	
2263	20c	Cable Car	.35	.20
a.		Imperf., pair	50.00	
2264	20.5c	Fire Engine (Bureau precancel in black)	.50	.40
2265	21c	Railroad Mail Car (Bureau precancel in red)	.40	.40
a.		Imperf., pair	42.50	
2266	24.1c	Tandem Bicycle (Bureau precancel in red)	.60	.45
1987, Booklet Stamps				
2267	22c	Congratulations	.65	.20
2268	22c	Get Well	.80	.20
2269	22c	Thank You	.80	.20
2270	22c	Love You, Dad	.80	.20
2271	22c	Best Wishes	.80	.20
2272	22c	Happy Birthday	.65	.20
2273	22c	Love You, Mother	1.40	.20
2274	22c	Keep in Touch	.80	.20
a.		Booklet pane of 10 (#2268-2271, 2273-2274, 2 each #2267, 2272)..	10.00	*5.00*
1987				
2275	22c	United Way	.40	.20
2276	22c	Flag & Fireworks	.40	.20
a.		Booklet pane of 20	8.50	—
b.		As "a", vert. pair, imperf. btwn.	*1,500.*	—
c.		As "a", miscut and inserted upside down into booklet cover, imperf. btwn. stamps and right selvage	—	
2277	(25c)	"E" & Earth, perf 11	.45	.20
2278	25c	Flag & Clouds, perf 11	.45	.20
Coil Stamps, Perf. 10 Vertically				
2279	(25c)	"E" & Earth (2277)	.45	.20
a.		Imperf., pair	*60.00*	—
2280	25c	Flag Over Yosemite, Green Trees ...	.45	.20
c.		Imperf., pair	10.00	
e.		Black trees	*700.00*	—

2252

2253

2254

2255

2256

2257

2258

2259

2260

2261

2262

2263

2264

2265

2266

HOW TO USE THIS BOOK

The number in the first column is its Scott number or identifying number. Following that is the denomination of the stamp and its color or description. Finally, the values, unused and used, are shown.

2275

2276

2277

2278

2280

2281

2283

2284

2285

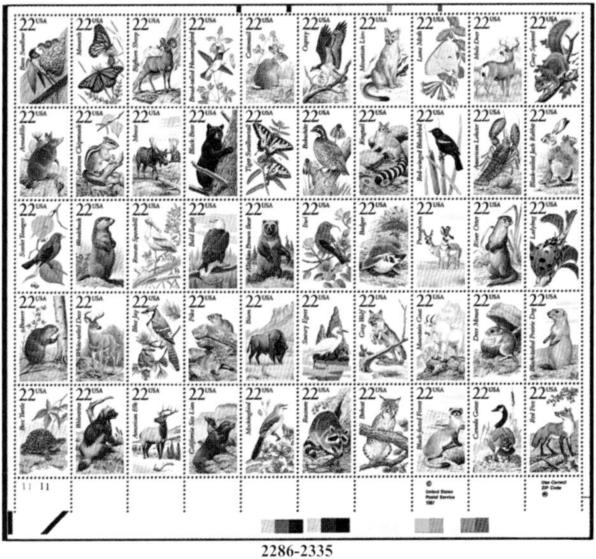
2286-2335

Scott No.		Description	Unused Value	Used Value
f.		Pair, imperf. btwn.	*450.00*	
2281	25c	Honeybee	.45	.20
a.		Imperf., pair	45.00	
b.		Black (engr.) omitted	*50.00*	
c.		Black (litho.) omitted	*450.00*	
d.		Pair, imperf. between	*700.00*	
e.		Yellow (litho.) omitted	*1,000.*	
Booklet Stamps				
2282	(25c)	"E" & Earth (2277), perf. 10	.50	.20
a.		Booklet pane of 10	6.50	3.50
2283	25c	Pheasant, multicolored	.50	.20
a.		Booklet pane of 10	6.00	3.50
b.	25c	multi, red removed from sky	6.50	.20
c.		As "b," booklet pane of 10	*65.00*	—
d.		As "a," horiz. imperf. btwn.	—	
2284	25c	Grosbeak	.50	.20
2285	25c	Owl	.50	.20
b.		Bklt. pane of 10, 5 each #2284-2285	5.00	3.50
d.		Pair, #2284-2285	1.10	.25
2285A	25c	Flag & Clouds (2278), perf. 10	.50	.20
c.		Booklet pane of 6	3.00	2.00
1987				
2286	22c	Barn swallow	1.00	.50
2287	22c	Monarch butterfly	1.00	.50
2288	22c	Bighorn sheep	1.00	.50
2289	22c	Broad-tailed hummingbird	1.00	.50
2290	22c	Cottontail	1.00	.50
2291	22c	Osprey	1.00	.50
2292	22c	Mountain lion	1.00	.50
2293	22c	Luna moth	1.00	.50
2294	22c	Mule deer	1.00	.50
2295	22c	Gray squirrel	1.00	.50
2296	22c	Armadillo	1.00	.50
2297	22c	Eastern chipmunk	1.00	.50
2298	22c	Moose	1.00	.50
2299	22c	Black bear	1.00	.50
2300	22c	Tiger swallowtail	1.00	.50
2301	22c	Bobwhite	1.00	.50
2302	22c	Ringtail	1.00	.50
2303	22c	Red-winged blackbird	1.00	.50
2304	22c	American lobster	1.00	.50
2305	22c	Black-tailed jack rabbit	1.00	.50
2306	22c	Scarlet tanager	1.00	.50
2307	22c	Woodchuck	1.00	.50
2308	22c	Roseate spoonbill	1.00	.50
2309	22c	Bald eagle	1.00	.50
2310	22c	Alaskan brown bear	1.00	.50
2311	22c	Iiwi	1.00	.50

Scott No.	Description	Unused Value	Used Value	/ / / / / /
2312	22c Badger	1.00	.50	☐☐☐☐☐
2313	22c Pronghorn	1.00	.50	☐☐☐☐☐
2314	22c River otter	1.00	.50	☐☐☐☐☐
2315	22c Ladybug	1.00	.50	☐☐☐☐☐
2316	22c Beaver	1.00	.50	☐☐☐☐☐
2317	22c White-tailed deer	1.00	.50	☐☐☐☐☐
2318	22c Blue jay	1.00	.50	☐☐☐☐☐
2319	22c Pika	1.00	.50	☐☐☐☐☐
2320	22c American Buffalo	1.00	.50	☐☐☐☐☐
2321	22c Snowy egret	1.00	.50	☐☐☐☐☐
2322	22c Gray wolf	1.00	.50	☐☐☐☐☐
2323	22c Mountain goat	1.00	.50	☐☐☐☐☐
2324	22c Deer mouse	1.00	.50	☐☐☐☐☐
2325	22c Black-tailed prairie dog	1.00	.50	☐☐☐☐☐
2326	22c Box turtle	1.00	.50	☐☐☐☐☐
2327	22c Wolverine	1.00	.50	☐☐☐☐☐
2328	22c American elk	1.00	.50	☐☐☐☐☐
2329	22c California sea lion	1.00	.50	☐☐☐☐☐
2330	22c Mockingbird	1.00	.50	☐☐☐☐☐
2331	22c Raccoon	1.00	.50	☐☐☐☐☐
2332	22c Bobcat	1.00	.50	☐☐☐☐☐
2333	22c Black-footed ferret	1.00	.50	☐☐☐☐☐
2334	22c Canada goose	1.00	.50	☐☐☐☐☐
2335	22c Red fox	1.00	.50	☐☐☐☐☐
a.	Pane of 50, #2286-2335	50.00	35.00	☐☐☐☐☐
	2286b-2335b, any single, red omitted	*2,500.*		☐☐☐☐☐
1987-90				
2336	22c Delaware Ratification	.60	.20	☐☐☐☐☐
2337	22c Pennsylvania Ratification	.60	.20	☐☐☐☐☐
2338	22c New Jersey Ratification	.60	.20	☐☐☐☐☐
a.	Black (engr.) omitted	*5,000.*		☐☐☐☐☐
2339	22c Georgia Ratification	.60	.20	☐☐☐☐☐
2340	22c Connecticut Ratification	.60	.20	☐☐☐☐☐
2341	22c Massachusetts Ratification	.60	.20	☐☐☐☐☐
2342	22c Maryland Ratification	.60	.20	☐☐☐☐☐
2343	25c South Carolina Ratification	.60	.20	☐☐☐☐☐
a.	Strip of 3, vert. imperf. btwn.	*12,500.*		☐☐☐☐☐
b.	Red missing (from perf. shift)	—		☐☐☐☐☐
2344	25c New Hampshire Ratification	.60	.20	☐☐☐☐☐
2345	25c Virginia Ratification	.60	.20	☐☐☐☐☐
2346	25c New York Ratification	.60	.20	☐☐☐☐☐
2347	25c North Carolina Ratification	.60	.20	☐☐☐☐☐
2348	25c Rhode Island Ratification	.60	.20	☐☐☐☐☐
1987				
2349	22c U.S.-Morocco Diplomatic Relations	.50	.20	☐☐☐☐☐
a.	Black (engr.) omitted	*250.00*		☐☐☐☐☐
2350	22c William Faulkner	.55	.20	☐☐☐☐☐
2351	22c Lacemaking - Upper Left	.45	.20	☐☐☐☐☐
2352	22c Lacemaking - Upper Right	.45	.20	☐☐☐☐☐

2336

2337

2338

2339

2340

2341

2342

2343

2344

2345

2346

2347

2348

2349

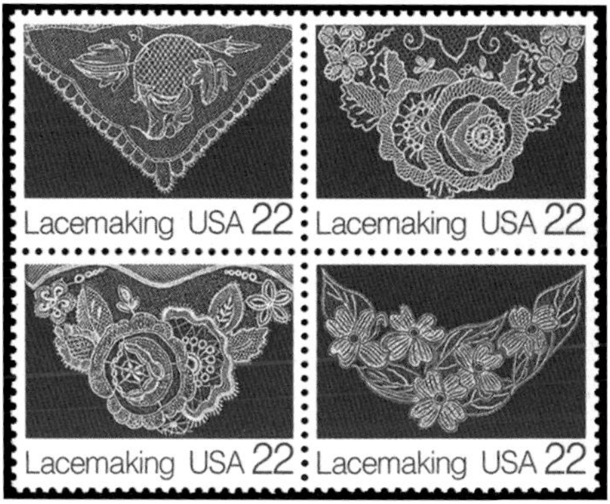

2351-2354

2350

2360

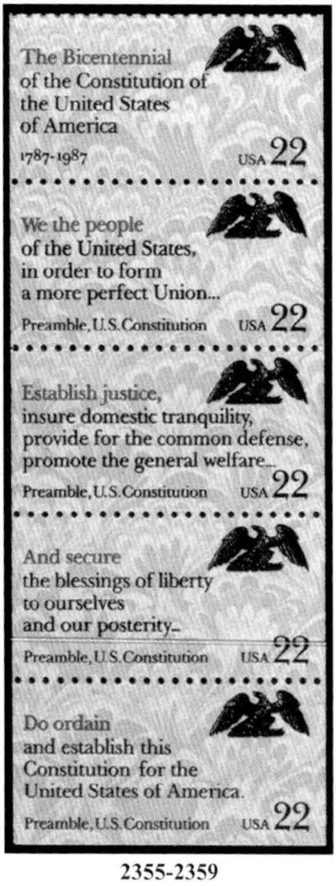

2355-2359

2367

2368

2361

2369

2362-2366

2370

2371

2376

2372-2375

Scott No.	Description	Unused Value	Used Value
2353	22c Lacemaking - Lower Left	.45	.20
2354	22c Lacemaking - Lower Right	.45	.20
a.	Block of 4, #2351-2354	1.90	1.90
b.	As "a," white omitted	*500.00*	
c.	Single stamp, white omitted	—	
2355	22c "The Bicentennial . . ."	.90	.20
a.	Grayish green (background) omitted	—	
2356	22c "We the People . . ."	.90	.20
a.	Grayish green (background) omitted	—	
2357	22c "Establish Justice, . . ."	.90	.20
a.	Grayish green (background) omitted	—	
2358	22c "And Secure . . ."	.90	.20
a.	Grayish green (background) omitted	—	
2359	22c "Do Ordain . . ."	.90	.20
a.	Bklt. pane of 5, #2355-2359	4.50	*2.25*
b.	Grayish green (background) omitted	—	
2360	22c Signing of the Constitution	.55	.20
2361	22c Certified Public Accounting	1.00	.20
a.	Black (engr.) omitted	*675.00*	
2362	22c Stourbridge Lion	.55	.20
2363	22c Best Friend of Charleston	.55	.20
2364	22c John Bull	.55	.20
2365	22c Brother Jonathan	.55	.20
a.	Red omitted	*1,100.*	225.00
2366	22c Gowan and Marx	.55	.20
a.	Booklet pane of 5, #2362-2366	2.75	*2.50*
b.	As "a," black omitted on #2366	—	
c.	As No. 2366, blue omitted	—	
2367	22c Christmas - Religious	.45	.20
2368	22c Christmas - Ornaments	.45	.20
1988			
2369	22c Olympics - Skiing	.50	.20
2370	22c Australia Bicentennial	.45	.20
2371	22c James Weldon Johnson	.50	.20
2372	22c Siamese, Exotic Shorthair Cats	.70	.20
2373	22c Abyssinian, Himalayan Cats	.70	.20
2374	22c Maine Coon, Burmese Cats	.70	.20
2375	22c American Shorthair, Persian Cats	.70	.20
a.	Block of 4, #2372-2375	2.80	1.90
2376	22c Knute Rockne	.50	.20
2377	25c Francis Ouimet	.60	.20
2378	25c Rose	.50	.20
a.	Imperf., pair	*2,000.*	
2379	45c Roses	.85	.20
2380	25c Olympics - Gymnastics Rings	.50	.20
2381	25c 1928 Locomobile	.80	.20
2382	25c 1929 Pierce-Arrow	.80	.20
2383	25c 1931 Cord	.80	.20

2377

2378

2379

2381-2385

2380

2390-2393

2386-2389

2394

2395

2396

2397

2398

2399

2400

2401

2402

2403

2404

2410

2411

2405-2409

2412

2413

2414

2415

Scott No.	Description	Unused Value	Used Value
2384	25c 1932 Packard	.80	.20
2385	25c 1935 Duesenberg	.80	.20
a.	Booklet pane of 5, #2381-2385	6.00	3.50
2386	25c Nathaniel Palmer	.65	.20
2387	25c Lt. Charles Wilkes	.65	.20
2388	25c Richard E. Byrd	.65	.20
2389	25c Lincoln Ellsworth	.65	.20
a.	Block of 4, #2386-2389	2.75	2.00
b.	Black omitted	*1,250.*	
c.	As "a," imperf. horiz.	*1,950.*	
2390	25c Deer	.75	.20
2391	25c Horse	.75	.20
2392	25c Camel	.75	.20
2393	25c Goat	.75	.20
a.	Block of 4, #2390-2393	3.00	2.00
b.	As "a," red omitted	—	
2394	$8.75 Eagle and Moon	13.50	8.00
2395	25c Happy Birthday	.50	.20
2396	25c Best Wishes	.50	.20
a.	Bklt. pane, 3 #2395 + 3 #2396 with gutter btwn.	3.50	3.25
2397	25c Thinking of You	.50	.20
2398	25c Love You	.50	.20
a.	Bklt. pane of 6, 3 #2397 + 3 #2398 with gutter btwn.	3.50	3.25
b.	As "a," imperf. horiz.	—	
c.	As "a," imperf.	—	
2399	25c Christmas - Religious	.50	.20
a.	Gold omitted	25.00	
2400	25c Christmas - Sleigh	.50	.20

1989

Scott No.	Description	Unused Value	Used Value
2401	25c Montana Statehood	.55	.20
2402	25c A. Philip Randolph	.50	.20
2403	25c North Dakota Statehood	.50	.20
2404	25c Washington Statehood	.50	.20
2405	25c Experiment	.50	.20
2406	25c Phoenix	.50	.20
2407	25c New Orleans	.50	.20
2408	25c Washington	.50	.20
2409	25c Walk in the Water	.50	.20
a.	Booklet pane of 5, #2405-2409	2.50	1.75
2410	25c World Stamp Expo '89	.50	.20
2411	25c Arturo Toscanini	.50	.20

1989-90

Scott No.	Description	Unused Value	Used Value
2412	25c House of Representatives	.50	.20
2413	25c Senate	.50	.20
2414	25c Executive Branch	.50	.20

2416

2417

2418

2419

2420

2421

2422-2425

2426

Scott No.		Description	Unused Value	Used Value	/ / / / / /
2415	25c	Supreme Court	.50	.20	
1989					
2416	25c	South Dakota Statehood	.60	.20	
2417	25c	Lou Gehrig	.60	.20	
2418	25c	Ernest Hemingway	.50	.20	
a.		Vert. pair, imperf. horiz.	*1,500.*		
2419	$2.40	Moon Landing	4.75	2.00	
a.		Black (engr.) omitted	*2,000.*		
b.		Imperf., pair	*650.00*		
c.		Black (litho.) omitted	*2,250.*		
2420	25c	Letter Carriers	.50	.20	
2421	25c	Bill of Rights	.50	.20	
a.		Black (engr.) omitted	*250.00*		
2422	25c	Tyrannosaurus Rex	.70	.20	
a.		Black (engr.) omitted	80.00	—	
2423	25c	Pteranodon	.70	.20	
a.		Black (engr.) omitted	80.00	—	
2424	25c	Stegosaurus	.70	.20	
a.		Black (engr.) omitted	80.00	—	
2425	25c	Brontosaurus	.70	.20	
a.		Black (engr.) omitted	80.00	—	
b.		Block of 4, #2422-2425	2.80	2.00	
c.		As "b," black (engr.) omitted	*400.00*		
2426	25c	Columbian Artifacts	.60	.20	
2427	25c	Christmas - Religious	.50	.20	
a.		Booklet pane of 10	5.00	3.50	
b.		Red (litho.) omitted	*650.00*		
2428	25c	Christmas - Sleigh, perf. 11	.50	.20	
a.		Vert. pair, imperf. horiz.	*750.00*		
Booklet Stamps, Perf. 11½ on 2 or 3 Sides					
2429	25c	Christmas - Sleigh (2428)	.50	.20	
a.		Booklet pane of 10	5.00	3.50	
b.		Vert. pair, imperf. btwn.	—		
c.		As "a," imperf. btwn.	—		
d.		As "a," Red omitted	*3,500.*		
e.		Imperf. pair	—		
Die cut, Self-adhesive					
2431	25c	Eagle and Shield	.50	.20	
a.		Booklet pane of 18	11.00		
b.		Vert. pair, no die cutting btwn.	*500.00*		
c.		Pair, no die cutting	*275.00*		
1989					
2433		World Stamp Expo '89, sheet of 4	11.00	11.00	
a.	90c	like No. 122	2.75	2.75	
b.	90c	like No. 132TC (blue frame, brown center)	2.75	2.75	

2427

2428

2431

2433

2439

2434-2437

2442

2440

2443

Scott No.	Description	Unused Value	Used Value	/ / / / / /
c.	90c like No. 132TC (green frame, blue center)	2.75	2.75	☐☐☐☐☐
d.	90c like No. 132TC (scarlet frame, blue center)	2.75	2.75	☐☐☐☐☐
2434	25c Stagecoach	.50	.20	☐☐☐☐☐
2435	25c Paddlewheel Steamer	.50	.20	☐☐☐☐☐
2436	25c Biplane	.50	.20	☐☐☐☐☐
2437	25c Automobile	.50	.20	☐☐☐☐☐
a.	Block of 4, #2434-2437	2.00	1.75	☐☐☐☐☐
b.	As "a," dark blue (engr.) omitted	*300.00*		☐☐☐☐☐
2438	UPU Congress, sheet of 4, imperf.	4.50	3.75	☐☐☐☐☐
a.	25c Stagecoach (2434)	1.10	.80	☐☐☐☐☐
b.	25c Paddlewheel Steamer (2435)	1.10	.80	☐☐☐☐☐
c.	25c Biplane (2436)	1.10	.80	☐☐☐☐☐
d.	25c Automobile (2437)	1.10	.80	☐☐☐☐☐
e.	Dark blue & gray (engr.) omitted	*5,000.*		☐☐☐☐☐
1990				
2439	25c Idaho Statehood	.55	.20	☐☐☐☐☐
2440	25c Love, perf. 12½ x 13	.50	.20	☐☐☐☐☐
a.	Imperf., pair	*675.00*		☐☐☐☐☐
Booklet Stamp, Perf. 11½ on 2 or 3 Sides				
2441	25c Love (2440)	.50	.20	☐☐☐☐☐
a.	Booklet pane of 10	5.00	3.50	☐☐☐☐☐
b.	As "a," bright pink omitted	*125.00*		☐☐☐☐☐
c.	As "b," single stamp	*1,500.*		☐☐☐☐☐
2442	25c Ida B. Wells	.75	.20	☐☐☐☐☐
2443	15c Beach Umbrella	.30	.20	☐☐☐☐☐
a.	Booklet pane of 10	3.00	2.00	☐☐☐☐☐
b.	As "a," blue omitted	*125.00*		☐☐☐☐☐
c.	As 2443, blue omitted	*1,250.*		☐☐☐☐☐
2444	25c Wyoming Statehood	.80	.20	☐☐☐☐☐
a.	Black (engr.) omitted	*1,250.*	—	☐☐☐☐☐
2445	25c The Wizard of Oz	1.50	.20	☐☐☐☐☐
2446	25c Gone With the Wind	1.50	.20	☐☐☐☐☐
2447	25c Beau Geste	1.50	.20	☐☐☐☐☐
2448	25c Stagecoach	1.50	.20	☐☐☐☐☐
a.	Block of 4, #2445-2448	6.00	3.50	☐☐☐☐☐
2449	25c Marianne Moore	.60	.20	☐☐☐☐☐
a.	All colors missing (from extraneous paper)	—		☐☐☐☐☐
1990-95, Coil Stamps, Perf. 10 Vertically				
2451	4c Steam Carriage, tagged	.20	.20	☐☐☐☐☐
a.	Imperf., pair	*525.00*		☐☐☐☐☐
b.	Untagged	.20	.20	☐☐☐☐☐
2452	5c Circus Wagon, engr., tagged	.20	.20	☐☐☐☐☐
a.	Untagged	.20	.20	☐☐☐☐☐

2444

2449

2445-2448

2451

2452

2453

2457

2464

2468

2470-2474

Scott No.	Description	Unused Value	Used Value	/ / / / / /
c.	Imperf., pair	*550.00*		
2452B	5c Circus Wagon (2452), photo.	.20	.20	
2452D	5c Circus Wagon with cent sign (2452).	.20	.20	
e.	Imperf., pair	*135.00*		
2453	5c Canoe, brown, engr. (Bureau precancel in gray)	.25	.20	
a.	Imperf., pair	*225.00*		
b.	Gray omitted		—	
2454	5c Canoe (2453), red, photo. (Bureau precancel in gray)	.30	.20	
2457	10c Tractor Trailer, engr. (Bureau precancel in gray)	.35	.20	
a.	Imperf., pair	*125.00*		
b.	All color omitted	—		
2458	10c Tractor Trailer (2457), photo. (Bureau precancel in black).	.45	.20	
2463	20c Cog Railway (2451)	.40	.20	
a.	Imperf., pair	*90.00*		
2464	23c Lunch Wagon	.45	.20	
b.	Imperf., pair	*110.00*		
2466	32c Ferryboat (2451)	.80	.20	
a.	Imperf., pair	*475.00*		
b.	Bright blue	3.00	2.25	
2468	$1 Seaplane	2.25	.50	
a.	Imperf., pair	*2,500.*	*1,350.*	

1990, Booklet Stamps

Scott No.	Description	Unused Value	Used Value	/ / / / / /
2470	25c Admiralty Head Lighthouse	1.90	.20	
2471	25c Cape Hatteras Lighthouse	1.90	.20	
2472	25c West Quoddy Head Lighthouse	1.90	.20	
2473	25c American Shoals Lighthouse	1.90	.20	
2474	25c Sandy Hook Lighthouse	1.90	.20	
a.	Bklt. pane of 5, #2470-2474	9.50	2.00	
b.	As "a," white (USA 25) omitted	100.00	—	

Die cut, Self-adhesive

Scott No.	Description	Unused Value	Used Value	/ / / / / /
2475	25c Flag	.55	.25	
a.	Pane of 12	6.60		

1990-95

Scott No.	Description	Unused Value	Used Value	/ / / / / /
2476	1c American Kestrel	.20	.20	
2477	1c American Kestrel with cent sign	.20	.20	
2478	3c Eastern Bluebird, no cent sign	.20	.20	
a.	Vert. pair, imperf. horiz.	—		
b.	Double impression of all colors except yellow	—		
2479	19c Fawn	.35	.20	
b.	Red omitted	*725.00*		
c.	Imperf., pair	*1,000.*		
2480	30c Cardinal	.60	.20	

2475

2476

2477

2478

2482

2483

2487

2488

2489

2490

2491

2496-2500

2501-2505

Scott No.	Description	Unused Value	Used Value	/ / / / / /
2481	45c Pumpkinseed Sunfish	.90	.20	
a.	Black (engr.) omitted	*375.00*	—	
2482	$2 Bobcat	3.50	1.25	
a.	Black (engr.) omitted	*225.00*		
1991-95, Booklet Stamps				
2483	20c Blue Jay	.50	.20	
a.	Booklet pane of 10	5.25	2.25	
b.	As "a," imperf.	—		
2484	29c Wood Duck, black denomination	.60	.20	
a.	Booklet pane of 10	6.00	3.75	
b.	Vert. pair, imperf. btwn.	*190.00*		
c.	As "b," bklt. pane of 10	*1,000.*		
f.	Vert. pair imperf. btwn. and with natural straight edge at top or bottom	—		
2485	29c Wood Duck (2484), red denomination	.60	.20	
a.	Booklet pane of 10	6.00	4.00	
b.	Vert. pair, imperf. btwn.	*3,000.*		
c.	Imperf., pair.	*2,000.*		
2486	29c African Violets	.60	.20	
a.	Booklet pane of 10	6.00	4.00	
2487	32c Peach	.65	.20	
2488	32c Pear	.65	.20	
a.	Booklet pane, 5 each #2487-2488	6.50	4.25	
b.	Pair, #2487-2488	1.30	.30	
1993-95, Booklet Stamps, Die cut, Self-adhesive				
2489	29c Red Squirrel	.65	.20	
a.	Booklet pane of 18	12.00		
b.	As "a," die cutting omitted	—		
2490	29c Rose, red, green & black	.65	.20	
a.	Booklet pane of 18	12.00		
2491	29c Pine Cone	.60	.20	
a.	Booklet pane of 18	11.00		
b.	Horiz. pair, no die cutting between.	*200.00*	*150.00*	
Serpentine Die Cut				
2492	32c Rose (2490), pink, green & black	.65	.20	
a.	Bklt. pane of 20 + label	13.00		
b.	Bklt. pane of 15 + label	9.75		
c.	Horiz. pair, no die cutting btwn.	—		
d.	As "a," 2 stamps and parts of 7 others printed on backing liner	—		
e.	Booklet pane of 14	21.00		
f.	Booklet pane of 16	21.00		
h.	Vertical pair, no die cutting btwn.	—		
2493	32c Peach (2487)	.65	.20	
2494	32c Pear (2488)	.65	.20	
a.	Bklt. pane, 10 each #2493-2494 + label	13.00		

2479

2480

2481

2484

2486

2506-2507

2508-2511

2512

2513

2514

2515

2517

2521

2522

Scott No.	Description	Unused Value	Used Value
b.	Pair, #2493-2494	1.30	
c.	As "b," die cutting omitted	—	

1995, Coil Stamps, Serpentine Die Cut Vert.

Scott No.	Description	Unused Value	Used Value
2495	32c Peach (2487)	2.00	.20
2495A	32c Pear (2488)	2.00	.20

1990

Scott No.	Description	Unused Value	Used Value
2496	25c Jesse Owens	.60	.20
2497	25c Ray Ewry	.60	.20
2498	25c Hazel Wightman	.60	.20
2499	25c Eddie Eagan	.60	.20
2500	25c Helene Madison	.60	.20
a.	Strip of 5, #2496-2500	3.25	2.50
b.	As "a," blue omitted	—	
2501	25c Assiniboin	1.50	.20
2502	25c Cheyenne	1.50	.20
2503	25c Comanche	1.50	.20
2504	25c Flathead	1.50	.20
2505	25c Shoshone	1.50	.20
a.	Bklt. pane, 2 each #2501-2505	15.00	*7.50*
b.	As "a," black (engr.) omitted	*3,500.*	
c.	Strip of 5, #2501-2505	7.50	2.50
d.	As "a," horiz. imperf. btwn.	—	
2506	25c Micronesia	.50	.20
2507	25c Marshall Islands	.50	.20
a.	Pair, #2506-2507	1.00	.75
b.	As "a," black (engr.) omitted	*2,750.*	
2508	25c Killer Whale	.55	.20
2509	25c Northern Sea Lion	.55	.20
2510	25c Sea Otter	.55	.20
2511	25c Common Dolphin	.55	.20
a.	Block of 4, #2508-2511	2.25	1.90
b.	As "a," black (engr.) omitted	*350.00*	
2512	25c Grand Canyon	.55	.20
2513	25c Dwight D. Eisenhower	.90	.20
a.	Imperf., pair	*2,250.*	
2514	25c Christmas - Religious	.50	.20
a.	Booklet pane of 10	5.00	3.25
2515	25c Christmas - Tree, perf. 11	.50	.20
a.	Vert. pair, imperf. horiz.	*900.00.*	
b.	All colors missing (from extraneous paper)	—	

Booklet Stamp, Perf. 11½ x11 on 2 or 3 Sides

Scott No.	Description	Unused Value	Used Value
2516	25c Christmas - Tree (2515)	.50	.20
a.	Booklet pane of 10	5.00	3.25

2523

2524

2528

2529

2530

2531

2531A

2532

2533

2534

2535

2537

2538

2544

2544A

Scott No.	Description	Unused Value	Used Value	/ / / / / /
1991				
2517	(29c) "F" & Flower, perf. 13, yellow, black, red & yellow green	.60	.20	☐☐☐☐☐
a.	Imperf., pair	*700.00*		☐☐☐☐☐
b.	Horiz. pair, imperf. vert.	*1,150.*		☐☐☐☐☐
Coil Stamp, Perf. 10 Vertically				
2518	(29c) "F" & Flower (2517), yellow, black, dull red & dark yellow green	.60	.20	☐☐☐☐☐
a.	Imperf., pair	27.50		☐☐☐☐☐
Booklet Stamps, Perf. 11 on 2 or 3 Sides				
2519	(29c) "F" & Flower (2517), yellow, black, dull red & dk green, bullseye perfs.	.60	.20	☐☐☐☐☐
a.	Booklet pane of 10	6.50	4.50	☐☐☐☐☐
b.	As "a," imperf. horiz.	—		☐☐☐☐☐
2520	(29c) "F" & Flower (2517), pale yellow, black, red & brt green	1.75	.20	☐☐☐☐☐
a.	Booklet pane of 10	18.00	4.50	☐☐☐☐☐
b.	As "a," imperf. horiz.	—		☐☐☐☐☐
c.	Horiz. pair, imperf. btwn.	*500.00*		☐☐☐☐☐
d.	Imperf. vert., pair	—		☐☐☐☐☐
1991				
2521	(4c) Text	.20	.20	☐☐☐☐☐
a.	Vert. pair, imperf. horiz.	95.00		☐☐☐☐☐
b.	Imperf., pair	60.00		☐☐☐☐☐
Die cut, Self-adhesive				
2522	(29c) "F" & Flag	.60	.25	☐☐☐☐☐
a.	Pane of 12	7.25		☐☐☐☐☐
Coil Stamps, Perf. 10 Vertically				
2523	29c Flag over Mt. Rushmore, blue, red & claret, engraved	.65	.20	☐☐☐☐☐
b.	Imperf., pair	20.00		☐☐☐☐☐
c.	Blue, red & brown	5.00	—	☐☐☐☐☐
2523A	29c Flag over Mt. Rushmore (2523), blue, red & brown, photogravure	.75	.20	☐☐☐☐☐
1991-92, Perf. 11				
2524	29c Flower, dull yellow, black, red & yellow green	.60	.20	☐☐☐☐☐
Perf. 13 x 12½				
2524A	29c Flower, dull yellow, black, red & yellow green (2524)	1.00	.20	☐☐☐☐☐
Coil Stamps, Rouletted 10 Vertically				
2525	29c Flower (2524), pale yellow, black, red & yellow green	.60	.20	☐☐☐☐☐

2539

2540

2541

2542

2543

2550

2545-2549

Scott No.	Description	Unused Value	Used Value	/ / / / / /
Perf. 10 Vertically				
2526	29c Flower (2524), pale yellow, black, red & yellow green	.80	.20	□□□□□
Booklet Stamp, Perf. 11 on 2 or 3 sides				
2527	29c Flower (2524), pale yellow, black, red & bright green	.60	.20	□□□□□
a.	Booklet pane of 10	6.00	3.50	□□□□□
b.	Horiz. pair, imperf. btwn.	—		□□□□□
c.	Horiz. pair, imperf. vert.	*165.00*		□□□□□
d.	As "a," imperf. horiz.	*750.00*		□□□□□
e.	As "a," imperf. vert.	—		□□□□□
1991				
2528	29c Flag & Olympic Rings	.60	.20	□□□□□
a.	Booklet pane of 10	6.00	3.50	□□□□□
c.	Vert. pair, imperf. btwn., perfed at top and bottom	*250.00*		□□□□□
d.	Vert. strip of 3, top or bottom pair imperf. btwn	—		□□□□□
e.	Vert. pair, imperf. horiz..	*700.00*		□□□□□
1991-94, Coil Stamps, Perf. 9.8 Vertically				
2529	19c Fishing Boat	.40	.20	□□□□□
a.	Type II (finer dot pattern), tagged...	.40	.20	□□□□□
b.	As "a," untagged	1.00	.40	□□□□□
2529C	19c Fishing Boat (2529), one loop of rope	.50	.20	□□□□□
Booklet Stamp, Perf. 10 on 2 or 3 Sides				
2530	19c Balloon	.40	.20	□□□□□
a.	Booklet pane of 10	4.00	2.75	□□□□□
1991				
2531	29c Flags on Parade	.60	.20	□□□□□
Die cut, Self-adhesive				
2531A	29c Liberty Torch	.60	.25	□□□□□
b.	Pane of 18	11.00		□□□□□
c.	Pair, imperf.	*1,750.*		□□□□□
1991				
2532	50c Switzerland	1.00	.25	□□□□□
a.	Vert. pair, imperf. horiz.	*2,250.*		□□□□□
2533	29c Vermont Statehood	.90	.20	□□□□□
2534	29c Savings Bonds	.60	.20	□□□□□
Perf. 12½ x13				
2535	29c Love	.60	.20	□□□□□
b.	Imperf., pair	*1,850.*		□□□□□
Perf. 11				
2535A	29c Love (2535)	.85	.20	□□□□□

2551

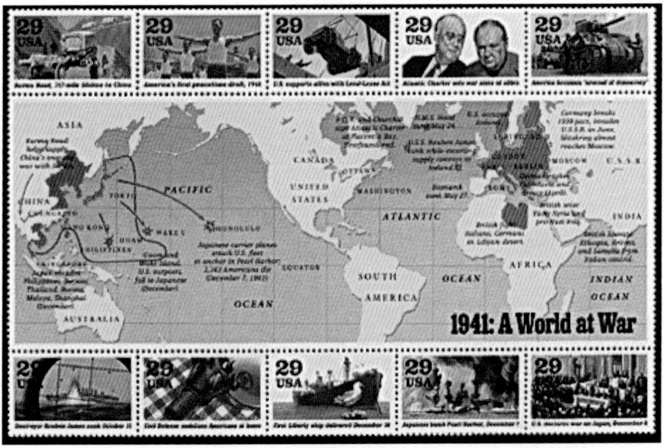

2559

2558

2560

2567

2561

Scott No.		Description	Unused Value	Used Value
Booklet Stamp, Perf. 11 on 2 or 3 Sides				
2536	29c	Love (2535)	.60	.20
a.		Booklet pane of 10	6.00	3.50
2537	52c	Love	.90	.20
2538	29c	William Saroyan	.60	.20
a.		All colors missing (from extraneous paper)	—	
b.		All colors except black missing (from extraneous paper)	—	
2539	$1	Eagle & Olympic Rings	2.00	.50
a.		Black omitted	—	
1991-95				
2540	$2.90	Eagle	6.00	1.50
a.		Vert. pair, imperf. horiz.	*1,000.*	
b.		Black (engr.) omitted	—	
2541	$9.95	Eagle	20.00	6.00
a.		Imperf., pair	—	
2542	$14	Eagle	25.00	15.00
a.		Red (engr. inscriptions) omitted	—	
2543	$2.90	Futuristic Space Shuttle	6.00	1.75
2544	$3	Space Shuttle *Challenger,* dated "1995"	5.75	1.75
b.		Dated "1996"	5.75	1.75
c.		Horiz. pair, imperf. btwn.	—	
d.		Imperf, pair.	*1,250.*	
2544A	$10.75	Space Shuttle *Endeavour*	20.00	9.00
1991				
2545	29c	Royal Wulff	2.50	.20
a.		Black omitted	—	
b.		Horiz. pair, imperf. btwn.	—	
2546	29c	Jock Scott	2.50	.20
a.		Black omitted	—	
2547	29c	Apte Tarpon Fly	2.50	.20
a.		Black omitted	—	
2548	29c	Lefty's Deceiver	2.50	.20
2549	29c	Muddler Minnow	2.50	.20
a.		Booklet pane of 5, #2545-2549	12.50	*3.50*
2550	29c	Cole Porter	.60	.20
a.		Vert. pair, imperf. horiz.	*500.00*	
2551	29c	Desert Shield & Desert Storm	.60	.20
a.		Vert. pair, imperf. horiz.	*1,250.*	
2552	29c	Desert Shield & Desert Storm (2551) 20½mm wide (from bklt. pane)	.60	.20
a.		Booklet pane of 5	3.00	*2.25*
2553	29c	Olympics - Pole Vault	.60	.20
2554	29c	Olympics - Discus	.60	.20
2555	29c	Olympics - Women's Sprints	.60	.20
2556	29c	Olympics - Javelin	.60	.20
2557	29c	Olympics - Women's Hurdles	.60	.20

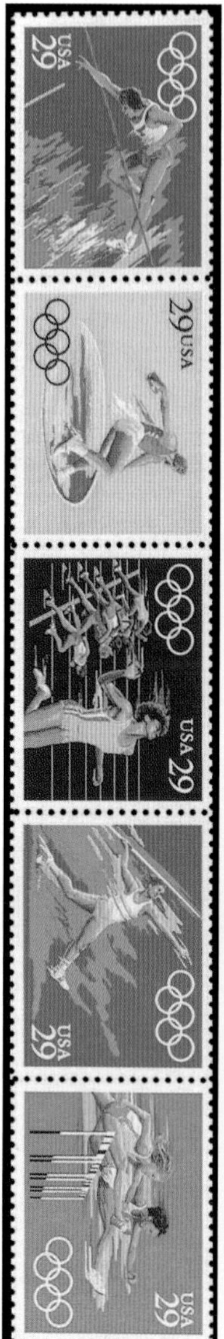

2553-2557

2562-2566

2568-2577

Scott No.		Description	Unused Value	Used Value	/ / / / / /
a.		Strip of #2553-2557	3.00	2.25	☐☐☐☐☐
2558	29c	Numismatics	.60	.20	☐☐☐☐☐
2559		World War II, block of 10	7.50	5.00	☐☐☐☐☐
a.-j.	29c	Any single	.75	.45	☐☐☐☐☐
k.		Black (engr.) omitted	*12,500.*		☐☐☐☐☐
2560	29c	Basketball	.60	.20	☐☐☐☐☐
2561	29c	District of Columbia	.60	.20	☐☐☐☐☐
a.		Black (engr.) omitted	*100.00*		☐☐☐☐☐
2562	29c	Laurel and Hardy	1.00	.20	☐☐☐☐☐
2563	29c	Bergen and McCarthy	1.00	.20	☐☐☐☐☐
2564	29c	Jack Benny	1.00	.20	☐☐☐☐☐
2565	29c	Fanny Brice	1.00	.20	☐☐☐☐☐
2566	29c	Abbott and Costello	1.00	.20	☐☐☐☐☐
a.		Booklet pane, 2 each #2562-2566	10.00	5.00	☐☐☐☐☐
b.		As "a," scarlet & bright violet (engr.) omitted	*550.00*		☐☐☐☐☐
c.		Strip of 5, #2562-2566	5.00	2.50	☐☐☐☐☐
2567	29c	Jan E. Matzeliger	.60	.20	☐☐☐☐☐
a.		Horiz. pair, imperf. vert.	*1,150.*		☐☐☐☐☐
b.		Vert. pair, imperf. horiz.	*1,150.*		☐☐☐☐☐
c.		Imperf. pair	*400.00*		☐☐☐☐☐
2568	29c	Mercury	1.10	.20	☐☐☐☐☐
2569	29c	Venus	1.10	.20	☐☐☐☐☐
2570	29c	Earth	1.10	.20	☐☐☐☐☐
2571	29c	Moon	1.10	.20	☐☐☐☐☐
2572	29c	Mars	1.10	.20	☐☐☐☐☐
2573	29c	Jupiter	1.10	.20	☐☐☐☐☐
2574	29c	Saturn	1.10	.20	☐☐☐☐☐
2575	29c	Uranus	1.10	.20	☐☐☐☐☐
2576	29c	Neptune	1.10	.20	☐☐☐☐☐
2577	29c	Pluto	1.10	.20	☐☐☐☐☐
a.		Booklet pane of 10, #2568-2577	10.00	4.50	☐☐☐☐☐
2578	(29c)	Christmas - Religious	.60	.20	☐☐☐☐☐
a.		Booklet pane of 10	6.00	3.25	☐☐☐☐☐
b.		As "a," single, red & black (engr.) omitted	*3,250.*		☐☐☐☐☐
2579	(29c)	Christmas - Santa in Chimney, perf 11	.60	.20	☐☐☐☐☐
a.		Horiz. pair, imperf. vert.	*225.00*		☐☐☐☐☐
b.		Vert. pair, imperf. horiz.	*375.00*		☐☐☐☐☐

Booklet Stamps, Size: 25 x 18½ mm, Perf. 11 on 2 or 3 sides

Scott No.		Description	Unused Value	Used Value	/ / / / / /
2580	(29c)	Christmas - Santa in Chimney (2579), Type I	2.25	.20	☐☐☐☐☐
2581	(29c)	Christmas - Santa in Chimney (2579), Type II	2.75	.20	☐☐☐☐☐
a.		Pair, #2580, 2581	5.00	.50	☐☐☐☐☐
b.		Bklt. pane, 2 each #2580, 2581	11.00	1.25	☐☐☐☐☐

The extreme left brick in the top row of chimney is missing on Type II, No. 2581.

2578

2579

2582

2583

2584

2585

2587

2592

2590

2593

2595

Scott No.		Description	Unused Value	Used Value
2582	(29c)	Christmas - Santa Checking List	.60	.20
a.		Booklet pane of 4	2.40	1.25
2583	(29c)	Christmas - Santa with Presents......	.60	.20
a.		Booklet pane of 4	2.40	1.25
2584	(29c)	Christmas - Santa at Fireplace	.60	.20
a.		Booklet pane of 4	2.40	1.25
2585	(29c)	Christmas - Santa and Sleigh..........	.60	.20
a.		Booklet pane of 4	2.40	1.25

1995, Perf. 11.2

2587	32c	James K. Polk	.65	.20

1994, Perf. 11.5

2590	$1	Surrender of Gen. John Burgoyne ..	1.90	.50
2592	$5	Washington and Jackson	8.00	2.50

1992-93, Booklet Stamps
Perf. 10 on 2 or 3 sides

2593	29c	Flag, black denomination	.60	.20
a.		Booklet pane of 10	6.00	4.25

Perf. 11 x 10 on 2 or 3 sides

2593B	29c	Flag, black denomination (2593) ...	1.70	.50
c.		Booklet pane of 10	17.00	7.50

Perf. 11 x 10 on 2 or 3 Sides

2594	29c	Flag (2593), red denomination........	.65	.20
a.		Booklet pane of 10	6.50	4.25
b.		Imperf., pair	900.00	

1992-94, Die cut, Self-adhesive

2595	29c	Eagle & Shield, brown denomination	.60	.25
a.		Booklet pane of 17 + label.............	13.00	
b.		Pair, no die cutting.........................	*135.00*	
c.		Brown (engr.) omitted	*350.00*	
d.		As "a," die cutting omitted.............	*1,150.*	
2596	29c	Eagle & Shield (2595), green denom.	.60	.25
a.		Booklet pane of 17 + label.............	12.00	
2597	29c	Eagle & Shield (2595), red denom.	.60	.25
a.		Booklet pane of 17 + label.............	10.50	
2598	29c	Eagle	.60	.20
a.		Booklet pane of 18	11.00	
b.		Coil with P#111.............................	—	5.00
2599	29c	Statue of Liberty............................	.60	.20
a.		Booklet pane of 18	11.00	
b.		Coil with P#D1111.........................	—	5.00

1991-93, Coil Stamps, Perf. 10 Vertically

2602	(10c)	Eagle & Shield (Bureau precancel, Bulk Rate, in blue)	.30	.20
a.		Imperf. pair	—	

2598

2599

2602

2603

2605

2606

2609

2618

2616

2617

2619

2611-2615

Scott No.	Description	Unused Value	Used Value	/ / / / / /
2603	(10c) Eagle & Shield, orange yellow & multi (Bureau precancel, Bulk Rate, in red)	.30	.20	
a.	Imperf., pair	20.00		
2604	(10c) Eagle & Shield (2603), gold & multi (Bureau precancel, Bulk Rate, in red)	.30	.20	
2605	23c Flag (Bureau precancel in blue)	.45	.40	
a.	Imperf., pair	—		
2606	23c Reflected Flag (Bureau precanceled)	.45	.40	
2607	23c Reflected Flag (2606), multi (Bureau precanceled)	.45	.40	
c.	Imperf., pair	70.00		
2608	23c Reflected Flag (2606), violet blue, red & black (Bureau precanceled)	.80	.40	
	On No. 2607 "First Class" is 9mm long. On No. 2608 "First Class" is 8½mm long.			
2609	29c Flag over White House	.60	.20	
a.	Imperf. pair	15.00		
b.	Pair, imperf. btwn.	90.00		
1992				
2611	29c Olympics - Ice Hockey	.60	.20	
2612	29c Olympics - Figure Skating	.60	.20	
2613	29c Olympics - Speed Skating	.60	.20	
2614	29c Olympics - Skiing	.60	.20	
2615	29c Olympics - Bobsledding	.60	.20	
a.	Strip of 5, #2611-2615	3.00	2.50	
2616	29c World Columbian Stamp Expo	.60	.20	
2617	29c W.E.B. DuBois	.60	.20	
2618	29c Love	.60	.20	
a.	Horiz. pair, imperf. vert.	*625.00*		
b.	As "a," green omitted on right stamp	*2,500.*		
2619	29c Olympic Baseball	.60	.20	
2620	29c Seeking Queen Isabella's Support	.60	.20	
2621	29c Crossing the Atlantic	.60	.20	
2622	29c Approaching Land	.60	.20	
2623	29c Coming Ashore	.60	.20	
a.	Block of 4, #2620-2623	2.40	2.00	
2624	First Sighting of Land, sheet of 3	2.00	1.25	
a.	1c deep blue (like No. 230)	.20	.20	
b.	4c ultramarine (like No. 233)	.20	.20	
c.	$1 salmon (like No. 241)	1.75	1.00	
2625	Claiming a New World (2624), sht. of 3	7.25	5.00	
a.	2c brown violet (like No. 231)	.20	.20	
b.	3c green (like No. 232)	.20	.20	
c.	$4 crimson lake (like No. 244)	7.00	4.00	
2626	Seeking Royal Support (2624), sheet of 3	1.60	1.25	
a.	5c chocolate (like No. 234)	.20	.20	

2620-2623

2624-2629

2630

Scott No.	Description	Unused Value	Used Value	/ / / / / /
b.	30c orange brown (like No. 239)	.60	.30	☐☐☐☐☐
c.	50c slate blue (like No. 240)	.90	.50	☐☐☐☐☐
2627	Royal Favor Restored (2624), sheet of 3	5.75	3.50	☐☐☐☐☐
a.	6c purple (like No. 235)	.20	.20	☐☐☐☐☐
b.	8c magenta (like No. 236)	.20	.20	☐☐☐☐☐
c.	$3 yellow green (like No. 243)	5.50	3.00	☐☐☐☐☐
2628	Reporting Discoveries (2624) Sht. of 3	4.00	3.00	☐☐☐☐☐
a.	10c black brown (like No. 237)	.20	.20	☐☐☐☐☐
b.	15c dark green (like No. 238)	.30	.20	☐☐☐☐☐
c.	$2 brown red (like No. 242)	3.50	2.00	☐☐☐☐☐
2629	$5 Christopher Columbus (2624), sheet of 1 (like No. 245)	8.75	6.00	☐☐☐☐☐
a.	$5 black, single stamp	8.50	5.00	☐☐☐☐☐
2630	29c New York Stock Exchange	.60	.20	☐☐☐☐☐
a.	Black missing (from extraneous paper)	—		☐☐☐☐☐
b.	Black missing (from a color misregistration)	—		☐☐☐☐☐
c.	Center inverted	*26,000.*		☐☐☐☐☐
2631	29c Cosmonaut	.60	.20	☐☐☐☐☐
2632	29c Astronaut	.60	.20	☐☐☐☐☐
2633	29c Apollo Modules	.60	.20	☐☐☐☐☐
2634	29c Soyuz	.60	.20	☐☐☐☐☐
a.	Block of 4, #2631-2634	2.40	1.90	☐☐☐☐☐
b.	As "a," yellow omitted	—		☐☐☐☐☐
2635	29c Alaska Highway	.60	.20	☐☐☐☐☐
a.	Black (engr.) omitted	*700.00*		☐☐☐☐☐
2636	29c Kentucky Statehood	.60	.20	☐☐☐☐☐
a.	Dark blue missing (from extraneous paper)	—		☐☐☐☐☐
b.	Dark blue and red missing (from extraneous paper)	—		☐☐☐☐☐
c.	All colors missing (from extraneous paper)	—		☐☐☐☐☐
2637	29c Olympics - Soccer	.60	.20	☐☐☐☐☐
2638	29c Olympics - Gymnastics	.60	.20	☐☐☐☐☐
2639	29c Olympics - Volleyball	.60	.20	☐☐☐☐☐
2640	29c Olympics - Boxing	.60	.20	☐☐☐☐☐
2641	29c Olympics - Swimming	.60	.20	☐☐☐☐☐
a.	Strip of 5, #2637-2641	3.00	2.50	☐☐☐☐☐
2642	29c Ruby-Throated Hummingbird	.60	.20	☐☐☐☐☐
2643	29c Broad-billed Hummingbird	.60	.20	☐☐☐☐☐
2644	29c Costa's Hummingbird	.60	.20	☐☐☐☐☐
2645	29c Rufous Hummingbird	.60	.20	☐☐☐☐☐
2646	29c Calliope Hummingbird	.60	.20	☐☐☐☐☐
a.	Booklet pane of 5, #2642-2646	3.00	*2.50*	☐☐☐☐☐
2647	29c Indian Paintbrush	.80	.60	☐☐☐☐☐
2648	29c Fragrant Water Lily	.80	.60	☐☐☐☐☐

2631-2634

2635

2636

2637-2641

2642-2646

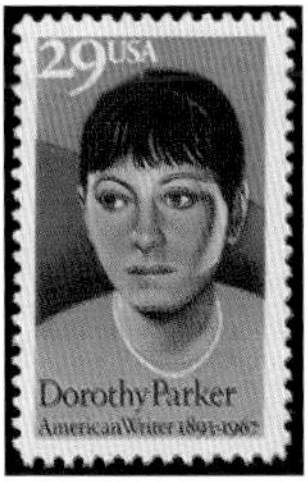

2698

2699

2700-2703

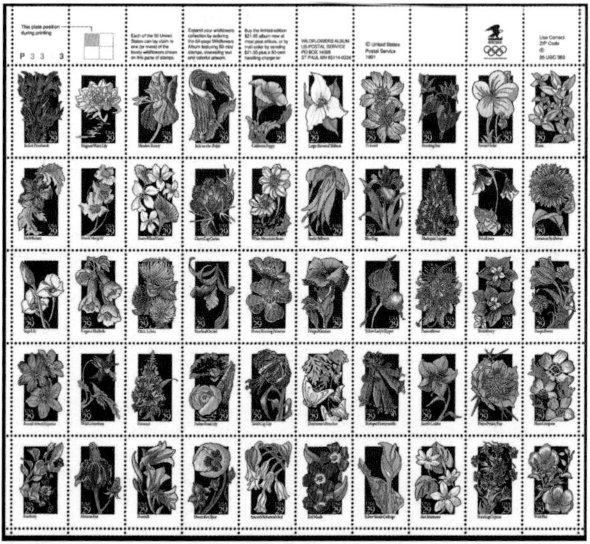

2647-2696

2697

Scott No.	Description	Unused Value	Used Value	/ / / / / /
2649	29c Meadow Beauty	.80	.60	☐☐☐☐☐
2650	29c Jack-in-the-Pulpit	.80	.60	☐☐☐☐☐
2651	29c California Poppy	.80	.60	☐☐☐☐☐
2652	29c Large-flowered Trillium	.80	.60	☐☐☐☐☐
2653	29c Tickseed	.80	.60	☐☐☐☐☐
2654	29c Shooting Star	.80	.60	☐☐☐☐☐
2655	29c Stream Violet	.80	.60	☐☐☐☐☐
2656	29c Bluets	.80	.60	☐☐☐☐☐
2657	29c Herb Robert	.80	.60	☐☐☐☐☐
2658	29c Marsh Marigold	.80	.60	☐☐☐☐☐
2659	29c Sweet White Violet	.80	.60	☐☐☐☐☐
2660	29c Claret Cup Cactus	.80	.60	☐☐☐☐☐
2661	29c White Mountain Avens	.80	.20	☐☐☐☐☐
2662	29c Sessile Bellwort	.80	.60	☐☐☐☐☐
2663	29c Blue Flag	.80	.60	☐☐☐☐☐
2664	29c Harlequin Lupine	.80	.60	☐☐☐☐☐
2665	29c Twinflower	.80	.60	☐☐☐☐☐
2666	29c Common Sunflower	.80	.60	☐☐☐☐☐
2667	29c Sego Lily	.80	.60	☐☐☐☐☐
2668	29c Virginia Bluebells	.80	.60	☐☐☐☐☐
2669	29c Ohia Lehua	.80	.60	☐☐☐☐☐
2670	29c Rosebud Orchid	.80	.60	☐☐☐☐☐
2671	29c Showy Evening Primrose	.80	.60	☐☐☐☐☐
2672	29c Fringed Gentian	.80	.60	☐☐☐☐☐
2673	29c Yellow Lady's Slipper	.80	.60	☐☐☐☐☐
2674	29c Passionflower	.80	.60	☐☐☐☐☐
2675	29c Bunchberry	.80	.60	☐☐☐☐☐
2676	29c Pasqueflower	.80	.60	☐☐☐☐☐
2677	29c Round-lobed Hepatica	.80	.60	☐☐☐☐☐
2678	29c Wild Columbine	.80	.60	☐☐☐☐☐
2679	29c Fireweed	.80	.60	☐☐☐☐☐
2680	29c Indian Pond Lily	.80	.60	☐☐☐☐☐
2681	29c Turk's Cap Lily	.80	.60	☐☐☐☐☐
2682	29c Dutchman's Breeches	.80	.60	☐☐☐☐☐
2683	29c Trumpet Honeysuckle	.80	.60	☐☐☐☐☐
2684	29c Jacobs Ladder	.80	.60	☐☐☐☐☐
2685	29c Plains Prickly Pear	.80	.60	☐☐☐☐☐
2686	29c Moss Campion	.80	.60	☐☐☐☐☐
2687	29c Bearberry	.80	.60	☐☐☐☐☐
2688	29c Mexican Hat	.80	.60	☐☐☐☐☐
2689	29c Harebell	.80	.60	☐☐☐☐☐
2690	29c Desert Five Spot	.80	.60	☐☐☐☐☐
2691	29c Smooth Solomon's Seal	.80	.60	☐☐☐☐☐
2692	29c Red Maids	.80	.60	☐☐☐☐☐
2693	29c Yellow Skunk Cabbage	.80	.60	☐☐☐☐☐
2694	29c Rue Anemone	.80	.20	☐☐☐☐☐
2695	29c Standing Cypress	.80	.60	☐☐☐☐☐
2696	29c Wild Flax	.80	.60	☐☐☐☐☐

2704

2705-2709

2724-2730

2710

2720

2722

2723

2711-2714

Scott No.		Description	Unused Value	Used Value
a.		Pane of 50, #2647-2696	40.00	—
2697		World War II, block of 10	7.50	5.00
a.-j.	29c	Any single	.75	.30
k.		Red (litho.) omitted	*5,000.*	
2698	29c	Dorothy Parker	.60	.20
2699	29c	Theodore von Karman	.60	.20
2700	29c	Azurite	.60	.20
2701	29c	Copper	.60	.20
2702	29c	Variscite	.60	.20
2703	29c	Wulfenite	.60	.20
a.		Block or strip of 4, #2700-2703	2.40	2.00
b.		As "a," silver (litho.) omitted	*7,750.*	
c.		As "a," red (litho.) omitted	—	
2704	29c	Juan Rodriguez Cabrillo	.60	.20
a.		Black (engr.) omitted	*3,250.*	
2705	29c	Giraffe	.65	.20
2706	29c	Giant Panda	.65	.20
2707	29c	Flamingo	.65	.20
2708	29c	King Penguins	.65	.20
2709	29c	White Bengal Tiger	.65	.20
a.		Booklet pane of 5, #2705-2709	3.25	*2.25*
b.		As "a," imperforate	*2,250.*	
2710	29c	Christmas - Religious	.60	.20
a.		Booklet pane of 10	6.00	3.50
2711	29c	Christmas - Horse	.75	.20
2712	29c	Christmas - Locomotive	.75	.20
2713	29c	Christmas - Fire Pumper	.75	.20
2714	29c	Christmas - Boat	.75	.20
a.		Block of 4, #2711-2714	3.00	1.10

Booklet Stamps, Perf. 11 on 2 or 3 sides

Scott No.		Description	Unused Value	Used Value
2715	29c	Christmas - Horse (2711)	.85	.20
2716	29c	Christmas - Locomotive (2712)	.85	.20
2717	29c	Christmas - Fire Pumper (2713)	.85	.20
2718	29c	Christmas - Boat (2714)	.85	.20
a.		Booklet pane of 4, #2715-2718	3.50	1.25
b.		As "a," imperf. horiz.	—	

Die cut, Self-adhesive

Scott No.		Description	Unused Value	Used Value
2719	29c	Christmas - Locomotive (2712)	.60	.20
a.		Booklet pane of 18	11.00	

1992

Scott No.		Description	Unused Value	Used Value
2720	29c	Year of the Rooster	.60	.20

1993 Issues

Scott No.		Description	Unused Value	Used Value
2721	29c	Elvis Presley, "Elvis" only (2724)	.60	.20
a.		Imperf, pair.	—	
2722	29c	Oklahoma!, no frameline	.60	.20

2741-2745

2746

2749

2755

2747

2748

2754

2750-2753

Scott No.	Description	Unused Value	Used Value
Perf. 10			
2723	29c Hank Williams, 27½mm inscription,	.75	.20
Perf. 11.2 x 11.5			
2723A	29c Hank Williams, 27½mm inscription (2723)	20.00	10.00
Perf. 10			
2724	29c Elvis Presley, with "Presley," no frameline	.70	.20
2725	29c Bill Haley	.70	.20
2726	29c Clyde McPhatter	.70	.20
2727	29c Ritchie Valens	.70	.20
2728	29c Otis Redding	.70	.20
2729	29c Buddy Holly	.70	.20
2730	29c Dinah Washington	.70	.20
a.	Vert. strip of 7, #2724-2730	5.50	
Booklet stamps, Perf. 11 Horiz., with Framelines			
2731	29c Presley (2724)	.60	.20
2732	29c Haley (2725)	.60	.20
2733	29c McPhatter (2726)	.60	.20
2734	29c Valens (2727)	.60	.20
2735	29c Redding (2728)	.60	.20
2736	29c Holly (2729)	.60	.20
2737	29c Washington (2730)	.60	.20
a.	Booklet pane, 2 #2731, 1 each #2732-2737	5.00	2.25
b.	Booklet pane, #2731, 2735-2737 + tab	2.40	1.50
2741	29c Ringed Planet	.60	.20
2742	29c Craft without Wings	.60	.20
2743	29c Astronauts	.60	.20
2744	29c Craft with Long Wings	.60	.20
2745	29c Craft with Short Wings	.60	.20
a.	Booklet pane of 5, #2741-2745	3.00	2.25
2746	29c Percy Lavon Julian	.60	.20
2747	29c Oregon Trail	.60	.20
b.	Blue omitted	—	
2748	29c World University Games	.60	.20
2749	29c Grace Kelly	.60	.20
2750	29c Clown	.60	.20
2751	29c Ringmaster	.60	.20
2752	29c Trapeze Artist	.60	.20
2753	29c Elephant	.60	.20
a.	Block of 4, #2750-2753	2.40	1.75
2754	29c Cherokee Strip Land Run	.60	.20
2755	29c Dean Acheson	.60	.20
2756	29c Steeplechase	.60	.20

2756-2759

2766

2760-2764

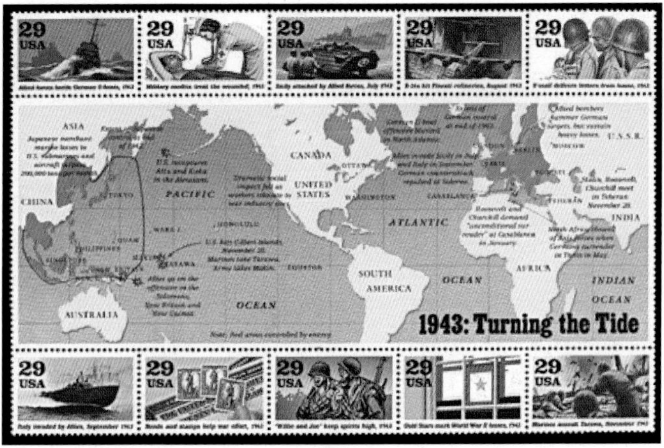

2765

2767-2770

2772-2774

2779-2782

2783-2784

2785-2788

2789

2791-2794

2804

2805

2806

Scott No.	Description	Unused Value	Used Value
2757	29c Thoroughbred Racing	.60	.20
2758	29c Harness Racing	.60	.20
2759	29c Polo	.60	.20
a.	Block of 4, #2756-2759	2.40	2.00
b.	As "a," black (engr.) omitted	*700.00*	
2760	29c Hyacinth	.75	.20
2761	29c Daffodil	.75	.20
2762	29c Tulip	.75	.20
2763	29c Iris	.75	.20
2764	29c Lilac	.75	.20
a.	Booklet pane of 5, #2760-2764	3.75	2.25
b.	As "a," black (engr.) omitted	*175.00*	
c.	As "a," imperf.	*1,000.*	
2765	World War II, block of 10	7.50	5.00
a.-j.	29c Any single	.75	.40
2766	29c Joe Louis	.60	.20
2767	29c Show Boat	.60	.20
2768	29c Porgy & Bess	.60	.20
2769	29c Oklahoma! with frameline	.60	.20
2770	29c My Fair Lady	.60	.20
a.	Booklet pane of 4, #2767-2770	2.75	2.25
2771	29c Hank Williams (2723), 27mm inscription	.75	.20
2772	29c Patsy Cline	.75	.20
2773	29c Carter Family	.75	.20
2774	29c Bob Wills	.75	.20
a.	Block or horiz. strip of 4, #2771-2774	3.00	1.75

Booklet stamps, Perf. 11 Horiz., with Frameline

Scott No.	Description	Unused Value	Used Value
2775	29c Hank Williams (2723), 22mm inscript.	.60	.20
2776	29c Carter Family	.60	.20
2777	29c Patsy Cline	.60	.20
2778	29c Bob Wills	.60	.20
a.	Booklet pane of 4, #2775-2778	2.50	2.00
2779	29c Benjamin Franklin	.60	.20
2780	29c Civil War Soldier	.60	.20
2781	29c Charles Lindbergh	.60	.20
2782	29c Stamps	.60	.20
a.	Block or strip of 4, #2779-2782	2.40	2.00
b.	As "a," black and maroon omitted	—	
c.	As "a," imperf.	*3,250.*	
2783	29c Recognizing Deafness	.60	.20
2784	29c American Sign Language	.60	.20
a.	Pair, #2783-2784	1.20	.75
2785	29c Rebecca of Sunnybrook Farm	.60	.20
2786	29c Little House on the Prairie	.60	.20
2787	29c Adventures of Huckleberry Finn	.60	.20

2807-2811

2812

2813

2814

2815

2816

2817

Scott No.	Description	Unused Value	Used Value
2788	29c Little Women	.60	.20
a.	Block or horiz. strip of 4, #2785-2788	2.40	2.00
2789	29c Christmas - Religious	.60	.20

Booklet Stamp, Perf. 11½ x 11 on 2 or 3 Sides, 18 x 25mm

Scott No.	Description	Unused Value	Used Value
2790	29c Christmas - Religious (2789)	.60	.20
a.	Booklet pane of 4	2.40	1.75
b.	Pair, imperf.	—	
c.	As "a," imperf.	—	

Perf. 11½

Scott No.	Description	Unused Value	Used Value
2791	29c Christmas - Jack-in-the-Box	.60	.20
2792	29c Christmas - Reindeer	.60	.20
2793	29c Christmas - Snowman	.60	.20
2794	29c Christmas - Toy Soldier	.60	.20
a.	Block or strip of 4, #2791-2794	2.40	2.00

Booklet Stamps, Perf. 11 x 10 on 2 or 3 Sides

Scott No.	Description	Unused Value	Used Value
2795	29c Christmas - Toy Soldier (2794)	.85	.20
2796	29c Christmas - Snowman (2793)	.85	.20
2797	29c Christmas - Reindeer (2792)	.85	.20
2798	29c Christmas - Jack-in-the-Box (2791)	.85	.20
a.	Booklet pane, 3 each #2795-2796, 2 each #2797-2798	8.50	4.00
b.	Booklet pane, 3 each #2797-2798, 2 each #2795-2796	8.50	4.00
c.	Block of 4, #2795-2798.	3.40	1.75

Die cut, Self-adhesive, 19½ x 26½mm

Scott No.	Description	Unused Value	Used Value
2799	29c Christmas - Snowman (2793)	.65	.20
2800	29c Christmas - Toy Soldier (2794)	.65	.20
2801	29c Christmas - Jack-in-the-Box (2791)	.65	.20
2802	29c Christmas - Reindeer (2792)	.65	.20
a.	Booklet pane, 3 each #2799-2802	8.00	
b.	Block of 4, #2799-2802	2.60	

Die cut, Self-adhesive, 17 x 20 mm

Scott No.	Description	Unused Value	Used Value
2803	29c Christmas - Snowman (2793)	.60	.20
a.	Booklet pane of 18	11.00	

Perf. 11

Scott No.	Description	Unused Value	Used Value
2804	29c Mariana Islands	.60	.20

Perf. 11.2

Scott No.	Description	Unused Value	Used Value
2805	29c Columbus' Landing in Puerto Rico	.60	.20
2806	29c AIDS Awareness	.60	.20
a.	Perf. 11 vert. on 1 or 2 sides	.70	.20
b.	As "a," booklet pane of 5	3.50	2.00

2819-2828

2829-2833

2818

2834

2835

2836

Scott No.	Description	Unused Value	Used Value	/ / / / / /
1994 Issues				
2807	29c Olympics - Slalom	.60	.20	
2808	29c Olympics - Luge	.60	.20	
2809	29c Olympics - Ice Dancing	.60	.20	
2810	29c Olympics - Cross-Country Skiing	.60	.20	
2811	29c Olympics - Ice Hockey	.60	.20	
a.	Strip of 5, #2807-2811	3.00	2.50	
2812	29c Edward R. Murrow	.60	.20	
Die cut, Self-adhesive				
2813	29c Love	.60	.20	
a.	Pane of 18	11.00		
b.	Coil with plate #B1	—	3.75	
Booklet stamp, Perf. 10.9 x 11.1				
2814	29c Love, photogravure	.60	.20	
a.	Booklet pane of 10	6.00	3.50	
b.	As "a," imperf.	—		
Perf. 11.1				
2814C	29c Love (2814), litho. & engr.	.70	.20	
2815	52c Love	1.00	.20	
2816	29c Dr. Allison Davis	.60	.20	
2817	29c Year of the Dog	.80	.20	
2818	29c Buffalo Soldier	.60	.20	
a.	Double impression of red brown (engr. inscriptions)	—		
2819	29c Rudolph Valentino	1.10	.30	
2820	29c Clara Bow	1.10	.30	
2821	29c Charlie Chaplin	1.10	.30	
2822	29c Lon Chaney	1.10	.30	
2823	29c John Gilbert	1.10	.30	
2824	29c Zasu Pitts	1.10	.30	
2825	29c Harold Lloyd	1.10	.30	
2826	29c Keystone Cops	1.10	.30	
2827	29c Theda Bara	1.10	.30	
2828	29c Buster Keaton	1.10	.30	
a.	Block of 10, #2819-2828	11.00	4.00	
b.	As "a," black (litho.) omitted	—		
c.	As "a," red, black & bright violet (litho.) omitted	—		
2829	29c Lily	.60	.20	
2830	29c Zinnia	.60	.20	
2831	29c Gladiola	.60	.20	
2832	29c Marigold	.60	.20	
2833	29c Rose	.60	.20	
a.	Booklet pane of 5, #2829-2833	3.00	2.25	
b.	As "a," imperf.	*800.00*		
c.	As "a," black (engr.) omitted	*225.00*		

2838a

2837

2839

2841a

2840

2843-2847

Scott No.	Description	Unused Value	Used Value	/ / / / / /
2834	29c World Cup Soccer	.60	.20	☐☐☐☐☐
2835	40c World Cup Soccer	.80	.20	☐☐☐☐☐
2836	50c World Cup Soccer	1.00	.20	☐☐☐☐☐
2837	World Cup Soccer, Sheet of 3, #a.-c. (like #2834-2836)	4.00	3.00	☐☐☐☐☐
2838	World War II, block of 10 (2765)	18.00	10.00	☐☐☐☐☐
a.-j.	29c Any single	1.80	.50	☐☐☐☐☐
2839	29c Norman Rockwell	.60	.20	☐☐☐☐☐
2840	Norman Rockwell, sheet of 4	4.50	2.75	☐☐☐☐☐
a.	50c Freedom from Want	1.10	.65	☐☐☐☐☐
b.	50c Freedom from Fear	1.10	.65	☐☐☐☐☐
c.	50c Freedom of Speech	1.10	.65	☐☐☐☐☐
d.	50c Freedom of Worship	1.10	.65	☐☐☐☐☐
2841	Moon Landing, sheet of 12	11.00	—	☐☐☐☐☐
a.	29c Single stamp	.90	.60	☐☐☐☐☐
2842	$9.95 Moon Landing	20.00	16.00	☐☐☐☐☐
2843	29c Hudson's General	.70	.20	☐☐☐☐☐
2844	29c McQueen's Jupiter	.70	.20	☐☐☐☐☐
2845	29c Eddy's No. 242	.70	.20	☐☐☐☐☐
2846	29c Ely's No. 10	.70	.20	☐☐☐☐☐
2847	29c Buchanan's No. 999	.70	.20	☐☐☐☐☐
a.	Booklet pane of 5, #2843-2847	3.50	2.00	☐☐☐☐☐
b.	As "a," imperf.	*2,500.*		☐☐☐☐☐
2848	29c George Meany	.60	.20	☐☐☐☐☐
2849	29c Al Jolson	.75	.20	☐☐☐☐☐
2850	29c Bing Crosby	.75	.20	☐☐☐☐☐
2851	29c Ethel Waters	.75	.20	☐☐☐☐☐
2852	29c Nat "King" Cole	.75	.20	☐☐☐☐☐
2853	29c Ethel Merman	.75	.20	☐☐☐☐☐
a.	Vert. strip of 5, #2849-2853	3.75	2.00	☐☐☐☐☐
b.	Pane of 20, imperf.	*4,600.*		☐☐☐☐☐
2854	29c Bessie Smith	1.60	.20	☐☐☐☐☐
2855	29c Muddy Waters	1.60	.20	☐☐☐☐☐
2856	29c Billie Holiday	1.60	.20	☐☐☐☐☐
2857	29c Robert Johnson	1.60	.20	☐☐☐☐☐
2858	29c Jimmy Rushing	1.60	.20	☐☐☐☐☐
2859	29c "Ma" Rainey	1.60	.20	☐☐☐☐☐
2860	29c Mildred Bailey	1.60	.20	☐☐☐☐☐
2861	29c Howlin' Wolf	1.60	.20	☐☐☐☐☐
a.	Block of 8, #2854-2861 +2 additional stamps	16.00	4.50	☐☐☐☐☐
2862	29c James Thurber	.75	.20	☐☐☐☐☐
2863	29c Motorboat	.75	.20	☐☐☐☐☐
2864	29c Ship	.75	.20	☐☐☐☐☐
2865	29c Ship's Wheel	.75	.20	☐☐☐☐☐

2854-2861

2849-2853

2842

2848

2862

2863-2866

2951-2954

2867

2868

2871

2872

2869

2873

2874

2876

Scott No.		Description	Unused Value	Used Value
2866	29c	Coral	.75	.20
a.		Block of 4, #2963-2966	3.00	1.50
b.		As "a," imperf	*1,000.*	
2867	29c	Black-necked Crane	.70	.20
2868	29c	Whooping Crane	.70	.20
a.		Pair, #2867-2868	1.40	.75
b.		Black and magenta (engr.) omitted	*1,650.*	
c.		As "a," double impression of engr. black (Birds' names and "USA") & magenta ("29")	*5,000.*	
d.		As "a," double impression of engr. black ("USA") & magenta ("29")	—	
2869		Legends of the West, pane of 20	15.00	10.00
a.-t.	29c	Any single	.75	.50
u.		As No. 2869, a.-e. imperf, f.-j. part perf.	—	
2870	29c	Legends of the West (2869), pane of 20	*275.00*	—
		Nos. 2869 and 2870 have different Bill Pickett stamps. Framelines on No. 2870 are thinner than on No. 2869.		
2871	29c	Christmas - Religious, perf. 11¼	.70	.20
2871A	29c	Christmas-Religious, perf. 9¾ x 11 (2871)	.60	.20
b.		Booklet Pane of 10	6.25	3.50
c.		Imperf. pair	*475.00*	
2872	29c	Christmas - Stocking	.60	.20
a.		Booklet pane of 20	12.50	4.00
b.		Imperf., pair	—	
c.		As "a," imperf horiz.	—	
d.		Quadruple impression of black, triple impression of blue, double impression of red and yellow, green normal...	—	
e.		Vert. pair, imperf. btwn.	—	
2873	29c	Christmas - Santa Claus	.70	.20
a.		Booklet pane of 12	8.50	
b.		Coil with plate #V1111	—	6.00
2874	29c	Christmas - Cardinal	.60	.20
a.		Booklet pane of 18	11.00	
2875	$2	Bureau of Engraving & Printing, Sheet of 4, perf. 11	16.00	13.50
a.		Single stamp (like No. 262)	4.00	2.00
2876	29c	Year of the Boar	.70	.20
2877	(3c)	Dove, tan, brt bl & red, thin inscript.	.20	.20
a.		Imperf., pair	*135.00*	
b.		Double impression of red	*190.00*	
2878	(3c)	Dove (2877), tan, dk blue & red, heavy inscriptions	.20	.20
2879	(20c)	Flag, black "G," yellow & multi	.40	.20

Scott No.		Description	Unused Value	Used Value	/ / / / / /
a.		Imperf pair	—		
2880	(20c)	Flag (2879), red "G," yellow & multi	.75	.20	
2881	(32c)	Flag, black "G" & multi, perf 11.2 x 11.1	1.25	.20	
a.		Booklet pane of 10	12.50	5.00	
2882	(32c)	Flag (2881), red "G" & multi	.60	.20	

Distance on No. 2882 from bottom of red G to top of flag immediately above is 13¾mm, on No. 2885 13½mm.

Booklet stamps

2883	(32c)	Flag (2881), black "G" & multi, perf.10 x 9.9	.65	.20	
a.		Booklet pane of 10	6.50	3.75	
2884	(32c)	Flag (2881), blue "G" & multi	.65	.20	
a.		Booklet pane of 10	6.50	3.75	
b.		As "a," imperf.	*1,700.*		
2885	(32c)	Flag (2881), red "G" & multi	.90	.20	
a.		Booklet pane of 10	9.00	4.50	
b.		Pair, imperf. vert.	—		
c.		Pair, imperf. btwn.	—		

Self-adhesive, Die Cut

2886	(32c)	Flag (2881), gray, blue, light blue, red & black	.75	.20	
a.		Booklet pane of 18	14.00		
b.		Coil with plate #V1111	—	10.00	
2887	(32c)	Flag (2881), black, blue & red	.75	.20	
a.		Booklet pane of 18	13.50		

No. 2886 has a small number of blue shading dots in white stripes immediately below the blue field. No. 2887 has noticeable blue shading.

1994-95, Coil Stamps, Perf. 9.8 Vert.

2888	(25c)	Flag, blue & multi	.90	.50	
2889	(32c)	Flag (2881), black "G" & multi	1.50	.20	
a.		Imperf., pair	*275.00*		
2890	(32c)	Flag (2881), blue "G" & multi	.65	.20	
2891	(32c)	Flag (2881), red "G" & multi	.85	.20	

Rouletted 9.8 Vert.

2892	(32c)	Flag (2881), red "G" & multi	.75	.20	

Perf. 9.8 Vert.

2893	(5c)	Flag, green & multi (Bureau precancel)	.50	.20	

1995

2897	32c	Flag over Porch	.65	.20	
a.		Imperf., vert. pair	*60.00*		

Coil Stamps

2902	(5c)	Butte, perf.	.20	.20	
a.		Imperf., pair	600.00		
2902B	(5c)	Butte (2902), Serpentine Die Cut Vert.	.35	.20	
2903	(5c)	Mountain, perf, purple & multi	.25	.20	
2904	(5c)	Mountain (2903), perf, blue & multi	.20	.20	

2875

2877

2879

2881

2888

2893

2897

2902

2905

2907

2908

2911

2919

2933

2934

2938

2940

2941

2942

2943

2948

2949

Scott No.		Description	Unused Value	Used Value
c.		Imperf., pair....................................	400.00	
2904A	(5c)	Mountain (2903), Serpentine Die Cut Vert., 11.2 Vert., purple & multi...	.20	.20
2904B	(5c)	Mountain (2903), Serpentine Die cut 9.8 vert.	.20	.20
2905	(10c)	Auto, perf., small "1995" date	.20	.20
a.		Large "1995" date..........................	.20	.20
b.		As "a," brown omitted, P#S33 single		—
2906	(10c)	Auto (2905), Serpentine Die Cut Vert.	.50	.20
2907	(10c)	Eagle and Shield (2603), Serpentine Die Cut Vert., gold & multi	.75	.20
2908	(15c)	Auto Tail Fin, perf., dk org yel & multi	.30	.30
2909	(15c)	Auto Tail Fin (2908), perf., buff & multi	.30	.30
2910	(15c)	Auto Tail Fin (2908), Serpentine Die Cut Vert., buff & multi	.30	.30

No. 2908 has dark bold colors and heavy shading lines, and heavily shaded chrome. No. 2909 has shinier chrome, more subdued colors and finer details.

Scott No.		Description	Unused Value	Used Value
2911	(25c)	Juke Box, dark red, dark yellow green & multi, perf.	.50	.50
a.		Imperf., pair....................................	*425.00*	
2912	(25c)	Juke Box (2911), brt org red, brt yel grn & multi, perf..........................	.50	.50
2912A	(25c)	Juke Box (2911), brt org red, brt yel grn & multi, Serpentine Die Cut 11.5 Vert.	.50	.50

No. 2911 has dark saturated colors, dark blue lines in music selection board, No. 2912 has bright colors, less shading and light blue lines in music selection board.

Scott No.		Description	Unused Value	Used Value
2912B	(25c)	Juke Box (2911) perf. 9.8 Vert......	.75	.50
2913	32c	Flag (2897), blue, tan, brown, red & lt blue, perf. 9.8 vert.	.65	.20
a.		Imperf., pair....................................	30.00	
2914	32c	Flag (2897), blue, yellow brown, red & gray, perf. 9.8 vert.	.80	.20

No. 2913 has light blue shading in flag, No. 2914 has pale gray shading.

Self-Adhesive, Serpentine Die Cut Vert.

Scott No.		Description	Unused Value	Used Value
2915	32c	Flag (2897), cut 8.7 vert.	1.25	.30
2915A	32c	Flag (2897), cut 9.8 vert., 10 or 11 "peaks" on each side....................	.65	.20
h.		Imperf., pair....................................	32.50	
i.		Tan omitted		*2,000.*
j.		Double die cutting..........................	30.00	
2915B	32c	Flag (2897), cut 11.5 vert.	1.00	*.90*
2915C	32c	Flag (2897), cut 10.9 vert.	2.00	.40
2915D	32c	Flag (2897), cut 9.8 vert., 9 and/or 10 "peaks" on each side	2.00	*.90*

Booklet Stamps, Perf. 10.8 x 9.8 on 2 or 3 sides

Scott No.		Description	Unused Value	Used Value
2916	32c	Flag (2897), blue, tan, brn, red & lt blue	.65	.20
a.		Booklet pane of 10.........................	6.50	3.25

2950

2955

2956

2967

2975

Scott No.		Description	Unused Value	Used Value	/ / / / / /
b.		As "a," imperf.	—		☐☐☐☐☐
Self-Adhesive					
2919	32c	Flag over Field, Die Cut	.65	.20	☐☐☐☐☐
a.		Booklet pane of 18	12.00		☐☐☐☐☐
b.		Vert. pair, no die cutting btwn.	—		☐☐☐☐☐
2920	32c	Flag (2897), large date, Serpentine Die Cut 8.7	.65	.20	☐☐☐☐☐
a.		Booklet pane of 20 + label	13.00		☐☐☐☐☐
b.		Small date	6.00	.35	☐☐☐☐☐
c.		As "b," booklet pane of 20 + label.	*120.00*		☐☐☐☐☐
f.		As No. 2920, pane of 15 + label	*10.00*		☐☐☐☐☐
h.		As No. 2920, booklet pane of 15	*50.00*		☐☐☐☐☐
i.		As No. 2920, imperf pair	—		☐☐☐☐☐
j.		Dark blue omitted (from #2920a)	*1,750.*		☐☐☐☐☐
k.		Vert. pair, die cutting missing btwn. (from perf. shift) (from No. 2920a)	—		☐☐☐☐☐
2920D	32c	Flag, Large date, Serpentine die cut 11.3 (2897)	.80	.25	☐☐☐☐☐
e.		Booklet pane of 10	8.00		☐☐☐☐☐
2921	32c	Flag (2897), dk blue, tan, brn, red & lt bl, Serpentine Die Cut 9.8 on 2 or 3 sides	.90	.20	☐☐☐☐☐
a.		Booklet pane of 10, dated red "1996"	9.00		☐☐☐☐☐
b.		As #2921, dated red "1997"	.75	.20	☐☐☐☐☐
c.		As "a," dated red "1997"	7.50		☐☐☐☐☐
d.		Booklet pane of 5 + label, dated red "1997"	7.00		☐☐☐☐☐
e.		As "a," die cutting omitted.	*200.00*		☐☐☐☐☐
1995-96 Great Americans					
2933	32c	Milton S. Hershey	.65	.20	☐☐☐☐☐
2934	32c	Cal Farley	.65	.25	☐☐☐☐☐
2935	32c	Henry R. Luce	.65	.35	☐☐☐☐☐
2936	32c	Lila and Dewitt Wallace, blue	.65	.35	☐☐☐☐☐
a.	32c	Light blue	.65	.35	☐☐☐☐☐
2938	46c	Ruth Benedict	.90	.30	☐☐☐☐☐
2940	55c	Dr. Alice Hamilton	1.10	.20	☐☐☐☐☐
a.		Imperf., pair	—		☐☐☐☐☐
2941	55c	Justin S. Morrill, Self-adhesive	1.10	.20	☐☐☐☐☐
2942	77c	Mary Breckinridge, Self-adhesive	1.50	.40	☐☐☐☐☐
2943	78c	Alice Paul, bright violet	1.60	.20	☐☐☐☐☐
a.	78c	Dull violet	1.60	.25	☐☐☐☐☐
b.	78c	Pale violet	1.75	.30	☐☐☐☐☐
Perf. 11.2					
2948	(32c)	Love	.65	.20	☐☐☐☐☐
Self-Adhesive					
2949	(32c)	Love	.65	.20	☐☐☐☐☐
a.		Booklet pane of 20 + label	13.00		☐☐☐☐☐
b.		Red (engr.) omitted	*275.00*		☐☐☐☐☐
c.		As "a," red (engr.) omitted	*5,500.*		☐☐☐☐☐
d.		Red (engr.) missing (from a color			

2999

3001

2976-2979

2980

2998

2981

Scott No.		Description	Unused Value	Used Value
		misregistration)	—	
2950	32c	Florida Statehood	.65	.20
2951	32c	Earth in Tub	.65	.20
2952	32c	Solar Energy	.65	.20
2953	32c	Tree Planting	.65	.20
2954	32c	Beach Clean-up	.65	.20
a.		Block of 4, #2951-2954	2.60	1.75
2955	32c	Richard M. Nixon	.65	.20
a.		Red (engr.) missing (from a color misregistration)	*950.00*	
2956	32c	Bessie Coleman	.85	.20
2957	32c	Love	.65	.20
2958	55c	Love	1.10	.20
Booklet stamps				
2959	32c	Love (2957), Perf 9.8 x 10.8	.65	.20
a.		Booklet pane of 10	6.50	3.25
b.		Imperf., pair	*100.00*	
Self-Adhesive				
2960	55c	Love	1.10	.20
a.		Booklet pane of 20 + label	22.50	
1995				
2961	32c	Volleyball	.65	.20
2962	32c	Softball	.65	.20
2963	32c	Bowling	.65	.20
2964	32c	Tennis	.65	.20
2965	32c	Golf	.65	.20
a.		Vert. strip of 5, #2961-2965	3.25	2.00
b.		As "a," imperf.	*2,250.*	
c.		As "a," yellow omitted	*2,000.*	
d.		As "a," yellow, blue & mag. omitted	*2,000.*	
2966	32c	Prisoners of War & Missing in Action	.65	.20
2967	32c	Marilyn Monroe	.85	.20
a.		Imperf., pair	*400.00*	
2968	32c	Texas Statehood	.75	.20
2969	32c	Split Rock Lighthouse	1.25	.30
2970	32c	St. Joseph Lighthouse	1.25	.30
2971	32c	Spectacle Reef Lighthouse	1.25	.30
2972	32c	Marblehead Lighthouse	1.25	.30
2973	32c	Thirty Mile Point Lighthouse	1.25	.30
a.		Booklet pane of 5, #2969-2973	6.25	*3.00*
2974	32c	United Nations	.65	.20
2975		Civil War, pane of 20	35.00	17.50
a.-t.	32c	Any single	1.50	.60
u.		As No. 2975, a-e imperf. f-j. part perf., others perf.	—	
v.		As No. 2975, k-t. imperf. f-j. part perf., others perf.	—	
w.		As No. 2975, imperf.	*1,500.*	
x.		Block of 9 (f-h, k-m, p-r) k-l & p-q		

2983-2992

3003

3002

3012

3013

2993-2997

Scott No.		Description	Unused Value	Used Value
		imperf. vert.	—	
y.		As No. 2975, a-b perf., c, f-h part perf., others imperf.	—	
z.		As No. 2975, o. & t. imperf., j., n. & s. part perf., others perf.	—	
2976	32c	Carousel Horses, upper left	.65	.20
2977	32c	Carousel Horses, upper right	.65	.20
2978	32c	Carousel Horses, lower left	.65	.20
2979	32c	Carousel Horses, lower right	.65	.20
a.		Block of 4, #2976-2979	2.60	2.00
2980	32c	Woman Suffrage	.65	.20
a.		Black (engr.) omitted	*375.00*	
b.		Imperf., pair	*1,250.*	
c.		Vert. pair, imperf. btwn. and at bottom	*750.00*	
2981		World War II, block of 10	15.00	7.50
a.-j.	32c	Any single	1.50	.50
2982	32c	Louis Armstrong, white denomination (2984)	.90	.25
2983	32c	Coleman Hawkins	2.25	.20
2984	32c	Louis Armstrong, black denom.	2.25	.20
2985	32c	James P. Johnson	2.25	.20
2986	32c	Jelly Roll Morton	2.25	.20
2987	32c	Charlie Parker	2.25	.20
2988	32c	Eubie Blake	2.25	.20
2989	32c	Charles Mingus	2.25	.20
2990	32c	Thelonious Monk	2.25	.20
2991	32c	John Coltrane	2.25	.20
2992	32c	Erroll Garner	2.25	.20
a.		Vertical block of 10, #2983-2992	23.00	7.50
b.		Pane of 20, dark blue omitted	—	
c.		Imperf., pair of Nos. 2991-2992	—	
2993	32c	Aster	.65	.20
2994	32c	Chrysanthemum	.65	.20
2995	32c	Dahlia	.65	.20
2996	32c	Hydrangea	.65	.20
2997	32c	Rudbeckia	.65	.20
a.		Booklet pane of 5, #2993-2997	3.25	2.25
b.		As "a," imperf.	*2,750.*	
2998	60c	Eddie Rickenbacker, small "1995" date	1.40	.50
a.	60c	Large "1995" date	2.00	.50
2999	32c	Republic of Palau	.65	.20
3000		Comic Strips, pane of 20	13.00	10.00
a.-t.	32c	Any single	.65	.50
u.		As No. 3000 a.-h. imperf., i.-l. part perf	—	
v.		As No. 3000 m.-t. imperf., i.-l. part perf	—	
w.		As No. 3000 a.-l. imperf., m.-t. imperf. vertically	—	
x.		As No. 3000, imperf	—	
3001	32c	Naval Academy	.65	.20

3000

3030

3032

3033

3036

3051

3052

Scott No.		Description	Unused Value	Used Value
3002	32c	Tennessee Williams	.65	.20
3003	32c	Christmas - Religious, perf. 11.2	.65	.20
c.		Blk (engr., denomination) omitted	*200.00*	
3003A	32c	Christmas -Religious, Perf. 9.8 x 10.9 from bklt pane (3003)	.65	.20
b.		Booklet pane of 10	6.50	4.00
3004	32c	Christmas - Santa, Chimney	.70	.20
3005	32c	Christmas - Child, Jumping Jack	.70	.20
3006	32c	Christmas - Child, Tree	.70	.20
3007	32c	Christmas - Santa, Sled	.70	.20
a.		Block or strip of 4	2.80	1.25
b.		Booklet pane of 10, 3 ea. #3004-3005, 2 ea. #3006-3007	8.00	4.00
c.		Booklet pane of 10, 2 ea. #3004-3005, 3 ea. #3006-3007	8.00	4.00
d.		As "a," imperf.	*475.00*	
e.		As "b," miscut and inserted upside down into booklet cover, with full bottom selvage.	—	

Booklet stamps, self-adhesive, Serpentine Die Cut

Scott No.		Description	Unused Value	Used Value
3008	32c	Christmas - Santa, Sled (3007)	.95	.20
3009	32c	Christmas - Child, Jumping Jack (3005)	.95	.20
3010	32c	Christmas - Santa, Chimney (3004)	.95	.20
3011	32c	Christmas - Child, Tree (3006)	.95	.20
a.		Booklet pane of 20, 5 ea. #3008-3011 + label	19.00	—
3012	32c	Christmas - Angel	.65	.20
a.		Booklet pane of 20 + label	13.00	—
b.		Vert. pair, no die cutting btwn.	—	
c.		Booklet pane of 15 + label, 1996	13.00	
d.		Booklet pane of 15	*30.00*	
3013	32c	Christmas - Children Sledding	.65	.20
a.		Booklet pane of 18	12.00	

Coil stamps, Serpentine Die Cut Vert.

Scott No.		Description	Unused Value	Used Value
3014	32c	Christmas - Santa, Sled (3007)	2.75	.30
3015	32c	Christmas - Child, Jumping Jack (3005)	2.75	.30
3016	32c	Christmas - Santa, Chimney (3004)	2.75	.30
3017	32c	Christmas - Child, Tree (3006)	2.75	.30
a.		Strip of 4, #3014-3017	11.00	
3018	32c	Christmas - Angel (3012)	1.10	.30
3019	32c	1893 Duryea	.90	.20
3020	32c	1894 Haynes	.90	.20
3021	32c	1898 Columbia	.90	.20
3022	32c	1899 Winton	.90	.20
3023	32c	1901 White	.90	.20
a.		Vert. or horiz. strip of 5, #3019-3023	4.50	2.00

1996 Issues

Scott No.		Description	Unused Value	Used Value
3024	32c	Utah Statehood	.75	.20

3019-3023

3004-3007

3024

3058

3025-3029

3059

3060

Scott No.		Description	Unused Value	Used Value
3025	32c	Crocus	.75	.20
3026	32c	Winter Aconite	.75	.20
3027	32c	Pansy	.75	.20
3028	32c	Snowdrop	.75	.20
3029	32c	Anemone	.75	.20
a.		Booklet pane of 5, #3025-3029	3.75	2.50
b.		As "a," imperf.	—	
Serpentine Die Cut 11.3, Self-adhesive				
3030	32c	Love	.65	.20
a.		Booklet pane of 20 + label	13.00	
b.		Booklet pane of 15 + label	10.00	
c.		Red (engr. "Love") omitted	*175.00*	
d.		Red (engr. "Love") missing (from a color misregistration)	—	
e.		Double impression of red (engr. "Love")	—	
f.		Die cutting omitted, pair	*275.00*	
g.		As "a," stamp 1-5 double impression of red (engr. "Love")	—	
Serpentine Die Cut				
3031	1c	American Kestrel, self-adhesive (2477)	.20	.20
3031A		American Kestrel, blue inscription and year	.20	.20
b.		Die cutting omitted, pair	—	
1996-98				
3032	2c	Red-headed Woodpecker	.20	.20
3033	3c	Eastern Bluebird with cent sign	.20	.20
3036	$1	Red Fox, self-adhesive, serp. die cut 11½ x 11¼	2.00	.50
a.		Serpentine die cut 11¾ x 11	2.75	.50
Coil Stamp, Perf. 9¾ Vert.				
3044	1c	American Kestrel (2477) with cent sign, small date	.20	.20
a.		Large date,	.20	.20
3045	2c	Red-headed Woodpecker, Coil	.20	.20
Serpentine Die Cut 10½ x 10¾, Booklet Stamp, Self-Adhesive				
3048	20c	Blue Jay (2483)	.40	.20
a.		Booklet pane of 10	4.00	
b.		Booklet pane of 4	25.00	
c.		Booklet pane of 6	40.00	
3049	32c	Rose, serp. die cut 11¼ x 11¾ (2490)	.65	.20
a.		Booklet pane of 20 + label	13.00	
b.		Booklet pane of 4	2.60	
c.		Booklet pane of 5 + label	3.50	
d.		Booklet pane of 6	6.00	
3050	20c	Ring-necked Pheasant, serp. die cut 11.25	.60	.20
a.		Booklet pane of 10	6.00	
b.		Serp. die cut 11	1.75	.20

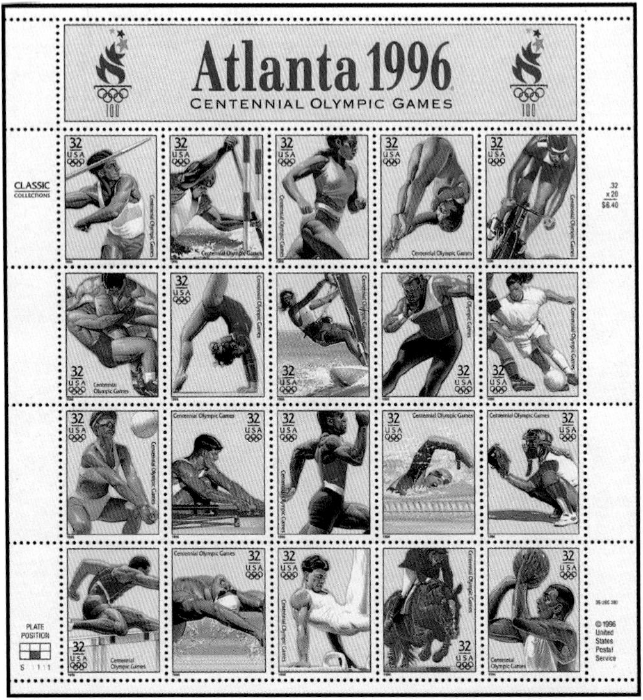

3068

3065

3061-3064

3066

Scott No.		Description	Unused Value	Used Value	/ / / / / /
c.		As "b," booklet pane of 10, all stamps upright	20.00		□□□□□
3051	20c	Ring-Necked Pheasant, serp. die cut 10.5 x 11, self-adhesive bklt. stamps (3050)	.75	.20	□□□□□
3051A	20c	Ring-Necked Pheasant, serp. die cut 10.6 x 10.4	6.00	.50	□□□□□
b.		Booklet pane of 5, 4 #3051, 1 #3051A turned sideways at top.	9.00		□□□□□
c.		Booklet pane of 5, 4 #3051, 1 #3051A turned sideways at bottom	9.00		□□□□□
Booklet Stamp, Serpentine Die Cut 11½ x 11¼					
3052	33c	Coral Pink Rose, serp. die cut 11.5 x 11.25	.90	.20	□□□□□
a.		Booklet pane of 4	3.60		□□□□□
b.		Booklet pane of 5 + label	4.50		□□□□□
c.		Booklet pane of 6	5.50		□□□□□
d.		Booklet pane of 20 + label	17.50		□□□□□
i.		Die cutting omitted, pair	—		□□□□□
Serpentine Die Cut 10¾ x 10½ on 2 or 3 sides, Booklet Stamp					
3052E	33c	Coral Pink Rose (3052)	.80	.20	□□□□□
f.		Booklet pane of 20	16.00		□□□□□
g.		Black ("33 USA," etc.) omitted	375.00		□□□□□
h.		As "f," all 12 stamps on one side with black ("33 USA," etc.) omitted	—		□□□□□
i.		Horiz. pair, die cutting omitted btwn.	—		□□□□□
Coil Stamp, Serpentine Die Cut 11½ Vert.					
3053	20c	Blue Jay (2483)	.50	.20	□□□□□
3054	32c	Yellow Rose, serp. die cut 9.75 vert.	.65	.20	□□□□□
a.		Die cutting omitted, pair	*85.00*		□□□□□
b.		Black, yellow & green omitted	—		□□□□□
c.		As "b," die cutting omitted, pair	—		□□□□□
d.		Black omitted	—		□□□□□
e.		As "d," die cutting omitted, pair	—		□□□□□
f.		All colors omitted, die cutting omitted	—		□□□□□
g.		Pair, die cutting omitted, containing one stamp each of "c" and "e"	—		□□□□□
3055	20c	Ring-Necked Pheasant, serp. die cut 9.75 vert. (3051)	.40	.20	□□□□□
a.		Die cutting omitted, pair	*150.00*		□□□□□
1996					
3058	32c	Ernest E. Just	.65	.20	□□□□□
3059	32c	Smithsonian Institution	.65	.20	□□□□□
3060	32c	Chinese New Year - Year of the Rat	.90	.20	□□□□□
a.		Imperf., pair	*725.00*		□□□□□
3061	32c	Eadweard Muybridge	.65	.20	□□□□□
3062	32c	Ottmar Mergenthaler	.65	.20	□□□□□
3063	32c	Frederic E. Ives	.65	.20	□□□□□

3067

3069

3070

3072-3076

3077-3080

3081

3082

3087

3088

3083-3086

3090

3095

3096-3099

3100-3103

3104

3106

3105

3107

3117

3108-3111

3118

Scott No.		Description	Unused Value	Used Value
3064	32c	William Dickson	.65	.20
a.		Block or strip of 4, #3061-3064	2.60	2.00
3065	32c	Fulbright Scholarship	.75	.20
3066	50c	Jacqueline Cochran	1.00	.40
a.		Black (engr.) omitted	55.00	
3067	32c	Marathon	.65	.20
3068		Olympic Games, pane of 20	14.00	10.00
a.-t.		Any single	.70	.50
u.		As. No. 3068, imperf.	*1,000.*	
v.		As No. 3068, back inscriptions omitted on a., f., k. & p., incorrect back inscriptions on others	—	
w.		As No. 3068, e. imperf., d., i.-j. part perf., all others perf.	—	
3069	32c	Georgia O'Keeffe	.85	.20
a.		Imperf., pair	*125.00*	
3070	32c	Tennessee Statehood, perf.	.65	.20
3071	32c	Tennessee Statehood (3070), serpentine die cut	.75	.30
a.		Booklet pane of 20	15.00	
b.		Horiz. pair, no die cutting btwn.	—	—
c.		Die cutting omitted, pair	—	
d.		Horiz. pair, die cutting omitted vert.	—	—
3072	32c	Fancy Dance	1.00	.20
3073	32c	Butterfly Dance	1.00	.20
3074	32c	Traditional Dance	1.00	.20
3075	32c	Raven Dance	1.00	.20
3076	32c	Hoop Dance	1.00	.20
a.		Strip of 5, #3072-3076	5.00	2.50
3077	32c	Eohippus	.65	.20
3078	32c	Woolly Mammoth	.65	.20
3079	32c	Mastodon	.65	.20
3080	32c	Saber-tooth Cat	.65	.20
a.		Block or Strip of 5, #3077-3080	2.60	2.00
3081	32c	Breast Cancer Awareness	.65	.20
3082	32c	James Dean	.65	.20
a.		Imperf., pair	*150.00*	
b.		As "a," red (USA 32c) missing (from a color misregistration) and tan (James Dean) omitted	—	
c.		As "a," tan (James Dean) omitted	—	
d.		As "a," top stamp red missing (from a color misregistration) and tan (James Dean) omitted, bottom stamp tan omitted	—	
e.		As No. 3082, pane of 20, right two columns perf., left three columns imperf.	*1,750.*	
3083	32c	Mighty Casey	.65	.20
3084	32c	Paul Bunyan	.65	.20

3119

3120

3121

3123

3124

3125

3126

3127

3130-3131

3134

3137

3139a

3143-3146

3140a

3141

3151

3152

Scott No.		Description	Unused Value	Used Value
3085	32c	John Henry	.65	.20
3086	32c	Pecos Bill	.65	.20
a.		Block or Strip of 5, #3083-3086	2.60	2.00
3087	32c	Centennial Olympic Games	.80	.20
3088	32c	Iowa Statehood, perf.	.80	.20
3089	32c	Iowa Statehood, self-adhesive (3088)	.70	.30
a.		Booklet pane of 20	14.00	
3090	32c	Rural Free Delivery, Centenary	.65	.20
3091	32c	Riverboats - "Robert E. Lee"	.65	.20
3092	32c	Riverboats - "Sylvan Dell"	.65	.20
3093	32c	Riverboats - "Far West"	.65	.20
3094	32c	Riverboats - "Rebecca Everingham"	.65	.20
3095	32c	Riverboats - "Bailey Gatzert"	.65	.20
a.		Vertical strip of 5, #3091-3095	3.25	
b.		Strip of 5, #3091-3095, with special die cutting	75.00	50.00
3096	32c	Count Basie	.75	.20
3097	32c	Tommy and Jimmy Dorsey	.75	.20
3098	32c	Glenn Miller	.75	.20
3099	32c	Benny Goodman	.75	.20
a.		Block or Strip of 4, #3096-3099	3.00	2.00
3100	32c	Harold Arlen	.75	.20
3101	32c	Johnny Mercer	.75	.20
3102	32c	Dorothy Fields	.75	.20
3103	32c	Hoagy Carmichael	.75	.20
a.		Block or Strip of 4, #3100-3103	3.00	2.00
3104	23c	F. Scott Fitzgerald	.55	.20
3105		Endangered Species, Pane of 15	10.50	8.00
a.-o.	32c	Any single	.70	.50
3106	32c	Computer Technology	.65	.20
3107	32c	Christmas - Madonna and Child	.65	.20
3108	32c	Christmas - Family at Fireplace	.65	.20
3109	32c	Christmas - Decorating Tree	.65	.20
3110	32c	Christmas - Dreaming of Santa Claus	.65	.20
3111	32c	Christmas - Holiday Shopping	.65	.20
a.		Block or Strip of 4, #3108-3111	2.60	1.75

Serpentine Die Cut 10, Self-Adhesive Booklet Stamps

Scott No.		Description	Unused Value	Used Value
3112	32c	Christmas - Madonna and Child (3107)	.75	.20
a.		Booklet pane of 20 + label	15.00	
b.		Die cutting omitted, pair	60.00	
c.		As "a," die cutting omitted	—	
3113	32c	Christmas - Family at Fireplace (3108)	.75	.20
3114	32c	Christmas - Decorating Tree (3109)	.75	.20
3115	32c	Christmas - Dreaming of Santa Claus (3110)	.75	.20
3116	32c	Christmas - Holiday Shopping (3111)	.75	.20
a.		Booklet pane of 20, 5 ea. #3113-3116	15.00	
b.		Strip of 4, #3113-3116, die cutting		

Scott No.		Description	Unused Value	Used Value
		omitted	*550.00*	
c.		Block of 6, die cutting omitted	*775.00*	
d.		As "a," die cutting omitted	*2,100.*	
Self-Adhesive, Die Cut				
3117	32c	Christmas - Skaters	.65	.20
a.		Booklet pane of 18	12.00	
3118	32c	Hanukkah	.65	.20
Perf. 11x11.1				
3119		Cycling, Souvenir Sheet of 2,	2.50	2.00
a.	50c	Orange and multi	1.25	1.00
b.	50c	Blue green and multi	1.25	1.00
1997 Issues				
3120	32c	Year of the Ox	.80	.20
3121	32c	Brig. Gen. Benjamin O. Davis, Sr.. self-adhesive	.70	.20
3122	32c	Statue of Liberty, self-adhesive (2599)	.70	.20
a.		Booklet pane of 20 + label	14.00	
b.		Booklet pane of 4	2.80	
c.		Booklet pane of 5 + label	3.75	
d.		Booklet pane of 6	4.25	
h.		As "a," die cutting omitted	—	
3122E	32c	Statue of Liberty, self-adhesive booklet stamp	1.50	.20
f.		Booklet pane of 20 + label	40.00	
g.		Booklet pane of 6	9.00	
3123	32c	Love - Swans, self-adhesive, booklet stamp	.65	.20
a.		Booklet pane of 20 + label	13.00	
b.		Die cutting omitted, pair	*135.00*	
c.		As "a," die cutting omitted	*1,350.*	
d.		As "a," black omitted	—	
3124	55c	Love - Swans, self-adhesive, booklet stamp	1.10	.20
a.		Booklet pane of 20 + label	22.00	
3125	32c	Helping Children Learn, self-adhesive	.65	.20
3126	32c	Merian Prints (citron), self-adhesive, booklet stamp	.65	.20
3127	32c	Merian Prints (pineapple), self-adhesive, booklet stamp	.65	.20
a.		Booklet pane, 10 ea. #3126-3127 + label	13.00	
b.		Pair, #3126-3127	1.30	
c.		Vert. pair, die cutting omitted btwn..	*475.00*	
3128	32c	Merian Botanical Prints, self-adhesive booklet stamp 18.5 x 24mm (3126)	1.00	.20
a.		Perf. 11.2 broken on right	3.00	.25

3153

3154-57

3158-3165

3168-3172

3166

3167

3173

Scott No.		Description	Unused Value	Used Value	/ / / / / /
b.		Booklet pane, 2 ea. #3128-3129 + 3128a	7.00		☐☐☐☐☐
3129	32c	Merian Botanical Prints, self-adhesive booklet stamp 18.5 x 24mm (3127)	1.00	.20	☐☐☐☐☐
a.		Perf. 11.2 broken on right	4.50	.35	☐☐☐☐☐
b.		Booklet pane, 2 ea. #3128-3129 + 3129a	9.00		☐☐☐☐☐
c.		Pair, #3128-3129	2.00		☐☐☐☐☐
3130	32c	Sailing Ship - Pacific '97	.65	.30	☐☐☐☐☐
3131	32c	Stagecoach - Pacific '97	.65	.30	☐☐☐☐☐
a.		Pair, #3130-3131	1.30	.75	☐☐☐☐☐
3132	32c	Juke Box, Imperf Coil (2911)	1.00	.50	☐☐☐☐☐
3133	32c	Flag Over Porch, Linerless Coil, serpentine die cut 9.9 vert. (2897)	1.50	.20	☐☐☐☐☐
3134	32c	Thornton Wilder - Literary Arts	.65	.20	☐☐☐☐☐
3135	32c	Raoul Wallenberg	.65	.20	☐☐☐☐☐
3136		Dinosaurs	10.00	8.00	☐☐☐☐☐
a.-o.	32c	Any single	.65	.50	☐☐☐☐☐
p.		As No. 3136, bottom seven stamps imperf.	*3,750.*		☐☐☐☐☐
q.		As No. 3136, top 8 stamps imperf.	*3,750.*		☐☐☐☐☐
r.		As No. 3136, all colors and tagging missing (from extraneous paper)	—		☐☐☐☐☐
3137		Bugs Bunny, self-adhesive pane of 10, die cutting does not extend through backing	6.75		☐☐☐☐☐
a.	32c	Single stamp	.65	.20	☐☐☐☐☐
b.		Pane of 9 #3137a	6.00		☐☐☐☐☐
c.		Pane of 1 #3137a	.65		☐☐☐☐☐
3138		Bugs Bunny, self-adhesive pane of 10, die cut through backing, right stamp with no die cutting	150.00		☐☐☐☐☐
a.	32c	Single stamp	3.50		☐☐☐☐☐
b.		Pane of 9 #3138a	32.50		☐☐☐☐☐
c.		Pane of 1, no die cutting	110.00		☐☐☐☐☐
3139	$6	Benjamin Franklin - Pacific '97, pane of 12	12.00	9.00	☐☐☐☐☐
a.	50c	Single stamp	1.00	.50	☐☐☐☐☐
3140	$7.20	Washington - Pacific '97, pane of 12	14.50	11.00	☐☐☐☐☐
a.	60c	Single stamp	1.20	.60	☐☐☐☐☐
3141	32c	Marshall Plan, 50th Anniversary	.65	.20	☐☐☐☐☐
3142		Classic American Aircraft, pane of 20	13.00	10.00	☐☐☐☐☐
a.-t.	32c	Any single	.65	.50	☐☐☐☐☐

1997 Perf. 11.2

3143	32c	Bear Bryant	.65	.25	☐☐☐☐☐
3144	32c	Pop Warner	.65	.25	☐☐☐☐☐

3174

3175

3176

3177

3179

3180

3178

3181

3182

3183

3184

Scott No.		Description	Unused Value	Used Value
3145	32c	Vince Lombardi	.65	.25
3146	32c	George Halas	.65	.25
a.		Block or strip of 4, #3143-3146	2.60	—
With Red Bar Above Coach's Name, Perf. 11				
3147	32c	Vince Lombardi	.65	.45
3148	32c	Bear Bryant	.65	.45
3149	32c	Pop Warner	.65	.45
3150	32c	George Halas	.65	.45
1997, July 28 Perf. 10.9x11.1				
3151		American Dolls, pane of 15	13.50	—
a.-o.	32c	Any single	.90	.60
1997, July 31 Perf. 11.1				
3152	32c	Humphrey Bogart (1899-1957)	.85	.20
1997, Aug. 21 Perf. 11.1				
3153	32c	*The Stars And Stripes Forever!*	.65	.20
1997 Perf. 11				
3154	32c	Lily Pons	.75	.20
3155	32c	Richard Tucker	.75	.20
3156	32c	Lawrence Tibbett	.75	.20
3157	32c	Rosa Ponselle	.75	.20
a.		Block or strip of 4, #3154-3157	3.00	2.00
3158	32c	Leopold Stokowski	1.10	.20
3159	32c	Arthur Fiedler	1.10	.20
3160	32c	George Szell	1.10	.20
3161	32c	Eugene Ormandy	1.10	.20
3162	32c	Samuel Barber	1.10	.20
3163	32c	Ferde Grofe	1.10	.20
3164	32c	Charles Ives	1.10	.20
3165	32c	Louis Moreau Gottschalk	1.10	.20
a.		Block of 8, #3158-3165	9.00	4.00
1997, Sept. 15 Perf. 11.2				
3166	32c	Padre Felix Varela (1788-1853)	.65	.20
1997, Sept. 18 Perf. 11.2 x 11.1				
3167	32c	Department Of The Air Force, 50th Anniv.	.65	.20
1997, Sept. 30 Perf. 10.2				
3168	32c	Lon Chaney as The Phantom of the Opera	.75	.20
3169	32c	Bela Lugosi as Dracula	.75	.20
3170	32c	Boris Karloff as Frankenstein's Monster	.75	.20
3171	32c	Boris Karloff as The Mummy	.75	.20
3172	32c	Lon Chaney, Jr. as The Wolf Man	.75	.20
a.		Strip of 5, #3168-3172	3.75	2.25
1997, Oct. 14 Serpentine Die Cut 11.4, Self-Adhesive				
3173	32c	First Supersonic Flight, 50th Anniv.	.65	.20
1997, Oct. 18 Perf. 11.1				

3185

3186

3187

3188

3193-3197

3198-3202

3192

Scott No.		Description	Unused Value	Used Value
3174	32c	Women In Military Service	.65	.20
1996, Oct. 22 Serpentine Die Cut 11, Self-Adhesive				
3175	32c	Kwanzaa	.65	.20
1997 Serpentine Die Cut 9.9 Booklet Stamps, Self-Adhesive				
3176	32c	Madonna and Child, by Sano di Pietro, self-adhesive booklet stamp	.65	.20
a.		Booklet pane of 20 + label	13.00	
Serpentine Die Cut 11.2 x 11.8 on 2, 3 or 4 Sides				
3177	32c	Holly	.65	.20
a.		Booklet pane of 20 + label	13.00	
b.		Booklet pane of 4	2.60	
c.		Booklet pane of 5 + label	3.25	
d.		Booklet pane of 6	3.90	
Souvenir Sheet 1997, Dec. 10 Perf. 11 x 11.1				
3178	$3	Mars Pathfinder	6.00	4.00
a.	$3	Single stamp	5.50	3.00
1998 Issues				
3179	32c	Year of the Tiger	.80	.20
3180	32c	Alpine Skiing	.70	.20
Self-Adhesive				
3181	32c	Madam C.J. Walker (1867-1919), Entrepreneur	.70	.20
Perf. 11.6				
3182		Celebrate The Century, 1900s, pane of 15	12.50	8.50
a.-o.	32c	any single	.80	.65
p.		Engraved red (No. 3182m, Gibson girl) omitted, in pane of 15	*3,000.*	
3183		Celebrate The Century, 1910s, pane of 15	12.50	8.50
a.-o.	32c	any single	.80	.65
p.		Nos. 3183g, 3183l-3183o imperf. in pane of 15	*7,000.*	
3184		Celebrate The Century, 1920s, pane of 15	12.50	8.50
a.-o.	32c	any single	.80	.65
3185	32c	Celebrate The Century, 1930s, pane of 15	12.50	8.50
a.-o.	32c	any single	.80	.65
3186		Celebrate The Century, 1940s, pane of 15	13.00	8.50
a.-o.	33c	any single	.85	.65
3187		Celebrate The Century, 1950s, pane of 15	13.00	8.50
a.-o.	33c	any single	.85	.65
1998-2000, Lithographed, Engraved (#3182m, 3183f, 3184m, 3185b, 3186k, 3187a, 3188c, 3189h), Perf. 11½				
3188		Celebrate The Century, 1960s, pane of 15	13.00	8.50
a.-o.	33c	any single	.85	.65
3189		Celebrate The Century, 1970s,		

3203

3204

3206

3207

3208

3209

3211

3212-3215

3216-3219

3220

3221

Scott No.		Description	Unused Value	Used Value
		pane of 15	13.00	8.50
a.-o.	33c	any single	.85	.65
3190		Celebrate The Century, 1980s, pane of 15	13.00	8.50
a.-o.	33c	any single	.85	.65
3191		Celebrate The Century, 1990s, pane of 15	13.00	8.50
a.-o.	33c	any single	.85	.65
1998, Feb. 15 Perf. 11.2 x 11				
3192	32c	*Remember The Maine*	.70	.20
1998, Mar. 19 Die Cut Perf 11.3, Self-Adhesive				
3193	32c	Southern Magnolia	.65	.20
3194	32c	Blue Paloverde	.65	.20
3195	32c	Yellow Poplar	.65	.20
3196	32c	Prairie Crab Apple	.65	.20
3197	32c	Pacific Dogwood	.65	.20
a.		Strip of 5, #3193-3197	3.25	
b.		As "a," die cutting omitted	—	
1998, Mar. 25 Perf. 10.2 Alexander Calder				
3198	32c	Black Cascade, 13 Verticals, 1959	.65	.20
3199	32c	Untitled, 1965	.65	.20
3200	32c	Rearing Stallion, 1928	.65	.20
3201	32c	Portrait of a Young Man, c. 1945	.65	.20
3202	32c	Un Effet du Japonais, 1945	.65	.20
a.		Strip of 5, #3198-3202	3.25	2.25
1998, Apr. 16 Serpentine Die Cut 11.7 x 10.9, Self-Adhesive				
3203	32c	Cinco De Mayo	.65	.20
1998, Apr. 27 Serpentine Die Cut 11.1, Self-Adhesive				
3204		Sylvester & Tweety, pane of 10	6.75	
a.	32c	any single	.65	.20
b.		Pane of 9 #3204a	6.00	
c.		Pane of 1 #3204a	.65	
3205		Pane of 10, right stamp with no die cutting	12.50	
a.	32c	single	1.00	
b.		Pane of 9 #3205a	*9.00*	
c.		Pane of 1, no die cutting	*2.00*	
1998, May 29 Serpentine Die Cut 10.8 x 10.9, Self-Adhesive				
3206	32c	Wisconsin Statehood	.65	.30
1998, June 5 Perf. 10 Vert., Coil Stamps				
3207	(5c)	Wetlands	.20	.20
3207A	(5c)	Wetlands, small dates, self-adhesive Coil	.20	.20
b.		Large date	.30	.20
3208	(25c)	Diner	.50	.50
3208A	(25c)	Diner, self-adhesive Coil	.50	.50

3222-3225

3230-3234

3226

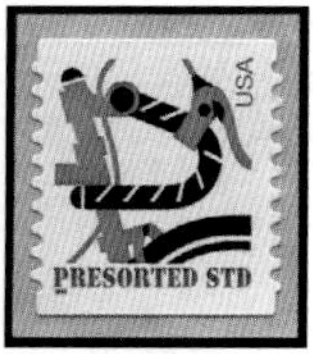

3228

3235

3237

Scott No.		Description	Unused Value	Used Value	/ / / / / /
1998, June 18 Perf. 12 x 12.4					
3209		1898 Trans-Mississippi Stamps, Cent., pane of 9	9.00	7.00	☐☐☐☐☐
a.	1c	green & black	.20	.20	☐☐☐☐☐
b.	2c	red brown & black	.20	.20	☐☐☐☐☐
c.	4c	orange & black	.20	.20	☐☐☐☐☐
d.	5c	blue & black	.20	.20	☐☐☐☐☐
e.	8c	dark lilac & black	.20	.20	☐☐☐☐☐
f.	10c	purple & black	.20	.20	☐☐☐☐☐
g.	50c	green & black	1.25	.60	☐☐☐☐☐
h.	$1	red & black	2.25	1.25	☐☐☐☐☐
i.	$2	red brown & black	4.25	2.50	☐☐☐☐☐
3210	$1	Pane of 9, #3209h	18.00	—	☐☐☐☐☐
1998, June 26 Perf. 11.2					
3211	32c	Berlin Airlift, 50th Anniv.	.65	.20	☐☐☐☐☐
1998, June 26 Perf. 10.1 x 10.2					
3212	32c	Huddie "Leadbelly" Ledbetter (1888-1949)	.75	.20	☐☐☐☐☐
3213	32c	Woody Guthrie (1912-67)	.75	.20	☐☐☐☐☐
3214	32c	Sonny Terry (1911-86)	.75	.20	☐☐☐☐☐
3215	32c	Josh White (1908-69)	.75	.20	☐☐☐☐☐
a.		Block or strip of 4, #3212-3215	3.00	2.00	☐☐☐☐☐
1998, July 15 Perf. 10.1 x 10.3					
3216	32c	Mahalia Jackson (1911-72)	.75	.20	☐☐☐☐☐
3217	32c	Roberta Martin (1917-69)	.75	.20	☐☐☐☐☐
3218	32c	Clara Ward (1924-73)	.75	.20	☐☐☐☐☐
3219	32c	Sister Rosetta Tharpe (1921-73)	.75	.20	☐☐☐☐☐
a.		Block or strip of 4, #3216-3219	3.00	2.00	☐☐☐☐☐
1998, June 26 Perf. 11.2					
3220	32c	La Mision de San Miguel de San Gabriel, Espanola, NM	.65	.20	☐☐☐☐☐
1998, July 22 Perf. 11.2					
3221	32c	Stephen Vincent Benet (1898-43)	.65	.20	☐☐☐☐☐
1998, July 29 Perf. 11.2					
3222	32c	Antillean Euphonia	.65	.20	☐☐☐☐☐
3223	32c	Green-throated Carib	.65	.20	☐☐☐☐☐
3224	32c	Crested Honeycreeper	.65	.20	☐☐☐☐☐
3225	32c	Cardinal Honeyeater	.65	.20	☐☐☐☐☐
a.		Block of 4, #3222-3225	2.60	2.00	☐☐☐☐☐
1998, Aug. 3 Perf. 11.1					
3226	32c	Alfred Hitchcock (1899-1980)	.75	.20	☐☐☐☐☐
1998, Aug. 5 Serpentine Die Cut 11.7, Self-Adhesive					
3227	32c	Organ & Tissue Donation	.65	.20	☐☐☐☐☐
3228	(10c)	Modern Bicycle, self-adhesive Coil, small "1998" year date	.20	.20	☐☐☐☐☐

3238-3242

3236

3243

3244

3245

3246

3247

3248

3257

3259

3260

Scott No.		Description	Unused Value	Used Value	/ / / / / /
a.		Large date	.25	.20	
3229	(10c)	Modern Bicycle coil	.20	.20	
3230	32c	Bright Eyes - Dog, self-adhesive	.75	.20	
3231	32c	Bright Eyes - Fish, self-adhesive	.75	.20	
3232	32c	Bright Eyes - Cat, self-adhesive	.75	.20	
3233	32c	Bright Eyes - Parakeet, self-adhesive	.75	.20	
3234	32c	Bright eyes - Hamster, self-adhesive	.75	.20	
a.		Strip of 5, #3230-3234	3.75		
3235	32c	Klondike Gold Rush Centennial	.65	.20	
3236	32c	American Art, pane of 20	15.00	17.50	
a.-t.		any single	.85	.85	
3237	32c	American Ballet	.65	.20	
3238	32c	Space Discovery - Space City	.65	.20	
3239	32c	Space Discovery - Space ship landing	.65	.20	
3240	32c	Space Discovery - Person in space suit	.65	.20	
3241	32c	Space Discovery - Space ship taking off	.65	.20	
3242	32c	Space Discovery - Large domed structure	.65	.20	
a.		Strip of 5, #3238-3242	3.25	2.25	
3243	32c	Giving and Sharing, self-adhesive	.65	.20	
3244	32c	Christmas - Madonna and Child, self-adhesive booklet stamp	.65	.20	
a.		Booklet pane of 20 + label	13.00		
b.		Die cutting omitted, pair	—		

Size: 22x25mm

Scott No.		Description	Unused Value	Used Value	
3245	32c	Wreath - Evergreen, self-adhesive booklet stamp	6.00	.20	
3246	32c	Wreath - Victorian, self-adhesive booklet stamp	6.00	.20	
3247	32c	Wreath - Chili Pepper, self-adhesive booklet stamp	6.00	.20	
3248	32c	Wreath - Tropical, self-adhesive booklet stamp	6.00	.20	
a.		Booklet pane of 4, #3245-3248	25.00		
b.		Booklet pane of 5, #3245-3246, 3248, 2 #3247 + label	32.50		
c.		Booklet pane of 6, #3247-3248, 2 each #3245-3246	40.00		
d.		As "a," die cutting omitted	—		
e.		As "b," die cutting omitted	—		
f.		As "c," die cutting omitted	—		

Size: 23x30mm

Scott No.		Description	Unused Value	Used Value	
3249	32c	Wreath (Large) - Evergreen, self-adhesive, serp. die cut 11.4 x 11.5	1.75	.20	
a.		Serp. die cut 11.7 x 11.6	2.25	.20	
3250	32c	Wreath (Large) - Victorian, self-adhesive, serp. die cut 11.4 x 11.5	1.75	.20	
a.		Serp. die cut 11.7 x 11.6	2.25	.20	

3261

3262

3272

3273

3274

3275

3276

3277

3283

3286

3270

3287

3288-3292

Scott No.		Description	Unused Value	Used Value	/ / / / / /
3251	32c	Wreath (Large) - Chili Pepper, self-adhesive, serp. die cut 11.4 x 11.5	1.75	.20	□□□□□
a.		Serp. die cut 11.7 x 11.7	2.25	.20	□□□□□
3252	32c	Wreath (Large) - Tropical, self-adhesive, serp. die cut 11.4 x 11.5	1.75	.20	□□□□□
a.		Serp. die cut 11.7 x 11.6	2.25	.20	□□□□□
b.		Block or strip of 4, #3249-3252	7.00		□□□□□
c.		Booklet pane, 5 each #3249-3252	35.00		□□□□□
d.		Block or strip of 4, #3249a-3252a	9.00		□□□□□
e.		Booklet pane, 5 each #3249a-3252a	45.00		□□□□□
f.		Block or strip of 4, red ("Greetings 32 USA" and "1998") omitted on #3249, 3252	*675.00*		□□□□□
g.		Block or strip of 4, #3249-3252, red ("Greetings 32 USA" and "1998") omitted on #3250, #3251	—		□□□□□
h.		As "b," die cutting omitted	—		□□□□□
i.		As "c," die cutting omitted	—		□□□□□
3257	(1c)	Weather Vane, white "USA"	.20	.20	□□□□□
a.		Black omitted	140.00		□□□□□
3258	(1c)	Weather Vane, pale blue "USA"	.20	.20	□□□□□
3259	22c	Uncle Sam, self-adhesive, Die Cut 10.8	.45	.20	□□□□□
a.		Die cut 10, 8 x 10.5	2.50	.25	□□□□□
b.		Vert. pair, #3259 & 3259a	3.50		□□□□□
3260	(33c)	Uncle Sam's Hat	.65	.20	□□□□□
3261	$3.20	Space Shuttle Landing, self-adhesive Priority Mail Rate	6.00	1.50	□□□□□
3262	$11.75	Piggyback Space Shuttle, self-adhesive Express Mail Rate	22.50	10.00	□□□□□
3263	22c	Uncle Sam, self-adhesive Coil	.45	.20	□□□□□
a.		Die cutting omitted, pair	—		□□□□□
3264	(33c)	Uncle Sam's Hat, coil	.65	.20	□□□□□
a.		Imperf., pair	—		□□□□□
3265	(33c)	Uncle Sam's Hat, self-adhesive coil, square corners	.80	.20	□□□□□
a.		Die cutting omitted, pair	70.00	—	□□□□□
b.		Red, omitted	*575.00*		□□□□□
c.		Black omitted	—		□□□□□
d.		Black omitted, die cutting omitted, pair	*575.00*		□□□□□
e.		Red omitted, die cutting omitted, pair	—		□□□□□
3266	(33c)	Uncle Sam's Hat, self-adhesive coil, rounded corners	1.75	.20	□□□□□
3267	(33c)	Uncle Sam's Hat, self-adhesive booklet stamp, serp die cut 9.9	.75	.20	□□□□□
a.		Booklet pane of 10	7.50		□□□□□
3268	(33c)	Uncle Sam's Hat, self-adhesive booklet stamp, serp. die cut 11¼	.75	.20	□□□□□
a.		Booklet pane of 10	7.50		□□□□□
b.		Serpentine die cut 11	.75	.20	□□□□□

3293

3308

3306

3314

3315

3310-3313

3316

Scott No.		Description	Unused Value	Used Value
c.		As "b," booklet pane of 20 + label.	15.00	
3269	(33c)	Uncle Sam's Hat, self-adhesive booklet stamp, serp. die cut 8	.65	.20
a.		Booklet pane of 18	12.00	
3270	(10c)	Eagle & Shield, coil stamp	.20	.20
a.		Large Date,	.45	.20 ...
3271	(10c)	Eagle & Shield, self-adhesive coil, Small Date	.20	.20
a.		Large Date	1.00	.20

1999 Issues

Scott No.		Description	Unused Value	Used Value
3272	33c	Chinese New Year - Year of the Rabbit	.80	.20
3273	33c	Malcolm X - Black Heritage, self-adhesive	.85	.20
3274	33c	Love, self-adhesive booklet stamp	.65	.20
a.		Booklet pane of 20	13.00	
b.		Die cutting omitted, pair	125.00	
c.		As "a," die cutting omitted	*1,250.*	
3275	55c	Love, self-adhesive	1.10	.20
3276	33c	Hospice Care	.65	.20
3277	33c	Flag and City	.70	.20
3278	33c	Flag and City, self-adhesive, serp. die cut 11 (3277)	.65	.20
a.		Booklet pane of 4	2.60	
b.		Booklet pane of 5 + label	3.25	
c.		Booklet pane of 6	3.90	
d.		Booklet pane of 10	12.50	
e.		Booklet pane of 20 + label	17.00	
h.		As "e," die cutting omitted.	—	
i.		Serpentine die cut 11¼	3.00	.20
j.		As "i," booklet pane of 10	30.00	
3278F	33c	Flag and City (3277), self-adhesive, serp. die cut 11½ x 11¾	1.25	.20
g.		Booklet pane of 20 + label	25.00	
3279	33c	Flag and City, self-adhesive booklet stamp, red date	.85	.20
a.		Booklet pane of 10	8.50	
3280	33c	Flag and City, Coil, small date	.65	.20
a.		Large date	1.25	.20
b.		Imperf, pair	—	
3281	33c	Flag and City, self-adhesive coil, square corners, large date	.65	.20
a.		Die cutting omitted, pair	30.00	
b.		Lt. blue and yellow omitted	*300.00*	
c.		Small date	.65	.20
e.		As "c," die cutting omitted, pair	—	
3282	33c	Flag and City, self-adhesive coil,		

3317-3320

3321-3324

3329

3330

3331

3325-3328

Scott No.		Description	Unused Value	Used Value	/ / / / / /
		rounded corners	.65	.20	
3283	33c	Flag and Chalkboard, self-adhesive booklet stamp	.65	.20	
a.		Booklet pane of 18	12.00		
3286	33c	Irish Immigration	.65	.20	
3287	33c	Alfred Lunt and Lynn Fontanne, Actors	.65	.20	
3288	33c	Arctic Hare	.85	.20	
3289	33c	Arctic Fox	.85	.20	
3290	33c	Snowy Owl	.85	.20	
3291	33c	Polar Bear	.85	.20	
3292	33c	Gray Wolf	.85	.20	
a.		Strip of 5, #3288-3292	4.25	—	
3293	33c	Sonoran Desert, self-adhesive pane of 10	6.50		
a.-j.		any single	.65	.50	
3294	33c	Blueberries, self-adhesive booklet stamp, dated "1999"	.85	.20	
a.		Dated "2000"	1.25	.20	
3295	33c	Raspberries, self-adhesive booklet stamp, dated "1999"	.85	.20	
a.		Dated "2000"	1.25	.20	
3296	33c	Strawberries, self-adhesive booklet stamp, dated "1999"	.85	.20	
a.		Dated "2000"	1.25	.20	
3297	33c	Blackberries, self-adhesive booklet stamp, dated "1999"	.85	.20	
a.		Dated 2000	1.25	.20	
b.		Booklet pane, 5 each #3294-3297 + label	17.00		
c.		Block of 4, #3294-3297	3.40		
d.		Booklet pane, 5 #3297e + label	25.00		
e.		Block of 4, #3294a-3297a	5.00		
3298	33c	Blueberries self-adhesive booklet stamp	.90	.20	
3299	33c	Raspberries, self-adhesive booklet stamp	.90	.20	
3300	33c	Strawberries, self-adhesive booklet stamp	.90	.20	
3301	33c	Blackberries, self-adhesive booklet stamp	.90	.20	
a.		Booklet pane of 4, #3298-3301,	3.60		
b.		Booklet pane of 5, #3298, 3299, 3301, 2 #3300 + label	4.50		
c.		Booklet pane of 6, #3300, 3301, 2 #3298, 3299	5.50		
d.		Block of 4, #3298-3301	3.40		
3302	33c	Blueberries, self-adhesive coil	1.00	.20	
3303	33c	Raspberries, self-adhesive coil	1.00	.20	
3304	33c	Strawberries, self-adhesive coil	1.00	.20	
3305	33c	Blackberries, self-adhesive coil	1.00	.20	
a.		Strip of 4, # 3302-3305	4.00		
3306		Daffy Duck, self-adhesive pane of 10	6.75		
a.	33c	any single	.65	.20	

3189

3190

3191

3332

3338

3333-3337

3339-3344

Scott No.		Description	Unused Value	Used Value
b.		Pane of 9 #3306a	6.00	
c.		Pane of 1 #3306a	.65	
3307		Daffy Duck, self-adhesive pane of 10, right stamp with no die cutting	14.00	
a.	33c	single	1.25	
b.		Pane of 9 #3307a	12.00	
c.		Pane of 1, no die cutting	1.75	
d.		As "a," vert. pair, imperf. between	—	
3308	33c	Ayn Rand - Literary Arts	.65	.20
3309	33c	Cinco de Mayo, self-adhesive	.70	.20
3310	33c	Tropical Flowers - Bird of Paradise, self-adhesive booklet stamp	.65	.20
3311	33c	Tropical Flowers - Royal Poinciana, self-adhesive booklet stamp	.65	.20
3312	33c	Tropical Flowers - Gloriosa Lily, self-adhesive booklet stamp	.65	.20
3313	33c	Tropical Flowers - Chinese Hibiscus, self-adhesive booklet stamp	.65	.20
a.		Block of 4, #3310-3313	2.60	
b.		Booklet pane of 20, 5 each #3310-3313	13.00	
3314	33c	John & William Bartram, self-adhesive	.65	.20
3315	33c	Prostate Cancer Awareness, self-adhesive	.65	.20
3316	33c	California Gold Rush 150th Anniversary	.65	.20
3317	33c	Aquarium Fish, self-adhesive	.65	.20
3318	33c	Aquarium Fish, self-adhesive	.65	.20
3319	33c	Aquarium Fish, self-adhesive	.65	.20
3320	33c	Aquarium Fish, self-adhesive	.65	.20
b.		Strip of 4, #3317-3320	2.60	
3321	33c	Extreme Sports - Skateboarding, self-adhesive	.75	.20
3322	33c	Extreme Sports - BMX Biking, self-adhesive	.75	.20
3323	33c	Extreme Sports - Snowboarding, self-adhesive	.75	.20
3324	33c	Extreme Sports - Inline Skating, self-adhesive	.75	.20
a.		Block or strip of 4, #3321-3324	3.00	
3325	33c	American Glass - Free-Blown Glass	1.50	.20
3326	33c	American Glass - Mold-Blown Glass	1.50	.20
3327	33c	American Glass - Pressed Glass	1.50	.20
3328	33c	American Glass - Art Glass	1.50	.20
a.		Strip or block of 4, #3325-3328	6.00	3.00
3329	33c	James Cagney - Legends of Hollywood	.80	.20
3330	55c	Gen. William "Billy" Mitchell	1.10	.30
3331	33c	Honoring Those Who Served, self-adhesive	.65	.20

1999, Lithographed, Perf. 11

Scott No.		Description	Unused Value	Used Value
3332	45c	Universal Postal Union	1.00	.45

3345-3350

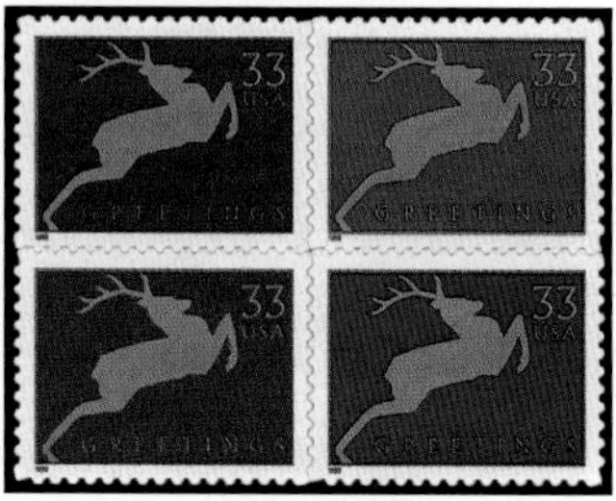

3356-3359

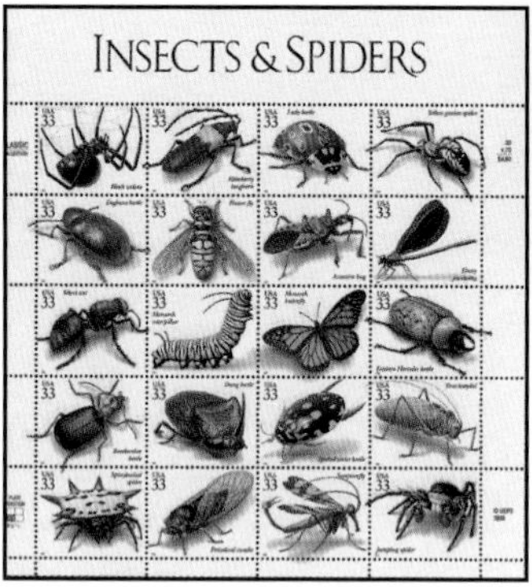

3351

3355

Scott No.		Description	Unused Value	Used Value	/ / / / / /
3333	33c	Famous Trains, Daylight	.75	.20	☐☐☐☐☐
3334	33c	Famous Trains, Congressional	.75	.20	☐☐☐☐☐
3335	33c	Famous Trains, 20th Century Limited	.75	.20	☐☐☐☐☐
3336	33c	Famous Trains, Hiawatha	.75	.20	☐☐☐☐☐
3337	33c	Famous Trains, Super Chief..........	.75	.20	☐☐☐☐☐
a.		Strip of 5, #3333-3337	3.75	—	☐☐☐☐☐
3338	33c	Frederick Law Olmsted, Landscape Architect....................	.70	.20	☐☐☐☐☐
3339	33c	Max Steiner	1.25	.20	☐☐☐☐☐
3340	33c	Dimitri Tiomkin.............................	1.25	.20	☐☐☐☐☐
3341	33c	Bernard Herrmann	1.25	.20	☐☐☐☐☐
3342	33c	Franz Waxman..............................	1.25	.20	☐☐☐☐☐
3343	33c	Alfred Newman	1.25	.20	☐☐☐☐☐
3344	33c	Erich Wolfgang Korngold	1.25	.20	☐☐☐☐☐
a.		Block of 6, #3339-3344	7.50	4.50	☐☐☐☐☐
3345	33c	Ira & George Gershwin	1.25	.20	☐☐☐☐☐
3346	33c	Alan Jay Lerner & Frederick Loewe	1.25	.20	☐☐☐☐☐
3347	33c	Lorenz Hart	1.25	.20	☐☐☐☐☐
3348	33c	Richard Rodgers & Oscar Hammerstein II	1.25	.20	☐☐☐☐☐
3349	33c	Meredith Willson..........................	1.25	.20	☐☐☐☐☐
3350	33c	Frank Loesser	1.25	.20	☐☐☐☐☐
a.		Block of 6, #3345-3350	7.50	4.50	☐☐☐☐☐
3351		Insects & Spiders, Pane of 20	13.00	10.00	☐☐☐☐☐
a.-t.	33c	any single......................................	.65	.50	☐☐☐☐☐
Serpentine Die Cut 11, Self-Adhesive					
3352	33c	Hanukkah......................................	.65	.20	☐☐☐☐☐
Coil Stamp Perf 9¾, Vertically					
3353	22c	Uncle Sam (3259).........................	.45	.20	☐☐☐☐☐
Perf. 11¼					
3354	33c	NATO, 50th Anniv.	.65	.20	☐☐☐☐☐
Serpentine Die Cut 11¼ on 2 or 3 sides, Self-Adhesive Booklet Stamp					
3355	33c	Madonna and Child, by Bartolomeo Vivarini	1.00	.20	☐☐☐☐☐
a.		Booklet pane of 20	20.00		☐☐☐☐☐
Serpentine Die Cut 11¼					
3356	33c	Deer, gold & red...........................	1.75	.20	☐☐☐☐☐
3357	33c	Deer, gold & blue	1.75	.20	☐☐☐☐☐
3358	33c	Deer, gold & purple	1.75	.20	☐☐☐☐☐
3359	33c	Deer, gold & green.......................	1.75	.20	☐☐☐☐☐
a.		Block or strip of 4, #3356-3359....	7.00		☐☐☐☐☐
Booklet Stamps					
Serpentine Die Cut 11¼ on 2, 3 or 4 sides					
3360	33c	Deer, gold & red (3356)................	1.60	.20	☐☐☐☐☐
3361	33c	Deer, gold & blue (3357)	1.60	.20	☐☐☐☐☐
3362	33c	Deer, gold & purple (3358)...........	1.60	.20	☐☐☐☐☐
3363	33c	Deer, gold & green (3359)............	1.60	.20	☐☐☐☐☐
a.		Booklet pane of 20, 5 each			

3369

3370

3371

3375a

3378

3379-3383

3384-3388

3389

3391

3390

3397

3393-3396

3398

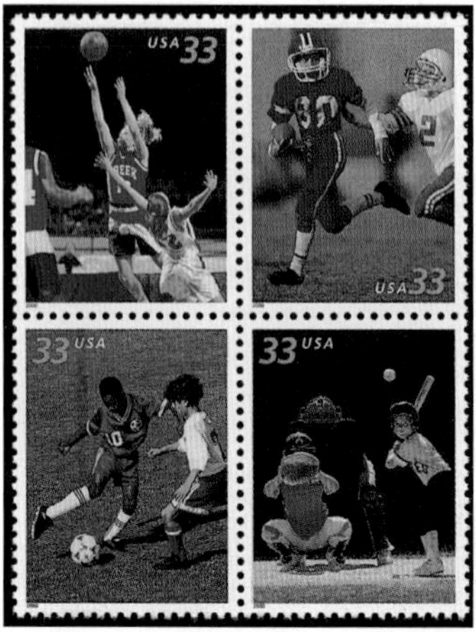

3399-3402

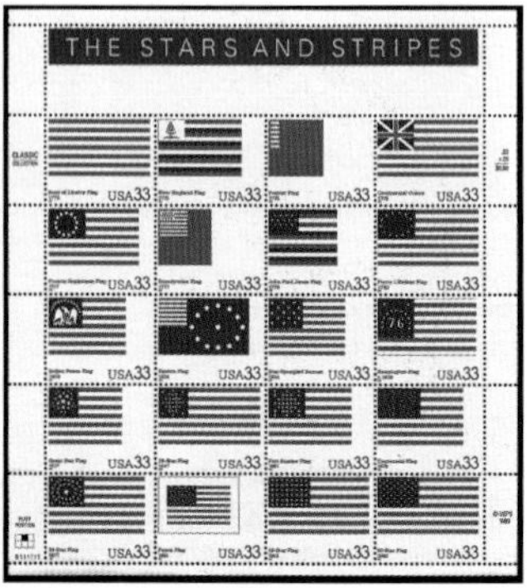

3403

3404-3407

3408

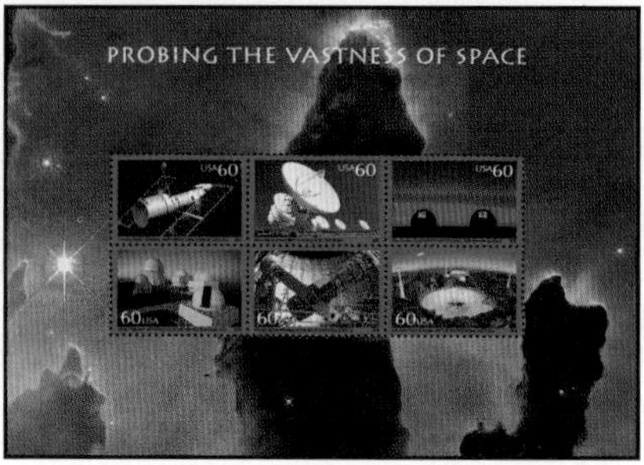

3409

Scott No.		Description	Unused Value	Used Value
		#3360-3363	32.50	
b.		Block of 4, #3360-3363	6.50	
c.		As "b," die cutting omitted	—	
d.		As "a," die cutting omitted	—	
Size: 21x19mm				
Serpentine Die Cut 11½ x11¼ on 2 or 3 sides				
3364	33c	Deer, gold & red (3356)	2.25	.20
3365	33c	Deer, gold & blue (3357)	2.25	.20
3366	33c	Deer, gold & purple (3358)	2.25	.20
3367	33c	Deer, gold & green (3359)	2.25	.20
a.		Booklet pane of 4, #3364-3367	9.00	
b.		Booklet pane of 5, #3364, 3366, 3367, 2 #3365 + label	11.25	
c.		Booklet pane of 6, #3365, 3367, 2 each #3364 & 3366	13.50	
d.		Block of 4, #3364-3367	9.00	
Photogravure, Serpentine Die Cut 11, Self-Adhesive				
3368	33c	Kwanzaa (3175)	.65	.20
Serpentine Die Cut 11¼, Self-Adhesive				
3369	33c	Year 2000, Baby New Year	.65	.20
2000 Issues				
3370	33c	Chinese New Year - Year of the Dragon	.80	.20
3371	33c	Patricia Roberts Harris, self-adhesive	.65	.20
Perf. 11				
3372	33c	Submarines, Los Angeles Class with microprinted "USPS" at base of sail	.75	.20
Booklet Stamps				
3373	22c	Submarines, S Class	1.25	.75
3374	33c	Submarines, Los Angeles Class, no microprinting	1.75	1.00
3375	55c	Submarines, Ohio Class	2.75	1.25
3376	60c	Submarines, USS Holland	3.00	1.50
3377	$3.20	Submarines, Gato Class	16.00	5.00
a.		Booklet pane of 5, #3373-3377	25.00	—
Serpentine Die Cut 11¼ x 11½, 11½ (horiz. stamps), Self-Adhesive				
3378		Pacific Coast Rain Forest, pane of 10	8.00	
a.-j.	33c	any single	.80	.50
Perf. 11 x 11¼				
3379	33c	Louise Nevelson, Sculptor, Silent Music I	.65	.20
3380	33c	Louise Nevelson, Sculptor, Royal Tide I	.65	.20
3381	33c	Louise Nevelson, Sculptor, Black Chord	.65	.20
3382	33c	Louise Nevelson, Sculptor, Nightsphere-Light	.65	.20

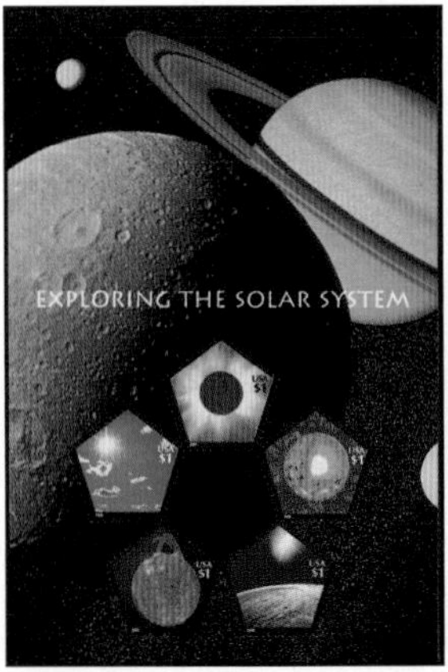

3410

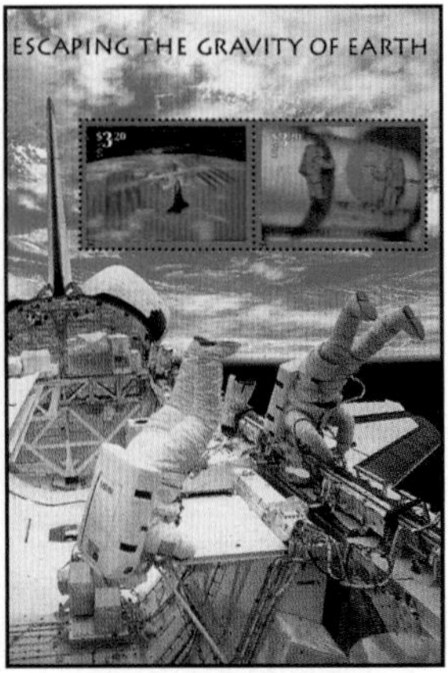

3411

3412

3413

3414-3417

Scott No.		Description	Unused Value	Used Value	/ / / / / /
3383	33c	Louise Nevelson, Sculptor, Dawn's Wedding Chapel I...........	.65	.20	☐☐☐☐☐
a.		Strip of 5, #3379-3383................	3.25	—	☐☐☐☐☐
Perf. 11					
3384	33c	Hubble Images, Eagle Nebula	.65	.20	☐☐☐☐☐
3385	33c	Hubble Images, Ring Nebula	.65	.20	☐☐☐☐☐
3386	33c	Hubble Images, Lagoon Nebula ..	.65	.20	☐☐☐☐☐
3387	33c	Hubble Images, Egg Nebula	.65	.20	☐☐☐☐☐
3388	33c	Hubble Images, Galaxy NGC 1316	.65	.20	☐☐☐☐☐
a.		Strip of 5, #3384-3388................	3.25	—	☐☐☐☐☐
b.		As "a," imperf................................	*1,250.*		☐☐☐☐☐
3389	33c	Samoan Double Canoe..................	.85	.20	☐☐☐☐☐
3390	33c	Library Of Congress, ...	.65	.20	☐☐☐☐☐
Serpentine Die Cut 11, Self-Adhesive					
3391		Road Runner & Wile E. Coyote, pane of 10	10.00		☐☐☐☐☐
a.	33c	single..	.85	.20	☐☐☐☐☐
b.		Pane of 9 #3391a..........................	8.00		☐☐☐☐☐
c.		Pane of 1 #3391a..........................	1.50		☐☐☐☐☐
d.		All die cutting omitted, pane of 10	*2,400.*		☐☐☐☐☐
3392		Road Runner & Wile E. Coyote, right stamp with no die cutting...	*40.00*		☐☐☐☐☐
a.	33c	single..	2.75		☐☐☐☐☐
b.		Pane of 9 #3392a..........................	30.00		☐☐☐☐☐
c.		Pane of 1, no die cutting.	5.00		☐☐☐☐☐
Perf. 11					
3393	33c	Maj. Gen. John L. Hines...............	.65	.20	☐☐☐☐☐
3394	33c	Gen. Omar N. Bradley..................	.65	.20	☐☐☐☐☐
3395	33c	Sgt. Alvin C. York	.65	.20	☐☐☐☐☐
3396	33c	Second Lt. Audie L. Murphy........	.65	.20	☐☐☐☐☐
a.		Block or strip of 4, #3393-3396...	2.60	—	
3397	33c	Summer Sports - Runners............	.65	.20	☐☐☐☐☐
Serpentine Die Cut 11½, Self-Adhesive					
3398	33c	Adoption.......................................	.75	.20	☐☐☐☐☐
a.		Die cutting omitted, pair	—		☐☐☐☐☐
Perf. 11					
3399	33c	Youth Team Sports, Basketball	.65	.20	☐☐☐☐☐
3400	33c	Youth Team Sports, Football........	.65	.20	☐☐☐☐☐
3401	33c	Youth Team Sports, Soccer	.65	.20	☐☐☐☐☐
3402	33c	Youth Team Sports, Baseball........	.65	.20	☐☐☐☐☐
a.		Block or strip of 4, #3399-3402...	2.60	—	☐☐☐☐☐
Perf. 10½ x 11					
3403		The Stars And Stripes, pane of 20	15.00	11.00	☐☐☐☐☐
a.-t.	33c	any single	.75	.50	☐☐☐☐☐

3420

3422

3426

3427

3427A

3428

3430

3431

3432A

3433

3434

3435

3438

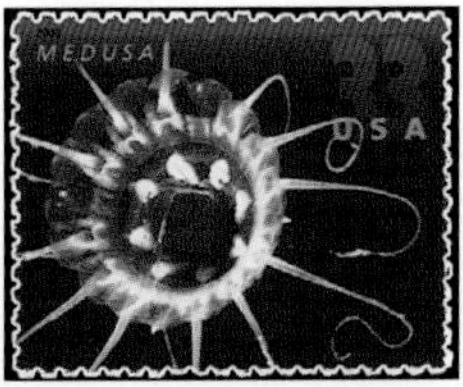

3443

3444

3445

3446

3447

3448

3451

3457

Scott No.	Description	Unused Value	Used Value
Photogravure, Serpentine Die Cut 8½ Horiz., Self-Adhesive Coil Stamps			
3404	33c Blueberries (3294)	2.50	.20
3405	33c Strawberries (3295)	2.50	.20
3406	33c Blackberries (3296)	2.50	.20
3407	33c Raspberries (3297)	2.50	.20
a.	Strip of 4, #3404-3407	10.00	
Serpentine Die Cut 11¼, Self-Adhesive			
3408	Legends Of Baseball, pane of 20	13.00	
a.-t.	33c any single	.65	.50
Souvenir Sheets			
3409	Probing the Vastness of Space, sheet of 6	12.50	7.00
a.-f.	60c any single	2.00	1.00
3410	Exploring the Solar System, sheet of 5 + label	16.00	10.00
a.-e.	$1 any single	3.00	1.75
f.	As No. 3410, imperf	*3,250.*	
g.	As No. 3410, with hologram from No. 3411b applied	—	
Untagged, Photogravure with Hologram Affixed			
3411	Escaping the Gravity of Earth, sheet of 2	21.00	10.00
a.-b.	$3.20 any single	10.00	4.00
c.	Hologram omitted on right stamp	—	
3412	$11.75 Space Achievement and Exploration	37.50	17.50
a.	$11.75 single	35.00	15.00
b.	Hologram omitted	—	
3413	$11.75 Landing on the Moon	37.50	17.50
a.	$11.75 single	35.00	15.00
b.	Double hologram	—	
Stampin' The Future – Children's Stamp Design Contest Winners, Serpentine Die Cut 11¼, Self-Adhesive			
3414	33c By Zachary Canter, Space Figures	.65	.20
3415	33c By Sarah Lipsey, Heart	.65	.20
3416	33c By Morgan Hill, "Mommy, Are We There Yet"	.65	.20
3417	33c By Ashley Young, Space Dog	.65	.20
a.	Horiz. strip of 4, #3414-3417	2.60	
2000-2009 Distinguished Americans Issue			
3420	10c Joseph W. Stilwell	.20	.20
a.	Imperf., pair	*350.00*	
3422	23c Wilma Rudolph, self-adhesive	.45	.20

Scott No.	Description	Unused Value	Used Value
3426	33c Claude Pepper	.65	.20
3427	58c Margaret Chase Smith, self-adhesive	1.25	.20
b.	Black (engr.) omitted	—	
3427A	59c James A. Michener, self-adhesive	1.25	.20
3428	63c Dr. Jonas Salk, self-adhesive	1.25	.20
a.	Black (litho.) omitted	—	
3430	75c Harriet Beecher Stowe, self-adhesive	1.50	.20
3431	76c Sen Hattie Caraway, self-adhesive, die cut 11	1.50	.20
3432	76c Hattie Caraway, die cut 11½ x 11 (3431)	3.50	2.00
3432A	76c Edward Trudeau, self-adhesive	1.50	.20
3432B	78c Mary Lasker, self-adhesive	1.60	.20
3433	83c Edna Ferber, self-adhesive	1.60	.30
3434	83c Edna Ferber, With Curving Shoulder, self-adhesive	1.60	.30
3435	87c Dr. Albert Sabin, self-adhesive	1.75	.30
3436	23c Wilma Rudolph, self-adhesive, booklet stamp, litho (3422)	.45	.20
a.	Booklet pane of 4	1.80	
b.	Booklet pane of 6	2.70	
c.	Booklet pane of 10	4.50	
d.	As "c," die cutting omitted	—	
2000 Commemoratives			
3438	33c California Statehood, 150th Anniv.	.75	.20
3439	33c Deep Sea Creatures - Fanfin Anglerfish	.65	.20
3440	33c Deep Sea Creatures - Sea Cucumber	.65	.20
3441	33c Deep Sea Creatures - Fangtooth	.65	.20
3442	33c Deep Sea Creatures - Amphipod	.65	.20
3443	33c Deep Sea Creatures - Medusa	.65	.20
a.	Vert. strip of 5, #3439-3443	3.25	2.00
3444	33c Literary Arts - Thomas Wolfe, Novelist	.65	.20
3445	33c White House, 200th Anniv.	1.00	.20
3446	33c Legends of Hollywood - Edward G. Robinson	1.10	.20
3447	(10c) New York Public Library Lion self-adhesive, coil stamp, "2000" year date	.20	.20
a.	"2003" year date	.20	.20
3448	(34c) Flag Over Farm, litho., perf 11¼	.75	.20
3449	(34c) Flag Over Farm, litho. self-adhesive	.70	1.00
3450	(34c) Flag Over Farm, photo., self-adhesive booklet stamp	.85	.20
a.	Booklet pane of 18	16.00	
b.	Die cutting omitted, pair	—	
3451	(34c) Statue of Liberty, self-adhesive booklet stamp	.70	.20
a.	Statue of Liberty, booklet pane of 20	14.00	

Scott No.		Description	Unused Value	Used Value	/ / / / / /
b.		Statue of Liberty, Booklet pane of 4	3.00		☐☐☐☐☐
c.		Statue of Liberty, booklet pane of 6	5.75		☐☐☐☐☐
d.		As "a," die cutting omitted............	—		☐☐☐☐☐
3452	(34c)	Statue of Liberty, coil stamp.........	.70	.20	☐☐☐☐☐
3453	(34c)	Statue of Liberty self-adhesive coil	.70	.20	☐☐☐☐☐
a.		Die cutting omitted, pair	*350.00*		☐☐☐☐☐
3454	(34c)	Flower, self-adhesive booklet stamp (purple background)	1.00	.20	☐☐☐☐☐
3455	(34c)	Flower, self-adhesive booklet stamp (tan background)........................	1.00	.20	☐☐☐☐☐
3456	(34c)	Flower, self-adhesive booklet stamp (green background)....................	1.00	.20	☐☐☐☐☐
3457	(34c)	Flower, self-adhesive booklet stamp (red background).........................	1.00	.20	☐☐☐☐☐
a.		Block of 4, #3454-3457	4.00		☐☐☐☐☐
b.		Booklet pane of 4, #3454-3457......	4.00		☐☐☐☐☐
c.		Booklet pane of 6, #3456, 3457, 2 each #3454-3455.....................	6.00		☐☐☐☐☐
d.		Booklet pane of 6, #3454, 3455, 2 each #3456-3457.....................	6.00		☐☐☐☐☐
e.		Booklet pane of 20, 5 each #3454-3457 + label....................	20.00		☐☐☐☐☐
3458	(34c)	Flower (purple bckgrnd), die cut 11.5 x 11.75	3.00	.25	☐☐☐☐☐
3459	(34c)	Flower (tan bckgrnd), die cut 11.5 x 11.75	3.00	.25	☐☐☐☐☐
3460	(34c)	Flower (green bckgrnd), die cut 11.5 x 11.75	3.00	.25	☐☐☐☐☐
3461	(34c)	Flower (red bckgrnd), die cut 11.5 x 11.75	3.00	.25	☐☐☐☐☐
a.		Block of 4, #3458-3461	12.00		☐☐☐☐☐
b.		Booklet pane of 20, 2 each #3461a, 3 each #3457a............................	36.50		☐☐☐☐☐
c.		Booklet pane of 20, 2 each #3457a, 3 each #3461a............................	45.00		☐☐☐☐☐
3462	(34c)	Flower (green bckgrnd), coil stamp	3.50	.20	☐☐☐☐☐
3463	(34c)	Flower (red bckgrnd), coil stamp..	3.50	.20	☐☐☐☐☐
3464	(34c)	Flower (tan bckgrnd), coil stamp..	3.50	.20	☐☐☐☐☐
3465	(34c)	Flower (purple bckgrnd), coil stamp	3.50	.20	☐☐☐☐☐
a.		Strip of 4, #3462-3465.................	14.00		☐☐☐☐☐
2001 Issues					
3466	34c	Statue of Liberty, self-adhesive coil (rounded corners).......................	.70	.20	☐☐☐☐☐
3467	21c	Buffalo, perf. 11¼ x 11	.50	.20	☐☐☐☐☐
3468	21c	American Buffalo, self-adhesive sheet stamp................................	.45	.20	☐☐☐☐☐
3468A	23c	George Washington, self-adhesive, serpentine die cut 11¼ x11¾....	.50	.20	☐☐☐☐☐

3467

3468

3468A

3471A

3472

3473

3475A

3484

3484A

3491

3495

3496

3499

3500

3501

Scott No.	Description	Unused Value	Used Value	/ / / / / /
3469	34c Flag Over Farm, perf 11.25 sheet stamp	.75	.20	□□□□□
3470	34c Flag Over Farm, self-adhesive sheet stamp	1.00	.20	□□□□□
3471	55c Eagle, self-adhesive, serpentine die cut 10¾	1.10	.20	□□□□□
3471A	57c Eagle, self-adhesive	1.10	.20	□□□□□
3472	$3.50 Capitol Dome	7.00	2.00	□□□□□
a.	Die cutting omitted, pair	—		□□□□□
3473	$12.25 Washington Monument	22.50	10.00	□□□□□
3475	21c American Buffalo, self-adhesive coil stamp	.50	.20	□□□□□
3475A	23c George Washington, self-adhesive, coil stamp, serpentine die cut 8½ Vert	.50	.20	□□□□□
3476	34c Statue of Liberty, perforated coil stamp	.70	.20	□□□□□
3477	34c Statue of Liberty, self-adhesive coil stamp (right angle corners)	.80	.20	□□□□□
a.	Die cutting omitted, pair	75.00		□□□□□
3478	34c Flower, self-adhesive coil stamp, die cut 8.5 vert.	.70	.20	□□□□□
3479	34c Flower , self-adhesive coil stamp, die cut 8.5 vert.	.70	.20	□□□□□
3480	34c Flowers, self-adhesive coil stamp, die cut 8.5 vert.	.70	.20	□□□□□
3481	34c Flowers, self-adhesive coil stamp, die cut 8.5 vert.	.70	.20	□□□□□
a.	Strip of 4, #3478-3481,	2.80		□□□□□
3482	20c George Washington, self-adhesive bklt stamp, die cut 11.25	.45	.20	□□□□□
a.	Booklet pane of 10	4.50		□□□□□
b.	Booklet pane of 4	1.80		□□□□□
c.	Booklet pane of 6	2.70		□□□□□
3483	20c George Washington, self-adhesive bklt stamp, die cut 10.5 x 11.25	5.00	1.25	□□□□□
a.	Booklet pane of 4, 2 #3482 at L, 2 #3483 at R	12.00		□□□□□
b.	Booklet pane of 6, 3 #3482 at L, 3 #3483 at R	20.00		□□□□□
c.	Booklet pane of 10, 5 #3482 at L, 5 #3483 at R	25.00		□□□□□
d.	Booklet pane of 4, 2 #3483 at L, 2 #3482 at R	12.00		□□□□□
e.	Booklet pane of 6, 3 #3483 at L, 3 #3482 at R	20.00		□□□□□
f.	Booklet pane of 10, 5 #3483 at L, 5 #3482 at R	25.00		□□□□□
g.	Pair, #3482 at L, #3483 at R	5.50		□□□□□
h.	Pair, #3483 at R, #3482 at L	5.50		□□□□□

Scott No.		Description	Unused Value	Used Value	/ / / / / /
3484	21c	Buffalo (3467), self-adhesive, booklet stamp, serpentine die cut 11¼ on 3 Sides	.50	.20	□□□□□
b.		Booklet pane of 4	2.00		□□□□□
c.		Booklet pane of 6	3.00		□□□□□
d.		Booklet pane of 10	5.00		□□□□□
3484A	21c	Buffalo, self-adhesive, booklet stamp ....serpentine die cut 10½ x 11¼	5.50	1.50	□□□□□
e.		Booklet pane of 4, 2 #3484 at L, 2 #3484A at R	12.00		□□□□□
f.		Booklet pane of 6, 3 #3484 at L, 3 #3484A at R,	20.00		□□□□□
g.		Booklet pane of 10, 5 #3484 at L, 5 #3484A at R	30.00		□□□□□
h.		Booklet pane of 4, 2 #3484A at L, 2 #3484 at R	12.00		□□□□□
i.		Booklet pane of 6, 3 #3484A at L, 3 #3484 at R	20.00		□□□□□
j.		Booklet pane of 10, 5 #3484A at L, 5 #3484 at R	30.00		□□□□□
k.		Pair, #3484 at L, #3484A at R	6.00		□□□□□
l.		Pair, #3484A at L, #3484 at R	6.00		□□□□□
3485	34c	Statue of Liberty, self-adhesive booklet stamp	.70	.20	□□□□□
a.		Booklet pane of 10	7.00		□□□□□
b.		Booklet pane of 20	14.00		□□□□□
c.		Booklet pane of 4	3.00		□□□□□
d.		Booklet pane of 6	4.50		□□□□□
e.		Die cutting omitted, pair (from No. 3485b)	—		□□□□□
f.		As "e," booklet pane of 20	—		□□□□□
3487	34c	Flower, self-adhesive booklet stamp, die cut 10¼ x 10¾	.75	.20	□□□□□
3488	34c	Flower, self-adhesive booklet stamp, die cut 10¼ x 10¾	.75	.20	□□□□□
3489	34c	Flower, self-adhesive booklet stamp, die cut 10¼ x 10¾	.75	.20	□□□□□
3490	34c	Flower, self-adhesive booklet stamp, die cut 10¼ x 10¾	.75	.20	□□□□□
a.		Block of 4, #3487-3490	3.00		□□□□□
b.		Booklet pane of 4, #3487-3490	3.00		□□□□□
c.		Booklet pane of 6, #3489-3490, 2 each #3487-3488	4.50		□□□□□
d.		Booklet pane of 6, #3487-3488, 2 each #3489-3490	4.50		□□□□□
e.		Booklet pane of 20, 5 each #3490a + label	15.00		□□□□□
3491	34c	Apple, self-adhesive booklet stamp, serpentine die cut 11¼	.70	.20	□□□□□

Scott No.		Description	Unused Value	Used Value	/ / / / / /
3492	34c	Orange, self-adhesive booklet stam	.70	.20	☐☐☐☐☐
a.		Pair, #3491-3492	1.40		☐☐☐☐☐
b.		Booklet pane, 10 each #3491-3492	14.00		☐☐☐☐☐
c.		As "a," black ("34 USA") omitted	—		☐☐☐☐☐
d.		As "a," die cutting omitted	—		☐☐☐☐☐
e.		As "b," die cutting omitted.	—		☐☐☐☐☐
f.		As "b," right four stamps yellow omitted	—		☐☐☐☐☐
3493	34c	Apple, self-adhesive booklet stamp, serpentine die cut 11½ x 10¾	1.25	.20	☐☐☐☐☐
3494	34c	Orange, self-adhesive booklet stamp	1.25	.20	☐☐☐☐☐
a.		Pair, #3493-3494	2.50		☐☐☐☐☐
b.		Booklet pane, 2 each #3493-3494	5.00		☐☐☐☐☐
c.		Booklet pane, 3 each #3493-3494, #3493 at UL	7.50		☐☐☐☐☐
d.		Booklet pane, 3 each #3493-3494, #3494 at UL	7.50		☐☐☐☐☐
3495	34c	Flag Over Farm, self-adhesive, booklet stamp (3469), serpentine die cut 8 on 2, 3 or 4 sides"	1.00	.20	☐☐☐☐☐
a.		Booklet pane of 18	18.00		☐☐☐☐☐
2001 Commemoratives					
3496	(34c)	Love - Rose, Apr. 20, 1763 Love letter by John Adams	.90	.20	☐☐☐☐☐
a.		Booklet pane of 20	18.00		☐☐☐☐☐
b.		Vert. pair, die cutting omitted btwn.	—		☐☐☐☐☐
3497	34c	Love - Rose and Apr 20, 1763 Love Letter by John Adams, self-adhesive	.90	.20	☐☐☐☐☐
a.		Booklet pane of 20	18.00		☐☐☐☐☐
b.		Vertical pair, die cutting omitted btwn.	—		☐☐☐☐☐
3498	34c	Love - Rose and Apr 20, 1763 Love Letter by John Adams, 18 x 21mm	1.00	.20	☐☐☐☐☐
a.		Booklet pane of 4	4.00		☐☐☐☐☐
b.		Booklet pane of 6	6.00		☐☐☐☐☐
3499	55c	Rose, Aug. 11 1763 Love Letter by Abigail Adams, self-adhesive	1.10	.20	☐☐☐☐☐
3500	34c	Chinese New Year - Year of the Snake	.75	.20	☐☐☐☐☐
3501	34c	Black Heritage, Roy Wilkins (1901-81), Civil Rights Leader	.70	.20	☐☐☐☐☐
3502		American Illustrators, pane of 20 .	17.50		☐☐☐☐☐
3502a-t		American Illustrators, any single ..	.85	.60	☐☐☐☐☐
3503	34c	Diabetes Awareness	.65	.20	☐☐☐☐☐
3504	34c	Nobel Prize, Centenary	.70	.20	☐☐☐☐☐
a.		Imperf., pair	—		☐☐☐☐☐
3505		Pan-American Expo Invert Stamps, Cent., pane	9.00	7.00	☐☐☐☐☐

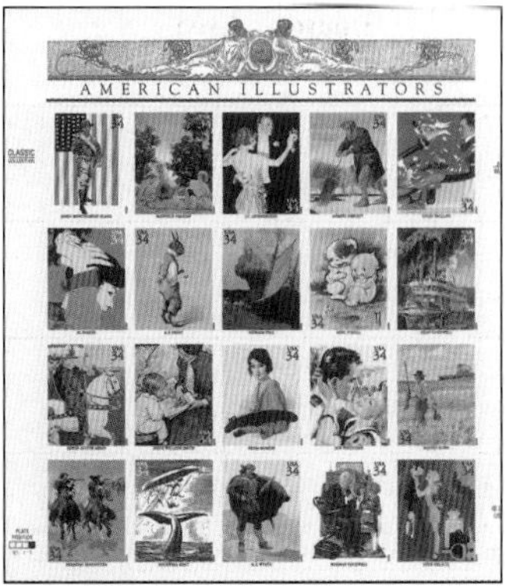

3502

3503

3505

3506

3504

3507

3508

3509

Scott No.		Description	Unused Value	Used Value	/ / / / / /
a.	1c	Pan-American Expo Invert Stamps, Cent. - Reproduction of Scott 294a	.60	.20	□□□□□
b.	2c	Pan-American Expo Invert Stamps, Cent. - Reproduction of Scott 295a	.60	.20	□□□□□
c.	4c	Pan-American Expo Invert Stamps, Cent. - Reproduction of Scott 296a	.60	.20	□□□□□
d.	80c	Pan-American Expo Invert Stamps, Cent. - Commemorative (cinderella) stamp depicting a buffalo............	1.75	.35	□□□□□
3506		Great Plains Prairie, pane of 10....	11.00		□□□□□
3506a-j	34c	Great Plains Prairie, any single.....	1.00	.50	□□□□□
3507	34c	Peanuts Comic Strip......................	.80	.20	□□□□□
3508	34c	Honoring Veterans, self-adhesive..	.75	.20	□□□□□
3509	34c	Frida Kahlo (1907-54), Painter, Self-Portrait................................	.75	.20	□□□□□
3510	34c	Legendary Playing Fields, Ebbets Field, self-adhesive......................	.90	.60	□□□□□
3511	34c	Legendary Playing Fields, Tiger Stadium, self-adhesive................	.90	.60	□□□□□
3512	34c	Legendary Playing Fields, Crosley Field, self-adhesive...............................	.90	.60	□□□□□
3513	34c	Legendary Playing Fields, Yankee Stadium, self-adhesive....	.90	.60	□□□□□
3514	34c	Legendary Playing Fields, Polo Grounds, self-adhesive................	.90	.60	□□□□□
3515	34c	Legendary Playing Fields, Forbes Field, self-adhesive...............................	.90	.60	□□□□□
3516	34c	Legendary Playing Fields, Fenway Park, self-adhesive...............................	.90	.60	□□□□□
3517	34c	Legendary Playing Fields, Comiskey Park, self-adhesive...............................	.90	.60	□□□□□
3518	34c	Legendary Playing Fields, Shibe Park, self-adhesive...............................	.90	.60	□□□□□
3519	34c	Legendary Playing fields, Wrigley Field, self-sdhesive...............................	.90	.60	□□□□□
a.		Legendary Playing fields, Block of 10, #3510-3519	9.00		□□□□□
3520	(10c)	Atlas Statue, New York City, self-adhesive coil stamp..............	.20	.20	□□□□□
3521	34c	Leonard Bernstein (1918-90), Conductor	.65	.20	□□□□□
3522	(15c)	Woody Wagon, self-adhesive coil stamp	.30	.20	□□□□□
3523	34c	Legends of Hollywood - Lucille Ball (1911-89), self-adhesive.............	1.00	.20	□□□□□
a.		Die cutting omitted, pair	*925.00*		□□□□□
3524	34c	American Treasures Series, Amish Quilts - Diamond in the Square, c. 1920, self-adhesive.................	.70	.20	□□□□□

3511

3520

3521

3522

3523

3524

3528

3532

3533

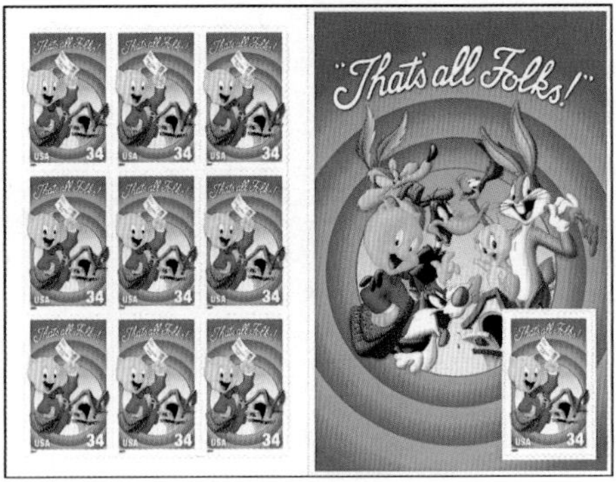

3534-3535

Scott No.		Description	Unused Value	Used Value	/ / / / / /
3525	34c	American Treasures Series, Amish Quilts - Lone Star, c. 1920, self-adhesive	.70	.20	
3526	34c	American Treasures Series, Amish Quilts - Sunshine and Shadow, c. 1910, self-adhesive..............................	.70	.20	
3527	34c	American Treasures Series, Amish Quilts - Double Ninepatch Variation, self-adhesive..............................	.70	.20	
a.		Block or strip of 4, #3524-3527....	2.80		
3528	34c	Carnivorous Plants - Venus Flytrap, self-adhesive..............................	.70	.20	
3529	34c	Carnivorous Plants - Yellow Trumpet, self-adhesive..............................	.70	.20	
3530	34c	Carnivorous Plants - Cobra Lily, self-adhesive..............................	.70	.20	
3531	34c	Carnivorous Plants - English Sundew, self-adhesive..............................	.70	.20	
a.		Block or strip of 4, #3528-3531....	2.80		
3532	34c	Eid - 'Eid Mubarak', self adhesive	.70	.20	
3533	34c	Enrico Fermi, Physicist, self-adhesive	.70	.20	
3534		That's All Folks! Porky Pig at Mailbox, Pane of 10, self-adhesive..........	7.00		
a.	34c	Single	.70	.20	
b.		Pane of 9, #3534a.........................	6.25		
c.		Pane of 1, #3534a.........................	.70		
3535		That's All Folks! Porky Pig at Mailbox, Pane of 10, self-adhesive, right stamp with no die cutting...	60.00		
a.	34c	Single	*3.00*		
b.		Pane of 9, #3535a.........................	*27.50*		
c.		Pane of 1, no die cutting..............	30.00		
3536	34c	Virgin and Child, by Lorenzo Costa, self-adhesive, booklet stamp, serpentine die cut 11½ on 2, 3, or 4 Sides..........................	.75	.20	
a.		Booklet pane of 20.......................	15.00		
3537	34c	Santa Claus, large date, self-adhesive serpentine die cut 10¾ x 11........	.70	.20	
a.		Small date (from booklet pane), self-adhesive, serp. die cut 10¾ x 11...................................	.80	.20	
b.		Large date (from booklet pane)	2.00	.20	
3538	34c	Santa Claus, large date, self-adhesive, serpentine die cut 10¾ x 11	.70	.20	
a.		Small date (from booklet pane), self-adhesive, serp. die cut 10¾ x 11...................................	.80	.20	
b.		Large date, (from booklet pane) ..	2.00	.20	

3536

3537

3538

3539

3540

3541

3542

3543

3544

3545

3546

3547

3548

3549

3549B

3550

3550A

3551

Scott No.		Description	Unused Value	Used Value
3539	34c	Santa Claus, large date, self-adhesive, serpentine die cut 10¾ x 11	.70	.20
a.		Small date (from booklet pane), self-adhesive, serp. die cut 10¾ x 11	.80	.20
b.		Large date (from booklet pane) ...	2.00	.20
3540	34c	Santa Claus, large date, self-adhesive, serpentine die cut 10¾ x 11	.70	.20
a.		Small date (from booklet pane), self-adhesive, serp. die cut 10¾ x 11	.80	.20
b.		Santa Claus, Block of 4, #3537-3540	2.80	
c.		Santa Claus, Block of 4, small date, #3537a-3540a	3.25	
d.		Santa Claus, Booklet pane, 5 #3540c + label	16.50	
e.		Large date (from booklet pane) ...	2.00	.20
f.		Block of 4, large date, #3537b-3539b, 3540e (from booklet pane)	8.00	
g.		Booklet pane of 20, 5 #3540f + label	40.00	
3541	34c	Santa Claus, Green and Red denominations, self-adhesive, serpentine die cut 11	.70	.20
3542	34c	Santa Claus, Green and Red denominations, Self-Adhesive, serpentine die cut 11	.70	.20
3543	34c	Santa Claus, Green and Red denominations, self-adhesive, serpentine die cut 11	.70	.20
3544	34c	Santa Claus, Green and Red denominations, self-adhesive, serpentine die cut 11	.70	.20
a.		Block of 4, #3541-3544	2.80	
b.		Booklet pane of 4, #3541-3544	2.80	
c.		Booklet pane of 6, #3543-3544, 2 #3541-3542	4.25	
d.		Booklet pane of 6, #3541-3542, 2 #3543-3544	4.25	
3545	34c	James Madison (1751-1836), Montpelier, self-adhesive............	.70	.20
3546	34c	Thanksgiving Cornicopia, self-adhesive	.70	.20
3547	34c	Hanukkah Type of 1996 (3118), self-adhesive	.70	.20
3548	34c	Kwanzaa Type of 1997 (3175), self-adhesive	.70	.20

3552

3553

3554

3555

3556

3557

3558

3559

3560

Scott No.		Description	Unused Value	Used Value	/ / / / / /
3549	34c	United We Stand, self-adhesive, booklet stamp, serpentine die cut 11¼ on 2, 3, or 4 sides......	.75	.20	☐☐☐☐☐
a.		Booklet pane of 20........................	15.00		☐☐☐☐☐
3549B	34c	United We Stand (3549), self-adhesive, booklet stamp, serpentine die cut 10½ x 10¾ on 2 or 3 Sides	.90	.20	☐☐☐☐☐
c.		Booklet pane of 4..........................	3.60		☐☐☐☐☐
d.		Booklet pane of 6..........................	5.40		☐☐☐☐☐
e.		Booklet pane of 20........................	18.00		☐☐☐☐☐
3550	34c	United We Stand (3549), self-adhesive, coil stamp, square corners,......... serpentine die cut 9¾ Vert.	1.10	.20	☐☐☐☐☐
3550A	34c	United We Stand (3549), self-adhesive, coil stamp, round corners, spaced, serpentine die cut 9¾ Vert.	1.10	.20	☐☐☐☐☐
3551	57c	Love Letters (3496), self-adhesive, serpentine die cut 11¼...............	1.10	.20	☐☐☐☐☐

2002 Issues

Scott No.		Description	Unused Value	Used Value	/ / / / / /
3552	34c	Winter Olympics - Ski Jumping, self-adhesive	.70	.20	☐☐☐☐☐
3553	34c	Winter Olympics - Snowboarding, self-adhesive	.70	.20	☐☐☐☐☐
3554	34c	Winter Olympics - Ice Hockey, self-adhesive	.70	.20	☐☐☐☐☐
3555	34c	Winter Olympics - Figure Skating, self-adhesive	.70	.20	☐☐☐☐☐
a.		Block or strip of 4, #3552-3555....	2.80		☐☐☐☐☐
b.		Die cutting inverted, pane of 20....	—		☐☐☐☐☐
c.		Die cutting omitted, block of 4	*825.00*		☐☐☐☐☐
3556	34c	Child and Adult, self-adhesive......	.70	.20	☐☐☐☐☐
3557	34c	Langston Hughes, Writer, self-adhesive	.70	.20	☐☐☐☐☐
a.		Die cutting omitted, pair	*1,250.*		☐☐☐☐☐
3558	34c	Happy Birthday, self-adhesive	.70	.20	☐☐☐☐☐
3559	34c	Year of the Horse, self-adhesive ...	.75	.20	☐☐☐☐☐
3560	34c	Military Academy Coat of Arms, self-adhesive	.70	.45	☐☐☐☐☐
3561	34c	Greetings from Alabama, self-adhesive	.70	.45	☐☐☐☐☐
3562	34c	Greetings from Alaska, self-adhesive	.70	.45	☐☐☐☐☐
3563	34c	Greetings from Arizona, self-adhesive	.70	.45	☐☐☐☐☐
3564	34c	Greetings from Arkansas, self-adhesive	.70	.45	☐☐☐☐☐
3565	34c	Greetings from California, self-adhesive	.70	.45	☐☐☐☐☐
3566	34c	Greetings from Colorado, self-adhesive	.70	.45	☐☐☐☐☐
3567	34c	Greetings from Connecticut, self-adhesive.............................	.70	.45	☐☐☐☐☐
3568	34c	Greetings from Delaware, self-adhesive	.70	.45	☐☐☐☐☐

3561

3562

3563

3564

3565

3566

3567

3568

3569

3570

3571

3572

3573

3574

3575

3576

3577

3578

3579

3580

3581 3582

3583 3584

3585 3586

3587 3588

3589 3590

Scott No.		Description	Unused Value	Used Value	/ / / / / /
3569	34c	Greetings from Florida, self-adhesive	.70	.45	☐☐☐☐☐
3570	34c	Greetings from Georgia, self-adhesive	.70	.45	☐☐☐☐☐
3571	34c	Greetings from Hawaii, self-adhesive	.70	.45	☐☐☐☐☐
3572	34c	Greetings from Idaho, self-adhesive	.70	.45	☐☐☐☐☐
3573	34c	Greetings from Illinois, self-adhesive	.70	.45	☐☐☐☐☐
3574	34c	Greetings from Indiana, self-adhesive	.70	.45	☐☐☐☐☐
3575	34c	Greetings from Iowa, self-adhesive	.70	.45	☐☐☐☐☐
3576	34c	Greetings from Kansas, self-adhesive	.70	.45	☐☐☐☐☐
3577	34c	Greetings from Kentucky, self-adhesive	.70	.45	☐☐☐☐☐
3578	34c	Greetings from Louisiana, self-adhesive	.70	.45	☐☐☐☐☐
3579	34c	Greetings from Maine, self-adhesive	.70	.45	☐☐☐☐☐
3580	34c	Greetings from Maryland, self-adhesive	.70	.45	☐☐☐☐☐
3581	34c	Greetings from Massachusetts, self-adhesive	.70	.45	☐☐☐☐☐
3582	34c	Greetings from Michigan, self-adhesive	.70	.45	☐☐☐☐☐
3583	34c	Greetings from Minnesota, self-adhesive	.70	.45	☐☐☐☐☐
3584	34c	Greetings from Mississippi, self-adhesive	.70	.45	☐☐☐☐☐
3585	34c	Greetings from Missouri, self-adhesive	.70	.45	☐☐☐☐☐
3586	34c	Greetings from Montana, self-adhesive	.70	.45	☐☐☐☐☐
3587	34c	Greetings from Nebraska, self-adhesive	.70	.45	☐☐☐☐☐
3588	34c	Greetings from Greetings from Nevada, self-adhesive	.70	.45	☐☐☐☐☐
3589	34c	Greetings from New Hampshire, self-adhesive	.70	.45	☐☐☐☐☐
3590	34c	Greetings from New Jersey, self-adhesive	.70	.45	☐☐☐☐☐
3591	34c	Greetings from New Mexico, self-adhesive	.70	.45	☐☐☐☐☐
3592	34c	Greetings from New York, self-adhesive	.70	.45	☐☐☐☐☐
3593	34c	Greetings from North Carolina, self-adhesive	.70	.45	☐☐☐☐☐
3594	34c	Greetings from North Dakota, self-adhesive	.70	.45	☐☐☐☐☐
3595	34c	Greetings from Ohio, self-adhesive	.70	.45	☐☐☐☐☐
3596	34c	Greetings from Oklahoma, self-adhesive	.70	.45	☐☐☐☐☐
3597	34c	Greetings from Oregon, self-adhesive	.70	.45	☐☐☐☐☐
3598	34c	Greetings from Pennsylvania, self-adhesive	.70	.45	☐☐☐☐☐
3599	34c	Greetings from Rhode Island, self-adhesive	.70	.45	☐☐☐☐☐
3600	34c	Greetings from South Carolina, self-adhesive	.70	.45	☐☐☐☐☐
3601	34c	Greetings from South Dakota, self-adhesive	.70	.45	☐☐☐☐☐
3602	34c	Greetings from Tennessee, self-adhesive	.70	.45	☐☐☐☐☐
3603	34c	Greetings from Texas, self-adhesive	.70	.45	☐☐☐☐☐
3604	34c	Greetings from Utah, self-adhesive	.70	.45	☐☐☐☐☐

3591

3592

3593

3594

3595

3596

3597

3598

3599

3600

3601

3602

3603

3604

3605

3606

3607

3608

3609

3610

3611

3612

3613-3614

3616-3617

3618-3619

3620-3621

3622

3623

3624

3625

3626

3627

3628

3629

3629F

3630

3631-3633

3632A

3634F

3635

3636

Scott No.		Description	Unused Value	Used Value	/ / / / / /
3605	34c	Greetings from Vermont, self-adhesive	.70	.45	☐☐☐☐☐
3606	34c	Greetings from Virginia, self-adhesive	.70	.45	☐☐☐☐☐
3607	34c	Greetings from Washington, self-adhesive	.70	.45	☐☐☐☐☐
3608	34c	Greetings from West Virginia, self-adhesive	.70	.45	☐☐☐☐☐
3609	34c	Greetings from Wisconsin, self-adhesive	.70	.45	☐☐☐☐☐
3610	34c	Greetings from Wyoming, self-adhesive	.70	.45	☐☐☐☐☐
a.		Greetings From America, pane of 50, #3561-3610	35.00		☐☐☐☐☐
3611		Longleaf Pine Forest, pane of 10, self-adhesive	16.00		☐☐☐☐☐
a.	34c	Bachman's sparrow,	1.60	.50	☐☐☐☐☐
b.	34c	Northern bobwhite, yellow pitcher plants	1.60	.50	☐☐☐☐☐
c.	34c	Fox squirrel, red-bellied woodpecker	1.60	.50	☐☐☐☐☐
d.	34c	Brown-headed nuthatch	1.60	.50	☐☐☐☐☐
e.	34c	Broadhead skink, yellow pitcher plants, pipeworts	1.60	.50	☐☐☐☐☐
f.	34c	Eastern towhee, yellow pitcher plants, Savannah meadow beauties, toothache grass	1.60	.50	☐☐☐☐☐
g.	34c	Gray fox, gopher tortoise	1.60	.50	☐☐☐☐☐
h.	34c	Blind click beetle, sweetbay, pine woods treefrog	1.60	.50	☐☐☐☐☐
i.	34c	Rosebud orchid, pipeworts, southern toad, yellow pitcher plants	1.60	.50	☐☐☐☐☐
j.	34c	Grass-pink orchid, yellow-sided skimmer, pipeworts, yellow pitcher plants	1.60	.50	☐☐☐☐☐
k.		As No. 3611, die cutting omitted..	*2,500.*		☐☐☐☐☐
3612	5c	Toleware Coffeepot, coil stamp, perf. 10 vert.	.20	.20	☐☐☐☐☐
a.		Imperf., pair	—		☐☐☐☐☐
3613	3c	Star, self-adhesive, serpentine die cut 11	.20	.20	☐☐☐☐☐
a.		Die cutting omitted, pair	—		☐☐☐☐☐
3614	3c	Star (3613), self-adhesive, serpentine die cut 10, year at lower right...	.20	.20	☐☐☐☐☐
3615	3c	Star, year at lower left	.20	.20	☐☐☐☐☐
3616	23c	Washington (3468A), perf. 11¼...	.50	.20	☐☐☐☐☐
3617	23c	Washington (3468A), self-adhesive, coil stamp, serpentine die cut 11¼	.45	.20	☐☐☐☐☐
a.		Die cutting omitted, pair	—		☐☐☐☐☐
3618	23c	Washington (3468A), booklet stamp, self-adhesive, serp. die cut 11¼	.50	.20	☐☐☐☐☐
a.		Booklet pane of 4	2.00		☐☐☐☐☐

Scott No.		Description	Unused Value	Used Value	/ / / / / /
b.		Booklet pane of 6	3.00		□□□□□
c.		Booklet pane of 10	5.00		□□□□□
3619	23c	Washington (3468A), booklet stamp, self-adhesive, serpentine die cut 10½ x11¼	4.00	1.75	□□□□□
a.		Booklet pane of 4, 2 #3619 at L, 2 #3618 at R	9.00		□□□□□
b.		Booklet pane of 6, 3 #3619 at L, 3 #3618 at R	14.00		□□□□□
c.		Booklet pane of 4, 2 #3618 at L, 2 #3619 at R	9.00		□□□□□
d.		Booklet pane of 6, 3 #3618 at L, 3 #3619 at R	14.00		□□□□□
e.		Booklet pane of 10, 5 #3619 at L, 5 #3618 at R	21.00		□□□□□
f.		Booklet pane of 10, 5 #3618 at L, 5 #3619 at R	21.00		□□□□□
g.		Pair, #3619 at L, #3618 at R	4.50		□□□□□
h.		Pair, #3618 at L, #3619 at R	4.50		□□□□□
3620	(37c)	Flag perf.11¼ x 11	.85	.20	□□□□□
3621	(37c)	Flag (3620), self-adhesive, serpentine die cut 11¼ x 11	1.00	.20	□□□□□
3622	(37c)	Flag (3620), coil stamp, self-adhesive, serpentine die cut 10 vert.	.75	.20	□□□□□
a.		Die cutting omitted, pair	—		□□□□□
3623	(37c)	Flag (3620), booklet stamps, self-adhesive, serpentine die cut 11¼	.75	.20	□□□□□
a.		Booklet pane of 20	15.00		□□□□□
3624	(37c)	Flag (3620), booklet stamp, self-adhesive, serpentine die cut 10½ x10¾	.75	.20	□□□□□
a.		Booklet pane of 4	3.00		□□□□□
b.		Booklet pane of 6	4.50		□□□□□
c.		Booklet pane of 20	15.00		□□□□□
3625	(37c)	Flag (3620), booklet stamp, self-adhesive, serp. die cut 8	.75	.20	□□□□□
a.		Booklet pane of 18	13.50		□□□□□
3626	(37c)	Toy Mail Wagon, self-adhesive, booklet stamp	.75	.20	□□□□□
3627	(37c)	Toy Locomotive, self-adhesive, booklet stamp	.75	.20	□□□□□
3628	(37c)	Toy Taxicab, self-adhesive, booklet stamp	.75	.20	□□□□□
3629	(37c)	Toy Fire Pumper, self-adhesive, booklet stamp	1.00	.20	□□□□□
a.		Block of 4, #3626-3629	3.00		□□□□□
b.		Booklet pane of 4, #3626-3629	3.00		□□□□□

Scott No.		Description	Unused Value	Used Value
c.		Booklet pane of 6, #3627, 3629, 2 each #3626, 3628	4.50	
d.		Booklet pane of 6, #3626, 3628, 2 each #3627, 3629	4.50	
e.		Booklet pane of 20, 5 each		
3629F	37c	Flag (3630), perf 11¼	.90	.20
3630	37c	Flag, self-adhesive, serpentine die cut 11¼ x 11	.90	.20
3631	37c	Flag (3630), coil stamp, perf. 10 vert.	.75	.20
3632	37c	Flag (3630), self-adhesive, coil stamp, serp. die cut 9¾ vert	.75	.20
b.		Die cutting omitted, pair	*55.00*	
3632A	37c	Flag (3630) self-adhesive, serp. die cut 10¼ vert	.75	.20
f.		Die cutting omitted, pair	—	
3632C	37c	Flag (3630), self-adhesive, coil stamp, serp. die cut 11¾ vert	1.00	.20
3633	37c	Flag (3630), self-adhesive, coil stamp, serpentine die cut 8½ vert., dated "2002," rounded corners	.75	.20
3633A	37c	Flag (3630), self-adhesive - coil Stamp, serp. die cut 8½ vert., square corners	2.00	.20
3633B	37c	Flag (3630), self-adhesive - coil Stamp, serp. die cut 9½ vert.	3.50	.20
3634	37c	Flag (3630), self-adhesive, booklet stamp, serp. die cut 11.1, dated "2002"	.75	.20
a.		Booklet pane of 10	7.50	
b.		Dated "2003"	.75	.20
c.		Booklet pane, 4 #3634b	3.00	
d.		Booklet pane, 6 #3635b	4.50	
e.		As No. 3634, die cut 11.3	.85	.25
f.		As "e," booklet pane of 10	8.50	
3635	37c	Flag (3630), self-adhesive, booklet stamp, serp. die cut 11¼	.75	.20
a.		Booklet pane of 20	15.00	
b.		Black omitted	—	
3636	37c	Flag (3630), self-adhesive, booklet stamp, serp. die cut 10½ x 10¾.	.75	.20
a.		Booklet pane of 4	3.00	
b.		Booklet pane of 6	4.50	
c.		Booklet pane of 20	15.00	
f.		As "c," 11 stamps and part of 12th stamp on reverse printed on backing liner, the 8 stamps on front side imperf.	—	
3636D	37c	Flag (3630), self-adhesive, booklet stamp, serp. die cut 11¼ x11 on 2 or 3 sides	1.10	.20

3638

3639

3640

3641

3642

3643

3644

3645

3646

3647

3648

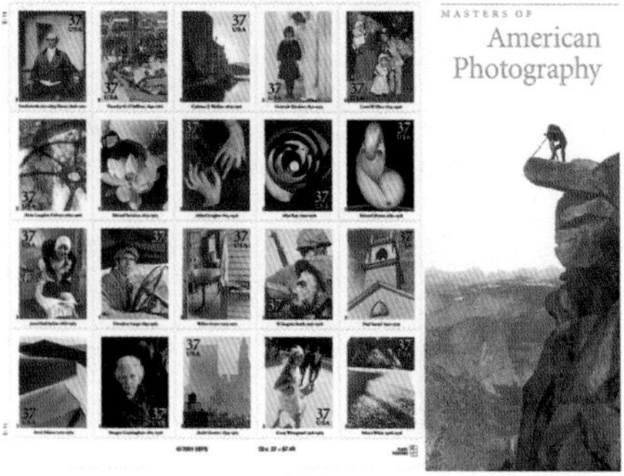

3649

Scott No.		Description	Unused Value	Used Value	/ / / / / /
e.		Booklet pane of 20	22.50		□□□□□
3637	37c	Flag self-adhesive, booklet stamp, serpentine die cut 8	.75	.20	□□□□□
a.		Booklet pane of 18	13.50		□□□□□
3638	37c	Toy Locomotive, coil	.85	.20	□□□□□
3639	37c	Toy Mail Wagon, coil	.85	.20	□□□□□
3640	37c	Toy Fire Pumper, coil	.85	.20	□□□□□
3641	37c	Toy Taxicab, coil	.85	.20	□□□□□
a.		Strip of 4, #3638-3641	3.40		□□□□□
3642	37c	Mail Wagon, booklet stamp, serp. die cut 11, dated "2002"	.75	.20	□□□□□
a.		Serp. die cut 11 x 11¼, dated '2003'	.75	.20	□□□□□
3643	37c	Locomotive, booklet stamp, serp. die cut 11, dated "2002"	.75	.20	□□□□□
a.		Serp. die cut 11 x 11¼, dated '2003'	.75	.20	□□□□□
3644	37c	Taxicab, booklet stamp, serp. die cut 11, dated "2002"	.75	.20	□□□□□
a.		Serp. die cut 11 x 11¼, dated '2003'	.75	.20	□□□□□
3645	37c	Fire Pumper, booklet stamp, serp. die cut 11, dated "2002"	.75	.20	□□□□□
a.		Block of 4, #3642-3645	3.00		□□□□□
b.		Booklet pane of 4, #3642-3645	3.00		□□□□□
c.		Booklet pane of 6, #3643, 3645, 2 each #3642, 3644	4.50		□□□□□
d.		Booklet pane of 6, #3642, 3644, 2 each #3643, 3645	4.50		□□□□□
e.		Booklet pane of 20, 5 each #3642-3645	15.00		□□□□□
f.		Serp. die cut 11 x 11¼, dated '2003'	.75	.20	□□□□□
g.		Block of 4, #3642a, 3643a, 3644a, 3645f	3.00		□□□□□
h.		Booklet pane of 20, 5 #3645g	15.00		□□□□□
3646	60c	Coverlet eagle, self-adhesive	1.25	.25	□□□□□
3647	$3.85	Jefferson Memorial, self-adhesive, serp. die cut 11¼	7.50	2.00	□□□□□
3647A	$3.85	Jefferson Memorial (3647), self-adhesive, serp. die cut 11 x 10¾	8.50	2.00	□□□□□
3648	$13.65	Capitol Dome	27.50	10.00	□□□□□
3649		Masters of American Photography, pane of 20, self-adhesive	15.00		□□□□□
a.	37c	Portrait of Daniel Webster, by Albert Sands	.75	.50	□□□□□
b.	37c	Gen. Ulysses S. Grant and Officers, by Timothy H. Olsullivan	.75	.50	□□□□□
c.	37c	Cape Horn, Columbia River, by Carleton E. Watkins	.75	.50	□□□□□
d.	37c	Blessed Art Thou Among Women, by Gertrude Kasebier	.75	.50	□□□□□

3650

3651

3652

3653

3654

3655

3656

3657

3658

3659

3660

Scott No.		Description	Unused Value	Used Value	/ / / / / /
e.	37c	Looking for Lost Luggage, Ellis Island, by Lewis W. Hine........................	.75	.50	☐☐☐☐☐
f.	37c	The Octopus, by Alvin Langdon Colburn	.75	.50	☐☐☐☐☐
g.	37c	Lotus, Mount Kisco, New York, by Edward Steichen	.75	.50	☐☐☐☐☐
h.	37c	Hands and Thimble, by Alfred Stieglitz	.75	.50	☐☐☐☐☐
i.	37c	Rayograph, by Man Ray................	.75	.50	☐☐☐☐☐
j.	37c	Two Shells, by Edward Weston.....	.75	.50	☐☐☐☐☐
k.	37c	My Corsage, by James VanDerZee	.75	.50	☐☐☐☐☐
l.	37c	Ditched, Stalled, and Stranded, San Joaquin Valley, California, by Dorothea Lange...........................	.75	.50	☐☐☐☐☐
m.	37c	Washroom and Dining Area of Floyd Burroughs' Home, Hale County, Alabama, by Walker Evans	.75	.50	☐☐☐☐☐
n.	37c	Frontline Soldier with Canteen, Saipan, by W. Eugene Smith.......	.75	.50	☐☐☐☐☐
o.	37c	Steeple, by Paul Strand	.75	.50	☐☐☐☐☐
p.	37c	Sand Dunes, Sunrise, by Ansel Adams	.75	.50	☐☐☐☐☐
q.	37c	Age and Its Symbols, by Imogen Cunningham................................	.75	.50	☐☐☐☐☐
r.	37c	New York Cityscape, by Andre Kertesz	.75	.50	☐☐☐☐☐
s.	37c	Photograph of pedestrians, by Garry Winogrand..................................	.75	.50	☐☐☐☐☐
t.	37c	Bristol, Vermont, by Minor White	.75	.50	☐☐☐☐☐
u.		As No. 3649, die cutting omitted..	—		☐☐☐☐☐
3650	37c	Scarlet and Louisiana Tanagers, self-adhesive................................	1.00	.20	☐☐☐☐☐
3651	37c	Harry Houdini (1874-1926), Magician, self-adhesive..............................	.75	.20	☐☐☐☐☐
3652	37c	Andy Warhol (1928-87), Artist - Self-Portrait, self-adhesive.........	.75	.20	☐☐☐☐☐
3653	37c	Teddy Bears, Centennial - Bruin Bear, c. 1907....................	1.00	.20	☐☐☐☐☐
3654	37c	Teddy Bears, Centennial - Stick Bear, 1920s.......................	1.00	.20	☐☐☐☐☐
3655	37c	Teddy Bears, Centennial - Bund Bear, c. 1948	1.00	.20	☐☐☐☐☐
3656	37c	Teddy Bears, Centennial - Ideal Bear, c. 1905.....................	1.00	.20	☐☐☐☐☐
a.		Block or vert. strip of 4, #3653-3656...............................	4.00		☐☐☐☐☐
3657	37c	Love, self-adhesive, booklet stamp	.75	.20	☐☐☐☐☐
a.		Booklet pane of 20.......................	15.00		☐☐☐☐☐
b.		As "a," silver ("Love 37 USA") missing on top 5 stamps (from color misregistration)................	*750.00*		☐☐☐☐☐
3658	60c	Love, self-adhesive......................	1.25	.25	☐☐☐☐☐

3661

3662

3663

3664

3665

3666

3667

3668

3669

3670

3671

3675

Scott No.	Description	Unused Value	Used Value	/ / / / / /
3659	37c Ogden Nash (1902-1987), Poet, self-adhesive	.75	.20	☐☐☐☐☐
3660	37c Duke Kahanamoku, 1890-1968, 'Father of Surfing' and Olympic Swimmer, self-adhesive	.75	.20	☐☐☐☐☐
3661	37c American Bats - Red Bat, self-adhesive	.75	.20	☐☐☐☐☐
3662	37c American Bats -Leaf-nosed Bat, self-adhesive	.75	.20	☐☐☐☐☐
3663	37c American Bats - Pallid Bat, self-adhesive	.75	.20	☐☐☐☐☐
3664	37c American Bat - Spotted Bat, self-adhesive	.75	.20	☐☐☐☐☐
a.	Block or horiz. strip of 4, #3661-3664	3.00		☐☐☐☐☐
3665	37c Women In Journalism - Nellie Bly (1864-1922), self-adhesive..	.75	.20	☐☐☐☐☐
3666	37c Women In Journalism - Ida M. Tarbell (1857-1944), self-adhesive	.75	.20	☐☐☐☐☐
3667	37c Women In Journalism - Ethel L. Payne (1911-91), self-adhesive	.75	.20	☐☐☐☐☐
3668	37c Women In Journalism - Marguerite Higgins (1920-66), self-adhesive	.75	.20	☐☐☐☐☐
a.	Block or horiz. strip of 4, #3665-3668	3.00		☐☐☐☐☐
3669	37c Irving Berlin, 1888-1989, Composer, self-adhesive	.75	.20	☐☐☐☐☐
3670	37c Neuter and Spay - Kitten, self-adhesive	1.00	.20	☐☐☐☐☐
3671	37c Neuter and Spay - Puppy, self-adhesive	1.00	.20	☐☐☐☐☐
a.	Horiz. or vert. pair, #3670-3671 ..	2.00		☐☐☐☐☐
3672	37c Hanukkah Type of 1996 (3118), self-adhesive	.75	.20	☐☐☐☐☐
3673	37c Kwanzaa Type of 1997 (3175) self-adhesive	.75	.20	☐☐☐☐☐
3674	37c Eid Type of 2001 (3532) self-adhesive	.75	.20	☐☐☐☐☐
3675	37c Christmas - Madonna and Child, by Jan Gossaert, self-adhesive, booklet stamp, 19x27mm design size	.75	.20	☐☐☐☐☐
a.	Booklet pane of 20......................	15.00		
3676	37c Snowman with Red and Green Plaid Scarf, self-adhesive...........	.90	.20	☐☐☐☐☐
3677	37c Snowman with Blue Plaid Scarf, self-adhesive	.90	.20	☐☐☐☐☐
3678	37c Snowman with Pipe, self-adhesive	.90	.20	☐☐☐☐☐
3679	37c Snowman with Top Hat, self-adhesive	.90	.20	☐☐☐☐☐
a.	Block or vert. strip of 4, #3676-3679	3.75		☐☐☐☐☐
3680	37c Snowman with Blue Plaid Scarf, self-adhesive, coil stamp............	2.00	.20	☐☐☐☐☐
3681	37c Snowman with Pipe, self-adhesive, coil stamp..................................	2.00	.20	☐☐☐☐☐

3676

3677

3678

3679

3680

3681

3682

3683

3692

3693

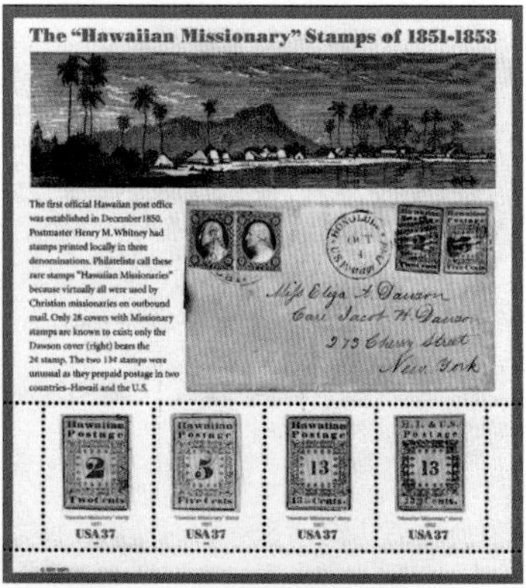

3694

3746

3747

3749

3748

3750

Scott No.		Description	Unused Value	Used Value	/ / / / / /
3682	37c	Snowman with Top Hat, self-adhesive, coil stamp............	2.00	.20	□□□□□
3683	37c	Snowman with Red and Green Plaid Scarf, self-adhesive, coil stamp	2.00	.20	□□□□□
a.		Strip of 4, #3680-3683................	8.00		□□□□□
3684	37c	Snowman with Red and Green Plaid Scarf, self-adhesive, booklet stamp, serp. die cut 10¾ x 11..................................	1.25	.20	□□□□□
3685	37c	Snowman with Blue Plaid Scarf, self-adhesive, booklet stamp, serp. die cut 10¾ x 11..............	1.25	.20	□□□□□
3686	37c	Snowman with Pipe, self-adhesive, booklet stamp, serp. die cut 10¾ x 11..................................	1.25	.20	□□□□□
3687	37c	Snowman with Top Hat, self-adhesive, booklet stamp, serp. die cut 10¾ x 11..............	1.25	.20	□□□□□
a.		Block of 4, #3684-3687..............	5.00		□□□□□
b.		Booklet pane, 5 #3687a + label...	25.00		□□□□□
3688	37c	Snowman with Blue Plaid Scarf, self-adhesive, booklet stamp, serp. die cut 11..........................	1.00	.20	□□□□□
3689	37c	Snowman with Blue Plaid Scarf, self-adhesive, booklet stamp, serp. die cut 11..........................	1.00	.20	□□□□□
3690	37c	Snowman with Pipe, self-adhesive, booklet stamp, serp. die cut 11..	1.00	.20	□□□□□
3691	37c	Snowman with Top Hat, self-adhesive, booklet stamp, serp. die cut 11..........................	1.00	.20	□□□□□
a.		Block of 4, #3688-3691..............	4.00		□□□□□
b.		Booklet pane of 4, #3688-3691 ...	4.00		□□□□□
c.		Booklet pane of 6, #3690-3691, 2 each #3688-3689....................	6.00		□□□□□
d.		Booklet pane of 6, #3688-3689, 2 each #3690-3691....................	6.00		□□□□□
3692	37c	Legends of Hollywood - Cary Grant (1904-86), Actor, self-adhesive..	1.00	.20	□□□□□
3693	5c	Sea Coast, self-adhesive, coil stamp, serpentine die cut 8½ vert.	.20	.20	□□□□□
3694		Hawaiian Missionary Stamps - Pane of 4..................................	3.50	2.50	□□□□□
a.	37c	2c stamp of 1851, Hawaii Scott 1	.85	.50	□□□□□
b.	37c	5c stamp of 1851, Hawaii Scott 2	.85	.50	□□□□□
c.	37c	13c stamp of 1851, Hawaii Scott 3	.85	.50	□□□□□
d.	37c	13c stamp of 1852, Hawaii Scott 4	.85	.50	□□□□□
3695	37c	Happy Birthday Type of 2002 (3558), self-adhesive.................	.75	.20	□□□□□

Scott No.	Description	Unused Value	Used Value	/ / / / / /
3696	37c Greetings From Alabama type (3561), self-adhesive..................	.75	.60	☐☐☐☐☐
3697	37c Greetings From Alaska type (3562), self-adhesive..................	.75	.60	☐☐☐☐☐
3698	37c Greetings From Arizona type (3563), self-adhesive..................	.75	.60	☐☐☐☐☐
3699	37c Greetings From Arkansas type (3564), self-adhesive..................	.75	.60	☐☐☐☐☐
3700	37c Greetings From California type (3565), self-adhesive..................	.75	.60	☐☐☐☐☐
3701	37c Greetings From Colorado type (3566), self-adhesive..................	.75	.60	☐☐☐☐☐
3702	37c Greetings From Connecticut type (3567), self-adhesive..................	.75	.60	☐☐☐☐☐
3703	37c Greetings From Delaware type (3568), self-adhesive..................	.75	.60	☐☐☐☐☐
3704	37c Greetings From Florida type (3569), self-adhesive..................	.75	.60	☐☐☐☐☐
3705	37c Greetings From Georgia type (3570), self-adhesive..................	.75	.60	☐☐☐☐☐
3706	37c Greetings From Hawaii type (3571), self-adhesive..................	.75	.60	☐☐☐☐☐
3707	37c Greetings From Idaho type (3572), self-adhesive..................	.75	.60	☐☐☐☐☐
3708	37c Greetings From Illinois type (3573), self-adhesive..................	.75	.60	☐☐☐☐☐
3709	37c Greetings From Indiana type (3574), self-adhesive..................	.75	.60	☐☐☐☐☐
3710	37c Greetings From Iowa type (3575), self-adhesive..................	.75	.60	☐☐☐☐☐
3711	37c Greetings From Kansas type (3576), self-adhesive..................	.75	.60	☐☐☐☐☐
3712	37c Greetings From Kentucky type (3577), self-adhesive..................	.75	.60	☐☐☐☐☐
3713	37c Greetings From Louisiana type (3578), self-adhesive..................	.75	.60	☐☐☐☐☐
3714	37c Greetings From Maine type (3579), self-adhesive..................	.75	.60	☐☐☐☐☐
3715	37c Greetings From Maryland type (3580), self-adhesive..................	.75	.60	☐☐☐☐☐
3716	37c Greetings From Massachusetts type (3581), self-adhesive..................	.75	.60	☐☐☐☐☐
3717	37c Greetings From Michigan type (3582), self-adhesive..................	.75	.60	☐☐☐☐☐
3718	37c Greetings From Minnesota type (3583), self-adhesive..................	.75	.60	☐☐☐☐☐
3719	37c Greetings From Mississippi type (3584), self-adhesive..................	.75	.60	☐☐☐☐☐

Scott No.	Description	Unused Value	Used Value	/ / / / / /
3720	37c Greetings From Missouri type (3585), self-adhesive.................	.75	.60	□□□□□
3721	37c Greetings From Montana type (3586), self-adhesive.................	.75	.60	□□□□□
3722	37c Greetings From Nebraska type (3587), self-adhesive.................	.75	.60	□□□□□
3723	37c Greetings From Nevada type (3588), self-adhesive.................	.75	.60	□□□□□
3724	37c Greetings From New Hampshire type (3589), self-adhesive..........	.75	.60	□□□□□
3725	37c Greetings From New Jersey type (3590), self-adhesive.................	.75	.60	□□□□□
3726	37c Greetings From New Mexico type (3591), self-adhesive.................	.75	.60	□□□□□
3727	37c Greetings From New York type (3592), self-adhesive.................	.75	.60	□□□□□
3728	37c Greetings From North Carolina type (3593), self-adhesive.................	.75	.60	□□□□□
3729	37c Greetings From North Dakota type (3594), self-adhesive.................	.75	.60	□□□□□
3730	37c Greetings From Ohio type (3595), self-adhesive	.75	.60	□□□□□
3731	37c Greetings From Oklahoma type (3596), self-adhesive.................	.75	.60	□□□□□
3732	37c Greetings From Oregon type (3597), self-adhesive.................	.75	.60	□□□□□
3733	37c Greetings From Pennsylvania type (3598), self-adhesive.................	.75	.60	□□□□□
3734	37c Greetings From Rhode Island type (3599), self-adhesive.................	.75	.60	□□□□□
3735	37c Greetings From South Carolina type (3600), self-adhesive.................	.75	.60	□□□□□
3736	37c Greetings From South Dakota type (3601), self-adhesive.................	.75	.60	□□□□□
3737	37c Greetings From Tennessee type (3602), self-adhesive.................	.75	.60	□□□□□
3738	37c Greetings From Texas type (3603), self-adhesive.................	.75	.60	□□□□□
3739	37c Greetings From Utah type (3604), self-adhesive.................	.75	.60	□□□□□
3740	37c Greetings From Vermont type (3605), self-adhesive.................	.75	.60	□□□□□
3741	37c Greetings From Virginia type (3606), self-adhesive.................	.75	.60	□□□□□
3742	37c Greetings From Washington type (3607), self-adhesive.................	.75	.60	□□□□□
3743	37c Greetings From West Virginia type (3608), self-adhesive.................	.75	.60	□□□□□

3753

3754

3755

3757

3756

3758

3762

3766

3770

3772

3771

3773

3774

3775

3776

Scott No.	Description	Unused Value	Used Value	/ / / / / /
3744	37c Greetings From Wisconsin type (3609), self-adhesive	.75	.60	□□□□□
3745	37c Greetings From Wyoming type (3610), self-adhesive	.75	.60	□□□□□
a.	Pane of 50, #3696-3745	37.50		□□□□□
2003 Issues				
3746	37c Black Heritage Series - Thurgood Marshall (1908-93), Supreme Court Justice, self-adhesive	.75	.20	□□□□□
3747	37c Chinese New Year - Year of the Ram, self-adhesive	.80	.20	□□□□□
3748	37c Literary Arts - Zora Neale Hurston (1891-1960), Writer, self-adhesive	.85	.20	□□□□□
3749	1c American Design Series - Tiffany Lamp (3758), self-adhesive	.20	.20	□□□□□
3749A	1c American Design Series - Tiffany Lamp (3758), self-adhesive, with "USPS" microprinting	.20	.20	□□□□□
3750	2c American Design Series - Navajo Necklace, self-adhesive, die cut 11	.20	.20	□□□□□
3751	2c American Design Series - Navajo Necklace (3750), self-adhesive, serp. die cut 11¼ x 11½	.20	.20	□□□□□
3752	2c American Design Series - Navajo Necklace (3750), self-adhesive, serp. die cut 11¼ x 11½, with "USPS" microprinting	.20	.20	□□□□□
3753	2c American Design Series - Navajo Necklace (3750), dated "2007," serp. die cut 11¼x10¾, self-adhesive, with "USPS" microprinting	.20	.20	□□□□□
3754	3c American Design Series - Silver Coffeepot, self-adhesive	.20	.20	□□□□□
3755	4c American Design Series - Chippendale Chair, self-adhesive	.20	.20	□□□□□
3756	5c American Design Series - Toleware Coffeepot (3612), self-adhesive serp. die cut 11¼ x 11¾	.20	.20	□□□□□
3756A	5c American Design Series - Toleware Coffeepot (3612), self-adhesive, serp. die cut 11¼ x 10¾	.20	.20	□□□□□
3757	10c American Design Series - American Clock, self-adhesive	.20	.20	□□□□□
a.	Die cutting omitted, pair	—		□□□□□
3758	1c American Design Series - Tiffany Lamp, coil stamp, dated "2003"	.20	.20	□□□□□
3758A	1c American Design Series - Tiffany Lamp (3758), coil stamp, dated "2008" with "USPS" microprinting	.20	.20	□□□□□

3777

3778

3779

3780

3781

3782

3783

3784

3786

3787

3788

3789

3790

3791

3792

Scott No.	Description	Unused Value	Used Value
3759	3c American Design Series - Silver Coffeepot (3754), coil stamp	.20	.20
3761	4c American Design Series - Chippendale Chair (3755), coil stamp	.20	.20
3762	10c American Design Series - American Clock (3757), coil stamp	.20	.20
3763	10c American Design Series - American Clock (3757), coil stamp	.20	.20
3766	$1 American Culture Series - Wisdom, Rockefeller Center, New York City, self-adhesive, dated "2003"	2.00	.40
a.	Dated "2008"	2.00	.40
3769	10c New York Public Library Lion Type of 2000 (3447), coil stamp, perf. 10 vert.	.20	.20
3770	10c Atlas Statue (3520), self-adhesive, coil stamp, serp. die cut 11 vert.	.20	.20
3771	80c Special Olympics - Athlete with Medal, self-adhesive	1.60	.35
3772	American Filmmaking: Behind The Scenes, pane of 10, self-adhesive	10.00	
a.	37c Screenwriting, segment of script from Gone With the Wind	1.00	.50
b.	37c Directing, John Cassavetes	1.00	.50
c.	37c Costume design, Edith Head	1.00	.50
d.	37c Music, Max Steiner working on score	1.00	.50
e.	37c Makeup, Jack Pierce working on Boris Karloff's makeup for Frankenstein	1.00	.50
f.	37c Art direction, Perry Ferguson working on sketch for Citizen Kane	1.00	.50
g.	37c Cinematography, Paul Hill, assistant cameraman for Nagana	1.00	.50
h.	37c Film Editing, J. Watson Webb editing the Razor's Edge	1.00	.50
i.	37c Special effects, Mark Siegel working on model for E.T. The Extra-Terrestrial	1.00	.50
j.	37c Sound, Gary Summers works on control panel	1.00	.50
3773	37c Ohio Statehood Bicentennial, self-adhesive	.75	.20
3774	37c Pelican Island National Wildlife Refuge, Cent. - Brown Pelican, self-adhesive	.75	.20
3775	5c Sea Coast Type of 2002 (3693), coil stamp, perf 9¾ vert., "2003" year date	.20	.20
3776	37c Old Glory - Uncle Sam on Bicycle with Liberty Flag, 20th Cent., self-adhesive, booklet stamp	.75	.50

3793

3802

3803

3804

3805

3806

3807

3808

3809

3810

3811

Scott No.	Description	Unused Value	Used Value
3777	37c Old Glory - 1888 Presidential Campaign Badge, self-adhesive, booklet stamp............................	.75	.50
3778	37c Old Glory - 1893 Silk Bookmark, self-adhesive, booklet stamp......	.75	.50
3779	37c Old Glory - Modern Hand Fan, self adhesive, booklet stamp......	.75	.50
3780	37c Old Glory - Carving of Woman with Flag and Sword, 19th Cent., self-adhesive, booklet stamp......	.75	.50
a.	Horiz. Strip of 5, #3776-3780......	3.75	
b.	Booklet pane, 2 #3780a	7.50	
3781	37c Cesar E. Chavez (1927-93), Labor Organizer, self-adhesive............	.75	.20
3782	37c Louisiana Purchase, Bicent., self-adhesive	.95	.40
3783	37c First Flight of Wright Brothers, Cent., self-adhesive..................	.75	.40
a.	Booklet pane of 9........................	6.75	
b.	Booklet pane of 1, booklet stamp	.75	
3784	37c Purple Heart, self-adhesive serp. die cut 11¼ x 10¾..........	.75	.20
b.	Printed on back of backing paper	—	
d.	Die cutting omitted, pair	—	
3784A	37c Purple Heart (3784), self-adhesive, serp. die cut 10¾ x 10¼..........	.75	.20
c.	Die cutting omitted, pane of 20 ...	*1,600.*	
3785	5c Sea Coast Type of 2002 (3693), self-adhesive, coil stamp, serp. die cut 9½ x 10.........................	.20	.20
a.	Serp. die cut 9¼ x 10	.20	.20
3786	37c Legends of Hollywood - Audrey Hepburn (1929-93), Actress, self-adhesive	1.00	.20
3787	37c Southeastern Lighthouses - Old Cape Henry, Virginia, self-adhesive....	1.10	.20
3788	37c Southeastern Lighthouses - Cape Lockout, North Carolina, self-adhesive	1.10	.20
a.	Bottom of 'USA' even with top of upper half-diamond of lighthouse, pos. 2......................	4.00	2.50
3789	37c Southeastern Lighthouses - Morris Island, South Carolina, self-adhesive....	1.10	.20
3790	37c Southeastern Lighthouses - Tybee Island, Georgia, self-adhesive	1.10	.20
3791	37c Southeastern Lighthouses - Hillsboro Inlet, Florida, self-adhesive	1.10	.20
a.	Strip of 5, #3587-3791................	5.50	

3812

3813

3814

3815

3816

3817

3818

3819

3820

3821

3822

3823

3824

3825

3826

3827

3828

Scott No.		Description	Unused Value	Used Value
b.		Strip of 5, #3767, 3788a, 3789-3791	9.50	
3792	25c	Eagle in gold on gray background, self-adhesive, coil stamp	.50	.20
a.		Dated "2005"	.50	.20
3793	25c	Red eagle on gold background, self-adhesive, coil stamp	.50	.20
a.		Dated "2005"	.50	.20
3794	25c	Eagle in gold on dull blue background, self-adhesive, coil stamp	.50	.20
a.		Dated "2005"	.50	.20
3795	25c	Prussian blue eagle on gold background, self-adhesive, coil stamp	.50	.20
a.		Dated "2005"	.50	.20
3796	25c	Eagle in gold on green background, self-adhesive, coil stamp	.50	.20
a.		Dated "2005"	.50	.20
3797	25c	Gray eagle on gold background, self-adhesive, coil stamp	.50	.20
a.		Dated "2005"	.50	.20
3798	25c	Eagle in gold on Prussian blue background, self-adhesive, coil stamp	.50	.20
a.		Dated "2005"	.50	.20
3799	25c	Dull blue eagle on gold background, self-adhesive, coil stamp	.50	.20
a.		Dated "2005"	.50	.20
3800	25c	Eagle in gold on red background, self-adhesive, coil stamp	.50	.20
a.		Dated "2005"	.50	.20
3801	25c	Green eagle on gold background, self-adhesive, coil stamp	.50	.20
a.		Strip of 10 #3792-3801	5.00	
b.		Dated "2005"	.50	.20
c.		Strip of 10, #3792a-3801b	5.00	
3802		Arctic Tundra, Pane of 10, self-adhesive	7.50	
a.	37c	Gyrfalcon	.75	.50
b.	37c	Gray wolf, vert.	.75	.50
c.	37c	Common raven, vert.	.75	.50
d.	37c	Musk oxen and caribou	.75	.50
e.	37c	Grizzly bears, caribou	.75	.50
f.	37c	Caribou, willow ptarmigans	.75	.50
g.	37c	Arctic ground squirrel, vert.	.75	.50
h.	37c	Willow ptarmigan, bearberry	.75	.50
i.	37c	Arctic grayling	.75	.50
j.	37c	Singing vole, thin-legged wolf spider, lingonberry, Labrador tea	.75	.50
3803	37c	Korean War Veterans Memorial, self-adhesive	.75	.20

3829

3829A

3831

3832

3833

3834

3835

3836

3837

3838

3839

Scott No.	Description	Unused Value	Used Value	/ / / / / /
3804	37c Mary Cassatt Paintings - Young Mother, 1888, self-adhesive, booklet stamp............................	.75	.20	☐☐☐☐☐
3805	37c Mary Cassatt Paintings - Children Playing on the Beach, 1884, self-adhesive, booklet stamp......	.75	.20	☐☐☐☐☐
3806	37c Mary Cassatt Paintings - On a Balcony, 1878-79, self-adhesive, booklet stamp............................	.75	.20	☐☐☐☐☐
3807	37c Mary Cassatt Paintings - Child in a Straw Hat, c. 1886, self-adhesive, booklet stamp......	.75	.20	☐☐☐☐☐
a.	Block of 4, #3804-3807	3.00		☐☐☐☐☐
b.	Booklet pane of 20, 5 each #3807a	15.00		☐☐☐☐☐
3808	37c Early Football Heroes - Bronko Nagurski (1908-90), self-adhesive	.75	.20	☐☐☐☐☐
3809	37c Early Football Heroes - Ernie Nevers (1903-96), self-adhesive	.75	.20	☐☐☐☐☐
3810	37c Early Football Heroes - Walter Camp (1859-1925), self-adhesive	.75	.20	☐☐☐☐☐
3811	37c Early Football Heroes - Red Grange (1903-91), self-adhesive	.75	.20	☐☐☐☐☐
a.	Block of 4, #3808-3811	3.00		☐☐☐☐☐
3812	37c Roy Acuff (1903-92), Country Music Artist, self-adhesive	.75	.20	☐☐☐☐☐
3813	37c District of Columbia, self-adhesive	.85	.20	☐☐☐☐☐
3814	37c Reptiles and Amphibians - Scarlet Kingsnake, self-adhesive	.80	.20	☐☐☐☐☐
3815	37c Reptiles and Amphibians - Blue-Spotted Salamander, self-adhesive	.80	.20	☐☐☐☐☐
3816	37c Reptiles and Amphibians - Reticulate Collared Lizard, self-adhesive	.80	.20	☐☐☐☐☐
3817	37c Reptiles and Amphibians - Orange Chorus Frog, self-adhesive	.80	.20	☐☐☐☐☐
3818	37c Reptiles and Amphibians - Ornate Box Turtle, self-adhesive	.80	.20	☐☐☐☐☐
a.	Vert. strip of 5, #3814-3818.........	3.75		☐☐☐☐☐
3819	37c George Washington (3468A), self-adhesive, serp. die cut 11....	1.00	.20	☐☐☐☐☐
3820	37c Christmas Type of 2002 (3675), self-adhesive, booklet stamp, 19½ x 28mm design size...........	.75	.20	☐☐☐☐☐
a.	Booklet pane of 20......................	15.00		☐☐☐☐☐
b.	Die cutting omitted, pair	—		☐☐☐☐☐
3821	37c Reindeer with Pan Pipes, self-adhesive, serp. die cut 11¾ x 11	.80	.20	☐☐☐☐☐
3822	37c Santa Claus with Drum, self-adhesive, serp. die cut 11¾ x 11..............	.80	.20	☐☐☐☐☐

3840

3841

3842

3843

3844

3845

3846

3847

3848

3849

3850

3851

3852

3853

3854

3855

3856

Scott No.	Description	Unused Value	Used Value	/ / / / / /
3823	37c Santa Claus with Trumpet, self-adhesive, serp. die cut 11¾ x 11	.80	.20	□□□□□
3824	37c Reindeer with Horn, self-adhesive, serp. die cut 11¾ x 11	.80	.20	□□□□□
a.	Book of 4, #3821-3824	3.20		□□□□□
b.	Booklet pane of 20, 5 each #3821-3824	16.00		□□□□□
3825	37c Reindeer with Pan Pipes, booklet stamp, serpentine die cut 10½ x 10¾	1.00	.20	□□□□□
3826	37c Santa Claus with Drum, booklet stamp, serpentine die cut 10½ x 10¾	1.00	.20	□□□□□
3827	37c Santa Claus with Trumpet, booklet stamp, serpentine die cut 10½ x 10¾	1.00	.20	□□□□□
3828	37c Reindeer with Horn, booklet stamp, serpentine die cut 10½ x 10¾	1.00	.20	□□□□□
a.	Block of 4, #3825-3828	4.00		□□□□□
b.	Booklet pane of 4, #3825-3828	4.00		□□□□□
c.	Booklet pane of 6, #3827-3828 2 each #3825-3826	6.00		□□□□□
d.	Booklet pane of 6, #3825-3826, 2 each #3827-3828	6.00		□□□□□
2003-05 Issues				
3829	37c Snowy Egret, self-adhesive, coil stamp, serp. die cut 8½ vert.	.75	.20	□□□□□
b.	Black omitted	—		□□□□□
3829A	37c Snowy Egret (3829), self-adhesive, coil stamp, serp. die cut 9½ vert..	.75	.20	□□□□□
3830	37c Snowy Egret (3829), self-adhesive, booklet stamp, serp. die cut 11½ x 11	.75	.20	□□□□□
a.	Booklet pane of 20	15.00		□□□□□
b.	Die cutting omitted, pair	—		□□□□□
c.	As "a," die cutting omitted	—		□□□□□
3830D	37c Snowy Egret (3829), self-adhesive, with "USPS" Microprinted on Bird's Breast	6.00	.50	□□□□□
e.	Booklet pane of 20	*120.00*		□□□□□
f.	Die cutting omitted, pair	*250.00*		□□□□□
g.	As "e," die cutting omitted	—		□□□□□
2004 Issues				
3831	37c Pacific Coral Reef - Marine Life, pane of 10, self-adhesive	7.50		□□□□□
a.	37c Emperor angelfish, blue coral, mound coral	.75	.20	□□□□□

3857

3858

3859

3860

3861

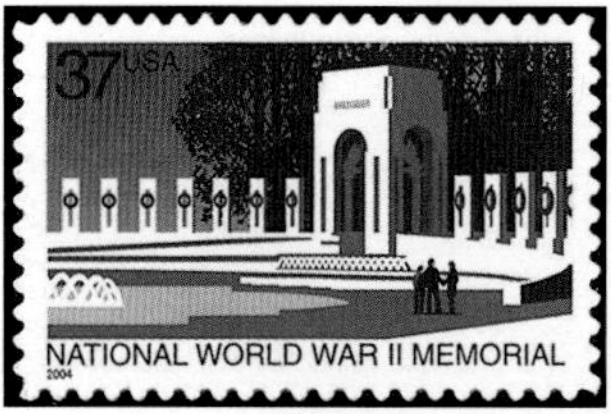

3862

3863

3865

3866

Scott No.	Description	Unused Value	Used Value	/ / / / / /
b.	37c Humphead wrasse, Moorish idol.	.75	.20	□□□□□
c.	37c Bumphead parrotfish	.75	.20	□□□□□
d.	37c Black-spotted puffer, threadfin butterflyfish, staghorn coral	.75	.20	□□□□□
e.	37c Hawksbill turtle, palette surgeonfish	.75	.20	□□□□□
f.	37c Pink amemonefish, magnificent sea anemone..............................	.75	.20	□□□□□
g.	37c Snowflake moray eel, spanish dance	.75	.20	□□□□□
h.	37c Lionfish.......................................	.75	.20	□□□□□
i.	37c Triton's trumpet...........................	.75	.20	□□□□□
j.	37c Oriental sweetlips, bluestreak cleaner wrasse, mushroom coral	.75	.20	□□□□□
3832	37c Chinese New Year - Year of the Monkey, self-adhesive	.75	.20	□□□□□
3833	37c Love - Candy Hearts, self-adhesive, booklet stamp............................	.75	.20	□□□□□
a.	Booklet pane of 20......................	15.00		□□□□□
3834	37c Black Heritage Series - Paul Robeson (1898-1976), Actor, Singer, Athlete and Activist, self-adhesive	.75	.20	□□□□□
3835	37c Theodor Seuss Geisel (Dr. Seuss), Children's Book Writer, and Book Characters, self-adhesive..	.85	.20	□□□□□
a.	Die cutting omitted, pair	*2,750.*		□□□□□
3836	37c Flowers: White Lilacs and Pink Roses, selfl-adhesive, booklet stamp...	.75	.20	□□□□□
a.	Booklet pane of 20......................	15.00		□□□□□
3837	60c Flowers: Five Varieties of Pink Roses, self-adhesive, booklet stamp...	1.25	.25	□□□□□
3838	37c U.S. Air Force Academy, 50th Anniv., self-adhesive	.75	.20	□□□□□
3839	37c Henry Mancini (1924-94), Composer, and Pink Panther, self-adhesive.	.75	.20	□□□□□
3840	37c American Choreographers, Martha Graham (1893-1991), self-adhesive	.75	.20	□□□□□
3841	37c American Choreographers, Alvin Ailey (1931-89), and Dancers, self-adhesive	.75	.20	□□□□□
3842	37c American Choreographers, Agnes de Mille (1909-93), and Dancers, self-adhesive	.75	.20	□□□□□
3843	37c American Choreographers, George Balanchine (1904-83), and Dancers, self-adhesive	.75	.20	□□□□□
a.	Horiz. strip of 4, #3840-3843	3.00		□□□□□
b.	Strip of 4, die cutting omitted......	*500.00*		□□□□□

3867

3868

3869

3870

3871

3876

3877

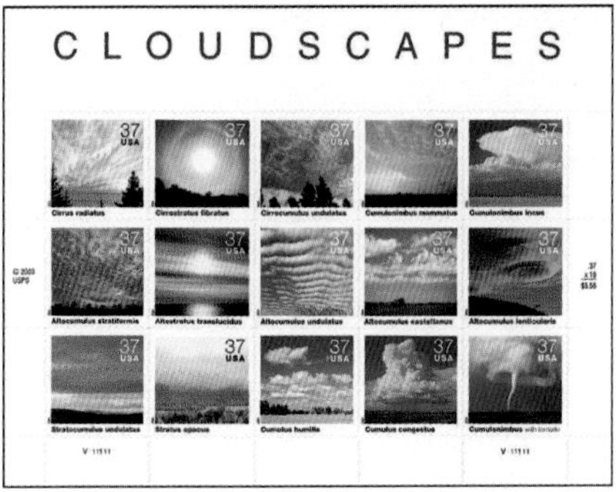

3878

3879

Scott No.	Description	Unused Value	Used Value	/ / / / / /
3844	25c Eagle Type of 2003 (3792), coil stamp, perf. 9¾ vert.	.65	.20	□□□□□
3845	25c Eagle Type of 2003 (3801), coil stamp, perf. 9¾ vert.	.65	.20	□□□□□
3846	25c Eagle Type of 2003 (3800), coil stamp, perf. 9¾ vert.	.65	.20	□□□□□
3847	25c Eagle Type of 2003 (3799), coil stamp, perf. 9¾ vert.	.65	.20	□□□□□
3848	25c Eagle Type of 2003 (3798), coil stamp, perf. 9¾ vert.	.65	.20	□□□□□
3849	25c Eagle Type of 2003 (3797), coil stamp, perf. 9¾ vert.	.65	.20	□□□□□
3850	25c Eagle Type of 2003 (3796), coil stamp, perf. 9¾ vert.	.65	.20	□□□□□
3851	25c Eagle Type of 2003 (3795), coil stamp, perf. 9¾ vert.	.65	.20	□□□□□
3852	25c Eagle Type of 2003 (3794), coil stamp, perf. 9¾ vert.	.65	.20	□□□□□
3853	25c Eagle Type of 2003 (3801), coil stamp, perf. 9¾ vert.	.65	.20	□□□□□
a.	25c Strip of 10, #3844-3853...............	6.50	—	□□□□□
3854	37c Lewis & Clark Expedition, Bicent., Meriwether Lewis (1774-1809) and William Clark (1770-1838), On Hill, self-adhesive	.90	.20	□□□□□
3855	37c Lewis & Clark Expedition, Bicent., Meriwether Lewis, self-adhesive, booklet stamp............................	.90	.45	□□□□□
3856	37c Lewis & Clark Expedition, Bicent., William Clark, self-adhesive, booklet stamp............................	.90	.45	□□□□□
a.	Horiz. or vert. Pair, #3855-3856..	1.80	—	□□□□□
b.	Booklet pane, 5 each #3855-3856	9.00	—	□□□□□
3857	37c Isamu Naguchi (1904-88), Sculptor, Akari 25N, self-adhesive............	.80	.20	□□□□□
3858	37c Isamu Naguchi (1904-88), Sculptor, Margaret la Farge Osborn, self-adhesive.....................................	.80	.20	□□□□□
3859	37c Isamu Naguchi (1904-88), Sculptor, Black Sun, self-adhesive............	.80	.20	□□□□□
3860	37c Isamu Naguchi (1904-88), Scultpor, Mother and Child, self-adhesive	.80	.20	□□□□□
3861	37c Isamu Naguchi (1904-88), Scultpor, Figure (Detail), self-adhesive	.80	.20	□□□□□
a.	Horiz. strip of 5, #3857-3861	4.00	—	□□□□□
3862	37c National World War II Memorial, self-adhesive	.75	.20	□□□□□

3880

3881

3882

3883

3884

3885

3886

3887

3888

3889

3890

3891

3892

3893

3894

Scott No.		Description	Unused Value	Used Value	/ / / / / /
3863	37c	Summer Olympic Games, Athens, Greece, Stylized Runner, self-adhesive	.75	.20	□□□□□
3864	5c	Sea Coast Type of 2002 (3693), coil stamp, perf. 9¾ vert., "2004" year date	.20	.20	□□□□□
3865	37c	Disney Characters: Goofy, Mickey Mouse, Donald Duck, self-adhesive	1.00	.20	□□□□□
3866	37c	Disney Characters: Bambi, Thumper, self-adhesive	1.00	.20	□□□□□
3867	37c	Disney Characters: Mufasa, Simba, self-adhesive	1.00	.20	□□□□□
3868	37c	Disney Characters: Jiminy Cricket, Pinocchio, self-adhesive	1.00	.20	□□□□□
a.		Block or vert. strip of 4, #3865-3868	4.00	—	□□□□□
3869	37c	U.S.S. Constellation, self-adhesive	.75	.20	□□□□□
3870	37c	R. Buckminster Fuller (1895-1983), Engineer; Time Magazine Cover Depicting Fuller, by Boris Artzybasheff, self-adhesive	.75	.20	□□□□□
3871	37c	Literary Arts - James Baldwin (1924-87), Writer, self-adhesive	.75	.20	□□□□□
3872	37c	Giant Magnolias, by M.J. Heade, self-adhesive	.70	.20	□□□□□
a.		Booklet pane of 20	15.00		□□□□□
b.		Die cutting omitted, pair	—		□□□□□
3873	37c	Art of the American Indian, pane of 10	19.00		□□□□□
a.-j.		Any single	1.90	.20	□□□□□
3874	5c	Sea Coast Type of 2002 (3693), self-adhesive, coil stamp, serp. die cut 10 vert., large "2003" date	.20	20	□□□□□
a.		Small "2003" date	.20	.20	□□□□□
3875	5c	Sea Coast Type of 2002 (3693), self-adhesive, coil stamp, serp. die cut 11½ vert., "2004" date	.20	.20	□□□□□
3876	37c	Legends of Hollywood - John Wayne (1907-79), Actor, self-adhesive	.75	.20	□□□□□
3877	37c	Sickle Cell Disease Awareness, self-adhesive	.75	.20	
3878		Cloudscapes, pane of 15, self-adhesive	12.50		□□□□□
a.	37c	Cirrus radiatus	.80	.20	□□□□□
b.	37c	Cirrostratus fibratus	.80	.20	□□□□□
c.	37c	Cirrocumulus undulatus	.80	.20	□□□□□

3895

3896

3897

3898

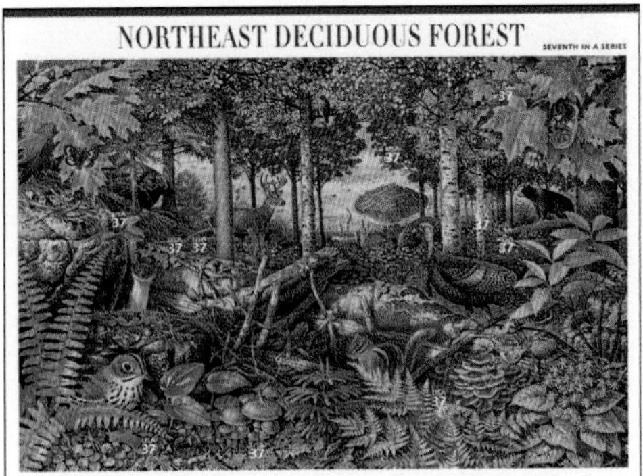

3899

Scott No.	Description	Unused Value	Used Value
d.	37c Cumulonimbus mammatus	.80	.20
e.	37c Cumolonimbus incus	.80	.20
f.	37c Altocumulus stratiformis.............	.80	.20
g.	37c Altostratus translucidus...............	.80	.20
h.	37c Altocumulus undulatus................	.80	.20
i.	37c Altocumullus castellanus.............	.80	.20
j.	37c Altocumulus lenticularis	.80	.20
k.	37c Stratocumulus undulatus.............	.80	.20
l.	37c Stratus opacus	.80	.20
m.	37c Cumulus humilis	.80	.20
n.	37c Cumulus congestus	.80	.20
o.	37c Cumulonimbus with tornado.......	.80	.20
3879	37c Christmas, Madonna and Child, self-adhesive, booklet stamp	.75	.20
a.	Booklet pane of 20	15.00	
b.	As "a," die cutting omitted...........	—	
3880	37c Hanukkah, Dreidel, self-adhesive	.75	.20
a.	Die cut applied to wrong side of stamp (hyphen hole cuts on face, die cut 10¾ on reverse).............	—	—
3881	37c Kwanzaa, self-adhesive................	.75	.20
3882	37c Literary Arts - Moss Hart (1904-61), Playwright, self-adhesive...............................	.80	.20
3883	37c Christmas, Purple Santa Ornament, self-adhesive.............	.90	.20
3884	37c Christmas, Green Santa Ornament, self-adhesive.............	.90	.20
3885	37c Christmas, Blue Santa Ornament, self-adhesive.............	.90	.20
3886	37c Christmas, Red Santa Ornament, self-adhesive.............	.90	.20
a.	Block or strip of 4, #3883-3886...	3.60	
b.	Booklet pane of 20, 5 #3886a	18.00	
3887	37c Christmas, Purple Santa Ornament, self-adhesive, booklet stamp, serp. die cut 10¼ x 10¾ on 2 or 3 sides	.90	.20
3888	37c Christmas, Green Santa Ornament, self-adhesive, booklet stamp, serp.die cut 10¼ x 10¾ on 2 or 3 sides	.90	.20
3889	37c Christmas, Blue Santa Ornament, self-adhesive, booklet stamp, serp.die cut 10¼ x 10¾ on 2 or 3 sides	.90	.20

3900

3901

3902

3903

3904

3905

3906

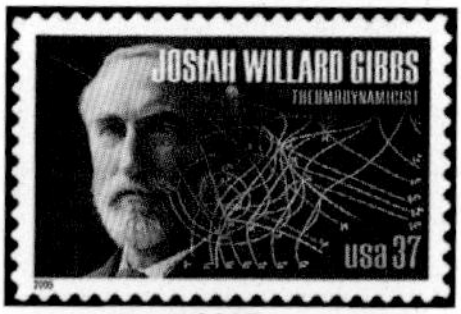

3907

3908

3909

3910

3911

Scott No.		Description	Unused Value	Used Value	/ / / / / /
3890	37c	Christmas, Red Santa Ornament, self-adhesive, booklet stamp, serp.die cut 10¼ x 10¾ on 2 or 3 sides	.90	.20	☐☐☐☐☐
a.		Block of 4, #3887-3890	3.60		☐☐☐☐☐
b.		Booklet pane of 4, #3887-3890,	3.60		☐☐☐☐☐
c.		Booklet pane of 6, #3889-3890, 2 each #3887-3888	5.50		☐☐☐☐☐
d.		Booklet pane of 6, #3887-3888, 2 each #3889-3890	5.50		☐☐☐☐☐
3891	37c	Christmas, Green Santa Ornament (3888), self-adhesive, booklet stamp, serp. die cut 8 on 2, 3 or 4 sides	1.10	.20	☐☐☐☐☐
3892	37c	Christmas, Purple Santa Ornament (3887), self-adhesive, booklet stamp, serp. die cut 8 on 2, 3 or 4 sides	1.10	.20	☐☐☐☐☐
3893	37c	Christmas, Red Santa Ornament (3890), self-adhesive, booklet stamp, serp. die cut 8 on 2, 3 or 4 sides	1.10	.20	☐☐☐☐☐
3894	37c	Christmas, Blue Santa Ornament (3889), self-adhesive, booklet stamp, serp. die cut 8 on 2, 3 or 4 sides	1.10	.20	☐☐☐☐☐
a.		Block of 4, #3891-3894	4.40		☐☐☐☐☐
b.		Booklet pane of 18, 6 each #3891, 3893, 3 each #3892, 3894	20.00		☐☐☐☐☐
2005 Issues					
3895		Chinese New Year - Types of 1992-2004, double sided pane of 24, 2 each #a-l, dated "2005", self-adhesive, serp. die cut 10¼.	18.00		☐☐☐☐☐
a.	37c	Rat	.75	.20	☐☐☐☐☐
b.	37c	Ox	.75	.20	☐☐☐☐☐
c.	37c	Tiger	.75	.20	☐☐☐☐☐
d.	37c	Rabbit	.75	.20	☐☐☐☐☐
e.	37c	Dragon	.75	.20	☐☐☐☐☐
f.	37c	Snake	.75	.20	☐☐☐☐☐
g.	37c	Horse	.75	.20	☐☐☐☐☐
h.	37c	Ram	.75	.20	☐☐☐☐☐
i.	37c	Monkey	.75	.20	☐☐☐☐☐
j.	37c	Rooster	.75	.20	☐☐☐☐☐
k.	37c	Dog	.75	.20	☐☐☐☐☐
l.	37c	Boar	.75	.20	☐☐☐☐☐

Scott No.		Description	Unused Value	Used Value	/ / / / / /
m.		As No. 3895, die cutting omitted on "a," "b," and "c" on reverse side	*1,250.*		□□□□□
2005 Issues					
3896	37c	Black Heritage Series - Marian Anderson (1897-1903), Singer, self-adhesive	.75	.20	□□□□□
3897	37c	Ronald Reagan (1911-2004), 40th President, self-adhesive	.75	.20	□□□□□
3898	37c	Love - Hand and Flower Bouquet, self-adhesive, booklet stamp	.75	.20	□□□□□
a.		Booklet pane of 20	15.00		□□□□□
3899		Northeast Deciduous Forest - Wildlife, pane of 10, self-adhesive	7.50		□□□□□
a.	37c	Eastern buckmoth, vert.	.75	.20	□□□□□
b.	37c	Red-shouldered hawk	.75	.20	□□□□□
c.	37c	Eastern red bat	.75	.20	□□□□□
d.	37c	White-tailed deer	.75	.20	□□□□□
e.	37c	Black bear	.75	.20	□□□□□
f.	37c	Long-tailed weasel, vert.	.75	.20	□□□□□
g.	37c	Wild turkey, vert.	.75	.20	□□□□□
h.	37c	Ovenbird, vert.	.75	.20	□□□□□
i.	37c	Red eft	.75	.20	□□□□□
j.	37c	Eastern Chipmunk	.75	.20	□□□□□
3900	37c	Spring Flowers, Hyacinth, self-adhesive, booklet stamp	.85	.20	□□□□□
3901	37c	Spring Flowers, Daffodil, self-adhesive, booklet stamp	.85	.20	□□□□□
3902	37c	Spring Flowers, Tulip, self-adhesive, booklet stamp	.85	.20	□□□□□
3903	37c	Spring Flowers, Iris, self-adhesive, booklet stamp	.85	.20	
a.		Block of 4, #3900-3903	3.40		□□□□□
b.		Booklet pane, 5 each #3900-3903	17.00		□□□□□
c.		As "b," die cutting omitted on side with 8 stamps	—		□□□□□
3904	37c	Literary Arts - Robert Penn Warren (1905-89), Writer, self-adhesive	.75	.20	□□□□□
3905	37c	Edgar Y. "Yip" Harburg (1896-1981), Lyricist, self-adhesive	.75	.20	□□□□□
3906	37c	American Scientists, Barbara McClintock (1902-92), Geneticist, self-adhesive	.75	.20	□□□□□

Scott No.		Description	Unused Value	Used Value	/ / / / / /
3907	37c	American Scientists, Josiah Willard Gibbs (1839-1903), Thermodynamicist, self-adhesive	.75	.20	□□□□□
3908	37c	American Scientists, John von Neumann (1903-57), Mathematician, self-adhesive	.75	.20	□□□□□
a.		Vert. pair, die cutting omitted, #3906 and 3908			□□□□□
3909	37c	American Scientists, Richard Feynman (1918-88), Physicist, self-adhesive	.75	.20	□□□□□
a.		Block or horiz. strip of 4, #3906-3909	3.00		□□□□□
b.		All colors omitted, tagging omitted, pane of 20	—		
c.		As "a," printing on back of stamps omitted	—		□□□□□
d.		Vert. pair, die cutting omitted, #3907 and 3909	—		□□□□□
3910		Modern American Architecture, pane of 12, self-adhesive	9.00		
a.	37c	Guggenheim Museum, New York	.75	.20	□□□□□
b.	37c	Chrysler Building, New York	.75	.20	□□□□□
c.	37c	Vanna Venturi House, Philadelphia	.75	.20	□□□□□
d.	37c	TWA Terminal, New York	.75	.20	□□□□□
e.	37c	Walt Disney Concert Hall, Los Angeles	.75	.20	□□□□□
f.	37c	860-880 Lake Shore Drive, Chicago	.75	.20	□□□□□
g.	37c	National Gallery of Art, Washington, DC	.75	.20	□□□□□
h.	37c	Glass House, New Canaan, CT	.75	.20	□□□□□
i.	37c	Yale Art and Architecture Building, New Haven, CT	.75	.20	□□□□□
j.	37c	High Museum of Art, Atlanta	.75	.20	□□□□□
k.	37c	Exeter Academy Library, Exeter, NH	.75	.20	□□□□□
l.	37c	Hancock Center, Chicago	.75	.20	□□□□□
m.		As No. 3910, orange yellow omitted	—	—	□□□□□
3911	37c	Legends of Hollywood - Henry Fonda (1905-82), Actor, self-adhesive	.90	.20	□□□□□

3912

3913

3914

3915

3916

3917

3918

3919

3920

3921

3922

3923

3924

3925

3926

3927

3928

3929

3930

3931

3932

3933

3934

3935

3936

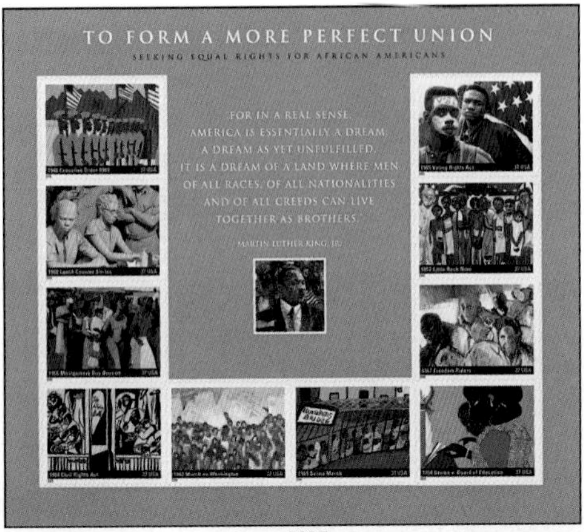

3937

3938

3939

3940

3941

3942

3943

Scott No.	Description	Unused Value	Used Value
3912	37c Disney Characters: Pluto, Mickey Mouse, self-adhesive.....	.75	.20
3913	37c Disney Characters: Mad Hatter, Alice, self-adhesive	.75	.20
3914	37c Disney Characters: Flounder, Ariel, self-adhesive....................	.75	.20
3915	37c Disney Characters: Snow White, Dopey, self-adhesive	.75	.20
a.	Block or vert. strip of 4 #3812-3815 ,,...	3.00	
b.	Die cutting omitted, pane of 20....	—	*1,400.*
c.	Printed on backing paper.............	—	
3916	37c Boeing 247, self-adhesive...........	.75	.20
3917	37c Consolidated PBY Catalina, self-adhesive..............................	.75	.20
3918	37c Grumman F6F Hellcat, self-adhesive............................	.75	.20
3919	37c Republic P-47 Thunderbolt, self-adhesive.............................	.75	.20
3920	37c Engineering and Research Corporation Ercoupe, self-adhesive.............................	.75	.20
3921	37c Lockheed P-80 Shooting Star, self-adhesive.............................	.75	.20
3922	37c Consolidated B-24 Liberator, self-adhesive.............................	.75	.20
3923	37c Boeing B-29 Superfortress, self-adhesive.............................	.75	.20
3924	37c Beechcraft 35 Bonanza, self-adhesive.............................	.75	.20
3925	37c Northrop YB-49 Flying Wing, self-adhesive.............................	.75	.20
a.	Block of 10, #3916-3925............	7.50	
3926	37c Rio Grande Blankets, self-adhesive, booklet stamp......	.75	.20
3927	37c Rio Grande Blankets, self-adhesive, booklet stamp......	.75	.20
3928	37c Rio Grande Blankets, self-adhesive, booklet stamp......	.75	.20
3929	37c Rio Grande Blankets, self-adhesive, booklet stamp......	.75	.20
a.	Block of 4, #3926-3929..............	3.00	
b.	Booklet pane, 5 each #3900-3903	15.00	
3930	37c Presidential Libraries Act, 50th Anniv., self-adhesive.........	.85	.20
3931	37c Sporty Cars of the 1950S, 1953 Studebaker Starliner, self-adhesive	.90	.20
3932	37c Sporty Cars of the 1950S, 1954 Kaiser Darrin, self-adhesive.......	.90	.20

3944

3945

3946

3947

3948

3949

3950

3951

Scott No.	Description	Unused Value	Used Value	/ / / / / /
3933	37c Sporty Cars of the 1950S, 1953 Chevrolet Corvette, self-adhesive	.90	.20	□□□□□
3934	37c Sporty Cars of the 1950S, 1952 Nash Healey, self-adhesive.........	.90	.20	□□□□□
3935	37c Sporty Cars of the 1950S, 1955 Ford Thunderbird, self-adhesive.	.90	.20	□□□□□
a.	37c Vert. strip of 5, #3931-3935..........	4.50		□□□□□
b.	37c Booklet pane of 20, #3931-3935..	18.00		□□□□□
3936	37c Arthur Ashe (1943-93), Tennis Player, self-adhesive....................	.75	.20	□□□□□
3937	To Form A More Perfect Union, pane of 10, self-adhesive	7.50		□□□□□
a.	37c 1948 Executive Order 9981 (Training for War, by William H. Johnson)................................	.75	.20	□□□□□
b.	37c 1965 Voting Rights Act (Youths on the Selma March, 1965, photograph by Bruce Davidson)...................	.75	.20	□□□□□
c.	37c 1960 Lunch Counter Sit-ins (National Civil Rights Museum exhibits, by Studio EIS)................................	.75	.20	□□□□□
d.	37c 1957 Little Rock Nine (America Cares, by George Hunt)	.75	.20	□□□□□
e.	37c 1955 Montgomery Bus Boycott (Walking, by Charles Alston).....	.75	.20	□□□□□
f.	37c 1961 Freedom Riders (Freedom Riders, by May Stevens).........................	.75	.20	□□□□□
g.	37c 1964 Civil Rights Act (Dixie Café, by Jacob Larence)...........................	.75	.20	□□□□□
h.	37c 1963 March on Washington (March on Washington, by Alma Thomas)	.75	.20	□□□□□
i.	37c 1965 Selma March (Selma March, by Bernice Sims)............................	.75	.20	□□□□□
j.	37c 1954 Brown v. Board of Education (The Lamp, by Romare Bearden)	.75	.20	□□□□□
3938	37c Child Health, self-adhesive...........	.75	.20	□□□□□
3939	37c Let's Dance, Merengue, self-adhesive	.75	.20	□□□□□
3940	37c Let's Dance, Salsa, self-adhesive..	.75	.20	□□□□□
3941	37c Let's Dance, Cha Cha Cha, self-adhesive...............................	.75	.20	□□□□□
3942	37c Let's Dance, Mambo, self-adhesive	.75	.20	□□□□□
a.	Vert. strip of 4	3.00		□□□□□
3943	37c Greta Garbo (1905-90), Actress, self-adhesive..............................	.75	.20	□□□□□
3944	Jim Henson and The Muppets, pane of 11, self-adhesive....................	8.25		□□□□□
a.	37c Kermit the Frog............................	.75	.20	□□□□□
b.	37c Fozzie Bear..................................	.75	.20	□□□□□

3952

3953

3954

3955

3956

3957

3958

3959

3960

3961

3962

3963

3964

Scott No.		Description	Unused Value	Used Value	/ / / / / /
c.	37c	Sam the Eagle and flag	.75	.20	□□□□□
d.	37c	Miss Piggy	.75	.20	□□□□□
e.	37c	Statler and Waldorf	.75	.20	□□□□□
f.	37c	The Swedish Chef and fruit	.75	.20	□□□□□
g.	37c	Animal	.75	.20	□□□□□
h.	37c	Dr. Bunsen Honeydew and Beaker	.75	.20	□□□□□
i.	37c	Rowlf the Dog	.75	.20	□□□□□
j.	37c	The Great Gonzo and Camilla the Chicken	.75	.20	□□□□□
k.	37c	Jim Henson	.75	.20	□□□□□
3945	37c	Constellations, Leo, self-adhesive	.75	.20	□□□□□
3946	37c	Constellations, Orion, self-adhesive	.75	.20	□□□□□
3947	37c	Constellations, Lyra, self-adhesive	.75	.20	□□□□□
3948	37c	Constellations, Pegasus, self-adhesive	.75	.20	□□□□□
a.		Block or vert. strip of 4, #3945-3948	3.00		□□□□□
b.		As "a," die cutting omitted	—		□□□□□
3949	37c	Christmas Cookies, Santa Claus, self-adhesive	.85	.20	□□□□□
3950	37c	Christmas Cookies, Snowmen, self-adhesive	.85	.20	□□□□□
3951	37c	Christmas Cookies, Angel, self-adhesive	.85	.20	□□□□□
3952	37c	Christmas Cookies, Elves, self-adhesive	.85	.20	□□□□□
a.		Block or vert. strip of 4, #3949-3952	3.50		
3953	37c	Christmas Cookies, Santa Claus (3949), self-adhesive, booklet stamp, serp. die cut 10¾ x 11 on 2 or 3 sides	.75	.20	□□□□□
3954	37c	Christmas Cookies, Snowmen (3950), self-adhesive, booklet stamp, serp. die cut 10¾ x 11 on 2 or 3 sides	.75	.20	□□□□□
3955	37c	Christmas Cookies, Angel (3951), self-adhesive, booklet stamp, serp. die cut 10¾ x 11 on 2 or 3 sides	.75	.20	□□□□□
3956	37c	Christmas Cookies, Elves (3952), self-adhesive, booklet stamp, serp. die cut 10¾ x 11 on 2 or 3 sides	.75	.20	□□□□□
a.		Block of 4, #3953-3956	3.00		
b.		Booklet pane of 20, 5 #3956a	15.00		□□□□□
3957	37c	Christmas Cookies, Santa Claus (3949), self-adhesive, booklet stamp, serp. die cut 10½ x 10¾ on 2 or 3 sides	1.50	.20	□□□□□
3958	37c	Christmas Cookies, Snowmen (3950), self-adhesive, booklet stamp, serp. die cut 10½ x 10¾ on 2 or 3 sides	1.50	.20	□□□□□

3965

3976

3978

3987

3988

3989

3990

3991

3992

3993

3994

3995

Scott No.		Description	Unused Value	Used Value	/ / / / / /
3959	37c	Christmas Cookies, Angel (3951), self-adhesive, booklet stamp, serp. die cut 10½ x 10¾ on 2 or 3 sides	1.50	.20	□□□□□
3960	37c	Christmas Cookies, Elves (3952), self-adhesive, booklet stamp, serp. die cut 10½ x 10¾ on 2 or 3 sides	1.50	.20	□□□□□
a.		Block of 4, #3957-3960	6.00		□□□□□
b.		Booklet pane of 4, #3957-3960	6.00		□□□□□
c.		Booklet pane of 6, #3957-3958, 2 each #3957-3958	9.00		□□□□□
d.		Booklet pane of 6, #3957-3958, 2 each #3959-3960	9.00		□□□□□
3961	37c	Distinguished Marines, Lt. Gen. John A. Lejeune (1867-1942), 2nd Infantry Division Insignia, self-adhesive..	1.00	.20	□□□□□
3962	37c	Distinguished Marines, Lt. Gen. Lewis B. Puller (1898-1971), 1st Marine Division Insignia, self-adhesive..	1.00	.20	□□□□□
3963	37c	Distinguished Marines, Sgt. John Basilone (1916-45), 5th Marine Division Insignia, self-adhesive..	1.00	.20	□□□□□
3964	37c	Distinguished Marines, Sgt. Major Daniel J. Daly (1873-1937), 73rd Marine Gun Company, 6th Marine Regiment Insignia, self-adhesive	1.00	.20	□□□□□
a.		Block or horiz. strip of 4, #3961-3964	4.00		□□□□□
2005-06 Issues					
3965	(39c)	Flag and Statue of Liberty, perf. 11¼	.80	.20	□□□□□
3966	(39c)	Flag and Statue of Liberty (3965), self-adhesive, serp. die cut 11¼ x10¾	.80	.20	□□□□□
a.		Booklet pane of 20........................	16.00		□□□□□
b.		As "a," die cutting omitted	—		□□□□□
3967	(39c)	Flag and Statue of Liberty (3965), coil stamp, perf. 9¾ vert............	.80	.20	□□□□□
3968	(39c)	Flag and Statue of Liberty (3965), self-adhesive, coil stamp, serp. die cut 8½ vert.	.80	.20	□□□□□
3969	(39c)	Flag and Statue of Liberty (3965), self-adhesive, coil stamp, serp. die cut 10¼ vert., dated 2006	.80	.20	□□□□□
3970	(39c)	Flag and Statue of Liberty (3965), self-adhesive, coil stamp, serp. die cut 9½ vert.	.80	.20	□□□□□
3972	(39c)	Flag and Statue of Liberty (3965), self-adhesive, booklet stamp, serp. die cut 11¼ x 10¾ on 2 or 3 sides	.80	.20	□□□□□
a.		Booklet pane of 20........................	16.00		□□□□□

3997

3996

3998

3999

4000

4001

4002

4003

4004

4005

4006

4007

4008

4009

4010

4011

4012

Scott No.	Description	Unused Value	Used Value	/ / / / / /
3973	(39c)Flag and Statue of Liberty (3965), self-adhesive, booklet stamp, serp. die cut 10¼ x 10¾ on 2 or 3 sides	.80	.20	□□□□□
a.	Booklet pane of 20........................	16.00		□□□□□
3974	(39c)Flag and Statue of Liberty (3965), self-adhesive, booklet stamp, serp. die cut 11¼ x 10¾ on 2 or 3 sides	.80	.20	□□□□□
a.	Booklet pane of 4..........................	3.20		□□□□□
b.	Booklet pane of 6..........................	4.80		□□□□□
3975	(39c)Flag and Statue of Liberty (3965), self-adhesive, booklet stamp, serp. die cut 8 on 2, 3, or 4 sides	.80	.20	□□□□□
a.	Booklet pane of 18........................	14.50		□□□□□

2006 Issues

Scott No.	Description	Unused Value	Used Value	/ / / / / /
3976	(39c)Birds, self-adhesive, booklet stamp, serp.die cut 11 on 2, 3, or 4 sides	.90	.20	□□□□□
3978	39c Flag and Statue of Liberty, self-adhesive, serp. die cut 11¼ x 10¾	.80	.20	□□□□□
a.	Booklet pane of 10........................	8.00		□□□□□
b.	Booklet pane of 20........................	16.00		□□□□□
c.	As "b," die cutting omitted on side with 8 stamps..............................	—		□□□□□
3979	39c Flag and Statue of Liberty (3978), coil stamp, perf. 10 vert.	.80	.20	□□□□□
3980	39c Flag and Statue of Liberty (3978), self-adhesive, coil stamp, serp. die cut 11 vert., no micro-print...	.80	.20	□□□□□
3981	39c Flag and Statue of Liberty (3978), self-adhesive, coil stamp, serp. die cut 9½ vert.	.80	.20	□□□□□
a.	Die cutting omitted, pair	—		□□□□□
3982	39c Flag and Statue of Liberty (3978), self-adhesive, coil stamp, serp. die cut 10¼ vert.	.80	.20	□□□□□
a.	Vert. pair, unslit btwn.	—		□□□□□
3983	39c Flag and Statue of Liberty (3978), self-adhesive, coil stamp, serp. die cut 8½ vert.	.80	.20	□□□□□
3985	39c Flag and Statue of Liberty (3978), self-adhesive, booklet stamp, serp. die cut 11¼ x 10¾ on 2 or 3 sides, no micro print................	.80	.20	□□□□□
a.	Booklet pane of 20........................	16.00		□□□□□
b.	Serp. die cut 11.1 on 2 or 3 sides.	.80	.20	□□□□□
c.	Booklet pane of 4 #3985b............	3.20		□□□□□
d.	Booklet pane of 6 #3985b............	4.80		□□□□□

4018

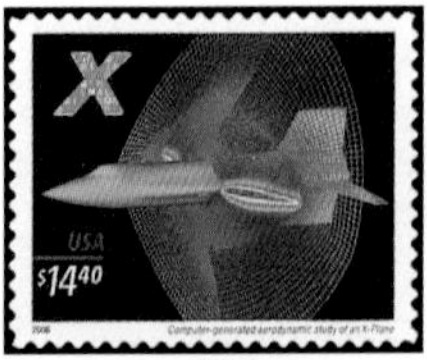

4019

4020

4021

4022

4023

4024

4025

4026

4027

4028

Scott No.		Description	Unused Value	Used Value	/ / / / / /
3987	39c	Children's Book Animals - The Very Hungry Caterpillar, from The Very Hungry Caterpillar, by Eric Carle, self-adhesive	.80	.20	
3988	39c	Children's Book Animals - Wilbur, from Charlotte's Web, by E.B. White, self-adhesive	.80	.20	
3989	39c	Children's Book Animals - Fox in Socks, from Fox in Socks, by Dr. Seuss, self-adhesive	.80	.20	
3990	39c	Children's Book Animals - Maisy, from Maisy's ABC, by Lucy Cousins, self-adhesive	.80	.20	
3991	39c	Children's Book Animals - Wild Thing, from Where the Wild Things Are, by Maurice Sendak, self-adhesive	.80	.20	
3992	39c	Children's Book Animals - Curious George, from Curious George, by Margaret and H.A. Rey, self-adhesive	.80	.20	
3993	39c	Children's Book Animals - Olivia, from Olivia, by Ian Falconer, self-adhesive	.80	.20	
3994	39c	Children's Book Animals - Frederick, from Frederick, by Leo Lionni, self-adhesive	.80	.20	
a.		Block of 8, #3987-3994	6.50		
3995	39c	2005 Winter Olympics, Turin, Italy, self-adhesive	.80	.20	
3996	39c	Black Heritage Series - Hattie McDaniel (1895-1952), Actress, self-adhesive	3.20		
3997		Chinese New Year - Types of 1992-2004, pane of 12, self-adhesive	9.75		
a.	39c	Rat	.80	.20	
b.	39c	Ox	.80	.20	
c.	39c	Tiger	.80	.20	
d.	39c	Rabbit	.80	.20	
e.	39c	Dragon	.80	.20	
f.	39c	Snake	.80	.20	
g.	39c	Horse	.80	.20	
h.	39c	Ram	.80	.20	
i.	39c	Monkey	.80	.20	
j.	39c	Rooster	.80	.20	
k.	39c	Dog	.80	.20	
l.	39c	Boar	.80	.20	
3998	39c	Wedding Doves, Dove Facing Left, self-adhesive, booklet stamp	.80	.20	
a.		Booklet pane of 20	16.00		
b.		As "a," die cutting omitted	—		

Scott No.		Description	Unused Value	Used Value	/ / / / / /
3999	63c	Wedding Doves, Dove Facing Right, self-adhesive, booklet stamp.......	1.40	.50	□□□□□
a.		Booklet pane, 20 each #3998-3999	45.00		□□□□□
b.		Horiz. pair, #3998-3999 with vert. gutter btwn.........................	2.25	1.00	□□□□□
4000	24c	Common Buckeye Butterfly.........	.50	.20	□□□□□
4001	24c	Common Buckeye Butterfly (4000), self-adhesive, serp. die cut 11	.55	.20	□□□□□
a.		Booklet stamp, serp. die cut 10¾ x 11¼ on 3 sides..................................	.50	.20	□□□□□
b.		Booklet pane of 10 #4001a...........	5.00		□□□□□
c.		Booklet pane of 4 #4001a.............	2.00		□□□□□
d.		Booklet pane of 6 #4001a.............	3.00		□□□□□
4002	24c	Common Buckeye Butterfly (4000), self-adhesive, coil stamp, serp. die cut 8½ horiz.	.50	.20	□□□□□
4003	39c	Crops of the Americas - Chili Peppers, self-adhesive, coil stamp, serp. die cut 10¼ horiz.	.85	.20	□□□□□
4004	39c	Crops of the Americas - Beans, self-adhesive, coil stamp, serp. die cut 10¼ horiz.	.85	.20	□□□□□
4005	39c	Crops of the Americas - Sunflower and Seeds, self-adhesive, coil stamp, serp. die cut 10¼ horiz.	.85	.20	□□□□□
4006	39c	Crops of the Americas - Squashes, self-adhesive, coil stamp, serp. die cut 10¼ horiz.	.85	.20	□□□□□
4007	39c	Crops of the Americas - Corn, self-adhesive, coil stamp, serp. die cut 10¼ horiz.	.85	.20	□□□□□
a.		Strip of 5, #4003-4007.................	4.25		□□□□□
4008	39c	Crops of the Americas - Corn (4007), self-adhesive, booklet stamp, serp. die cut 10¾ x 10¼.....................	.80	.20	□□□□□
4009	39c	Crops of the Americas - Squash (4006), self-adhesive, booklet stamp, serp. die cut 10¾ x 10¼.....................	.80	.20	□□□□□
4010	39c	Crops of the Americas - Sunflower and Seeds (4005), self-adhesive, booklet stamp, serp. die cut 10¾ x 10¼ .	.80	.20	□□□□□
4011	39c	Crops of the Americas - Beans (4004), self-adhesive, booklet stamp, serp. die cut 10¾ x 10¼	.80	.20	□□□□□
4012	39c	Crops of the Americas - Chili Peppers (4003), self-adhesive, booklet stamp, serp. die cut 10¾ x 10¼............	.80	.20	□□□□□
a.		Horiz. strip of 5, #4008-4012.......	4.00		□□□□□

Scott No.		Description	Unused Value	Used Value
b.		Booklet pane, 4 each #4008-4012	16.00	
4013	39c	Crops of the Americas - Chili Peppers (4003), self-adhesive, booklet stamp, serp. die cut 10¾ x 11¼	.90	.20
4014	39c	Crops of the Americas - Corn (4007), self-adhesive, booklet stamp, serp. die cut 10¾ x 11¼	.90	.20
4015	39c	Crops of the Americas - Squash (4006), self-adhesive, booklet stamp, serp. die cut 10¾ x 11¼	.90	.20
4016	39c	Crops of the Americas - Sunflower and Seeds (4005), self-adhesive, booklet stamp, serp. die cut 10¾ x 11¼ .	.90	.20
a.		Booklet pane of 4, #4013-4016....	3.60	
4017	39c	Crops of the Americas - Beans (4004), booklet stamp, serp. die cut 10¾ x 11¼	.90	.20
a.		Horiz. strip of 5, #4013-4017	4.50	
b.		Booklet pane of 4, #4013-4015, 4017	3.60	
c.		Booklet pane of 6, #4013-4016, 2 #40174	5.50	
d.		Booklet pane of 6, #4013-4015, 4017, 2 #4016......................................	5.50	
4018	4.05	X-Planes, self-adhesive................	8.00	5.00
a.		Silver foil ("X") omitted..............	—	
4019	14.40	X-Planes, self-adhesive................	27.50	15.00
4020	39c	Sugar Ray Robinson (1921-89), Boxer, self-adhesive....................	.80	.20
4021	39c	Benjamin Franklin (1706-90), Statesman, self-adhesive.............	1.10	.20
4022	39c	Benjamin Franklin (1706-90), Scientist, self-adhesive................	1.10	.20
4023	39c	Benjamin Franklin (1706-90), Printer, self-adhesive..................	1.10	.20
4024	39c	Benjamin Franklin (1706-90), Postmaster, self-adhesive	1.10	.20
a.		Block or horiz. strip of 4..............	4.40	
4025	39c	Disney Characters: Mickey and Minnie Mouse, self-adhesive......	.80	.20
4026	39c	Disney Characters: Cinderella and Prince Charming, self-adhesive..	.80	.20
4027	39c	Disney Characters: Beauty and the Beast, self-adhesive....................	.80	.20
4028	39c	Disney Characters: Lady and Tramp, self-adhesive..............................	.80	.20
a.		Block or vert. strip of 4, #4025-4028	3.20	
4029	39c	Birds, self-adhesive, booklet stamp, serp. die cut 11...........................	.80	.20
a.		Booklet pane of 20.......................	16.00	

4029

4030

4031

4032

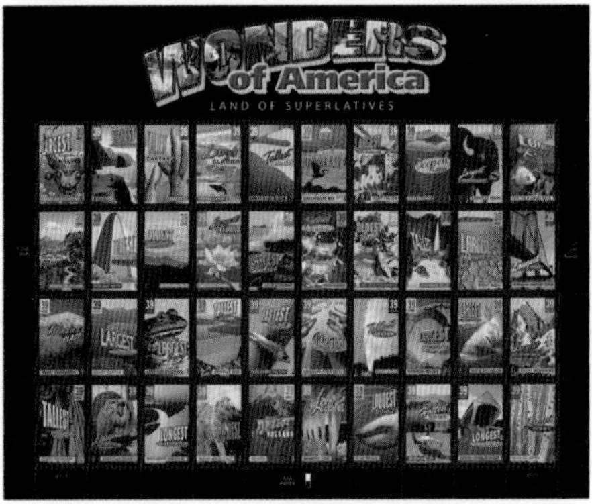

4072a

4073

Scott No.	Description	Unused Value	Used Value	/ / / / / /
4030	39c Literary Arts, Katherine Anne Porter (1890-1980), Author, self-adhesive	.80	.20	□□□□□
4031	39c Amber Alert, Mother and Child, self-adhesive	.80	.20	□□□□□
4032	39c Purple Heart Type of 2003 (3784), self-adhesive	.80	.20	□□□□□
4033	39c Wonders of America, American alligator, largest reptile, self-adhesive	.80	.45	□□□□□
4034	39c Wonders of America, Moloka'I, highest sea cliffs, self-adhesive	.80	.45	□□□□□
4035	39c Wonders of America, Saguaro, tallest cactus, self-adhesive	.80	.45	□□□□□
4036	39c Wonders of America, Bering Glacier, largest glacier, self-adhesive	.80	.45	□□□□□
4037	39c Wonders of America, Great Sand Dunes, tallest dunes, self-adhesive	.80	.45	□□□□□
4038	39c Wonders of America, Chesapeake Bay, largest estuary, self-adhesive	.80	.45	□□□□□
4039	39c Wonders of America, Cliff Palace, largest cliff dwelling, self-adhesive	.80	.45	□□□□□
4040	39c Wonders of America, Crater Lake, deepest lake, self-adhesive	.80	.45	□□□□□
4041	39c Wonders of America, American bison, largest land mammal, self-adhesive	.80	.45	□□□□□
4042	39c Wonders of America, Off the Florida Keys, longest reef, self-adhesive	.80	.45	□□□□□
4043	39c Wonders of America, Pacific Crest Trail, longest hiking trail, self-adhesive	.80	.45	□□□□□
4044	39c Wonders of America, Gateway Arch, tallest man-made monument, self-adhesive	.80	.45	□□□□□
4045	39c Wonders of America, Appalachians, oldest mountains, self-adhesive	.80	.45	□□□□□
4046	39c Wonders of America, American lotus, largest flower, self-adhesive	.80	.45	□□□□□
4047	39c Wonders of America, Lake Superior, largest lake, self-adhesive	.80	.45	□□□□□
4048	39c Wonders of America, Pronghorn, fastest land animal, self-adhesive	.80	.45	□□□□□
4049	39c Wonders of America, Bristlecone pines, oldest trees, self-adhesive	.80	.45	□□□□□
4050	39c Wonders of America, Yosemite Falls, tallest waterfall, self-adhesive	.80	.45	□□□□□
4051	39c Wonders of America, Great Basin, largest desert, self-adhesive	.80	.45	□□□□□
4052	39c Wonders of America, Verrazano-Narrows Bridge, longest span, self-adhesive	.80	.45	□□□□□

4074

4075

4076

Scott No.	Description	Unused Value	Used Value
4053	39c Wonders of America, Mount Washington, windiest place, self-adhesive	.80	.45
4054	39c Wonders of America, Grand Canyon, largest canyon, self-adhesive	.80	.45
4055	39c Wonders of America, American bullfrog, largest frog, self-adhesive	.80	.45
4056	39c Wonders of America, Oroville Dam, tallest dam, self-adhesive	.80	.45
4057	39c Wonders of America, Peregrine falcon, fastest bird, self-adhesive	.80	.45
4058	39c Wonders of America, Mississippi River Delta, largest delta, self-adhesive	.80	.45
4059	39c Wonders of America, Steamboat, tallest geyser, self-adhesive	.80	.45
4060	39c Wonders of America, Rainbow Bridge, largest natural bridge, self-adhesive	.80	.45
4061	39c Wonders of America, White sturgeon, largest freshwater fish, self-adhesive	.80	.45
4062	39c Wonders of America, Rocky Mountains, longest mountain chain, self-adhesive	.80	.45
4063	39c Wonders of America, Coast redwoods, tallest trees, self-adhesive	.80	.45
4064	39c Wonders of America, American beaver, largest rodent, self-adhesive	.80	.45
4065	39c Wonders of America, Mississippi-Missouri, longest river system, self-adhesive	.80	.45
4066	39c Wonders of America, Mount Wai'ale'ale, rainiest spot, self-adhesive	.80	.45
4067	39c Wonders of America, Kilauea, most active volcano, self-adhesive	.80	.45
4068	39c Wonders of America, Mammoth Cave, longest cave, self-adhesive	.80	.45
4069	39c Wonders of America, Blue whale, loudest animal, self-adhesive	.80	.45
4070	39c Wonders of America, Death Valley, hottest spot, self-adhesive	.80	.45
4071	39c Wonders of America, Cornish-Windsor Bridge, longest covered bridge, self-adhesive	.80	.45
4072	39c Wonders of America, Quaking aspen, largest plant, self-adhesive	.80	.45
a.	Pane of 40, #4033-4072	32.00	
4073	39c Exploration of East Coast By Samuel De Champlain, 400th Anniv., Ship and Map, self-adhesive, serp. die cut 10¾	.85	.20

4077

4080

4081

4082

4083

4084

Scott No.	Description	Unused Value	Used Value	/ / / / / /
4074	39c Exploration of East Coast By Samuel De Champlain, 400th Anniv., Ship and Map, Souvenir Sheet, 2 each #4074a, Canada #2156a	8.00	2.00	□□□□□
a.	Sheet single, USA, perf. 11	1.75	.20	□□□□□
4075	Washington 2006 World Philatelic Exhibition, Souvenir Sheet, pane of 3	16.00	6.00	□□□□□
a.	1.00 Reproduction of 1922 issue, Scott 571	2.00	.50	□□□□□
b.	2.00 Reproduction of 1922 issue, Scott 572	4.00	1.00	□□□□□
c.	5.00 Reproduction of 1922 issue, Scott 573	10.00	2.50	□□□□□
4076	Distinguished American Diplomats, Souvenir Sheet, self-adhesive, pane of 6	4.80		□□□□□
a.	39c Robett D. Murphy (1894-1978)	.80	.20	□□□□□
b.	39c Frances E. Willis (1899-1983)	.80	.20	□□□□□
c.	39c Hiram Bingham IV (1903-88)	.80	.20	□□□□□
d.	39c Philip C. Habib (1920-92)	.80	.20	□□□□□
e.	39c Charles E. Bohlen (1904-74)	.80	.20	□□□□□
f.	39c Clifton R. Wharton, Sr. (1899-1990)	.80	.20	□□□□□
4077	39c Legends of Hollywood - Judy Garland (1922-69), Actress, self-adhesive	.85	.20	□□□□□
a.	Pair, die cutting omitted	—		□□□□□
4078	39c Ronald Reagan Type of 2005 (3897), self-adhesive	.80	.20	□□□□□
4079	39c Happy Birthday Type of 2002 (3558), self-adhesive	.80	.20	□□□□□
4080	39c Baseball Sluggers, Roy Campanella (1921-93), self-adhesive	.80	.20	□□□□□
4081	39c Baseball Sluggers, Hank Greenberg (1911-86), self-adhesive	.80	.20	□□□□□
4082	39c Baseball Sluggers, Mel Ott (1909-58), self-adhesive	.80	.20	□□□□□
4083	39c Baseball Sluggers, Mickey Mantle (1931-95), self-adhesive	.80	.20	□□□□□
a.	Block or vert. strip of 4, #4080-4083	3.20		□□□□□
4084	D.C. Comics Superheroes, pane of 20, self-adhesive	16.00		□□□□□
a.	39c Superman	.80	.20	□□□□□
b.	39c Green Lantern	.80	.20	□□□□□
c.	39c Wonder Woman	.80	.20	□□□□□
d.	39c Green Arrow	.80	.20	□□□□□
e.	39c Batman	.80	.20	□□□□□
f.	39c The Flash	.80	.20	□□□□□
g.	39c Plastic Man	.80	.20	□□□□□
h.	39c Aquaman	.80	.20	□□□□□
i.	39c Supergirl	.80	.20	□□□□□
j.	39c Hawkman	.80	.20	□□□□□

4085

4086

4087

4088

4089

4090

4091

4092

4093

4094

4095

4096

4097

4098

Scott No.	Description	Unused Value	Used Value	/ / / / / /
k.	39c Cover of Superman #11	.80	.20	☐☐☐☐☐
l.	39c Cover of Green Lantern #4	.80	.20	☐☐☐☐☐
m.	39c Cover of Wonder Woman #22, Second Series	.80	.20	☐☐☐☐☐
n.	39c Cover of Green Arrow #15	.80	.20	☐☐☐☐☐
o.	39c Cover of Batman #1	.80	.20	☐☐☐☐☐
p.	39c Cover of The Flash #111	.80	.20	☐☐☐☐☐
q.	39c Cover of Plastic Man #4	.80	.20	☐☐☐☐☐
r.	39c Cover of Aquaman #5, of 5	.80	.20	☐☐☐☐☐
s.	39c Cover of The Daring New Adventures of Supergirl #1	.80	.20	☐☐☐☐☐
t.	39c Cover of The Brave and the Bold Presents Hawkman #36	.80	.20	☐☐☐☐☐
4085	39c Motorcycles - 1940 Indian Four, self-adhesive	1.00	.20	☐☐☐☐☐
4086	39c Motorcycles - 1918 Cleveland, self-adhesive	1.00	.20	☐☐☐☐☐
4087	39c Motorcycles - Generic "Chopper", c.1970, self-adhesive	1.00	.20	☐☐☐☐☐
4088	39c Motorcycles - 1965 Harley-Davidson Electra-Glide, self-adhesive	1.00	.20	☐☐☐☐☐
a.	Block or horiz. strip of 4, #4085-4088	4.00		☐☐☐☐☐
4089	39c American Treasures Series, Quilts - Housetop Variation, By Mary Lee Bendolph, self-adhesive	1.00	.20	☐☐☐☐☐
4090	39c American Treasures Series, Quilts - Pig In A Pen Medallion, By Minnie Sue Coleman, self-adhesive	1.00	.20	☐☐☐☐☐
4091	39c American Treasures Series, Quilts - Nine Patch, By Ruth P. Mosely, self-adhesive	1.00	.20	☐☐☐☐☐
4092	39c American Treasures Series, Quilts - Housetop Four Block Half Log Cabin Variation, By Lottie Mooney, self-adhesive	1.00	.20	☐☐☐☐☐
4093	39c American Treasures Series, Quilts - Roman Stripes Variation, By Loretta Pettway, self-adhesive	1.00	.20	☐☐☐☐☐
4094	39c American Treasures Series, Quilts - Chinese Coins Variation, By Arlonzia Pettway, self-adhesive	1.00	.20	☐☐☐☐☐
4095	39c American Treasures Series, Quilts - Blocks And Strips, By Annie Mae Young, self-adhesive	1.00	.20	☐☐☐☐☐
4096	39c American Treasures Series, Quilts - Medallion, By Loretta Pettway, self-adhesive	1.00	.20	☐☐☐☐☐

4099

4100

4101

4102

4103

4104

4117

4118

4119

4120

4121

4122

Scott No.	Description	Unused Value	Used Value	/ / / / / /
4097	39c American Treasures Series, Quilts - Bars And String-Pieced Columns, By Jessie T. Pettway, self-adhesive	1.00	.20	□□□□□
4098	39c American Treasures Series, Quilts - Medallion With Checkerboard Center, By Patty Ann Williams, self-adhesive	1.00	.20	□□□□□
a.	Block of 10, #4089-4098	10.00		□□□□□
b.	Booklet pane of 20, 2 each #4089-4098	20.00		□□□□□
4099	Southern Florida Wetland, Wildlife, pane of 10, self-adhesive	8.00		□□□□□
a.	39c Snail Kite	.80	.20	□□□□□
b.	39c Wood Storks	.80	.20	□□□□□
c.	39c Florida Panther	.80	.20	□□□□□
d.	39c Bald Eagle	.80	.20	□□□□□
e.	39c American Crocodile	.80	.20	□□□□□
f.	39c Roseate Spoonbills	.80	.20	□□□□□
g.	39c Everglades Mink	.80	.20	□□□□□
h.	39c Cape Sable Seaside Sparrow	.80	.20	□□□□□
i.	39c American Alligator	.80	.20	□□□□□
j.	39c White Ibis	.80	.20	□□□□□
4100	39c Christmas, Madonna and Child with Bird, by Ignacio Chacon, self-adhesive, booklet stamp	.80	.20	□□□□□
a.	Booklet pane of 20	16.00		□□□□□
4101	39c Christmas - Snowflake, self-adhesive, booklet stamp, serp. die cut 11¼ x 11, base of denomination higher than year date	.90	.20	□□□□□
4102	39c Christmas - Snowflake, self-adhesive, booklet stamp, serp. die cut 11¼ x 11, base of denomination higher than year date	.90	.20	□□□□□
4103	39c Christmas - Snowflake, self-adhesive, booklet stamp, serp. die cut 11¼ x 11, base of denomination higher than year date	.90	.20	□□□□□
4104	39c Christmas - Snowflake, self-adhesive, booklet stamp, serp. die cut 11¼ x 11, base of denomination higher than year date	.90	.20	□□□□□
a.	Block or vert. strip of 4, # 4101-4104	3.60		□□□□□
4105	39c Christmas - Snowflake (4101), self-adhesive, booklet stamp, serp. die cut 11¼ x 11½ on 2 or 3 sides, base of denomination even with year date	.80	.20	□□□□□

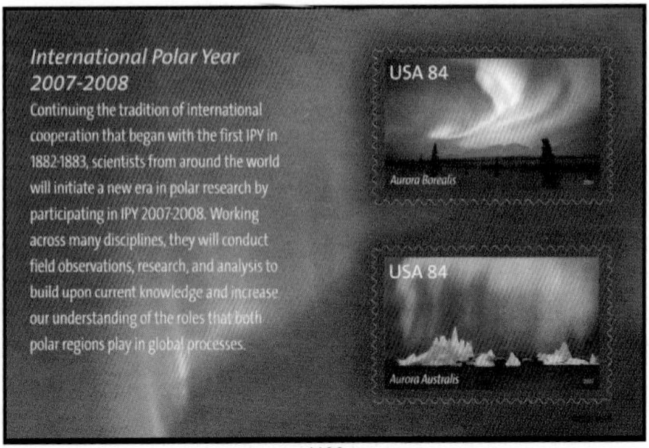

4123

4124

4125

4126

4127

4128

4129

Scott No.	Description	Unused Value	Used Value	/ / / / / /
4106	39c Christmas - Snowflake (4102), self-adhesive, booklet stamp, serp. die cut 11¼ x 11½ on 2 or 3 sides, base of denomination even with year date	.80	.20	☐☐☐☐☐
4107	39c Christmas - Snowflake (4103), self-adhesive, booklet stamp, serp. die cut 11¼ x 11½ on 2 or 3 sides, base of denomination even with year date	.80	.20	☐☐☐☐☐
4108	39c Christmas - Snowflake (4104), self-adhesive, booklet stamp, serp. die cut 11¼ x 11½ on 2 or 3 sides, base of denomination even with year date	.80	.20	☐☐☐☐☐
a.	Block of 4, # 4105-4108	3.20		
b.	Booklet pane of 20, 5 #4108a	16.00		☐☐☐☐☐
4109	39c Christmas - Snowflake (4101), self-adhesive, booklet stamp, serp. die cut 11¼ x 11 on 2 or 3 sides, base of denomination even with year date	.90	.20	☐☐☐☐☐
4110	39c Christmas - Snowflake (4102), self-adhesive, booklet stamp, serp. die cut 11¼ x 11 on 2 or 3 sides, base of denomination even with year date	.90	.20	☐☐☐☐☐
4111	39c Christmas - Snowflake (4103), self-adhesive, booklet stamp, serp. die cut 11¼ x 11 on 2 or 3 sides, base of denomination even with year date	.90	.20	☐☐☐☐☐
4112	39c Christmas - Snowflake (4104), self-adhesive, booklet stamp, serp. die cut 11¼ x 11 on 2 or 3 sides, base of denomination even with year date	.90	.20	☐☐☐☐☐
a.	Block of 4, # 4109-4112	3.60		☐☐☐☐☐
b.	Booklet pane of 4, # 4109-4112	3.60		☐☐☐☐☐
c.	Booklet pane of 6, # 4111-4112, 2 each # 4109-4110	5.50		☐☐☐☐☐
d.	Booklet pane of 6, # 4109-4110, 2 each # 4111-4112	5.50		☐☐☐☐☐
4113	39c Christmas - Snowflake (4101), self-adhesive, booklet stamp, serp. die cut 8 on 2, 3 or 4 sides	1.00	.20	☐☐☐☐☐
4114	39c Christmas - Snowflake (4102), self-adhesive, booklet stamp, serp. die cut 8 on 2, 3 or 4 sides	1.00	.20	☐☐☐☐☐

Scott No.	Description	Unused Value	Used Value	/ / / / / /
4115	39c Christmas - Snowflake (4103), self-adhesive, booklet stamp, serp. die cut 8 on 2, 3 or 4 sides	1.00	.20	□□□□□
4116	39c Christmas - Snowflake (4104), self-adhesive, booklet stamp, serp. die cut 8 on 2, 3 or 4 sides	1.00	.20	□□□□□
a.	Block of 4, # 4113-4116...............	4.00		□□□□□
b.	Booklet pane of 18, 4 each # 4114, 4116, 5 each # 4113, 4115	20.00		□□□□□
4117	39c Eid Type of 2001 (3532), self-adhesive	.80	.20	□□□□□
4118	39c Hanukkah Type of 2004 (3880), self-adhesive...............................	.80	.20	□□□□□
4119	39c Kwanzaa Type of 2004 (3881), self-adhesive...............................	.80	.20	□□□□□
2007 Issues				
4120	39c Black Heritage Series - Ella Fitzgerald (1917-96), Singer, self-adhesive.	.80	.20	□□□□□
4121	39c Oklahoma Statehood, self-adhesive	.80	.20	□□□□□
4122	39c Love - Hershey's Kiss, self-adhesive, booklet stamp, serp. die cut 10¾ x 11 on 2, 3 or 4 sides........................	.80	.20	□□□□□
a.	Booklet pane of 20.......................	16.00		□□□□□
4123	International Polar Year, souvenir sheet, pane of 2, self-adhesive	3.50		□□□□□
a.	84c International Polar Year - Aurora Borealis	1.75	.50	□□□□□
b.	84c International Polar Year - Aurora Australis	1.75	.50	□□□□□
4124	39c Literary Arts - Henry Wadsworth Longfellow (1807-82), Poet, self-adhesive..............................	.80	.20	□□□□□
4125	(41c) Forever Stamp - Liberty Bell, self-adhesive, booklet stamp, serp. die cut 11¼ x 10¾ on 2 or 3 sides, large microprinting, bell 16mm wide, dated 2007.................................	.85	.20	□□□□□
a.	Booklet pane of 20.......................	17.00		□□□□□
b.	(42c) Dated 2008................................	.85	.20	□□□□□
c.	Booklet pane of 20 #4125b	17.00		□□□□□
d.	As "c," copper ("FOREVER") omitted	—		□□□□□
e.	As "c," copper ("FOREVER") omitted on side with 12 stamps, copper splatters on side with 8 stamps	—		□□□□□
4126	(41c) Forever Stamp - Liberty Bell, self-adhesive, booklet stamp, serp. die cut 11¼ X 10¾ on 2 or 3 sides, small microprinting, bell 16mm wide, dated 2007.................................	.85	.20	□□□□□

Scott No.	Description	Unused Value	Used Value
a.	Booklet pane of 20	17.00	
b.	(42c) Dated 2008	.85	.20
c.	Booklet pane of 20 #4126b	17.00	
4127	(41c) Forever Stamp - Liberty Bell, self-adhesive, booklet stamp, serp. die cut 11¼ x 10¾ on 2 or 3 sides, medium microprinting, bell 15mm wide	.90	.20
a.	Booklet pane of 20	18.00	
b.	Booklet pane of 4	3.60	
c.	Booklet pane of 6	5.50	
d.	(42c) Dated "2008"	.90	.20
e.	Booklet pane of 20, #4127d	18.00	
f.	(42c) Dated 2008, date in smaller type	.85	.20
g.	Booklet pane of 4 #4127f	3.40	
h.	Booklet pane of 6 #4127f	5.10	
i.	(44c) Dated 2009 in copper	.90	.20
j.	Booklet pane of 20 #4127i	18.00	
4128	(41c) Forever Stamp - Liberty Bell, self-adhesive, booklet stamps, serp. die cut 8 on 2, 3 or 4 sides, large microprinting, bell 16mm wide, dated 2007	.85	.20
a.	Booklet pane of 18	15.50	
b.	(42c) Dated 2009	.85	.20
c.	Booklet pane of 18 #4128b	15.50	
4129	41c Flag, perf. 11¼	.85	.40
4130	41c Flag (4129), self-adhesive, serp. die cut 11¼ x 10¾	.85	.20
4131	41c Flag (4129), coil stamp, perf. 9¾ vert.	.85	.40
4132	41c Flag (4129), self-adhesive, coil stamp, serp. die cut 9½ Vert., with perpendicular corners	.85	.20
4133	41c Flag (4129), self-adhesive, coil stamp, serp. die cut 11 vert.	.85	.20
a.	Die cutting omitted, pair	—	
4134	41c Flag (4129), self-adhesive, coil stamp, serp. die cut 8½ vert.	.85	.20
4135	41c Flag (4129), self-adhesive, coil stamp, serp. die cut 11 vert., with rounded corners	.85	.40
4136	41c Settlement of Jamestown, self-adhesive	1.00	.20
4137	26c Wildlife - Florida Panther, perf. 11¼ x 11	.55	.20
4138	17c Wildlife - Bighorn Sheep, self-adhesive, serp. die cut 11	.45	.20
4139	26c Wildlife - Florida Panther (4137), self-adhesive, serp. die cut 11¼ x 11	.55	.20
4140	17c Wildlife - Bighorn Sheep (4138), self-adhesive, coil stamp, serpentine die cut 11 vert.	.35	.20

4136

4137

4138

4143

4144

4145

4146

4147

4148

4149

4150

4151

4152

4153

4154

4155

4156

4157

4159

4160

4161

4162

4163

Scott No.	Description	Unused Value	Used Value	/ / / / / /
4141	26c Wildlife - Florida Panther (4137), self-adhesive, coil stamp, serp. die cut 11 vert.	.55	.20	
a.	Die cutting omitted, pair	—		
4142	26c Wildlife - Florida Panther (4137), self-adhesive, booklet stamp, serp. die cut 11¼ x 11 on 3 sides	.55	.20	
a.	Booklet pane of 10	5.50		
4143	Premiere of Movie "Star Wars," 30th Anniv., pane of 15, self-adhesive	13.00		
a.	41c Darth Vader	.85	.20	
b.	41c Millennium Falcon	.85	.20	
c.	41c Emperor Palpatine	.85	.20	
d.	41c Anakin Skywalker and Obi-Wan Kenobi	.85	.20	
e.	41c Luke Skywalker	.85	.20	
f.	41c Princess Leia and R2-D2	.85	.20	
g.	41c C-3PO	.85	.20	
h.	41c Queen Padme Amidala	.85	.20	
i.	41c Obi-Wan Kenobi	.85	.20	
j.	41c Boba Fett	.85	.20	
k.	41c Darth Maul	.85	.20	
l.	41c Chewbacca and Han Solo	.85	.20	
m.	41c X-wing Starfighter	.85	.20	
n.	41c Yoda	.85	.20	
o.	41c Stormtroopers	.85	.20	
4144	$4.60 Air Force One, self-adhesive	9.25	5.00	
a.	Black (engr.) omitted	—		
4145	$16.25 Marine One, self-adhesive	27.50	16.00	
4146	41c Pacific Lighthouses - Diamond Head Lighthouse, Hawaii, self-adhesive	1.20	.20	
4147	41c Pacific Lighthouses - Five Finger Lighthouse, Alaska, self-adhesive	1.20	.20	
4148	41c Pacific Lighthouses - Grays Habor Lighthouse, Washington, self-adhesive	1.20	.20	
4149	41c Pacific Lighthouses - Umpqua River Lighthouse, Oregon, self-adhesive	1.20	.20	
4150	41c Pacific Lighthouses - St. George Reef Lighthouse, California, self-adhesive	1.20	.20	
a.	Horiz, Strip of 5, #4146-4150	6.00		
4151	41c Wedding Heart, self-adhesive, booklet stamp	.85	.20	
a.	Booklet pane of 20	17.00		
4152	58c Wedding Heart, self-adhesive	1.25	.25	
4153	41c Pollination - Purple Nightshade, Morrison's Bumblebee, Type I, self-adhesive, booklet stamp	.85	.20	
a.	Type II, bee at right straight edge.	.85	.20	

4165

4166

4167

4168

4169

4170

4171

4172

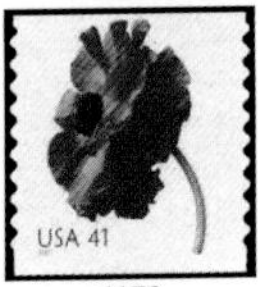

4173

4174

4175

4186

4192

4193

4196

4194

4195

Scott No.		Description	Unused Value	Used Value
4154	41c	Pollination - Hummingbird Trumpet, Calliope Hummingbird, Type I, self-adhesive, booklet stamp	.85	.20
a.		Type II, bird at left straight edge ..	.85	.20
4155	41c	Pollination - Saguaro, Lesser Long-nosed Bat, Type I, self-adhesive, booklet stamp	.85	.20
a.		Type II, bat at right straight edge..	.85	.20
4156	41c	Pollination - Prairie Ironweed, Southern Dogface Butterfly, Type I, self-adhesive, booklet stamp...........................	.85	.20
a.		Type II, butterfly at left straight edge	.85	.20
b.		Block of 4, #4153-4156................	3.40	
c.		Block of 4, #4153a-4156a	3.40	
d.		Booklet pane of 20, 3 each #4153-4156, 2 each #4153a-4156a	17.00	
4157	(10c)	Patriotic Banner, self-adhesive, coil stamp, serp. die cut 11 vert., photo.	.20	.20
4158	(10c)	Patriotic Banner (4157), self-adhesive, coil stamp, serp. die cut 11¾ vert., litho.	.20	.20
4159		Marvel Comics Superheroes, pane of 20, self-adhesive	17.00	
a.	41c	Spider-Man....................................	.85	.20
b.	41c	The Hulk.......................................	.85	.20
c.	41c	Sub-Mariner	.85	.20
d.	41c	The Thing	.85	.20
e.	41c	Captain America...........................	.85	.20
f.	41c	Silver Surfer	.85	.20
g.	41c	Spider-Woman..............................	.85	.20
h.	41c	Iron Man.......................................	.85	.20
i.	41c	Elektra	.85	.20
j.	41c	Wolverine	.85	.20
k.	41c	Cover of The Amazing Spider-Man #1	.85	.20
l.	41c	Cover of The Incredible Hulk #1..	.85	.20
m.	41c	Cover of Sub-Mariner #1	.85	.20
n.	41c	Cover of The Fantastic Four #3	.85	.20
o.	41c	Cover of Captain America #100...	.85	.20
p.	41c	Cover of The Silver Surfer #1.......	.85	.20
q.	41c	Cover of Marvel Spotlight on The Spider-Woman #32..............	.85	.20
r.	41c	Cover of Iron Man #1	.85	.20
s.	41c	Cover of Daredevil #176 Featuring Elektra.........................	.85	.20
t.	41c	Cover of The X-Men #1................	.85	.20
4160	41c	Vintage Mahogany Speedboats - 1915 Hutchinson, self-adhesive .	.85	.20
4161	41c	Vintage Mahogany Speedboats - 1954 Chris-Craft, self-adhesive..	.85	.20

4198

4199

4200

4201

4203

4204

4205

4206

Scott No.	Description	Unused Value	Used Value	/ / / / / /
4162	41c Vintage Mahogany Speedboats - 1939 Hacker-Craft, self-adhesive	.85	.20	□□□□□
4163	41c Vintage Mahogany Speedboats - 1931 Gar Wood, self-adhesive....	.85	.20	□□□□□
a.	Horiz. strip of 4, #4160-4163	3.40		□□□□□
4164	41c Purple Heart Type of 2003 (3784), self-adhesive..............................	.85	.20	□□□□□
4165	41c American Treasures Series - Magnolia & Irises, Stained Glass by Louis Comfort Tiffany, self-adhesive, booklet stamp	.85	.20	□□□□□
a.	Booklet pane of 20........................	17.00		□□□□□
4166	41c Flowers - Iris, self-adhesive, coil stamp	.85	.20	□□□□□
4167	41c Flowers - Dahlia, self-adhesive, coil stamp..................................	.85	.20	□□□□□
4168	41c Flowers - Magnolia, self-adhesive, coil stamp..................................	.85	.20	□□□□□
4169	41c Flowers - Red Gerbera Daisy, self-adhesive, coil stamp............	.85	.20	□□□□□
4170	41c Flowers - Coneflower, self-adhesive, coil stamp..................................	.85	.20	□□□□□
4171	41c Flowers - Tulip, self-adhesive, coil stamp..................................	.85	.20	□□□□□
4172	41c Flowers - Water Lily, self-adhesive, coil stamp..................................	.85	.20	□□□□□
4173	41c Flowers - Poppy, self-adhesive, coil stamp..................................	.85	.20	□□□□□
4174	41c Flowers - Chrysanthemum, self-adhesive, coil stamp............	.85	.20	□□□□□
4175	41c Flowers - Orange Gerbera Daisy, self-adhesive, coil stamp............	.85	.20	□□□□□
a.	Strip of 10, #4166-4175...............	8.50		□□□□□
4176	41c Flowers - Chrysanthemum (4174), self-adhesive, booklet stamp, serp. die cut 11¼ x 11½ on 2 or 3 sides	.85	.20	□□□□□
4177	41c Flowers - Orange Gerbera Daisy (4175), self-adhesive, booklet stamp, serp. die cut 11¼ x 11½ on 2 or 3 sides	.85	.20	□□□□□
4178	41c Flowers - Iris (4166), self-adhesive, booklet stamp, serp. die cut 11¼ x 11½ on 2 or 3 sides	.85	.20	□□□□□
4179	41c Flowers - Dahlia (4167), self-adhesive, booklet stamp, serp. die cut 11¼ x 11½ on 2 or 3 sides	.85	.20	□□□□□
4180	41c Flowers - Magnolia (4168), self-adhesive, booklet stamp, serp. die cut 11¼ x 11½ on 2 or 3 sides...........................	.85	.20	□□□□□
4181	41c Flowers - Red Gerbera Daisy (4169), self-adhesive, booklet stamp, serp. die cut 11¼ x 11½ on 2 or 3 sides	.85	.20	□□□□□

Scott No.	Description	Unused Value	Used Value	/ / / / / /
4182	41c Flowers - Water Lily (4172), self-adhesive, booklet stamp, serp. die cut 11¼ x 11½ on 2 or 3 sides	.85	.20	□□□□□
4183	41c Flowers - Poppy (4173), self-adhesive, booklet stamp, serp. die cut 11¼ x 11½ on 2 or 3 sides	.85	.20	□□□□□
4184	41c Flowers - Coneflower (4170), self-adhesive, booklet stamp, serp. die cut 11¼ x 11½ on 2 or 3 sides	.85	.20	□□□□□
4185	41c Flowers - Tulip (4171), self-adhesive, booklet stamp, serp. die cut 11¼ x 11½ on 2 or 3 sides	.85	.20	□□□□□
a.	Booklet pane of 20, 2 each #4176-4185	17.00		□□□□□
4186	41c Flag, self-adhesive, coil stamp, serp. die cut 9½ vert., with "USPS" microprinted on right side of flagpole	.85	.20	□□□□□
4187	41c Flag (4186), self-adhesive, coil stamp, serp. die cut 11 vert., with "USPS" microprinted on left side of flagpole	.85	.20	□□□□□
4188	41c Flag (4186), self-adhesive, coil stamp, serp. die cut 8½ vert.	.85	.20	□□□□□
4189	41c Flag (4186), self-adhesive, coil stamp, serp. die cut 11 vert., with rounded corners	.85	.20	□□□□□
4190	41c Flag (4186), self-adhesive, booklet stamp, serp. die cut 11¼ x 10¾ on 2 or 3 sides, with "USPS" mircoprinted on right side of flagpole	.85	.20	□□□□□
a.	Booklet pane of 10	8.50		□□□□□
4191	41c Flag (4186), self-adhesive, booklet stamp, serp. die cut 11¼ x 10¾ on 2 or 3 sides, with "USPS" microprinted on left side of flagpole	.85	.20	□□□□□
a.	Booklet pane of 20	17.00		□□□□□
4192	41c Disney Characters - Mickey Mouse, self-adhesive	.85	.20	□□□□□
4193	41c Disney Characters - Peter Pan and Tinker Bell, self-adhesive	.85	.20	□□□□□
4194	41c Disney Characters - Dumbo and Timothy Mouse, self-adhesive	.85	.20	□□□□□
4195	41c Disney Characters - Aladdin and Genie, self-adhesive	.85	.20	□□□□□
a.	Block of 4, #4192-4195	3.40		□□□□□
4196	41c Celebrate, self-adhesive	.85	.20	□□□□□
4197	41c Legends of Hollywood - James Stewart (1908-97), self-adhesive	.85	.20	□□□□□
4198	Alpine Tundra - Wildlife, pane of 10, self-adhesive	8.50		□□□□□
a.	41c Elk	.85	.20	□□□□□

Scott No.	Description	Unused Value	Used Value	/ / / / / /
b.	41c Golden eagle	.85	.20	☐☐☐☐☐
c.	41c Yellow-bellied marmot	.85	.20	☐☐☐☐☐
d.	41c American pika	.85	.20	☐☐☐☐☐
e.	41c Bighorn sheep	.85	.20	☐☐☐☐☐
f.	41c Magdalena alpine butterfly	.85	.20	☐☐☐☐☐
g.	41c White-tailed ptarmigan	.85	.20	☐☐☐☐☐
h.	41c Rocky Mountain parnassian butterfly	.85	.20	☐☐☐☐☐
i.	41c Melissa arctic butterfly	.85	.20	☐☐☐☐☐
j.	41c Brown-capped rosy-finch	.85	.20	☐☐☐☐☐
4199	41c Gerald R. Ford (1913-2006), 38th President, self-adhesive	.85	.20	☐☐☐☐☐
4200	41c Jury Duty - Twelve Jurors, self-adhesive	.85	.20	☐☐☐☐☐
4201	41c Mendez vs. Westminster, 60th Anniv., self-adhesive	.85	.20	☐☐☐☐☐
4202	41c Eid Type of 2001 (3532), self-adhesive	.85	.20	☐☐☐☐☐
4203	41c Auroras - Aurora Borealis, self-adhesive	1.00	.20	☐☐☐☐☐
4204	41c Auroras - Aurora Australis, self-adhesive	1.00	.20	☐☐☐☐☐
a.	Horiz. or vert. pair, #4203-4204	2.00		☐☐☐☐☐
4205	41c Yoda, self-adhesive	.85	.20	☐☐☐☐☐
4206	41c Christmas - Madonna of the Carnation, by Bernardino Luini, self-adhesive, booklet stamp	.85	.20	☐☐☐☐☐
a.	Booklet pane of 20	17.00		☐☐☐☐☐
4207	41c Christmas - Knit Reindeer, self-adhesive, serp. die cut 10¾	.85	.20	☐☐☐☐☐
4208	41c Christmas - Knit Christmas Tree, self-adhesive, serp. die cut 10¾	.85	.20	☐☐☐☐☐
4209	41c Christmas - Knit Snowman, self-adhesive, serp. die cut 10¾	.85	.20	☐☐☐☐☐
4210	41c Christmas - Knit Bear, self-adhesive, serp. die cut 10¾	.85	.20	☐☐☐☐☐
a.	Block or vert. strip of 4, #4207-4210	3.40		☐☐☐☐☐
b.	Booklet pane of 20, 5 each #4207-4210	17.00		☐☐☐☐☐
4211	41c Christmas - Knit Reindeer (4207), self-adhesive, booklet stamp, serp. die cut 11¼ x 11 on 2 or 3 sides	.85	.20	☐☐☐☐☐
4212	41c Christmas - Knit Christmas Tree (4208), self-adhesive, booklet stamp, serp. die cut 11¼ x 11 on 2 or 3 sides	.85	.20	☐☐☐☐☐
4213	41c Christmas - Knit Snowman (4209), self-adhesive, booklet stamp, serp. die cut 11¼ x 11 on 2 or 3 sides	.85	.20	☐☐☐☐☐
4214	41c Christmas - Knit Bear (4210), self-adhesive, booklet stamp, serp. die cut 11¼ x 11 on 2 or 3 sides	.85	.20	☐☐☐☐☐
a.	Block of 4, #4211-4214	3.40		☐☐☐☐☐
b.	Booklet pane of 4, #4211-4214	3.40		☐☐☐☐☐

4207

4208

4209

4210

4221

4222

4223

4224

4225

4226

4227

4228

4229

4230

4231

Scott No.		Description	Unused Value	Used Value	/ / / / / /
c.		Booklet pane of 6, #4213-4214, 2 each #4211-4212	5.10		
d.		Booklet pane of 6, #4211-4212, 2 each #4213-4214	5.10		
4215	41c	Christmas - Knit Reindeer (4207), self-adhesive, booklet stamp, serp. die cut 8 on 2, 3 or 4 sides	.85	.20	
4216	41c	Christmas - Knit Christmas Tree (4208), self-adhesive, booklet stamp, serp. die cut 8 on 2, 3 or 4 sides	.85	.20	
4217	41c	Christmas - Knit Snowman (4209), self-adhesive, booklet stamp, serp. die cut 8 on 2, 3 or 4 sides	.85	.20	
4218	41c	Christmas - Knit Bear (4210), self-adhesive, booklet stamp, serp. die cut 8 on 2, 3 or 4 sides	.85	.20	
a.		Block of 4, #4215-4218	3.40		
b.		Booklet pane of 18, 4 each #4215, 4218, 5 each #4216, 4217	15.50		
4219	41c	Hanukkah Type of 2004 (3880), self-adhesive	.85	.20	
4220	41c	Kwanzaa Type of 2004 (3881), self-adhesive	.85	.20	
2008 Issues					
4221	41c	Chinese New Year - Year of the Rat, lanterns, self-adhesive	.85	.20	
4222	41c	Black Heritage Series - Charles W. Chesnutt (1858-1932), Writer, self-adhesive	.85	.20	
4223	41c	Literary Arts Series - Marjorie Kinnan Rawlings (1896-1953), Writer, self-adhesive	.85	.20	
4224	41c	American Scientists - Gerty Cori (1896-1957), Biochemist, self-adhesive	.85	.20	
4225	41c	American Scientists - Linus Pauling (1901-94), Structural Chemist, self-adhesive	.85	.20	
4226	41c	American Scientists - Edwin Hubble (1889-1953), Astronomer, self-adhesive	.85	.20	
4227	41c	American Scientists - John Bardeen (1908-91), Theoretical Physicist, self-adhesive	.85	.20	
a.		Horiz. strip of 4, #4224-4227	3.40		
4228	42c	Flag at Dusk, coil stamp	.85	.40	
4229	42c	Flag at Night, coil stamp	.85	.40	
4230	42c	Flag at Dawn, coil stamp	.85	.40	
4231	42c	Flag at Midday, coil stamp	.85	.40	
a.		Horiz. strip of 4, #4228-4231	3.40	1.60	

4248

4249

4250

4251

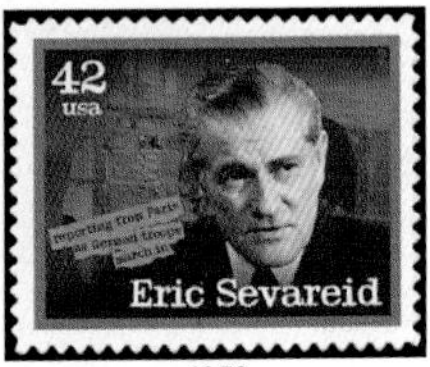

4252

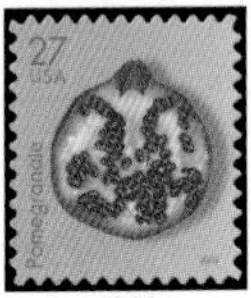

4253

4254

4255

4256

4257

4265

4266

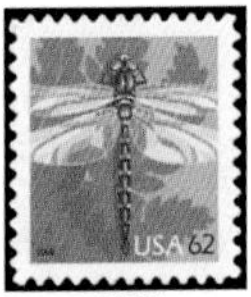

4267

Scott No.	Description	Unused Value	Used Value	/ / / / / /
4232	42c Flag at Dusk (4228), self-adhesive, coil stamp, serp. die cut 9½ vert.	.85	.20	□□□□□
4233	42c Flag at Night (4229), self-adhesive, coil stamp, serp. die cut 9½ vert.	.85	.20	□□□□□
4234	42c Flag at Dawn (4230), self-adhesive, coil stamp, serp. die cut 9½ vert.	.85	.20	□□□□□
4235	42c Flag at Midday (4231), self-adhesive, coil stamp, serp. die cut 9½ vert.	.85	.20	□□□□□
a.	Horiz. strip of 4, #4232-4235	3.40		□□□□□
4236	42c Flag at Dusk (4228), self-adhesive, coil stamp, serp. die cut 11 vert., with perpendicular corners.........	.85	.20	□□□□□
4237	42c Flag at Night (4229), self-adhesive, coil stamp, serp. die cut 11 vert., with perpendicular corners.........	.85	.20	□□□□□
4238	42c Flag at Dawn (4230), self-adhesive, coil stamp, serp. die cut 11 vert., with perpendicular corners.........	.85	.20	□□□□□
4239	42c Flag at Midday (4231), self-adhesive, coil stamp, serp. die cut 11 vert., with perpendicular corners.........	.85	.20	□□□□□
a.	Horiz. strip of 4, #4236-4239	3.40		□□□□□
4240	42c Flag at Dusk (4228), self-adhesive, coil stamp, serp. die cut 8½ vert.	.85	.20	□□□□□
4241	42c Flag at Night (4229), self-adhesive, coil stamp, serp. die cut 8½ vert.	.85	.20	□□□□□
4242	42c Flag at Dawn (4230), self-adhesive, coil stamp, serp. die cut 8½ vert.	.85	.20	□□□□□
4243	42c Flag at Midday (4231), self-adhesive, coil stamp, serp. die cut 8½ vert.	.85	.20	□□□□□
a.	Horiz. strip of 4, #4240-4243	3.40		□□□□□
4244	42c Flag at Dusk (4228), self-adhesive, coil stamp, serp. die cut 11 vert., with rounded corners..................	.85	.20	□□□□□
4245	42c Flag at Night (4229), self-adhesive, coil stamp, serp. die cut 11 vert., with rounded corners..................	.85	.20	□□□□□
4246	42c Flag at Dawn (4230), self-adhesive, coil stamp, serp. die cut 11 vert., with rounded corners..................	.85	.20	□□□□□
4247	42c Flag at Midday (4231), self-adhesive, coil stamp, serp. die cut 11 vert., with rounded corners..................	.85	.20	□□□□□
a.	Horiz. strip of 4, #4244-4247	3.40		□□□□□
4248	42c American Journalists - Martha Gellhorn (1908-98), self-adhesive	.85	.20	□□□□□
4249	42c American Journalists - John Hersey (1914-93), self-adhesive	.85	.20	□□□□□

4268

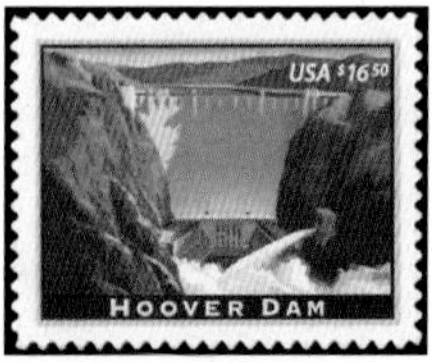

4269

4270

4271

4272

4273

4274

4275

4276

4277

4278

4279

4280

Scott No.	Description	Unused Value	Used Value	/ / / / / /
4250	42c American Journalists - George Polk (1913-48), self-adhesive	.85	.20	□□□□□
4251	42c American Journalists - Ruben Salazar (1928-70), self-adhesive	.85	.20	□□□□□
4252	42c American Journalists - Eric Sevareid (1912 92), self-adhesive	.85	.20	□□□□□
a.	Vert. strip of 5, #4248-4252..........	4.25		□□□□□
4253	27c Tropical Fruit - Pomegranate, self-adhesive...............................	.55	.20	□□□□□
4254	27c Tropical Fruit - Star Fruit, self-adhesive	.55	.20	□□□□□
4255	27c Tropical Fruit - Kiwi, self-adhesive	.55	.20	□□□□□
4256	27c Tropical Fruit - Papaya, self-adhesive	.55	.20	□□□□□
4257	27c Tropical Fruit - Guava, self-adhesive	.55	.20	□□□□□
a.	Horiz. strip of 5, #4253-4257	2.75		□□□□□
4258	27c Tropical Fruit - Pomegranate (4253), self-adhesive, coil stamp............	.55	.20	□□□□□
4259	27c Tropical Fruit - Star Fruit (4254), self-adhesive, coil stamp............	.55	.20	□□□□□
4260	27c Tropical Fruit - Kiwi (4255), self-adhesive, coil stamp............	.55	.20	□□□□□
4261	27c Tropical Fruit - Papaya (4256), self-adhesive, coil stamp............	.55	.20	□□□□□
4262	27c Tropical Fruit - Guava (4257), self-adhesive, coil stamp............	.55	.20	□□□□□
a.	Horiz. strip of 5, #4258-4262	2.75		□□□□□
4263	42c Purple Heart Type of 2003 (3784)	.85	.25	□□□□□
4264	42c Purple Heart Type of 2003 (3784), self-adhesive...............................	.85	.20	□□□□□
4265	42c Frank Sinatra (1915-98), Singer and Actor, self-adhesive	.85	.20	□□□□□
4266	42c Minnesota Statehood, 150th Anniv. - Bridge Over Mississippi River, self-adhesive...............................	.85	.20	□□□□□
4267	62c Dragonfly, self-adhesive...............	1.25	0.20	□□□□□
4268	$4.80 American Landmarks - Mount Rushmore, self-adhesive.	9.75	5.00	□□□□□
4269	$16.50 American Landmarks - Hoover Dam, self-adhesive.....................	30.00	17.00	□□□□□
4270	42c Love - Man carrying heart, self-adhesive, booklet stamp	.85	.20	□□□□□
a.	Booklet pane of 20.......................	17.00		□□□□□
4271	42c Wedding Heart, self-adhesive, booklet stamp............................	.85	.20	□□□□□
a.	Booklet pane of 20.......................	17.00		□□□□□
4272	59c Wedding Heart, self-adhesive.......	1.25	.25	□□□□□
4273	42c Flags Of Our Nation - American flag and clouds, self-adhesive, coil stamp	.85	.25	□□□□□

4281

4282

4283

4284

4285

4286

4287

4288

4289

4290

4291

4292

Scott No.	Description	Unused Value	Used Value	/ / / / / /
4274	42c Flags Of Our Nation - Alabama flag and shrimp boat, self-adhesive, coil stamp..................................	.85	.25	☐☐☐☐☐
4275	42c Flags Of Our Nation - Alaska flag and humpback whale, self-adhesive, coil stamp..................................	.85	.25	☐☐☐☐☐
4276	42c Flags Of Our Nation - American Samoa flag and island peaks and trees, self-adhesive, coil stamp...	.85	.25	☐☐☐☐☐
4277	42c Flags Of Our Nation - Arizona flag and saguaro cacti, self-adhesive, coil stamp..................................	.85	.25	☐☐☐☐☐
a.	Strip of 5, #4273-4277.................	4.25		☐☐☐☐☐
4278	42c Flags Of Our Nation - Arkansas flag and wood duck, self-adhesive, coil stamp..................................	.85	.25	☐☐☐☐☐
4279	42c Flags Of Our Nation - California flag and coast, self-adhesive, coil stamp	.85	.25	☐☐☐☐☐
4280	42c Flags Of Our Nation - Colorado flag and mountain, self-adhesive, coil stamp..................................	.85	.25	☐☐☐☐☐
4281	42c Flags Of Our Nation - Connecticut flag, sailboats and buoy, self-adhesive, coil stamp..................................	.85	.25	☐☐☐☐☐
4282	42c Flags Of Our Nation - Delaware flag and beach, self-adhesive, coil stamp	.85	.25	☐☐☐☐☐
a.	Strip of 5, #4278-4282.................	4.25		☐☐☐☐☐
b.	Plate # set of 10, #4277a + 4282a	8.50		☐☐☐☐☐
4283	42c Flags Of Our Nation - District of Columbia flag and cherry tree, self-adhesive, coil stamp............	.85	.25	☐☐☐☐☐
4284	42c Flags Of Our Nation - Florida flag and anhinga, self-adhesive, coil stamp..................................	.85	.25	☐☐☐☐☐
4285	42c Flags Of Our Nation - Georgia flag, fence and lamppost, self-adhesive, coil stamp..................................	.85	.25	☐☐☐☐☐
4286	42c Flags Of Our Nation - Guam flag, fish and tropicbird, self-adhesive, coil stamp..................................	.85	.25	☐☐☐☐☐
4287	42c Flags Of Our Nation - Hawaii flag and ohia lehua flowers, self-adhesive, coil stamp..................................	.85	.25	☐☐☐☐☐
a.	Strip of 5, #4283-4287.................	4.25		☐☐☐☐☐
4288	42c Flags Of Our Nation - Idaho flag and rainbow trout, self-adhesive, coil stamp..................................	.85	.25	☐☐☐☐☐

CHARLES+RAY EAMES
ARCHITECTURE • FURNITURE • FILM • GRAPHIC DESIGN • INDUSTRIAL DESIGN • SCULPTURE • TOYS • EXHIBITS
4333

42
USA
4334

Scott No.		Description	Unused Value	Used Value	/ / / / / /
4289		42c Flags Of Our Nation - Illinois flag and windmill, self-adhesive, coil stamp	.85	.25	☐☐☐☐☐
4290		42c Flags Of Our Nation - Indiana flag and tractor, self-adhesive, coil stamp	.85	.25	☐☐☐☐☐
4291		42c Flags Of Our Nation - Iowa flag, farm field and cornstalks, self-adhesive, coil stamp	.85	.25	☐☐☐☐☐
4292		42c Flags Of Our Nation - Kansas flag and farm buildings, self-adhesive, coil stamp	.85	.25	☐☐☐☐☐
	a.	Strip of 5, #4288-4292	4.25		☐☐☐☐☐
	b.	Plate # set of 10, #4287a +4192a.	8.50		☐☐☐☐☐
4333		Charles (1907-78) and Ray (1912-88) Eames, Designers, self-adhesive, pane of 16	15.00		☐☐☐☐☐
	a.	42c Christmas card depicting Charles and Ray Eames	.85	.20	☐☐☐☐☐
	b.	42c "Crosspatch" fabric design	.85	.20	☐☐☐☐☐
	c.	42c Stacking chairs	.85	.20	☐☐☐☐☐
	d.	42c Case Study House #8, Pacific Palisades, CA	.85	.20	☐☐☐☐☐
	e.	42c Wire-base table	.85	.20	☐☐☐☐☐
	f.	42c Lounge chair and ottoman	.85	.20	☐☐☐☐☐
	g.	42c Hang-it-all	.85	.20	☐☐☐☐☐
	h.	42c La Chaise	.85	.20	☐☐☐☐☐
	i.	42c Scene from film, "Tops"	.85	.20	☐☐☐☐☐
	j.	42c Wire mesh chair	.85	.20	☐☐☐☐☐
	k.	42c Cover of May 1943 edition of California Arts & Architecture magazine	.85	.20	☐☐☐☐☐
	l.	42c House of Cards	.85	.20	☐☐☐☐☐
	m.	42c Molded plywood sculpture	.85	.20	☐☐☐☐☐
	n.	42c Eames Storage Unit	.85	.20	☐☐☐☐☐
	o.	42c Aluminum group chair	.85	.20	☐☐☐☐☐
	p.	42c Molded plywood chair	.85	.20	☐☐☐☐☐
4334		42c Summer Olympic Games, Beijing, China - Gymnast, self-adhesive.	.85	.20	☐☐☐☐☐
4335		42c Celebrate type of 2007 (4196), self-adhesive	.85	.20	☐☐☐☐☐
4336		42c Vintage Black Cinema - Poster for Black and Tan, self-adhesive	.85	.20	☐☐☐☐☐
4337		42c Vintage Black Cinema - Poster for The Sport Of The Gods, self-adhesive	.85	.20	☐☐☐☐☐
4338		42c Vintage Black Cinema - Poster for Prinsesse Tam-Tam, self-adhesive	.85	.20	☐☐☐☐☐
4339		42c Vintage Black Cinema - Poster for Caldonia, self-adhesive	.85	.20	☐☐☐☐☐

4336

4337

4338

4339

4340

4341

4342

4343

4344

4345

Scott No.	Description	Unused Value	Used Value	/ / / / / /
4340	42c Vintage Black Cinema - Poster for Hallelujah, self-adhesive............	.85	.20	
a.	Horiz. strip of 5, #4336-4340.......	4.25		
4341	42c Take Me Out To The Ballgame, Centenary, self-adhesive............	.85	.20	
4342	42c The Art Of Disney: Imagination - Pongo and Pup, self-adhesive.....	.85	.20	
4343	42c The Art Of Disney: Imagination - Steamboat Willie, self-adhesive.	.85	.20	
4344	42c The Art Of Disney: Imagination - Princess Aurora, Flora, Fauna and Merryweather, self-adhesive.......	.85	.20	
4345	42c The Art Of Disney: Imagination - Mowgli and Baloo, self-adhesive	.85	.20	
a.	Block of 4, #4342-4345...............	3.40		
4346	42c American Treasures Series - Valley of the Yosemite, by Albert Bierstadt, self-adhesive, booklet stamp	.85	.20	
a.	Booklet pane of 20.......................	17.00		
4347	42c Sunflower, self-adhesive, booklet stamp	.85	.20	
a.	Booklet pane of 20.......................	17.00		
4348	(5c) Sea Coast type of 2002 (3693), coil stamp, perf. 9½ vert............	.20	.20	
4349	42c Latin Jazz, self-adhesive..............	.85	.20	
4350	42c Legends Of Hollywood - Bette Davis (1908-89), Actress, self-adhesive	.85	.20	
4351	42c Eid Type of 2001 (3532), self-adhesive	.85	.20	
4352	Great Lakes Dunes - Wildlife, pane of 10, self-adhesive...........	8.50		
a.	42c Vesper sparrow............................	.85	.20	
b.	42c Red fox .85................................	.20		
c.	42c Piping plover..............................	.85	.20	
d.	42c Eastern hognose snake.................	.85	.20	
e.	42c Common mergansers....................	.85	.20	
f.	42c Spotted sandpiper.........................	.85	.20	
g.	42c Tiger beetle..................................	.85	.20	
h.	42c White-footed mouse.....................	.85	.20	
i.	42c Piping plover nestlings.................	.85	.20	
j.	42c Red admiral butterfly....................	.85	.20	
4353	42c Automobiles of the 1950s - 1959 Cadillac Eldorado, self-adhesive	.85	.20	
4354	42c Automobiles of the 1950s - 1957 Studebaker Golden Hawk, self-adhesive..............................	.85	.20	
4355	42c Automobiles of the 1950s - 1957 Pontiac Safari, self-adhesive.......	.85	.20	
4356	42c Automobiles of the 1950s - 1957 Lincoln Premiere, self-adhesive.	.85	.20	

4346

4347

4349

4350

4352

4353

4354

4355

4356

4357

4358

4359

4360

4361

4362

4363

4364

4365

4366

4367

4374

4375

4376

4377

4378

4379

4380

4381

4382

4383

Scott No.		Description	Unused Value	Used Value
4357	42c	Automobiles Of The 1950s - 1957 Chrysler 300C, self-adhesive	.85	.20
a.		Vert. strip of 5, #4353-4357..........	4.25	
4358	42c	Alzheimer's Disease Awareness, self-adhesive..............................	.85	.20
4359	42c	Christmas - Virgin and Child with the young John the Baptist, by Sandro Botticelli, self-adhesive, booklet stamp............................	.85	.20
a.		Booklet pane of 20........................	17.00	
b.		Die cutting omitted, pair	—	
4360	42c	Christmas - Drummer Nutcracker, self-adhesive, booklet stamp, serp. die cut 10¾ x 11 on 2 or 3 sides	.85	.20
4361	42c	Christmas - Santa Claus Nutcracker, self-adhesive, booklet stamp, serp. die cut 10¾ x 11 on 2 or 3 sides	.85	.20
4362	42c	Christmas - King Nutcracker, self-adhesive, booklet stamp, serp. die cut 10¾ x 11 on 2 or 3 sides	.85	.20
4363	42c	Christmas - Soldier Nutcracker, self-adhesive, booklet stamp, serp. die cut 10¾ x 11 on 2 or 3 sides	.85	.20
a.		Block of 4, #4360-4363	3.40	
b.		Booklet pane of 20, 5 each #4360-4363	17.00	
4364	42c	Christmas - Drummer Nutcracker, self-adhesive, booklet stamp, serp. die cut 11¼ x 11 on 2 or 3 sides	.85	.20
4365	42c	Christmas - Santa Claus Nutcracker, self-adhesive, booklet stamp, serp. die cut 11¼ x 11 on 2 or 3 sides	.85	.20
4366	42c	Christmas - King Nutcracker, self-adhesive, booklet stamp, serp. die cut 11¼ x 11 on 2 or 3 sides	.85	.20
4367	42c	Christmas - Soldier Nutcracker, self-adhesive, booklet stamp, serp. die cut 11¼ x 11 on 2 or 3 sides	.85	.20
a.		Block of 4, #4364-4367	3.40	
b.		Booklet pane of 4, #4364-4367	3.40	
c.		Booklet pane of 6, #4366-4367, 2 each #4364-4365	5.10	
d.		Booklet pane of 6, #4364-4365, 2 each #4366-4367	5.10	
4368	42c	Christmas - Drummer Nutcracker, self-adhesive, booklet stamp, serp. die cut 8 on 2, 3 or 4 sides	.85	.20

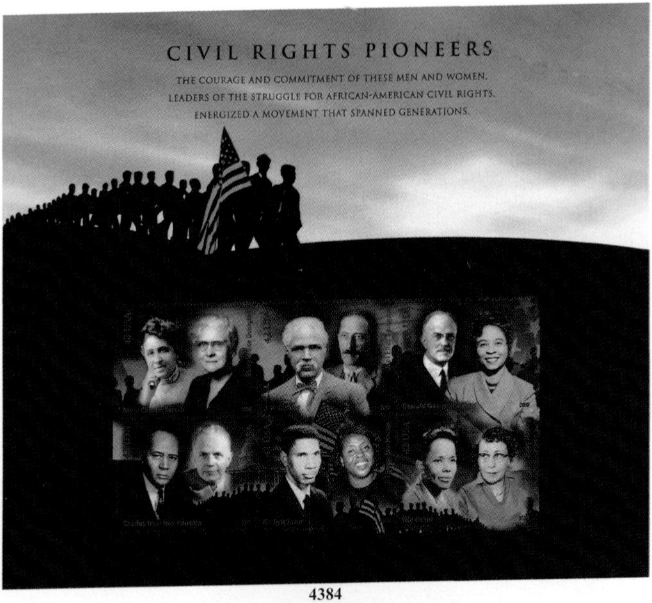

4384

4386

4387

4388

4389

4391

Scott No.	Description	Unused Value	Used Value	/ / / / / /
4369	42c Christmas - Santa Claus Nutcracker, self-adhesive, booklet stamp, serp. die cut 8 on 2, 3 or 4 sides	.85	.20	□□□□□
4370	42c Christmas - King Nutcracker, self-adhesive, booklet stamp, serp. dic cut 8 on 2, 3 or 4 sides	.85	.20	□□□□□
4371	42c Christmas - Soldier Nutcracker, self-adhesive, booklet stamp, serp. die cut 8 on 2, 3 or 4 sides	.85	.20	□□□□□
a.	Block of 4, #4368-4371	3.40		□□□□□
b.	Booklet pane of 18, 5 each #4368-4369, 4 each #4370-4371	15.50		□□□□□
4372	42c Hanukkah type of 2004 (3880), self-adhesive...............................	.85	.20	□□□□□
4373	42c Kwanzaa type of 2004 (3881), self-adhesive...............................	.85	.20	□□□□□
2009 Issues				
4374	42c Alaska Statehood, self-adhesive ...	.85	.20	□□□□□
4375	42c Chinese New Year - Year of the Ox, self-adhesive...............................	.85	.20	□□□□□
4376	42c Oregon Statehood, 150th Anniv., self-adhesive...............................	.85	.20	□□□□□
4377	42c Edgar Allan Poe (1809-49), Writer, self-adhesive...............................	.85	.20	□□□□□
4378	42c American Landmarks - Redwood Forest, self-adhesive...	10.00	5.00	□□□□□
4379	42c American Landmarks - Old Faithful, self-adhesive...............................	32.50	18.00	□□□□□
4380	42c Abraham Lincoln (1809-65), 16th President - Lincoln As Rail-splitter, self-adhesive	.85	.20	□□□□□
4381	42c Abraham Lincoln (1809-65), 16th President - Lincoln As Lawyer, self-adhesive...............................	.85	.20	□□□□□
4382	42c Abraham Lincoln (1809-65), 16th President - Lincoln As Politician, self-adhesive...............................	.85	.20	□□□□□
4383	42c Abraham Lincoln (1809-65), 16th President - Lincoln As President, self-adhesive...............................	.85	.20	□□□□□
a.	Horiz. strip of, #4380-4383	3.40		□□□□□
4384	Civil Rights Pioneers, pane of 6, self-adhesive...............................	5.10		□□□□□
a.	42c Mary Terrell (1863-1954), writer; Mary White Ovington (1865-1951), journalist....................................	.85	.20	□□□□□

4397

4398

4399

4400

4401

4402

4403

Scott No.	Description	Unused Value	Used Value	/ / / / / /
b.	42c J.R. Clifford (1848-1933), attorney; Joel Elias Spingarn (1875-1939), educator	.85	.20	☐☐☐☐☐
c.	42c Oswald Garrison Villard (1872-1949), co-founder of National Association for the Advancement of Colored People (NAACP); Daisy Gatson Bates (1914-99), mentor of black Little Rock Central High School students	.85	.20	☐☐☐☐☐
d.	42c Charles Hamilton Houston (1895-1950), lawyer; Walter White (1893-1955), chief secretary of NAACP	.85	.20	☐☐☐☐☐
e.	42c Medgar Evans (1925-63), assassinated Mississippi NAACP field secretary; Fannie Lou Hamer (1917-77), voting rights activist	.85	.20	☐☐☐☐☐
f.	42c Ella Baker (1903-86), activist; Ruby Hurley (1909-80), NAACP southeast regional director	.85	.20	☐☐☐☐☐
4385	(10c) Patriotic Banner Type of 2007 (4157), self-adhesive, coil stamp, perf 9¾ vert	.20	.20	☐☐☐☐☐
4386	61c Literary Arts - Richard Wright (1908-60), author, self-adhesive	1.25	.20	☐☐☐☐☐
4387	28c Wildlife - Polar Bear, self-adhesive	.60	.20	☐☐☐☐☐
4388	64c Wildlife - Dolphin, self-adhesive..	1.40	.25	☐☐☐☐☐
4389	28c Wildlife - Polar Bear, self-adhesive, coil stamp	.60	.20	☐☐☐☐☐
4390	44c Purple Heart type of 2003 (3784), self-adhesive	.90	.20	☐☐☐☐☐
4391	44c Flag, coil stamp, perf. 9¾ vert	.90	.20	☐☐☐☐☐
4392	44c Flag, coil stamp (4391), self-adhesive, with pointed corners, serp. die cut 11 vert	.90	.20	☐☐☐☐☐
4393	44c Flag (4391), coil stamp, self-adhesive, serp. die cut 9½ vert	.90	.20	☐☐☐☐☐
4394	44c Flag (4391), coil stamp, self-adhesive, serp. die cut 8½ vert	.90	.20	☐☐☐☐☐
4395	44c Flag (4391), coil stamp, self-adhesive, with rounded corners, serp. die cut 11 vert	.90	.20	☐☐☐☐☐
4396	44c Flag (4391), booklet stamp, self-adhesive, serp. die cut 11¼ x 10¾ on 3 sides	.90	.20	☐☐☐☐☐
a.	Booklet pane of 10	9.00		☐☐☐☐☐
4397	44c Weddings - Wedding Rings, self-adhesive	.90	.20	☐☐☐☐☐
4398	61c Weddings - Wedding Cake, self-adhesive	1.25	.25	☐☐☐☐☐

4404

4405

4406

4408

B1

B2

B3

Scott No.	Description	Unused Value	Used Value	/ / / / / /
4399	44c The Simpsons Television Show, 20th Anniv. - Homer Simpson, self-adhesive, booklet stamp	.90	.20	☐☐☐☐☐
4400	44c The Simpsons Television Show, 20th Anniv. - Marge Simpson, self-adhesive, booklet stamp	.90	.20	☐☐☐☐☐
4401	44c The Simpsons Television Show, 20th Anniv. - Bart Simpson, self-adhesive, booklet stamp	.90	.20	☐☐☐☐☐
4402	44c The Simpsons Television Show, 20th Anniv. - Lisa Simpson, self-adhesive, booklet stamp	.90	.20	☐☐☐☐☐
4403	44c The Simpsons Television Show, 20th Anniv. - Maggie Simpson, self-adhesive, booklet stamp	.90	.20	☐☐☐☐☐
a.	Horiz. strip of 5, #4399-4403	4.50		☐☐☐☐☐
b.	Booklet pane of 20, 4 each #4399-4403	18.00		☐☐☐☐☐
4404	44c Love - Kings of Hearts, self-adhesive, booklet stamp.............................	.90	.20	☐☐☐☐☐
4405	44c Love - Queen of Hearts, self-adhesive, booklet stamp..............................	.90	.20	☐☐☐☐☐
a.	Horiz. or vert. pair #4404-4405....	1.80		☐☐☐☐☐
b.	Booklet pane of 20, 10 each #4404-4405	18.00		☐☐☐☐☐
4406	44c Bob Hope (1903-2003), Actor and Comedian, self-adhesive.............	.90	.20	☐☐☐☐☐
4407	44c Celebrate type of 2007 (4196), self-adhesive................................	.90	.20	☐☐☐☐☐
4408	44c Black Heritage - Anna Julia Cooper (1858-1964), educator, self-adhesive	.90	.20	☐☐☐☐☐

SEMI-POSTAL STAMPS

1998, July 29

B1	(32c+8c) Breast Cancer Research, self-adhesive	.80	.20	☐☐☐☐☐

2002, June 7

B2	(34c+11c) Heroes of 2001, Firemen Atop World Trade Center Rubble, self-adhesive	.80	.35	☐☐☐☐☐

2003, Oct. 8

B3	(37c+8c) Stop Family Violence, self-adhesive	.85	.45	☐☐☐☐☐

C1

C4

C5

C6

C7

C10

C11

C12

C13

C14

C15

C18

C20

C21

C23

Scott No.	Description	Unused Value	Used Value	/ / / / / /
AIR POST STAMPS				
1918				
C1	6c Curtiss Jenny, orange	65.00	30.00	☐☐☐☐☐
C2	16c Curtiss Jenny (C1), green	70.00	35.00	☐☐☐☐☐
C3	24c Curtiss Jenny (C1), car rose & blue	70.00	35.00	☐☐☐☐☐
a.	Center inverted	*500,000.*		☐☐☐☐☐
1923				
C4	8c Propeller	21.00	14.00	☐☐☐☐☐
C5	16c Air Service Emblem	70.00	30.00	☐☐☐☐☐
C6	24c Biplane	75.00	30.00	☐☐☐☐☐
1926-30				
C7	10c Map & Planes, dark blue	2.50	.35	☐☐☐☐☐
C8	15c Map & Planes (C7), olive brown	2.75	2.50	☐☐☐☐☐
C9	20c Map & Planes (C7), yellow green	7.00	2.00	☐☐☐☐☐
C10	10c "Spirit of St. Louis"	7.00	2.50	☐☐☐☐☐
a.	Booklet pane of 3	80.00	*65.00*	☐☐☐☐☐
C11	5c Beacon	5.00	.75	☐☐☐☐☐
a.	Vertical pair, imperf. btwn.	*7,000.*		☐☐☐☐☐
C12	5c Winged Globe, violet, perf. 11	9.50	.50	☐☐☐☐☐
a.	Horiz. pair, imperf. btwn.	*4,500.*		☐☐☐☐☐
1930				
C13	65c Zeppelin over Atlantic	225.00	150.00	☐☐☐☐☐
C14	$1.30 Zeppelin between Continents	475.00	350.00	☐☐☐☐☐
C15	$2.60 Zeppelin passing Globe	675.00	550.00	☐☐☐☐☐
1931-32, Perf. 10½ x 11				
C16	5c Winged Globe (C12), violet	5.00	.60	☐☐☐☐☐
C17	8c Winged Globe (C12), olive bister	2.25	.40	☐☐☐☐☐
1933				
C18	50c Century of Progress	55.00	55.00	☐☐☐☐☐
1934				
C19	6c Winged Globe (C12), dull orange	3.50	.25	☐☐☐☐☐
1935				
C20	25c Transpacific (dated 1935), blue	1.40	1.00	☐☐☐☐☐
1937				
C21	20c Transpacific (no date), green	11.00	1.75	☐☐☐☐☐
C22	50c Transpacific (C21), carmine	11.00	5.00	☐☐☐☐☐
1938				
C23	6c Eagle & Shield	.50	.20	☐☐☐☐☐
a.	Vert. pair, imperf. horiz.	325.00		☐☐☐☐☐
b.	Horiz. pair, imperf. vert	*12,500.*		☐☐☐☐☐

C24

C25

C33

C32

C34

C35

C36

C40

C38

C42

C43

C44

C45

C46

C47

Scott No.	Description	Unused Value	Used Value	/ / / / / /
1939				
C24	30c Winged Globe (inscribed "Transatlantic"), dull blue	12.00	1.50	☐☐☐☐☐
1941-44				
C25	6c Airplane, carmine	.20	.20	☐☐☐☐☐
a.	Booklet pane of 3	5.00	1.50	☐☐☐☐☐
b.	Horiz. pair, imperf. btwn.	*2,250.*		☐☐☐☐☐
C26	8c Airplane (C25), olive green	.20	.20	☐☐☐☐☐
a.	All color omitted	—		☐☐☐☐☐
C27	10c Airplane (C25), violet	1.25	.20	☐☐☐☐☐
C28	15c Airplane (C25), brown carmine	2.25	.35	☐☐☐☐☐
C29	20c Airplane (C25), bright green	2.25	.30	☐☐☐☐☐
C30	30c Airplane (C25), blue	2.25	.35	☐☐☐☐☐
C31	50c Airplane (C25), orange	11.00	3.25	☐☐☐☐☐
1946				
C32	5c DC-4 Skymaster (entire plane)	.20	.20	☐☐☐☐☐
1947, Perf. 10½ x 11				
C33	5c DC-4 Skymaster	.20	.20	☐☐☐☐☐
C34	10c Pan American Union Building	.25	.20	☐☐☐☐☐
C35	15c Statue of Liberty	.35	.20	☐☐☐☐☐
a.	Horiz. pair, imperf. btwn.	*2,750.*		☐☐☐☐☐
C36	25c San Francisco-Oakland Bay Bridge	.90	.20	☐☐☐☐☐
1948, Coil Stamp, Perf. 10 Horizontally				
C37	5c DC-4 Skymaster (C33)	1.00	.80	☐☐☐☐☐
1948				
C38	5c New York City	.20	.20	☐☐☐☐☐
1949, Perf. 10½ x 11				
C39	6c DC-4 Skymaster (C33)	.20	.20	☐☐☐☐☐
a.	Booklet pane of 6	10.00	5.00	☐☐☐☐☐
1949				
C40	6c Alexandria Bicentennial	.20	.20	☐☐☐☐☐
Coil Stamp, Perf. 10 Horizontally				
C41	6c DC-4 Skymaster (C33)	3.00	.20	☐☐☐☐☐
1949				
C42	10c Universal Postal Union	.20	.20	☐☐☐☐☐
C43	15c Universal Postal Union	.30	.25	☐☐☐☐☐
C44	25c Universal Postal Union	.60	.40	☐☐☐☐☐
C45	6c Wright Brothers	.20	.20	☐☐☐☐☐
1952-58				
C46	80c Diamond Head, Hawaii	4.75	1.25	☐☐☐☐☐
C47	6c Powered Flight	.20	.20	☐☐☐☐☐

C48

C49

C51

C53

C55

C57

C58

C59

C63-Redrawn

C54

C56

C68

C70

C64

C66

C67

C69

Scott No.	Description	Unused Value	Used Value	/ / / / / /
C48	4c Eagle, bright blue	.20	.20	□□□□□
C49	6c Air Force	.20	.20	□□□□□
C50	5c Eagle (C48), red	.20	.20	□□□□□
Perf. 10½x11				
C51	7c Jet, blue	.20	.20	□□□□□
a.	Booklet pane of 6	9.00	7.00	□□□□□
Coil Stamp, Perf. 10 Horizontally				
C52	7c Jet (C51), blue	2.00	.20	□□□□□
1959				
C53	7c Alaska Statehood	.20	.20	□□□□□
C54	7c Balloon Jupiter	.30	.20	□□□□□
C55	7c Hawaii Statehood	.20	.20	□□□□□
C56	10c Pan American Games	.25	.25	□□□□□
1959-66				
C57	10c Liberty Bell, black & green	1.00	.70	□□□□□
C58	15c Statue of Liberty, black & orange	.35	.20	□□□□□
C59	25c Abraham Lincoln, black & maroon, untagged	.50	.20	□□□□□
a.	Tagged	.60	.30	□□□□□
Perf. 10½ x 11				
C60	7c Jet (C51), carmine	.20	.20	□□□□□
a.	Booklet pane of 6	10.00	8.00	□□□□□
b.	Vert. pair, imperf. btwn. (from booklet pane)	*5,500.*	—	□□□□□
Coil Stamp, Perf. 10 Horizontally				
C61	7c Jet (C51), carmine	4.00	.25	□□□□□
1961-67				
C62	13c Liberty Bell (C57), black & red, untagged	.40	.20	□□□□□
a.	Tagged	.75	.50	□□□□□
C63	15c Statue of Liberty (redrawn), blk & org, untagged	.30	.20	□□□□□
a.	Tagged	.35	.20	□□□□□
b.	As "a," horiz. pair, imperf. vert.	*15,000.*		□□□□□
c.	As "a," horiz. pair, imperf. btwn. and at left	*2,750.*		□□□□□
d.	All color omitted	—		□□□□□
Perf. 10½ x 11				
C64	8c Jet & Capitol, untagged	.20	.20	□□□□□
a.	Tagged	.20	.20	□□□□□
b.	Booklet pane 5 + label, tagged	7.00	3.00	□□□□□
c.	As "b," tagged	2.00	.75	□□□□□
Coil Stamp, Perf. 10 Horizontally				
C65	8c Jet & Capitol (C64), untagged	.40	.20	□□□□□
a.	Tagged	.35	.20	□□□□□

C72

C77

C78

C79

C71

C76

C84

C74

C75

C80

C85

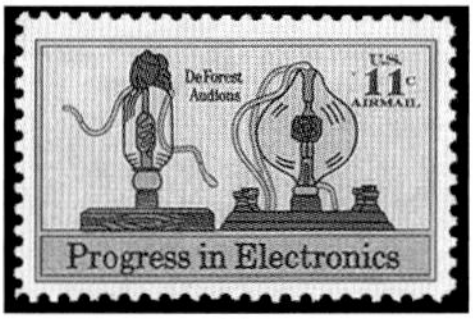

C86

C87

C88

C89

C90

C97

Scott No.	Description	Unused Value	Used Value	/ / / / / /
1963-67				
C66	15c Montgomery Blair	.60	.55	☐☐☐☐☐
C67	6c Eagle, untagged	.20	.20	☐☐☐☐☐
a.	Tagged	4.00	3.00	☐☐☐☐☐
C68	8c Amelia Earhart	.20	.20	☐☐☐☐☐
C69	8c Robert H. Goddard	.40	.20	☐☐☐☐☐
C70	8c Alaska Purchase	.25	.20	☐☐☐☐☐
C71	20c Columbia Jays by Audubon	.80	.20	☐☐☐☐☐
1968, Perf. 11 x 10½				
C72	10c Star Runway	.20	.20	☐☐☐☐☐
b.	Booklet pane of 8	2.00	.75	☐☐☐☐☐
c.	Booklet pane of 5 + label	3.75	.75	☐☐☐☐☐
d.	Vert. pair, imperf. btwn. (from booklet pane)	*4,000.*	—	☐☐☐☐☐
Coil Stamp, Perf. 10 Vertically				
C73	10c Star Runway (C72)	.30	.20	☐☐☐☐☐
a.	Imperf., pair	*550.00*		☐☐☐☐☐
1968				
C74	10c 50th Anniversary of Air Mail	.25	.20	☐☐☐☐☐
C75	20c "USA" & Jet, red, blue & black	.35	.20	☐☐☐☐☐
1969				
C76	10c Moon Landing	.25	.20	☐☐☐☐☐
a.	Rose red (litho.) omitted	*500.00*	—	☐☐☐☐☐
1971-73				
C77	9c Delta Wing Plane	.20	.20	☐☐☐☐☐
C78	11c Jet, tagged	.20	.20	☐☐☐☐☐
a.	Booklet pane of 4 + 2 labels	1.25	.75	☐☐☐☐☐
b.	Untagged (Bureau precanceled)	.85	.85	☐☐☐☐☐
C79	13c Winged Envelope, tagged	.25	.20	☐☐☐☐☐
a.	Booklet pane of 5 + label	1.50	.75	☐☐☐☐☐
b.	Untagged (Bureau precanceled)	.85	.85	☐☐☐☐☐
C80	17c Statue of Liberty	.35	.20	☐☐☐☐☐
C81	21c "USA" & Jet (C75), red, blue & black	.40	.20	☐☐☐☐☐
b.	Black (engr.) omitted	*2,750.*		☐☐☐☐☐
Coil Stamps, Perf. 10 Vertically				
C82	11c Jet (C78)	.25	.20	☐☐☐☐☐
a.	Imperf., pair	*250.00*		☐☐☐☐☐
C83	13c Winged Envelope (C79)	.30	.20	☐☐☐☐☐
a.	Imperf., pair	*65.00*		☐☐☐☐☐
1972-74				
C84	11c City of Refuge	.20	.20	☐☐☐☐☐
a.	Blue & green (litho.) omitted	*750.00*		☐☐☐☐☐
C85	11c Olympics - Skiing	.20	.20	☐☐☐☐☐

C91-C92

C93-C94

C95-C96

C99

C98

C100

C108

C113

C114

C115

C116

C117

C118

C119

Scott No.	Description	Unused Value	Used Value	/ / / / / /
C86	11c Progress in Electronics	.30	.20	☐☐☐☐☐
a.	Vermilion & olive (litho.) omitted	*825.00*		☐☐☐☐☐
c.	Olive omitted	*1,150.*		☐☐☐☐☐
C87	18c Statue of Liberty	.35	.30	☐☐☐☐☐
C88	26c Mt. Rushmore	.60	.20	☐☐☐☐☐
1976				
C89	25c Plane & Globes	.50	.20	☐☐☐☐☐
C90	31c Plane, Globes & Flag	.60	.20	☐☐☐☐☐
1978				
C91	31c Wright Brothers - Portraits at top	.65	.30	☐☐☐☐☐
C92	31c Wright Brothers - Plane at top	.65	.30	☐☐☐☐☐
a.	Vertical pair, #C91-C92	1.30	1.20	☐☐☐☐☐
b.	As "a," ultra & black (engr.) omitted	*600.00*		☐☐☐☐☐
c.	As "a," black (engr.) omitted	*2,500.*		☐☐☐☐☐
d.	As "a," black, yel, mag, blue & brown (litho.) omitted	*2,250.*		☐☐☐☐☐
1979				
C93	21c Octave Chanute - Portrait at top	.70	.35	☐☐☐☐☐
C94	21c Octave Chanute - Plane at top	.70	.35	☐☐☐☐☐
a.	Vertical pair, #C93-C94	1.40	1.20	☐☐☐☐☐
b.	As "a," ultra & black (engr.) omitted	*4,500.*		☐☐☐☐☐
C95	25c Wiley Post - Portrait at top	1.10	.45	☐☐☐☐☐
C96	25c Wiley Post - Plane at top	1.10	.45	☐☐☐☐☐
a.	Vertical pair, #C95-C96	2.25	1.50	☐☐☐☐☐
C97	31c Olympics - High Jump	.70	.30	☐☐☐☐☐
1980				
C98	40c Philip Mazzei, perf. 11	.80	.20	☐☐☐☐☐
b.	Imperf., pair	*3,500.*		☐☐☐☐☐
C98A	40c Philip Mazzei, perf. 10½ x 11¼ ('82) (C98)	8.00	1.50	☐☐☐☐☐
c.	Horiz. pair, imperf. vert.	*4,250.*		☐☐☐☐☐
C99	28c Blanche Stuart Scott	.60	.20	☐☐☐☐☐
a.	Imperf., pair	*2,350.*		☐☐☐☐☐
C100	35c Glenn Curtiss	.65	.20	☐☐☐☐☐
a.	Light blue (background) omitted	*2,000.*		☐☐☐☐☐
1983				
C101	28c Olympics - Women's Gymnastics	1.00	.30	☐☐☐☐☐
C102	28c Olympics - Hurdles	1.00	.30	☐☐☐☐☐
C103	28c Olympics - Women's Basketball	1.00	.30	☐☐☐☐☐
C104	28c Olympics - Soccer	1.00	.30	☐☐☐☐☐
a.	Block of 4, #C101-C104	4.25	2.50	☐☐☐☐☐
b.	As "a," imperf. vert.	*7,500.*		☐☐☐☐☐
C105	40c Olympics - Shot put, Perf. 11.2 bullseye	.90	.40	☐☐☐☐☐
a.	Perf. 11 line	1.00	.45	☐☐☐☐☐

C120

C121

C122-C125

C127

C128

C130

C131

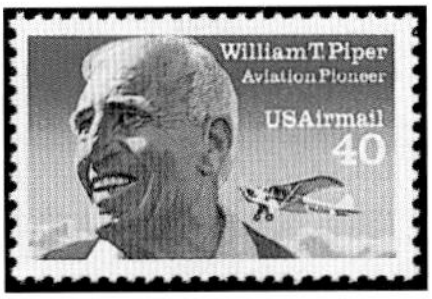

C132

C133

C134

C135

C136

C137

C138

Scott No.	Description	Unused Value	Used Value	/ / / / / /
C106	40c Olympics - Gymnast, Perf. 11.2 bullseye	.90	.40	□□□□□
a.	Perf. 11 line	1.00	.45	□□□□□
C107	40c Olympics - Swimmer, Perf. 11.2 bullseye	.90	.40	□□□□□
a.	Perf. 11 line	1.00	.45	□□□□□
C108	40c Olympics - Weightlifting, perf. 11.2 bullseye	.90	.40	□□□□□
a.	Perf. 11 line	1.00	.45	□□□□□
b.	Block of 4, #C105-C108	4.25	3.00	□□□□□
c.	Block of 4, #C105a-C108a	5.00	4.00	□□□□□
d.	Block of 4, imperf.	*1,000.*		□□□□□
C109	35c Olympics - Women's fencing	.90	.55	□□□□□
C110	35c Olympics - Cycling	.90	.55	□□□□□
C111	35c Olympics - Women's volleyball	.90	.55	□□□□□
C112	35c Olympics - Pole vaulting	.90	.55	□□□□□
a.	Block of 4, #C109-C112	4.00	3.25	□□□□□
1985				
C113	33c Alfred V. Verville	.65	.20	□□□□□
a.	Imperf., pair	*825.00*		□□□□□
C114	39c Lawrence & Elmer Sperry	.80	.25	□□□□□
a.	Imperf., pair	*1,750.*		□□□□□
C115	44c Transpacific Airmail	.85	.25	□□□□□
a.	Imperf., pair	*750.00*		□□□□□
C116	44c Father Junipero Serra	1.00	.35	□□□□□
a.	Imperf., pair	*1,300.*		□□□□□
1988				
C117	44c Settling of New Sweden	1.00	.25	□□□□□
C118	45c Samuel P. Langley	.90	.20	□□□□□
C119	36c Igor Sikorsky	.70	.25	□□□□□
a.	Red, dk blue & black (engr.) omitted	*3,000.*		□□□□□
1989				
C120	45c French Revolution	.95	.20	□□□□□
C121	45c Carved Figure	.90	.20	□□□□□
C122	45c Futuristic Space Craft	1.00	.50	□□□□□
C123	45c Futuristic Hover Car	1.00	.50	□□□□□
C124	45c Futuristic Moon Rover	1.00	.50	□□□□□
C125	45c Space Shuttle	1.00	.50	□□□□□
a.	Block of 4, #C122-C125	4.00	3.00	□□□□□
b.	As "a.," light blue (engr.) omitted	*725.00*		□□□□□
C126	UPU Congress, sheet of 4, imperf.	5.00	4.00	□□□□□
a.	45c Futuristic Space Craft (C122)	1.25	.50	□□□□□
b.	45c Futuristic Hover Car (C123)	1.25	.50	□□□□□
c.	45c Futuristic Moon Rover (C124)	1.25	.50	□□□□□
d.	45c Space Shuttle (C125)	1.25	.50	□□□□□
1990				
C127	45c Tropical Coast	.90	.20	□□□□□

Scott No.	Description	Unused Value	Used Value
1991, Perf. 11			
C128	50c Harriet Quimby, perf. 11	1.00	.25
a.	Vert. pair, imperf. horiz.	1,500.	
b.	Perf. 11.2	1.10	.25
C129	40c William T. Piper (C132), hair does not touch top edge	.80	.20
C130	50c Antarctic Treaty	1.00	.35
C131	50c Bering Land Bridge	1.00	.35
1993, Perf. 11.2			
C132	40c Piper, hair touches top edge	2.75	.65
C133	48c Niagara Falls, self-adhesive	.95	.20
C134	40c Rio Grande, self-adhesive	.80	.60
2000-05			
C135	60c Grand Canyon, self-adhesive	1.25	.25
a.	Imperf, pair	*2,250.*	
C136	70c Nine-Mile Prairie, Nebraska, self-adhesive	1.40	.30
C137	80c Mt. McKinley, self-adhesive	1.60	.35
C138	60c Arcadia National Park, self-adhesive, serpentine die cut 11¼ x 11½, dated "2001"	1.25	.25
a.	Dated "2001," serp. die cut 11.5x11.9	1.25	.25
b.	Dated "2005," serp. die cut 11.5x11.9	1.25	.25
c.	As "b," printed on back of backing paper	—	
C139	63c Scenic American Landscapes - Bryce Canyon National Park, self-adhesive	1.25	0.25
a.	Die cutting omitted, pair	—	
C140	75c Scenic American Landscapes - Great Smoky Mountains National Park, self-adhesive	1.50	0.35
a.	Die cutting omitted, pair	—	
C141	84c Scenic American Landscapes - Yosemite National Park, self-adhesive	1.75	0.35
2007			
C142	69c Scenic American Landscapes - Okefenokee Swamp, self-adhesive	1.40	0.30
C143	90c Scenic American Landscapes - Hagatna Bay, self-adhesive	1.80	0.40
2008			
C144	72c Scenic American Landscapes - 13-Mile Woods, self-adhesive	1.50	0.30
C145	94c Scenic American Landscapes - Trunk Bay, self-adhesive	1.90	0.45

C139

C140

C141

C142

C143

C144

C145

C146

C147

CE1

E1

E3

E4

E6

E12

E7

E14

Scott No.	Description	Unused Value	Used Value	/ / / / / /
2009				
C146	79c Scenic American Landscapes - Zion National Park, self-adhesive.	1.60	0.35	☐☐☐☐☐
C147	98c Scenic American Landscapes - Grand Teton National Park, self-adhesive	2.00	0.45	☐☐☐☐☐
AIR POST SPECIAL DELIVERY STAMPS				
1934, Perf. 11				
CE1	16c Great Seal, dark blue	.60	.70	☐☐☐☐☐
1936				
CE2	16c Great Seal (CE1), red & blue	.40	.25	☐☐☐☐☐
a.	Horiz. pair, imperf. vert.	*3,750.*		☐☐☐☐☐
SPECIAL DELIVERY STAMPS				
1885-93				
E1	10c Messenger Running, blue	550.00	75.00	☐☐☐☐☐
E2	10c Messenger Running, "Post Office" Curved (E3), blue	500.00	40.00	☐☐☐☐☐
E3	10c Messenger Running, orange	290.00	45.00	☐☐☐☐☐
1894, Line under "TEN CENTS"				
E4	10c Messenger Running, blue	900.00	75.00	☐☐☐☐☐
1895, Watermark 191				
E5	10c Messenger Running (E4), blue	210.00	10.00	☐☐☐☐☐
b.	Printed on both sides	—		☐☐☐☐☐
1902				
E6	10c Bicycle Messenger, ultramarine	230.00	10.00	☐☐☐☐☐
a.	10c blue	250.00	10.00	☐☐☐☐☐
1908				
E7	10c Helmet of Mercury	70.00	45.00	☐☐☐☐☐
1911, Watermark 190, Perf. 12				
E8	10c Bicycle Messenger (E6), ultramarine	110.00	10.00	☐☐☐☐☐
b.	10c violet blue	125.00	12.00	☐☐☐☐☐
1914, Perf. 10				
E9	10c Bicycle Messenger (E6), ultramarine	190.00	12.00	☐☐☐☐☐
a.	10c blue	240.00	15.00	☐☐☐☐☐
1916, Perf. 10, Unwatermarked				
E10	10c Bicycle Messenger (E6), pale ultra..	320.00	45.00	☐☐☐☐☐
a.	10c blue	350.00	50.00	☐☐☐☐☐
1917-25, Perf. 11				
E11	10c Bicycle Messenger (E6), ultramarine	20.00	.75	☐☐☐☐☐
b.	10c gray violet	30.00	3.00	☐☐☐☐☐

E20

E22

Scott No.	Description	Unused Value	Used Value	/ / / / / /
c.	10c blue	65.00	4.00	☐☐☐☐☐
d.	Perf. 10 at left	—		☐☐☐☐☐
E12	10c Motorcycle Delivery, gray violet	50.00	1.25	☐☐☐☐☐
a.	10c deep ultramarine	60.00	2.50	☐☐☐☐☐
E13	15c Motorcycle Delivery (E12), dp orange	30.00	2.00	☐☐☐☐☐
E14	20c Post Office Truck	2.00	1.00	☐☐☐☐☐
1927-51, Perf. 11 x 10½				
E15	10c Motorcycle Delivery (E12), gray violet	.65	.25	☐☐☐☐☐
a.	10c red lilac	.65	.25	☐☐☐☐☐
b.	10c gray lilac	.65	.25	☐☐☐☐☐
c.	Horiz. pair, imperf. btwn.	300.00		☐☐☐☐☐
E16	15c Motorcycle Delivery (E12), orange	.70	.25	☐☐☐☐☐
E17	13c Motorcycle Delivery (E12), blue	.60	.20	☐☐☐☐☐
E18	17c Motorcycle Delivery (E12), yellow	3.50	2.50	☐☐☐☐☐
E19	20c Post Office Truck	1.25	.20	☐☐☐☐☐
1954-57				
E20	20c Hands & Letter, deep blue	.40	.20	☐☐☐☐☐
E21	30c Hands & Letter (E20), lake	.50	.20	☐☐☐☐☐
1969-71				
E22	45c Arrows, carmine & violet blue	1.25	.25	☐☐☐☐☐
E23	60c Arrows (E22), violet blue & carmine	1.25	.20	☐☐☐☐☐

F1

FA1

Scott No.	Description	Unused Value	Used Value	/ / / / / /
REGISTRATION STAMP				
1911				
F1	10c Eagle	80.00	13.00	☐☐☐☐☐
CERTIFIED MAIL STAMP				
1955				
FA1	15c Mailman	.60	.40	☐☐☐☐☐

J1

J29

J69

J87

J88

Scott No.	Description	Unused Value	Used Value

POSTAGE DUE STAMPS

1879, Perf. 12

Scott No.	Description	Unused Value	Used Value
J1	1c Numeral, brown	95.00	14.00
J2	2c Numeral (J1), brown	425.00	18.00
J3	3c Numeral (J1), brown	105.00	6.00
J4	5c Numeral (J1), brown	825.00	70.00
J5	10c Numeral (J1), brown	1,000.00	70.00
a.	Imperf., pair	*3,000.*	
J6	30c Numeral (J1), brown	400.00	65.00
J7	50c Numeral (J1), brown	650.00	90.00

1879, Special Printing

Scott No.	Description	Unused Value	Used Value
J8	1c Numeral (J1), deep brown	*22,500.*	
J9	2c Numeral (J1), deep brown	*19,000.*	
J10	3c Numeral (J1), deep brown	*25,000.*	
J11	5c Numeral (J1), deep brown	*15,000.*	
J12	10c Numeral (J1), deep brown	*9,000.*	
J13	30c Numeral (J1), deep brown	*10,000.*	
J14	50c Numeral (J1), deep brown	*9,000.*	

1884-89

Scott No.	Description	Unused Value	Used Value
J15	1c Numeral (J1), red brown	75.00	7.00
J16	2c Numeral (J1), red brown	90.00	6.00
J17	2c Numeral (J1), red brown	1,150.	300.00
J18	5c Numeral (J1), red brown	625.00	45.00
J19	10c Numeral (J1), red brown	625.00	35.00
J20	30c Numeral (J1), red brown	225.00	60.00
J21	50c Numeral (J1), red brown	1,900.	225.00

1891-93

Scott No.	Description	Unused Value	Used Value
J22	1c Numeral (J1), bright claret	35.00	2.00

Scott No.	Description	Unused Value	Used Value	/ / / / / /
J23	2c Numeral (J1), bright claret	37.50	2.00	☐☐☐☐☐
J24	3c Numeral (J1), bright claret	75.00	16.00	☐☐☐☐☐
J25	5c Numeral (J1), bright claret	110.00	16.00	☐☐☐☐☐
J26	10c Numeral (J1), bright claret	180.00	30.00	☐☐☐☐☐
J27	30c Numeral (J1), bright claret	650.00	225.00	☐☐☐☐☐
J28	50c Numeral (J1), bright claret	700.00	210.00	☐☐☐☐☐
1894				
J29	1c Numeral, vermilion	2,750.	725.00	☐☐☐☐☐
J30	2c Numeral (J29), vermilion	850.00	350.00	☐☐☐☐☐
J31	1c Numeral (J29), deep claret	80.00	12.00	☐☐☐☐☐
b.	Vert. pair, imperf. horiz.	—		☐☐☐☐☐
J32	2c Numeral (J29), deep claret	70.00	10.00	☐☐☐☐☐
J33	3c Numeral (J29), deep claret	220.00	50.00	☐☐☐☐☐
J34	5c Numeral (J29), deep claret	350.00	55.00	☐☐☐☐☐
J35	10c Numeral (J29), deep clare	400.00	40.00	☐☐☐☐☐
J36	30c Numeral (J29), deep claret	600.00	250.00	☐☐☐☐☐
a.	30c carmine	750.00	275.00	☐☐☐☐☐
b.	30c pale rose	500.00	200.00	☐☐☐☐☐
J37	50c Numeral (J29), deep claret	2,000.	800.00	☐☐☐☐☐
a.	50c pale rose	1,800.	725.00	☐☐☐☐☐
1895, Watermark 191				
J38	1c Numeral (J29), deep claret	15.00	1.00	☐☐☐☐☐
J39	2c Numeral (J29), deep claret	15.00	1.00	☐☐☐☐☐
J40	3c Numeral (J29), deep claret	110.00	5.00	☐☐☐☐☐
J41	5c Numeral (J29), deep claret	120.00	5.00	☐☐☐☐☐
J42	10c Numeral (J29), deep claret	120.00	7.50	☐☐☐☐☐
J43	30c Numeral (J29), deep claret	700.00	75.00	☐☐☐☐☐
J44	50c Numeral (J29), deep claret	450.00	60.00	☐☐☐☐☐
1910-12, Watermark 190				
J45	1c Numeral (J29), deep claret	45.00	5.00	☐☐☐☐☐
a.	1c rose carmine	40.00	5.00	☐☐☐☐☐
J46	2c Numeral (J29), deep claret	45.00	2.00	☐☐☐☐☐
a.	2c rose carmine	40.00	2.00	☐☐☐☐☐
J47	3c Numeral (J29), deep claret	675.00	60.00	☐☐☐☐☐
J48	5c Numeral (J29), deep claret	130.00	12.00	☐☐☐☐☐
a.	5c rose carmine	130.00	12.00	☐☐☐☐☐
J49	10c Numeral (J29), deep claret	140.00	20.00	☐☐☐☐☐
a.	10c rose carmine	140.00	20.00	☐☐☐☐☐
J50	50c Numeral (J29), deep claret	1,150.	175.00	☐☐☐☐☐
1914-15, Perf. 10				
J52	1c Numeral (J29), carmine lake	90.00	15.00	☐☐☐☐☐
a.	1c dull rose	95.00	15.00	☐☐☐☐☐
J53	2c Numeral (J29), carmine lake	70.00	1.00	☐☐☐☐☐
a.	2c dull rose	75.00	2.00	☐☐☐☐☐
b.	2c vermilion	75.00	2.00	☐☐☐☐☐

Scott No.	Description	Unused Value	Used Value	/ / / / / /
J54	3c Numeral (J29), carmine lake	1,150.	75.00	☐☐☐☐☐
a.	3c dull rose	1,100.	75.00	☐☐☐☐☐
J55	5c Numeral (J29), carmine lake	55.00	6.00	☐☐☐☐☐
a.	5c dull rose	50.00	4.00	☐☐☐☐☐
J56	10c Numeral (J29), carmine lake	85.00	4.00	☐☐☐☐☐
a.	10c dull rose	90.00	5.00	☐☐☐☐☐
J57	30c Numeral (J29), carmine lake	250.00	55.00	☐☐☐☐☐
J58	50c Numeral (J29), carmine lake	*12,500.*	1,500.	☐☐☐☐☐
1916, Perf. 10, Unwatermarked				
J59	1c Numeral (J29), rose	4,500.	725.00	☐☐☐☐☐
J60	2c Numeral (J29), rose	300.00	75.00	☐☐☐☐☐
1917, Perf. 11				
J61	1c Numeral (J29), carmine rose	3.00	.25	☐☐☐☐☐
a.	1c rose red	3.00	.25	☐☐☐☐☐
b.	1c deep claret	3.00	.25	☐☐☐☐☐
J62	2c Numeral (J29), carmine rose	3.00	.25	☐☐☐☐☐
a.	2c rose red	3.00	.25	☐☐☐☐☐
b.	2c deep claret	3.00	.25	☐☐☐☐☐
J63	3c Numeral (J29), carmine rose	15.00	.80	☐☐☐☐☐
a.	3c rose red	15.00	.80	☐☐☐☐☐
b.	3c deep claret	15.00	.80	☐☐☐☐☐
J64	5c Numeral (J29), carmine	12.50	.80	☐☐☐☐☐
a.	5c rose red	12.50	.80	☐☐☐☐☐
b.	5c deep claret	12.50	.80	☐☐☐☐☐
J65	10c Numeral (J29), carmine rose	25.00	1.00	☐☐☐☐☐
a.	10c rose red	25.00	1.00	☐☐☐☐☐
b.	10c deep claret	25.00	1.00	☐☐☐☐☐
J66	30c Numeral (J29), carmine rose	90.00	2.00	☐☐☐☐☐
a.	30c deep claret	90.00	2.00	☐☐☐☐☐
b.	As "a," perf. 10 at top, precanceled	—	*21,000.*	☐☐☐☐☐
J67	50c Numeral (J29), carmine rose	150.00	1.00	☐☐☐☐☐
a.	50c rose red	150.00	1.00	☐☐☐☐☐
b.	50c deep claret	150.00	1.00	☐☐☐☐☐
1925				
J68	½c Numeral (J29), dull red	1.00	.25	☐☐☐☐☐
1930-31, Perf. 11				
J69	½c Numeral, carmine	4.50	1.90	☐☐☐☐☐
J70	1c Numeral (J69), carmine	3.00	.35	☐☐☐☐☐
J71	2c Numeral (J69), carmine	4.00	.35	☐☐☐☐☐
J72	3c Numeral (J69), carmine	21.00	2.75	☐☐☐☐☐
J73	5c Numeral (J69), carmine	19.00	5.00	☐☐☐☐☐
J74	10c Numeral (J69), carmine	45.00	2.00	☐☐☐☐☐
J75	30c Numeral (J69), carmine	150.00	4.00	☐☐☐☐☐
J76	50c Numeral (J69), carmine	200.00	2.00	☐☐☐☐☐
J77	$1 Numeral, carmine	35.00	.35	☐☐☐☐☐
a.	$1 scarlet	30.00	.35	☐☐☐☐☐

Scott No.	Description	Unused Value	Used Value	/ / / / / /
J78	$5 Numeral (J77), carmine	40.00	.35	□□□□□
a.	$5 scarlet	35.00	.35	□□□□□
1931-56, Perf. 11x10½, 10½x11				
J79	½c Numeral (J69), dull carmine	.90	.20	□□□□□
a.	½c scarlet	.90	.20	□□□□□
J80	1c Numeral (J69), dull carmine	.20	.20	□□□□□
a.	1c scarlet	.20	.20	□□□□□
J81	2c Numeral (J69), dull carmine	.20	.20	□□□□□
a.	2c scarlet	.20	.20	□□□□□
J82	3c Numeral (J69), dull carmine	.25	.20	□□□□□
a.	3c scarlet	.25	.20	□□□□□
J83	5c Numeral (J69), dull carmine	.40	.20	□□□□□
a.	5c scarlet	.40	.20	□□□□□
J84	10c Numeral (J69), dull carmine	1.10	.20	□□□□□
a.	10c scarlet	1.10	.20	□□□□□
J85	30c Numeral (J69), dull carmine	7.50	.25	□□□□□
a.	30c scarlet	7.50	.25	□□□□□
J86	50c Numeral (J69), dull carmine	9.00	.25	□□□□□
a.	50c scarlet	9.00	.25	□□□□□
J87	$1 Numeral (J77), scarlet	30.00	.25	□□□□□
1959, Black numerals				
J88	½c Numeral, carmine rose	1.50	1.10	□□□□□
J89	1c Numeral (J88), carmine rose	.20	.20	□□□□□
a.	"1 CENT" omitted	225.00		□□□□□
b.	Pair, one without "1 CENT"	*400.00*		□□□□□
J90	2c Numeral (J88), carmine rose	.20	.20	□□□□□
J91	3c Numeral (J88), carmine rose	.20	.20	□□□□□
a.	Pair, one without "3 CENTS"	*675.00*		□□□□□
J92	4c Numeral (J88), carmine rose	.20	.20	□□□□□
J93	5c Numeral (J88), carmine rose	.20	.20	□□□□□
a.	Pair, one without "5 CENTS"	*1,500.*		□□□□□
J94	6c Numeral (J88), carmine rose	.20	.20	□□□□□
a.	Pair, one without "6 CENTS"	*850.00*		□□□□□
J95	7c Numeral (J88), carmine rose	.20	.20	□□□□□
J96	8c Numeral (J88), carmine rose	.20	.20	□□□□□
a.	Pair, one without "8 CENTS"	*850.00*		□□□□□
J97	10c Numeral (J88), carmine rose	.20	.20	□□□□□
J98	30c Numeral (J88), carmine rose	.75	.20	□□□□□
J99	50c Numeral (J88), carmine rose	1.10	.20	□□□□□
J100	$1 Numeral (J88), carmine rose	2.00	.20	□□□□□
J101	$5 Numeral (J88), carmine rose	9.00	.20	□□□□□
1978				
J102	11c Numeral (J88), carmine rose	.25	.20	□□□□□
J103	13c Numeral (J88), carmine rose	.25	.20	□□□□□
1985				
J104	17c Numeral (J88), carmine rose	.40	.35	□□□□□

United States Stamps
of 1917-19
Surcharged

SHANGHAI
2¢
CHINA

Scott No.	Description	Unused Value	Used Value
U.S. OFFICES IN CHINA			
1919			
K1	2c on 1c Washington, green	25.00	*60.00*
K2	4c on 2c Washington, rose, type I	25.00	*60.00*
K3	6c on 3c Washington, violet, type II	60.00	*130.00*
K4	8c on 4c Washington, brown	60.00	*130.00*
K5	10c on 5c Washington, blue	65.00	*130.00*
K6	12c on 6c Washington, red orange	85.00	*190.00*
K7	14c on 7c Washington, black	87.50	*190.00*
K8	16c on 8c Washington, olive bister	70.00	*145.00*
a.	16c on 8c olive green	60.00	*125.00*
K9	18c on 9c Franklin, salmon red	65.00	*160.00*
K10	20c on 10c Franklin, orange yellow	60.00	*130.00*
K11	24c on 12c Franklin, brown carmine	80.00	*150.00*
a.	24c on 12c claret brown	110.00	*200.00*
K12	30c on 15c Franklin, gray	87.50	*220.00*
K13	40c on 20c Franklin, deep ultramarine	130.00	*310.00*
K14	60c on 30c Franklin, orange red	120.00	*260.00*
K15	$1 on 50c Franklin, light violet	575.00	*875.00*
K16	$2 on $1 Franklin, violet brown	450.00	*725.00*
a.	Double surcharge	*8,500.*	*8,000.*

Nos. 498 and 528B
Surcharged

SHANGHAI
2 Cts.
CHINA

Scott No.	Description	Unused Value	Used Value
1922, Surcharged locally			
K17	2c on 1c Washington, green	110.00	*200.00*
K18	4c on 2c Washington, carmine, type VII	100.00	*175.00*
a.	"SHANGHAI" omitted	*7,500.*	
b.	"CHINA" only	*15,000.*	

O1

O68

O47

O121

O127

O138A

O144

Scott No.	Description	Unused Value	Used Value
OFFICIAL STAMPS			
AGRICULTURE DEPT.			
Continental Bank Note Printings, Thin Hard Paper			
O1	1c Franklin, yellow	280.00	180.00
O2	2c Jackson (O1), yellow	240.00	85.00
O3	3c Washington (O1), yellow	220.00	16.00
O4	6c Lincoln (O1), yellow	260.00	60.00
O5	10c Jefferson (O1), yellow	525.00	200.00
O6	12c Clay (O1), yellow	450.00	260.00
O7	15c Webster (O1), yellow	425.00	230.00
O8	24c Scott (O1), yellow	425.00	220.00
O9	30c Hamilton (O1), yellow	550.00	270.00
EXECUTIVE DEPT.			
O10	1c Franklin (O1), carmine	850.00	475.00
O11	2c Jackson (O1), carmine	550.00	240.00
O12	3c Washington (O1), carmine	700.00	210.00
a.	3c violet rose	700.00	210.00
O13	6c Lincoln (O1), carmine	900.00	550.00
O14	10c Jefferson (O1), carmine	1,200.	650.00
INTERIOR DEPT.			
O15	1c Franklin (O1), vermilion	75.00	10.00
O16	2c Jackson (O1), vermilion	70.00	12.00
O17	3c Washington (O1), vermilion	80.00	6.00
O18	6c Lincoln (O1), vermilion	70.00	10.00
O19	10c Jefferson (O1), vermilion	70.00	20.00
O20	12c Clay (O1), vermilion	90.00	12.00

Scott No.	Description	Unused Value	Used Value
O21	15c Webster (O1), vermilion	200.00	25.00
O22	24c Scott (O1), vermilion	180.00	20.00
a.	Double impression		—
O23	30c Hamilton (O1), vermilion	290.00	20.00
O24	90c Perry (O1), vermilion	325.00	50.00

JUSTICE DEPT.

Scott No.	Description	Unused Value	Used Value
O25	1c Franklin (O1), purple	250.00	100.00
O26	2c Jackson (O1), purple	310.00	110.00
O27	3c Washington (O1), purple	320.00	35.00
O28	6c Lincoln (O1), purple	310.00	45.00
O29	10c Jefferson (O1), purple	310.00	100.00
O30	12c Clay (O1), purple	260.00	75.00
O31	15c Webster (O1), purple	475.00	200.00
O32	24c Scott (O1), purple	1,250.	425.00
O33	30c Hamilton (O1), purple	1,300.	350.00
O34	90c Perry (O1), purple	1,900.	900.00

NAVY DEPT.

Scott No.	Description	Unused Value	Used Value
O35	1c Franklin (O1), ultramarine	160.00	50.00
a.	1c dull blue	160.00	50.00
O36	2c Jackson (O1), ultramarine	160.00	25.00
a.	2c dull blue	160.00	25.00
O37	3c Washington (O1), ultramarine	170.00	15.00
a.	3c dull blue	170.00	15.00
O38	6c Lincoln (O1), ultramarine	150.00	25.00
a.	6c dull blue	150.00	25.00
O39	7c Stanton (O1), ultramarine	650.00	230.00
a.	7c dull blue	650.00	230.00
O40	10c Jefferson (O1), ultramarine	210.00	45.00
a.	10c dull blue	210.00	45.00
O41	12c Clay (O1), ultramarine	220.00	45.00
O42	15c Webster (O1), ultramarine	375.00	75.00
O43	24c Scott (O1), ultramarine	400.00	85.00
a.	24c dull blue	375.00	80.00
O44	30c Hamilton (O1), ultramarine	325.00	50.00
O45	90c Perry (O1), ultramarine	1,050.	375.00
a.	Double impression		*20,000.*

POST OFFICE DEPT.

Scott No.	Description	Unused Value	Used Value
O47	1c Numeral, black	25.00	12.00
O48	2c Numeral (O47), black	30.00	10.00
a.	Double impression	600.00	400.00
O49	3c Numeral (O47), black	10.00	2.00
a.	Printed on both sides		*7,500.*
O50	6c Numeral (O47), black	30.00	8.00
a.	Diagonal half used as 3c on cover		*5,000.*
O51	10c Numeral (O47), black	140.00	55.00
O52	12c Numeral (O47), black	120.00	12.00

Scott No.	Description	Unused Value	Used Value	/ / / / / /
O53	15c Numeral (O47), black	140.00	20.00	☐☐☐☐☐
O54	24c Numeral (O47), black	200.00	25.00	☐☐☐☐☐
O55	30c Numeral (O47), black	200.00	25.00	☐☐☐☐☐
O56	90c Numeral (O47), black	220.00	25.00	☐☐☐☐☐
STATE DEPT.				
O57	1c Franklin (O1), bright green	260.00	75.00	☐☐☐☐☐
O58	2c Jackson (O1), dark green	310.00	100.00	☐☐☐☐☐
O59	3c Washington (O1), bright green	220.00	25.00	☐☐☐☐☐
O60	6c Lincoln (O1), bright green	220.00	30.00	☐☐☐☐☐
O61	7c Stanton (O1), dark green	290.00	65.00	☐☐☐☐☐
O62	10c Jefferson (O1), dark green	230.00	55.00	☐☐☐☐☐
O63	12c Clay (O1), dark green	310.00	125.00	☐☐☐☐☐
O64	15c Webster (O1), dark green	320.00	90.00	☐☐☐☐☐
O65	24c Scott (O1), dark green	525.00	230.00	☐☐☐☐☐
O66	30c Hamilton (O1), dark green	500.00	180.00	☐☐☐☐☐
O67	90c Perry (O1), dark green	1,050.	325.00	☐☐☐☐☐
O68	$2 Seward, green & black	1,500.	1,500.	☐☐☐☐☐
O69	$5 Seward (O68), green & black	7,750.	12,000.	☐☐☐☐☐
O70	$10 Seward (O68), green & black	5,000.	7,000.	☐☐☐☐☐
O71	$20 Seward (O68), green & black	5,250.	5,000.	☐☐☐☐☐
TREASURY DEPT.				
O72	1c Franklin (O1), brown	120.00	10.00	☐☐☐☐☐
O73	2c Jackson (O1), brown	125.00	8.00	☐☐☐☐☐
O74	3c Washington (O1), brown	110.00	2.00	☐☐☐☐☐
a.	Double impression		*5,000.*	☐☐☐☐☐
O75	6c Lincoln (O1), brown	120.00	4.00	☐☐☐☐☐
O76	7c Stanton (O1), brown	250.00	35.00	☐☐☐☐☐
O77	10c Jefferson (O1), brown	240.00	12.00	☐☐☐☐☐
O78	12c Clay (O1), brown	300.00	10.00	☐☐☐☐☐
O79	15c Webster (O1), brown	300.00	12.00	☐☐☐☐☐
O80	24c Scott (O1), brown	675.00	100.00	☐☐☐☐☐
O81	30c Hamilton (O1), brown	400.00	12.00	☐☐☐☐☐
O82	90c Perry (O1), brown	400.00	15.00	☐☐☐☐☐
WAR DEPT.				
O83	1c Franklin (O1), rose	240.00	15.00	☐☐☐☐☐
O84	2c Jackson (O1), rose	240.00	15.00	☐☐☐☐☐
O85	3c Washington (O1), rose	240.00	5.00	☐☐☐☐☐
O86	6c Lincoln (O1), rose	625.00	10.00	☐☐☐☐☐
O87	7c Stanton (O1), rose	160.00	90.00	☐☐☐☐☐
O88	10c Jefferson (O1), rose	140.00	25.00	☐☐☐☐☐
O89	12c Clay (O1), rose	275.00	12.00	☐☐☐☐☐
O90	15c Webster (O1), rose	85.00	15.00	☐☐☐☐☐
O91	24c Scott (O1), rose	85.00	12.00	☐☐☐☐☐
O92	30c Hamilton (O1), rose	130.00	12.00	☐☐☐☐☐
O93	90c Perry (O1), rose	225.00	50.00	☐☐☐☐☐

Scott No.	Description	Unused Value	Used Value	/ / / / / /
AGRICULTURE DEPT.				
1879, American Bank Note Co. Printings, Soft Porous Paper				
O94	1c Franklin (O1), yellow, no gum	6,000.		☐☐☐☐☐
O95	3c Washington (O1), yellow	550.00	100.00	☐☐☐☐☐
INTERIOR DEPT.				
O96	1c Franklin (O1), vermilion	300.00	275.00	☐☐☐☐☐
O97	2c Jackson (O1), vermilion	10.00	3.00	☐☐☐☐☐
O98	3c Washington (O1), vermilion	10.00	3.00	☐☐☐☐☐
O99	6c Lincoln (O1), vermilion	10.00	12.50	☐☐☐☐☐
O100	10c Jefferson (O1), vermilion	110.00	75.00	☐☐☐☐☐
O101	12c Clay (O1), vermilion	230.00	115.00	☐☐☐☐☐
O102	15c Webster (O1), vermilion	400.00	260.00	☐☐☐☐☐
O103	24c Scott (O1), vermilion	4,500.	—	☐☐☐☐☐
JUSTICE DEPT.				
O106	3c Washington (O1), bluish purple	175.00	100.00	☐☐☐☐☐
O107	6c Lincoln (O1), bluish purple	475.00	275.00	☐☐☐☐☐
POST OFFICE DEPT.				
O108	3c Numeral (O47), black	30.00	10.00	☐☐☐☐☐
TREASURY DEPT.				
O109	3c Washington (O1), brown	80.00	10.00	☐☐☐☐☐
O110	6c Lincoln (O1), brown	200.00	50.00	☐☐☐☐☐
O111	10c Jefferson (O1), brown	260.00	80.00	☐☐☐☐☐
O112	30c Hamilton (O1), brown	2,400.	425.00	☐☐☐☐☐
O113	90c Perry (O1), brown	5,500.	525.00	☐☐☐☐☐
WAR DEPT.				
O114	1c Franklin (O1), rose red	6.00	4.00	☐☐☐☐☐
O115	2c Jackson (O1), rose red	12.00	4.00	☐☐☐☐☐
O116	3c Washington (O1), rose red	12.00	2.00	☐☐☐☐☐
a.	Imperf., pair	*5,000.*		☐☐☐☐☐
b.	Double impression	*6,500.*		☐☐☐☐☐
O117	6c Lincoln (O1), rose red	11.00	3.00	☐☐☐☐☐
O118	10c Jefferson (O1), rose red	65.00	50.00	☐☐☐☐☐
O119	12c Clay (O1), rose red	60.00	14.00	☐☐☐☐☐
O120	30c Hamilton (O1), rose red	225.00	100.00	☐☐☐☐☐
1875, SPECIAL PRINTINGS, Ovptd. "SPECIMEN" (Type D)				
Thin hard white paper				
AGRICULTURE DEPT., Carmine Overprint				
O1S	1c Franklin (O1), yellow	30.00		☐☐☐☐☐
a.	"Sepcimen" error	2,500.		☐☐☐☐☐
b.	Horiz. Ribbed paper	37.50		☐☐☐☐☐
c.	Small dotted "i" in "Specimen"	400.00		☐☐☐☐☐
O2S	2c Jackson (O1), yellow	55.00		☐☐☐☐☐
a.	"Sepcimen" error	3,000.		☐☐☐☐☐

Scott No.	Description	Unused Value	Used Value
O3S	3c Washington (O1), yellow	300.00	
a.	"Sepcimen" error	*11,000.*	
O4S	6c Lincoln (O1), yellow	325.00	
a.	"Sepcimen" error	*17,500.*	
O5S	10c Jefferson (O1), yellow	325.00	
a.	"Sepcimen" error	*17,500.*	
O6S	12c Clay (O1), yellow	325.00	
a.	"Sepcimen" error	*11,000.*	
O7S	15c Webster (O1), yellow	325.00	
a.	"Sepcimen" error	*11,000.*	
O8S	24c Scott (O1), yellow	325.00	
a.	"Sepcimen" error	*11,000.*	
O9S	30c Hamilton (O1), yellow	325.00	
a.	"Sepcimen" error	*13,500.*	
EXECUTIVE DEPT., Blue Overprint			
O10S	1c Franklin (O1), carmine	30.00	
a.	Horiz. Ribbed paper	35.00	
b.	Small dotted "i" in "Specimen"	500.00	
O11S	2c Jackson (O1), carmine	55.00	
O12S	3c Washington (O1), carmine	67.50	
O13S	6c Lincoln (O1), carmine	67.50	
O14S	10c Jefferson (O1), carmine	67.50	
INTERIOR DEPT., Blue Overprint			
O15S	1c Franklin (O1), vermilion	55.00	
O16S	2c Jackson (O1), vermilion	120.00	
a.	"Sepcimen" error	*10,000.*	
O17S	3c Washington (O1), vermilion	1,400.	
O18S	6c Lincoln (O1), vermilion	1,400.	
O19S	10c Jefferson (O1), vermilion	1,400.	
O20S	12c Clay (O1), vermilion	1,400.	
O21S	15c Webster (O1), vermilion	1,400.	
O22S	24c Scott (O1), vermilion	1,400.	
O23S	30c Hamilton (O1), vermilion	1,400.	
O24S	90c Perry (O1), vermilion	1,400.	
JUSTICE DEPT., Blue Overprint			
O25S	1c Franklin (O1), purple	30.00	
a.	"Sepcimen" error	1,900.	
b.	Horiz. Ribbed paper	35.00	
c.	Small dotted "i" in "Specimen"	500.00	
O26S	2c Jackson (O1), purple	55.00	
a.	"Sepcimen" error	2,500.	
O27S	3c Washington (O1), purple	900.00	
a.	"Sepcimen" error	*8,750.*	
O28S	6c Lincoln (O1), purple	900.00	
O29S	10c Jefferson (O1), purple	900.00	
O30S	12c Clay (O1), purple	900.00	

Scott No.	Description	Unused Value	Used Value	/ / / / / /
a.	"Sepcimen" error	*15,000.*		☐☐☐☐☐
O31S	15c Webster (O1), purple	900.00		☐☐☐☐☐
a.	"Sepcimen" error	*13,500.*		☐☐☐☐☐
O32S	24c Scott (O1), purple	900.00		☐☐☐☐☐
a.	"Sepcimen" error	*15,000.*		☐☐☐☐☐
O33S	30c Hamilton (O1), purple	900.00		☐☐☐☐☐
a.	"Sepcimen" error	*13,500.*		☐☐☐☐☐
O34S	90c Perry (O1), purple	900.00		☐☐☐☐☐
NAVY DEPT., Carmine Overprint				
O35S	1c Franklin (O1), ultramarine	32.50		☐☐☐☐☐
a.	"Sepcimen" error	2,500.		☐☐☐☐☐
O36S	2c Jackson (O1), ultramarine	60.00		☐☐☐☐☐
a.	"Sepcimen" error	3,250.		☐☐☐☐☐
O37S	3c Washington (O1), ultramarine	1,000.		☐☐☐☐☐
O38S	6c Lincoln (O1), ultramarine	1,100.		☐☐☐☐☐
O39S	7c Stanton (O1), ultramarine	450.00		☐☐☐☐☐
a.	"Sepcimen" error	8,250.		☐☐☐☐☐
O40S	10c Jefferson (O1), ultramarine	1,100.		☐☐☐☐☐
a.	"Sepcimen" error	*17,500.*		☐☐☐☐☐
O41S	12c Clay (O1), ultramarine	1,000.		☐☐☐☐☐
a.	"Sepcimen" error	*17,500.*		☐☐☐☐☐
O42S	15c Webster (O1), ultramarine	1,000.		☐☐☐☐☐
a.	"Sepcimen" error	*13,500.*		☐☐☐☐☐
O43S	24c Scott (O1), ultramarine	1,000.		☐☐☐☐☐
a.	"Sepcimen" error	*13,500.*		☐☐☐☐☐
O44S	30c Hamilton (O1), ultramarine	1,000.		☐☐☐☐☐
a.	"Sepcimen" error	*17,500.*		☐☐☐☐☐
O45S	90c Perry (O1), ultramarine	1,000.		☐☐☐☐☐
POST OFFICE DEPT., Carmine Overprint				
O47S	1c Numeral (O47), black	42.50		☐☐☐☐☐
a.	"Sepcimen" error	1,900.		☐☐☐☐☐
b.	Inverted overprint	*2,500.*		☐☐☐☐☐
O48S	2c Numeral (O47), black	250.00		☐☐☐☐☐
a.	"Sepcimen" error	3,250.		☐☐☐☐☐
O49S	3c Numeral (O47), black	1,200.		☐☐☐☐☐
a.	"Sepcimen" error	—		☐☐☐☐☐
O50S	6c Numeral (O47), black	1,100.		☐☐☐☐☐
O51S	10c Numeral (O47), black	900.00		☐☐☐☐☐
a.	"Sepcimen" error	*11,000.*		☐☐☐☐☐
O52S	12c Numeral (O47), black	1,000.		☐☐☐☐☐
O53S	15c Numeral (O47), black	1,100.		☐☐☐☐☐
a.	"Sepcimen" error	*13,500.*		☐☐☐☐☐
O54S	24c Numeral (O47), black	1,100.		☐☐☐☐☐
a.	"Sepcimen" error	*11,000.*		☐☐☐☐☐
O55S	30c Numeral (O47), black	1,200.		☐☐☐☐☐
O56S	90c Numeral (O47), black	1,100.		☐☐☐☐☐
a.	"Sepcimen" error	—		☐☐☐☐☐

Scott No.	Description	Unused Value	Used Value
STATE DEPT., Carmine Overprint			
O57S	1c Franklin (O1), bluish green	30.00	
a.	"Sepcimen" error	1,900.	
b.	Horiz. Ribbed paper	35.00	
c.	Small dotted "i" in "Specimen"	550.00	
d.	Double overprint	3,800.	
O58S	2c Jackson (O1), dark green	90.00	
a.	"Sepcimen" error	2,500.	
O59S	3c Washington (O1), bright green	120.00	
a.	"Sepcimen" error	6,000.	
O60S	6c Lincoln (O1), bright green	275.00	
a.	"Sepcimen" error	8,250.	
O61S	7c Stanton (O1), dark green	120.00	
a.	"Sepcimen" error	8,250.	
O62S	10c Jefferson (O1), dark green	500.00	
a.	"Sepcimen" error	*17,500.*	
O63S	12c Clay (O1), dark green	550.00	
a.	"Sepcimen" error	*11,000.*	
O64S	15c Webster (O1), dark green	550.00	
O65S	24c Scott (O1), dark green	550.00	
a.	"Sepcimen" error	*11,000.*	
O66S	30c Hamilton (O1), dark green	550.00	
a.	"Sepcimen" error	*15,000.*	
O67S	90c Perry (O1), dark green	550.00	
a.	"Sepcimen" error	*11,000.*	
O68S	$2 Seward (O68), green & black	*20,000.*	
O69S	$5 Seward (O68), green & black	*25,000.*	
O70S	$10 Seward (O68), green & black	*50,000.*	
O71S	$20 Seward (O68), green & black	*85,000.*	
TREASURY DEPT., Blue Overprint			
O72S	1c Franklin (O1), brown	75.00	
O73S	2c Jackson (O1), brown	350.00	
O74S	3c Washington (O1), brown	1,400.	
O75S	6c Lincoln (O1), brown	1,400.	
O76S	7c Stanton (O1), brown	850.00	
O77S	10c Jefferson (O1), brown	1,350.	
O78S	12c Clay (O1), brown	1,350.	
O79S	15c Webster (O1), brown	1,350.	
O80S	24c Scott (O1), brown	1,350.	
O81S	30c Hamilton (O1), brown	1,350.	
O82S	90c Perry (O1), brown	1,350.	
WAR DEPT., Blue Overprint			
O83S	1c Franklin (O1), deep rose	30.00	
a.	"Sepcimen" error	1,600.	
O84S	2c Jackson (O1), deep rose	120.00	
a.	"Sepcimen" error	2,000.	
O85S	3c Washington (O1), deep rose	1,000.	

Scott No.	Description	Unused Value	Used Value
a.	"Sepcimen" error	*11,000.*	
O86S	6c Lincoln (O1), deep rose	1,000.	
a.	"Sepcimen" error	*25,000.*	
O87S	7c Stanton (O1), deep rose	325.00	
a.	"Sepcimen" error	10,000.	
O88S	10c Jefferson (O1), deep rose	1,000.	
a.	"Sepcimen" error	*13,500.*	
O89S	12c Clay (O1), deep rose	1,000.	
a.	"Sepcimen" error	*13,500.*	
O90S	15c Webster (O1), deep rose	1,000.	
a.	"Sepcimen" error	*13,500.*	
O91S	24c Scott (O1), deep rose	1,000.	
a.	"Sepcimen" error	*13,500.*	
O92S	30c Hamilton (O1), deep rose	1,000.	
a.	"Sepcimen" error	*13,500.*	
O93S	90c Perry (O1), deep rose	1,000.	
a.	"Sepcimen" error	*13,500.*	

Soft, porous paper

EXECUTIVE DEPT., Blue Overprint

Scott No.	Description	Unused Value	Used Value
O10xS	1c Franklin (O1), violet rose	95.00	

NAVY DEPT., Carmine Overprint

Scott No.	Description	Unused Value	Used Value
O35xS	1c Franklin (O1), gray blue	100.00	
a.	Double overprint	1,200.	

STATE DEPT., Carmine Overprint

Scott No.	Description	Unused Value	Used Value
O57xS	1c Franklin (O1), yellow green	180.00	

OFFICIAL POSTAL SAVINGS MAIL

1911, Watermark 191

Scott No.	Description	Unused Value	Used Value
O121	2c Text, black	17.50	2.00
O122	50c Text (O121), dark green	160.00	60.00
O123	$1 Text (O121), ultramarine	200.00	15.00

Watermark 190

Scott No.	Description	Unused Value	Used Value
O124	1c Text (O121), dark violet	10.00	2.00
O125	2c Text (O121), black	55.00	7.00
O126	10c Text (O121), carmine	20.00	2.00

1983-85

Scott No.	Description	Unused Value	Used Value
O127	1c Great Seal	.20	.20
O128	4c Great Seal (O127)	.20	.25
O129	13c Great Seal (O127)	.50	*15.00*
O129A	14c Great Seal (O127)	.45	.50
O130	17c Great Seal (O127)	.60	.40
O132	$1 Great Seal (O127)	2.25	1.00
O133	$5 Great Seal (O127)	9.50	5.00

Coil Stamps, Perf 10 Vertically

Scott No.	Description	Unused Value	Used Value
O135	20c Great Seal (O127)	1.75	2.00
a.	Imperf., pair	*2,000.*	
O136	22c Great Seal (O127)	1.00	*2.00*

Scott No.	Description	Unused Value	Used Value	/ / / / / /
1985				
O138	(14c) Great Seal (O127), inscribed "Postal Card Rate D"	5.25	*10.00*	□□□□□
1985-88, Coil Stamps, Perf. 10 Vertically				
O138A	15c Great Seal, frame line completely around design	.50	.50	□□□□□
O138B	20c Great Seal (O138A)	.50	.30	□□□□□
O139	(22c) Great Seal (O127), inscribed "Domestic Letter Rate D"	5.25	*10.00*	□□□□□
O140	(25c) Great Seal (O138A), inscribed "Domestic Letter Rate E"	.75	*2.00*	□□□□□
O141	25c Great Seal (O138A)	.65	.50	□□□□□
a.	Imperf., pair	*1,250.*	—	□□□□□
1989				
O143	1c Great Seal (O138A)	.20	.20	□□□□□
1991, Coil Stamps, Perf. 10 Vertically				
O144	(29c) Great Seal	.80	.50	□□□□□
O145	29c Great Seal (O138A)	.70	.30	□□□□□
1991-93				
O146	4c Great Seal (O138A)	.20	.30	□□□□□
O146A	10c Great Seal (O138A)	.30	.30	□□□□□
O147	19c Great Seal (O138A)	.40	.50	□□□□□
O148	23c Great Seal (O138A)	.50	.30	□□□□□
O151	$1 Great Seal (O138A)	5.00	.75	□□□□□
Coil Stamps, Perf. 10 Vertically				
O152	(32c) Great Seal (O144), inscribed "G"	.65	.50	□□□□□
O153	32c Great Seal (O138A), with micro text	1.50	.50	□□□□□
1995				
O154	1c Great Seal (O138A), with micro text	.20	*.50*	□□□□□
O155	20c Great Seal (O138A), with micro text	.55	*.50*	□□□□□
O156	23c Great Seal (O138A), with micro text	.60	.50	□□□□□
1999, Oct. 8 Perf. 9¾ Vertically Coil Stamp				
O157	33c Great Seal (O138A), with micro text	1.25	—	□□□□□
2001-2006				
O158	34c Great Seal (O138A), coil stamp	1.25	.50	□□□□□
O159	37c Great Seal (O138A), coil stamp	.70	.50	□□□□□
O160	39c Great Seal (O138A), coil stamp	.80	.50	□□□□□
O161	$1 Great Seal (O138A), background is crosshatched lines	2.00	.90	□□□□□
2007				
O162	41c Great Seal (O138A), coil stamp	1.00	.50	□□□□□
2009, Feb. 24, Serpentine Die Cut 11½ x 10¾				
O163	1c Great Seal (O138A), self-adhesive	0.20	0.20	□□□□□

PR1

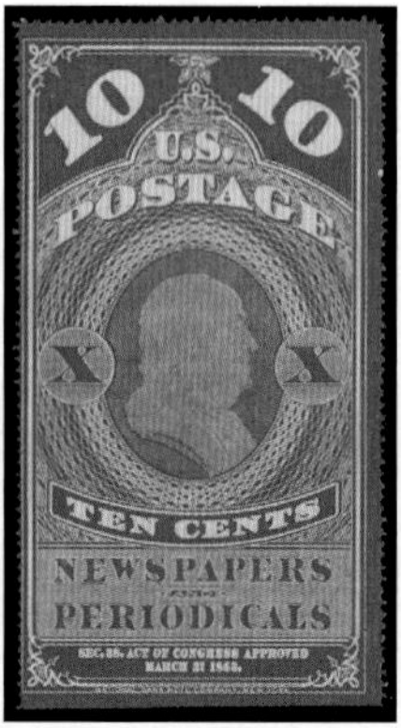

PR2

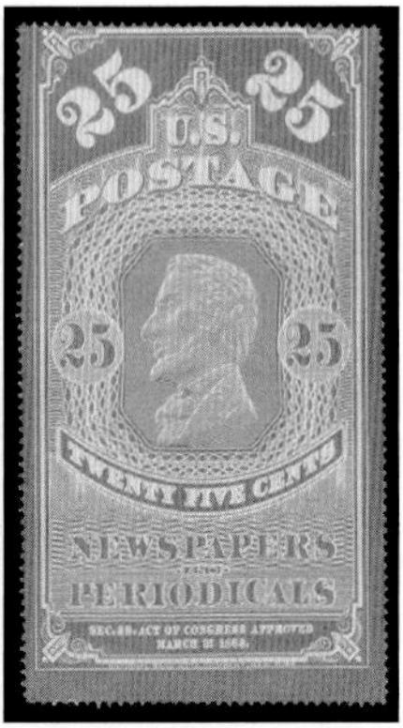

PR3

PR9

PR16

PR24

PR25

PR26

PR27

PR28

PR29

PR30

PR31

PR32

PR102

PR106

PR108

PR109

PR110

PR111

PR112

PR113

HOW TO USE THIS BOOK

In cases where two or more Scott numbers share a common design, the illustration shows the first Scott number that bears that design. Subsequent Scott numbers showing the same design will have the first Scott number in parentheses following the description to guide the user to the correct design.

Scott No.	Description	Unused Value	Used Value	/ / / / / /
NEWSPAPER STAMPS				
1865, Thin Hard Paper, No Gum				
PR1	5c Washington, dark blue	750.00	*2,000.*	☐☐☐☐☐
a.	5c light blue	1,000.00	—	☐☐☐☐☐
PR2	10c Franklin, blue green	300.00	*1,800.*	☐☐☐☐☐
a.	10c green	300.00	*1,800.*	☐☐☐☐☐
b.	Pelure paper	350.00	*1,800.*	☐☐☐☐☐
PR3	25c Lincoln, orange red	375.00	*2,400.*	☐☐☐☐☐
a.	25c carmine red	350.00	*2,400.*	☐☐☐☐☐
b.	Pelure paper	375.00		☐☐☐☐☐
White Border, Yellowish Paper				
PR4	5c Washington (PR1), light blue	325.00	2,400.	☐☐☐☐☐
a.	5c dark blue	325.00	—	☐☐☐☐☐
b.	Pelure paper	375.00	—	☐☐☐☐☐
1875, Reprints, Hard White Paper, No Gum				
PR5	5c Washington (PR1), dull blue	225.00		☐☐☐☐☐
a.	Printed on both sides	*5,750.*		☐☐☐☐☐
PR6	10c Franklin (PR2), dark bluish green	250.00		☐☐☐☐☐
a.	Printed on both sides	*4,250.*		☐☐☐☐☐
PR7	25c Lincoln (PR3), dark carmine	250.00		☐☐☐☐☐
1881, Reprint, Soft Porous Paper, White Border				
PR8	5c Washington (PR1), dark blue	750.00		☐☐☐☐☐
1875, Thin Hard Paper				
PR9	2c Statue of Freedom, black	280.00	30.00	☐☐☐☐☐
PR10	3c Statue of Freedom (PR9), black	280.00	32.50	☐☐☐☐☐
PR11	4c Statue of Freedom (PR9), black	280.00	30.00	☐☐☐☐☐
PR12	6c Statue of Freedom (PR9), black	280.00	32.50	☐☐☐☐☐
PR13	8c Statue of Freedom (PR9), black	325.00	47.50	☐☐☐☐☐
PR14	9c Statue of Freedom (PR9), black	475.00	95.00	☐☐☐☐☐
PR15	10c Statue of Freedom (PR9), black	350.00	37.50	☐☐☐☐☐
PR16	12c "Justice" (PR16), rose	800.00	100.00	☐☐☐☐☐
PR17	24c "Justice" (PR16), rose	875.00	125.00	☐☐☐☐☐
PR18	36c "Justice" (PR16), rose	875.00	150.00	☐☐☐☐☐
PR19	48c "Justice" (PR16), rose	1,250.	200.00	☐☐☐☐☐
PR20	60c "Justice" (PR16), rose	1,250.	115.00	☐☐☐☐☐
PR21	72c "Justice" (PR16), rose	1,250.	250.00	☐☐☐☐☐
PR22	84c "Justice" (PR16), rose	1,850.	375.00	☐☐☐☐☐
PR23	96c "Justice" (PR16), rose	1,350.	250.00	☐☐☐☐☐
PR24	$1.92 Ceres, dark brown	1,650.	250.00	☐☐☐☐☐
PR25	$3 "Victory," vermilion	1,800.	450.00	☐☐☐☐☐
PR26	$6 Clio, ultramarine	3,600.	550.00	☐☐☐☐☐
PR27	$9 Minerva, yellow orange	4,000.	600.00	☐☐☐☐☐
PR28	$12 Vesta, blue green	4,500.	750.00	☐☐☐☐☐
PR29	$24 "Peace," dark gray violet	4,750.	800.00	☐☐☐☐☐

Scott No.	Description	Unused Value	Used Value	/ / / / / /
PR30	$36 "Commerce," brown rose.................	5,000.	950.00	☐☐☐☐☐
PR31	$48 Hebe, red rose..................................	6,250.	1,150.	☐☐☐☐☐
PR32	$60 Indian Maiden, violet.......................	6,500.	1,250.	☐☐☐☐☐

1875, Special Printing, Hard White Paper, No Gum

PR33	2c Statue of Freedom (PR9), gray black	600.00		☐☐☐☐☐
a.	Horiz. ribbed paper..........................	450.00		☐☐☐☐☐
PR34	3c Statue of Freedom (PR9), gray black	600.00		☐☐☐☐☐
a.	Horiz. ribbed paper..........................	450.00		☐☐☐☐☐
PR35	4c Statue of Freedom (PR9), gray black	650.00		☐☐☐☐☐
a.	Horiz. ribbed paper..........................	900.00		☐☐☐☐☐
PR36	6c Statue of Freedom (PR9), gray black	850.00		☐☐☐☐☐
PR37	8c Statue of Freedom (PR9), gray black	950.00		☐☐☐☐☐
PR38	9c Statue of Freedom (PR9), gray black	1,050.		☐☐☐☐☐
PR39	10c Statue of Freedom (PR9), gray black	1,300.		☐☐☐☐☐
a.	Horiz. ribbed paper..........................	—		☐☐☐☐☐
PR40	12c "Justice" (PR16), pale rose	1,500.		☐☐☐☐☐
PR41	24c "Justice" (PR16), pale rose	2,100.		☐☐☐☐☐
PR42	36c "Justice" (PR16), pale rose	2,800.		☐☐☐☐☐
PR43	48c "Justice" (PR16), pale rose	4,000.		☐☐☐☐☐
PR44	60c "Justice" (PR16), pale rose	4,000.		☐☐☐☐☐
PR45	72c "Justice" (PR16), pale rose	4,500.		☐☐☐☐☐
PR46	84c "Justice" (PR16), pale rose	*5,000.*		☐☐☐☐☐
PR47	96c "Justice" (PR16), pale rose	*8,500.*		☐☐☐☐☐
PR48	$1.92 Ceres (PR24), dark brown	*22,500.*		☐☐☐☐☐
PR49	$3 "Victory" (PR25), vermilion............	*45,000.*		☐☐☐☐☐
PR50	$6 Clio (PR26), ultramarine..................	*80,000.*		☐☐☐☐☐
PR51	$9 Minerva (PR27), yellow orange.......	*160,000.*		☐☐☐☐☐
PR52	$12 Vesta (PR28), blue green..................	*125,000.*		☐☐☐☐☐
PR53	$24 "Peace" (PR29), dark gray violet.....	—		☐☐☐☐☐
PR54	$36 "Commerce" (PR30), brown rose....	*250,000.*		☐☐☐☐☐
PR55	$48 Hebe (PR31), red brown	—		☐☐☐☐☐
PR56	$60 Indian Maiden (PR32), violet	—		☐☐☐☐☐

1879, Soft Porous Paper

PR57	2c Statue of Freedom (PR9), black.......	50.00	8.50	☐☐☐☐☐
PR58	3c Statue of Freedom (PR9), black.......	60.00	10.50	☐☐☐☐☐
PR59	4c Statue of Freedom (PR9), black.......	60.00	10.50	☐☐☐☐☐
PR60	6c Statue of Freedom (PR9), black.......	105.00	21.00	☐☐☐☐☐
PR61	8c Statue of Freedom (PR9), black.......	115.00	21.00	☐☐☐☐☐
PR62	10c Statue of Freedom (PR9), black.......	115.00	21.00	☐☐☐☐☐
PR63	12c "Justice" (PR16), red........................	475.00	85.00	☐☐☐☐☐
PR64	24c "Justice" (PR16), red........................	475.00	85.00	☐☐☐☐☐
PR65	36c "Justice" (PR16), red........................	1,000.	240.00	☐☐☐☐☐
PR66	48c "Justice" (PR16), red	1,000.	180.00	☐☐☐☐☐
PR67	60c "Justice" (PR16), red	1,000.	160.00	☐☐☐☐☐
a.	Imperf., pair	*4,000.*		☐☐☐☐☐
PR68	72c "Justice" (PR16), red	1,250.	300.00	☐☐☐☐☐
PR69	84c "Justice" (PR16), red	1,250.	225.00	☐☐☐☐☐

Scott No.	Description	Unused Value	Used Value	/ / / / / /
PR70	96c "Justice" (PR16), red	1,200.	160.00	
PR71	$1.92 Ceres (PR24), pale brown	550.00	135.00	
PR72	$3 "Victory" (PR25), red vermilion	625.00	150.00	
PR73	$6 Clio (PR26), blue	1,050.	230.00	
PR74	$9 Minerva (PR27), orange	800.00	160.00	
PR75	$12 Vesta (PR28), yellow green	850.00	210.00	
PR76	$24 "Peace" (PR29), dark violet	800.00	260.00	
PR77	$36 "Commerce" (PR30), Indian red	850.00	280.00	
PR78	$48 Hebe (PR31), yellow brown	900.00	390.00	
PR79	$60 Indian Maiden (PR32), purple	850.00	360.00	
1883, Special Printing				
PR80	2c Statue of Freedom (PR9), intense black	1,350.		
1885				
PR81	1c Statue of Freedom (PR9), black	85.00	8.50	
PR82	12c "Justice" (PR16), carmine	180.00	20.00	
PR83	24c "Justice" (PR16), carmine	180.00	22.50	
PR84	36c "Justice" (PR16), carmine	280.00	37.50	
PR85	48c "Justice" (PR16), carmine	400.00	55.00	
PR86	60c "Justice" (PR16), carmine	525.00	80.00	
PR87	72c "Justice" (PR16), carmine	525.00	85.00	
PR88	84c "Justice" (PR16), carmine	800.00	200.00	
PR89	96c "Justice" (PR16), carmine	700.00	160.00	
1894				
PR90	1c Statue of Freedom (PR9), intense black	425.00	*750.00*	
PR91	2c Statue of Freedom (PR9), intense black	475.00		
PR92	4c Statue of Freedom (PR9), intense black	500.00	—	
PR93	6c Statue of Freedom (PR9), intense black	3,750.		
PR94	10c Statue of Freedom (PR9), intense black	1,150.		
PR95	12c "Justice" (PR16), pink	2,600.	*1,500.*	
PR96	24c "Justice" (PR16), pink	3,750.	*1,750.*	
PR97	36c "Justice" (PR16), pink	*50,000.*		
PR98	60c "Justice" (PR16), pink	*55,000.*	*7,500.*	
PR99	96c "Justice" (PR16), pink	*52,500.*		
PR100	$3 "Victory" (PR25), scarlet	*60,000.*		
PR101	$6 Clio (PR26), pale blue	*60,000.*	—	
1895				
PR102	1c Statue of Freedom, black	230.00	100.00	
PR103	2c Statue of Freedom (PR102), black	230.00	100.00	
PR104	5c Statue of Freedom (PR102), black	300.00	150.00	

Scott No.	Description	Unused Value	Used Value
PR105	10c Statue of Freedom (PR102), black	550.00	350.00
PR106	25c "Justice," carmine	750.00	500.00
PR107	50c "Justice" (PR106), carmine	1,500.	600.00
PR108	$2 "Victory"	1,500.	600.00
PR109	$5 Clio, ultramarine	2,100.	1,100.
PR110	$10 Vesta	2,500.	1,300.
PR111	$20 "Peace"	3,250.	2,000.
PR112	$50 "Commerce"	2,900.	750.00
PR113	$100 Indian Maiden	3,500.	2,500.

1895-97, Watermark 191

Scott No.	Description	Unused Value	Used Value
PR114	1c Statue of Freedom (PR102), black	8.00	*25.00*
PR115	2c Statue of Freedom (PR102), black	8.00	*25.00*
PR116	5c Statue of Freedom (PR102), black	13.00	*40.00*
PR117	10c Statue of Freedom (PR102), black	13.00	*25.00*
PR118	25c "Justice" (PR106), carmine	20.00	*65.00*
PR119	50c "Justice" (PR106), carmine	25.00	*75.00*
PR120	$2 "Victory" (PR108)	30.00	*110.00*
PR121	$5 Clio (PR109), dark blue	40.00	*160.00*
a.	$5 light blue	200.00	*500.00*
PR122	$10 Vesta (PR110)	42.50	*160.00*
PR123	$20 "Peace" (PR111)	45.00	*180.00*
PR124	$50 "Commerce" (PR112)	75.00	*225.00*
PR125	$100 Indian Maiden (PR113)	65.00	*240.00*

Q1

Q2

Q3

Q4

Q5

Q6

Q7

Q8

Q9

Q10

Q11

Q12

JQ1

QE1

Scott No.	Description	Unused Value	Used Value
PARCEL POST STAMPS			
1913			
Q1	1c Post Office Clerk	5.25	1.75
Q2	2c City Carrier	6.00	1.40
Q3	3c Railway Postal Clerk	12.00	6.50
Q4	4c Rural Carrier	35.00	3.50
Q5	5c Mail Train	30.00	2.50
Q6	10c Steamship & Mail Tender	47.50	3.50
Q7	15c Automobile Service	62.50	15.00
Q8	20c Airplane Carrying Mail	135.00	30.00
Q9	25c Manufacturing	62.50	8.50
Q10	50c Dairying	275.00	50.00
Q11	75c Harvesting	95.00	40.00
Q12	$1 Fruit Growing	325.00	45.00
PARCEL POST POSTAGE DUE STAMPS			
1912			
JQ1	1c Numeral, dark green	9.50	4.50
JQ2	2c Numeral (JQ1), dark green	75.00	17.50
JQ3	5c Numeral (JQ1), dark green	12.50	5.50
JQ4	10c Numeral (JQ1), dark green	150.00	45.00
JQ5	25c Numeral (JQ1), dark green	85.00	5.00
SPECIAL HANDLING STAMPS			
1925-28			
QE1	10c Numeral, yellow green	2.00	1.00
QE2	15c Numeral (QE1), yellow green	2.25	.90
QE3	20c Numeral (QE1), yellow green	3.75	1.50
QE4	25c Numeral (QE1), deep green	20.00	3.75
a.	25c yellow green	16.50	15.00

CVP1

CVP3

CVP31

CVP32

CVP34

CVP35

CVP39

CVP43

CVP54

Scott No.	Description	Unused Value	Used Value	/ / / / / /
COMPUTER VENDED POSTAGE				
1989, Aug. 23, Washington, D.C., Machine 82				
CVP1 25c	USA, 1st Class	6.00	—	
a.	1st day dated, serial #12501-15500	4.50	—	
b.	1st day dated, serial #00001-12500	4.50	—	
c.	1st day dated, serial over #27500	—	—	
CVP2 $1	USA (CVP1), 3rd Class	—	—	
a.	1st day dated, serial #24501-27500	—	—	
b.	1st day dated, serial over #27500	—	—	
CVP3 $1.69	Bar code, Parcel Post	—	—	
a.	1st day dated, serial #21501-24500	—	—	
b.	1st day dated, serial over #27500	—	—	
CVP4 $2.40	USA (CVP1), Priority Mail	—	—	
a.	1st day dated, serial #18501-21500	—	—	
b.	Priority Mail ($2.74), with bar code	*100.00*		
c.	1st day dated, serial over #27500	—	—	
CVP5 $8.75	USA (CVP1), Express Mail	—	—	
a.	1st day dated, serial #15501-18500	—	—	
b.	1st day dated, serial over #27500	—	—	
	Nos. 1a-5a	82.50	—	
Washington, D.C., Machine 83				
CVP6 25c	USA (CVP1), 1st Class	6.00	—	
a.	1st day dated, serial #12501-15500.	4.50	—	
b.	1st day dated, serial #00001-12500.	4.50	—	
c.	1st day dated, serial over #27500	—	—	
CVP7 $1	USA (CVP1), 3rd Class	—	—	
a.	1st day dated, serial #24501-27500	—	—	
b.	1st day dated, serial over #27500	—	—	
CVP8 $1.69	Bar Code (CVP3), Parcel Post	—	—	
a.	1st day dated, serial #21501-24500	—	—	
b.	1st day dated, serial over #27500	—	—	
CVP9 $2.40	USA (CVP1), Priority Mail	—	—	
a.	1st day dated, serial #18501-21500	—	—	
b.	1st day dated, serial over #27500	—	—	
c.	Priority Mail ($2.74), with bar code	*100.00*		
CVP10 $8.75	USA (CVP1), Express Mail	—	—	
a.	1st day dated, serial #15501-18500	—	—	
b.	1st day dated, serial over #27500	—	—	
	Nos. 6a-10a	57.50	—	
1989, Sept. 1, Kensington, MD, Machine 82				
CVP11 25c	USA (CVP1), 1st Class	6.00	—	
a.	1st day dated, serial #12501-15500	4.50	—	
b.	1st day dated, serial #00001-12500	4.50	—	
c.	1st day dated, serial over #27500	—	—	
CVP12 $1	USA (CVP1), 3rd Class	—	—	
a.	1st day dated, serial #24501-27500	—	—	
b.	1st day dated, serial over #27500	—	—	
CVP13 $1.69	Bar Code (CVP3), Parcel Post	—	—	

Scott No.	Description	Unused Value	Used Value	/ / / / / /
a.	1st day dated, serial #21501-24500	—	—	
b.	1st day dated, serial over #27500...	—	—	
CVP14 $2.40	USA (CVP1), Priority Mail..........	—	—	
a.	1st day dated, serial #18501-21500	—	—	
b.	1st day dated, serial over #27500...	—	—	
c.	Priority Mail ($2.74), with bar code	*100.00*		
CVP15 $8.75	USA (CVP1), Express Mail..........	—	—	
a.	1st day dated, serial #15501-18500	—	—	
b.	1st day dated, serial over #27500...	—	—	
	Nos. 11a-15a..................................	57.50	—	
	Nos. 1b-11b..................................	9.00	—	
Kensington, MD, Machine 83				
CVP16 25c	USA (CVP1), 1st Class..................	6.00	—	
a.	1st day dated, serial #12501-15500	4.50	—	
b.	1st day dated, serial #00001-12500	4.50	—	
c.	1st day dated, serial over #27500...	—	—	
CVP17 $1	USA (CVP1), 3rd Class................	—	—	
a.	1st day dated, serial #24501-27500	—	—	
b.	1st day dated, serial over #27500..	—	—	
CVP18 $1.69	Bar Code (CVP3), Parcel Post......	—	—	
a.	1st day dated, serial #21501-24500	—	—	
b.	1st day dated, serial over #27500..	—	—	
CVP19 $2.40	USA (CVP1), Priority Mail..........	—	—	
a.	1st day dated, serial #18501-21500	—	—	
b.	1st day dated, serial over #27500..	—	—	
c.	Priority Mail ($2.74), with bar code	100.00		
CVP20 $8.75	USA (CVP1), Express Mail.........	—	—	
a.	1st day dated, serial #15501-18500............................	—	—	
b.	1st day dated, serial over #27500.	—	—	
	Nos. 16a-20a...............................	57.50	—	
	Nos. 6b, 16b................................	9.00	—	
1989, Nov., Washington, D.C., Machine 11				
CVP21 25c	USA (CVP1), 1st Class...............	*150.00*		
a.	1st Class, with bar code	—		
CVP22 $1	USA (CVP1), 3rd Class..............	*500.00*		
CVP23 $1.69	Bar Code (CVP3), Parcel Post......	*500.00*		
CVP24 $2.40	USA (CVP1), Priority Mail..........	*500.00*		
a.	Priority Mail ($2.74), with bar code	—		
CVP25 $8.75	USA (CVP1), Express Mail.........	*500.00*		
Washington, D.C., Machine 12				
CVP26 25c	USA (CVP1), 1st Class...............	*150.00*		
CVP27 $1	USA (CVP1), 3rd Class..............	—		
CVP28 $1.69	Bar Code (CVP3), Parcel Post......	—		
CVP29 $2.40	USA (CVP1), Priority Mail..........	—		
a.	Priority Mail ($2.74), with bar code	—		
CVP30 $8.75	USA (CVP1), Express Mail.........	—		

Scott No.	Description	Unused Value	Used Value	/ / / / / /
1992, Coil Stamp				
CVP31 29c	Shield, red & blue, Type I	.75	.25	□□□□□
b.	Type II	.90	.40	□□□□□
	Type I has small serifed numerals preceded by an asterisk 1½ mm across. Type II has large sans-serif numerals preceded by an asterisk 2 mm across.			
1994, Coil Stamp				
CVP32 29c	Shield, red & blue.........................	.70	.35	□□□□□
1996, Coil Stamp				
CVP33 32c	Shield (32), bright red & blue dated "1996"	.60	.25	□□□□□
CVP34 33c	NCR Automated Postal machine .	*22.50*	—	□□□□□
CVP35 33c	IBM Postal machine	—	—	□□□□□
a.	With Priority Mail inscription......	—	—	□□□□□
1999				
CVP34 33c	NCR Automated Postal Machine	50.00	—	□□□□□
a.	With Priority Mail inscription.....	—	—	□□□□□
b.	With Express Mail inscription	—	—	□□□□□
1999, May 7				
CVP35 33c	IBM Postal Machine, Microprinting Above Red Orange Line, numbers only at LL, square corners	150.00	—	□□□□□
	Round corners	7.50	—	□□□□□
a.	"Priority Mail" at LL, square corners......................................	150.00	—	□□□□□
	Round corners	—	—	
b.	"Priority Mail AS" at LL, square corners	150.00	—	□□□□□
	Round corners	—	—	□□□□□
CVP36 33c	IBM Postal Machine (CVP35), No Microprinting Above Red Orange Line, numbers only at LL, square corners................	175.00	—	□□□□□
	Round corners	10.00	—	□□□□□
a.	"Priority Mail" at LL, square corners......................................	125.00	—	□□□□□
	Round corners	—	—	□□□□□
b.	"Priority Mail AS" at LL, square corners	125.00	—	□□□□□
	Round corners	—	—	□□□□□
CVP37 33c	IBM Postal Machine (CVP35), numbers only at LL	3.75	—	□□□□□
a.	"Priority Mail" at LL	5.00	—	□□□□□
b.	"Priority Mail AS" at LL...........	5.00	—	□□□□□
2001				
CVP39 34c	Simplypostage.com	—	—	□□□□□
CVP40 34c	Simplypostage.com, with machine number (CVP39)	—	—	□□□□□

CVP55

CVP56

CVP57

CVP66A

CVP69

CVP78

CVP79

HOW TO USE THIS BOOK

In cases where two or more Scott numbers share a common design, the illustration shows the first Scott number that bears that design. Subsequent Scott numbers showing the same design will have the first Scott number in parentheses following the description to guide the user to the correct design.

Scott No.	Description	Unused Value	Used Value	/ / / / / /
CVP41 34c	Simplypostage.com, Eagle and stars (CVP39)	—	—	□□□□□
CVP42 34c	Simplypostage.com, Eagle and Stars, with machine number (CVP39)	—	20.00	□□□□□
2002, June - 2003				
CVP43 21c	Neopostage.com	—	—	□□□□□
a.	Booklet pane of 10	—		□□□□□
CVP44 23c	Neopostage.com (CVP43)	—	—	□□□□□
a.	Booklet pane of 10	—		□□□□□
CVP45 34c	black, blue & orange, (CVP43)	—	—	□□□□□
a.	Booklet pane of 10	—		□□□□□
CVP46 37c	Neopostage.com (CVP43)	—	—	□□□□□
a.	Booklet pane of 10	—		□□□□□
CVP47 50c	Neopostage.com (CVP43)	—	—	□□□□□
a.	Booklet pane of 10	—		□□□□□
CVP48 60c	Neopostage.com (CVP43)	—	—	□□□□□
a.	Booklet pane of 10	—		□□□□□
CVP49 70c	Neopostage.com (CVP43)	—	—	□□□□□
a.	Booklet pane of 10	—		□□□□□
CVP50 80c	Neopostage.com (CVP43)	—	—	□□□□□
a.	Booklet pane of 10	—		□□□□□
CVP51 $3.50	black, blue & orange	—	—	□□□□□
a.	Booklet pane of 1	—		□□□□□
b.	Booklet pane of 2	—		□□□□□
c.	Booklet pane of 5	—		□□□□□
d.	Booklet pane of 10	—		□□□□□
CVP52 $3.85	Neopostage.com (CVP43)	—	—	□□□□□
a.	Booklet pane of 1	—		□□□□□
b.	Booklet pane of 2	—		□□□□□
c.	Booklet pane of 5	—		□□□□□
d.	Booklet pane of 10	—		□□□□□
CVP53 $13.65	Neopostage.com (CVP43)	—	—	□□□□□
a.	Booklet pane of 1	—		□□□□□
b.	Booklet pane of 2	—		□□□□□
c.	Booklet pane of 5	—		□□□□□
d.	Booklet pane of 10	—		□□□□□
2004, Apr. 14				
CVP54 37c	IBM Pitney Bowes	5.75	—	□□□□□
a.	With First Class Mail inscription	2.50	—	□□□□□
b.	With Priority Mail inscription	2.50	—	□□□□□
c.	With Parcel Post inscription	2.50	—	□□□□□
d.	With International inscription	2.50	—	□□□□□
CVP55 37c	IBM Pitney Bowes, US Postage	2.50	—	□□□□□
a.	With First Class Mail inscription	—	—	□□□□□
b.	With Priority Mail inscription	—	—	□□□□□
c.	With Parcel Post inscription	—	—	□□□□□
d.	With International inscription	—	—	□□□□□

Scott No.	Description	Unused Value	Used Value
2004, Nov. 19 -2008			
CVP56 37c	IBM Pitney Bowes	2.50	.25
a.	With Priority inscription	3.00	—
b.	With Parcel Post inscription	3.00	—
c.	With Express inscription	3.00	—
CVP57 37c	IBM Pitney Bowes	1.00	.25
a.	With Priority inscription	1.25	—
b.	With Parcel Post inscription	1.25	—
c.	With Express inscription	1.25	—
d.	With Int Air LP inscription	1.25	—
e.	With "FCM Letter" inscription	1.25	—
f.	With "FCM Flat" inscription	1.25	—
g.	With "FCM Parcel" inscription	1.25	—
h.	With "FCM Intl." inscription	1.25	—
i.	With "FCM Lg Env" inscription	1.25	—
j.	With "PM Fr Env" inscription	1.25	—
k.	With "PM Fr Box" inscription	1.25	—
l.	With "PM Lfr Box" inscription	1.25	—
m.	With "Exp Fr Env" inscription	1.25	—
n.	With "FCMI Ltr" inscription	1.25	—
o.	With "FCMI L Env" inscription	1.25	—
CVP58 60c	IBM Pitney Bowes, with "IM" and Numbers (CVP57)	3.00	.50
CVP59 80c	IBM Pitney Bowes, with "IM" and Numbers (CVP57)	3.75	.50
CVP60 $3.85	IBM Pitney Bowes, with "PM" and Numbers (CVP57)	15.00	.50
CVP61 $13.65	IBM Pitney Bowes, with "EM" and Numbers (CVP57)	42.50	1.00
CVP62 $1	IBM Pitney Bowes, with "IB" and Numbers (CVP57)	4.00	.25
2006			
CVP63 48c	IBM Pitney Bowes, with "IM" and Numbers (CVP57)	1.25	.40
CVP64 63c	IBM Pitney Bowes, with "IM" and Numbers (CVP57)	1.50	.50
CVP65 84c	IBM Pitney Bowes, with "IM" and Numbers(CVP57)	2.00	.50
CVP66 $4.05	IBM Pitney Bowes, with "PM" and Numbers (CVP57)	9.50	1.00
CVP66A $8.10	IBM Pitney Bowes, with "PM" and Numbers (CVP57)	35.00	1.00
CVP67 $14.40	IBM Pitney Bowes, with "EM" and Numbers (CVP57)	30.00	1.00
2006-2008			
CVP69 39c	IBM Pitney Bowes, No inscription under encryption	1.00	.25
a.	With "Priority" inscription	1.25	—

Scott No.	Description	Unused Value	Used Value
b.	With "Parcel Post" inscription	1.25	—
c.	With "Express" inscription	1.25	—
d.	With "FCM Flat" inscription	1.25	—
e.	With "FCM Parcel" inscription...	1.25	—
f.	With "FCM Lg Env" inscription.	1.25	—
g.	With "PM Fr Env" inscription.....	1.25	—
h.	With "PM Fr Box" inscription	1.25	—
i.	With "PM Lfr Box" inscription...	1.25	—
j.	With "Exp Fr Env" inscription....	1.25	—
2006-07			
CVP70 39c	IBM Pitney Bowes, with "IB" and Numbers (CVP57)..............	1.00	.50
CVP71 41c	IBM Pitney Bowes, with "IB" and Numbers (CVP57)..............	1.00	.50
CVP72 69c	IBM Pitney Bowes, with "IB" and Numbers (CVP57)..............	1.40	.70
CVP73 61c	IBM Pitney Bowes, with "IM" and Numbers (CVP57)..............	1.25	.50
CVP74 90c	IBM Pitney Bowes, with "IM" and Numbers (CVP57)..............	1.90	.95
2006, Dec.			
CVP75 41c	IBM Pitney Bowes, black & pink, with "First Class Mail" inscription	—	—
a.	With "Mailed From Zip Code..." inscription	0.20	—
b.	With "Postcard" inscription	0.55	—
c.	With "First Class Mail Intl" inscription	1.25	—
d.	With "Parcel Post" inscription	7.50	—
e.	With "Priority" inscription..........	9.25	—
f.	With "Express Mail" inscription.	33.00	—
2008			
CVP76 94c	IBM Pitney Bowes, with IM and numbers (CVP57)..............	2.00	0.60
CVP77 $1.20	IBM Pitney Bowes, with IM and numbers (CVP57)..............	2.40	1.25
CVP78 42c	IBM Pitney Bowes, black & pink, with rounded corners................	—	—
CVP79 42c	IBM Pitney Bowes, black & pink, with perpendicular corners	—	—

POSTAL CARDS

1990, July 5, Postal Buddy Machine

CVUX1	15c Eagle....................................	6.00	*10.00*

1991, Feb. 3, Postal Buddy Machine

CVUX2	19c Eagle (CVUX1)...................	3.00	*8.00*

1992, Nov. 13, Postal Buddy Machine

CVUX3	19c Star	6.00	*15.00*

1CVP1

1CVP2

1CVP10

1CVP16

1CVP22

1CVP32

1CVP37

1CVP38

1CVP39

1CVP43

1CVP47

1CVP51

1CVP55

1CVP59

1CVP60

1CVP61

1CVP62

1CVP63

1CVP64

1CVP65

1CVP66

1CVP67

1CVP68

1CVP69

Scott No.	Description	Unused Value	Used Value

PERSONAL COMPUTER POSTAGE

2000, Simply Postage

1CVP1 33c	Simplypostage.com	—	—

2002, Stamps.com

1CVP2 37c	Flag and star	4.00	3.00
a.	"First Class" below "US Postage".	2.75	2.00
b.	"Priority" below "US Postage"	8.25	2.50
c.	"Express" below "US Postage"	25.00	5.00
d.	"Media Mail" below "US Postage"	7.75	2.50
e.	"Parcel Post" below "US Postage"	7.75	2.50
f.	"Bound Printed Matter" below "US Postage"	7.75	2.50
g.	"BPM" below "US Postage"	7.75	2.50
1CVP2A 37c	Flag and star	7.00	3.00
a.	"First Class" below zip code	2.75	2.00
b.	"Priority" below zip code	8.25	2.50
c.	"Express" below zip code	25.00	5.00
d.	"Media Mail" below zip code	7.75	2.50
e.	"Parcel Post" below zip code	7.75	2.50
1CVP3 37c	Heart	4.00	4.00
a.	"First Class" below "US Postage".	2.75	2.00
b.	"Priority" below "US Postage"	8.25	2.50
c.	"Express" below "US Postage"	25.00	5.00
d.	"Media Mail" below "US Postage"	7.75	2.50
e.	"Parcel Post" below "US Postage"	7.75	2.50
f.	"Bound Printed Matter" below "US Postage"	7.75	2.50
g.	""BPM"" below "US Postage"	7.75	2.50

2003, June, Stamps.com

1CVP4 37c	Statue of Liberty and Flag	3.50	2.00
a.	"First Class" below "US Postage".	3.25	2.00
b.	"Priority" below "US Postage"	8.00	1.00
c.	"Express" below "US Postage"	25.00	3.00
d.	"Media Mail" below "US Postage"	7.50	1.00
e.	"Parcel Post" below "US Postage"	7.50	1.00
f.	"Bound Printed Matter" below "US Postage"	7.50	1.00
g.	""BPM"" below "US Postage"	7.50	1.00
1CVP5 37c	Liberty Bell and Flag	3.50	2.00
a.	"First Class" below "US Postage".	3.25	2.00
b.	"Priority" below "US Postage"	8.00	1.00
c.	"Express" below "US Postage"	25.00	3.00
d.	"Media Mail" below "US Postage"	7.50	1.00
e.	"Parcel Post" below "US Postage"	7.50	1.00
f.	"Bound Printed Matter" below "US Postage"	7.50	1.00
g.	""BPM"" below "US Postage"	7.50	1.00
1CVP6 37c	Eagle and Flag	3.50	2.00

Scott No.	Description	Unused Value	Used Value	/ / / / / /
a.	"First Class" below "US Postage".	3.25	2.00	☐☐☐☐☐
b.	"Priority" below "US Postage"	8.00	1.00	☐☐☐☐☐
c.	"Express" below "US Postage".....	25.00	3.00	☐☐☐☐☐
d.	"Media Mail" below "US Postage"	7.50	1.00	☐☐☐☐☐
e.	"Parcel Post" below "US Postage"	7.50	1.00	☐☐☐☐☐
f.	"Bound Printed Matter" below "US Postage"...............................	7.50	1.00	☐☐☐☐☐
g.	"BPM" below "US Postage".........	7.50	1.00	☐☐☐☐☐
1CVP7 37c	George Washington and Flag........	3.50	2.00	☐☐☐☐☐
a.	"First Class" below "US Postage".	3.25	.20	☐☐☐☐☐
b.	"Priority" below "US Postage"	8.00	1.00	☐☐☐☐☐
c.	"Express" below "US Postage".....	25.00	3.00	☐☐☐☐☐
d.	"Media Mail" below "US Postage"	7.50	1.00	☐☐☐☐☐
e.	"Parcel Post" below "US Postage"	7.50	1.00	☐☐☐☐☐
f.	"Bound Printed Matter" below "US Postage"...............................	7.50	1.00	☐☐☐☐☐
g.	"BPM" below "US Postage".........	7.50	1.00	☐☐☐☐☐
1CVP8 37c	Capitol Building and Flag.............	3.50	2.00	☐☐☐☐☐
a.	"First Class" below "US Postage".	3.25	.20	☐☐☐☐☐
b.	"Priority" below "US Postage"	8.00	1.00	☐☐☐☐☐
c.	"Express" below "US Postage".....	25.00	3.00	☐☐☐☐☐
d.	"Media Mail" below "US Postage"	7.50	1.00	☐☐☐☐☐
e.	"Parcel Post" below "US Postage"	7.50	1.00	☐☐☐☐☐
f.	"Bound Printed Matter" below "US Postage"...............................	7.50	1.00	☐☐☐☐☐
g.	"BPM" below "US Postage".........	7.50	1.00	☐☐☐☐☐
h.	Strip of 5, #1CVP4-1CVP8...........	17.50		☐☐☐☐☐
1CVP9 37c	Flag and Star type of 2002 (1CVP2) Redrawn with Stamps.com in upper case letters.........................	3.00	1.50	☐☐☐☐☐
a.	"First Class" below "US Postage".	2.00	.20	☐☐☐☐☐
b.	"Priority" below "US Postage"	8.00	1.00	☐☐☐☐☐
c.	"Express" below "US Postage".....	25.00	3.00	☐☐☐☐☐
d.	"Media Mail" below "US Postage"	7.50	1.00	☐☐☐☐☐
e.	"Parcel Post" below "US Postage"	7.50	1.00	☐☐☐☐☐
f.	"Bound Printed Matter" below "US Postage"...............................	7.50	1.00	☐☐☐☐☐
g.	"BPM" below "US Postage".........	7.50	1.00	☐☐☐☐☐
2003, Dec., Stamps.com				
1CVP10 37c	Snowman..	3.00	1.50	☐☐☐☐☐
a.	"First Class" below "US Postage".	2.00	1.00	☐☐☐☐☐
b.	"Priority" below "US Postage"	8.00	1.00	☐☐☐☐☐
c.	"Express" below "US Postage".....	25.00	3.00	☐☐☐☐☐
d.	"Media Mail" below "US Postage"	7.50	1.00	☐☐☐☐☐
e.	"Parcel Post" below "US Postage"	7.50	1.00	☐☐☐☐☐
f.	"Bound Printed Matter" below "US Postage"...............................	7.50	1.00	☐☐☐☐☐
g.	"BPM" below "US Postage".........	7.50	1.00	☐☐☐☐☐

Scott No.	Description	Unused Value	Used Value	/ / / / / /
1CVP11 37c	Snowflakes	3.00	1.50	☐☐☐☐☐
a.	"First Class" below "US Postage".	2.00	1.00	☐☐☐☐☐
b.	"Priority" below "US Postage"	8.00	1.00	☐☐☐☐☐
c.	"Express" below "US Postage"	25.00	3.00	☐☐☐☐☐
d.	"Media Mail" below "US Postage"	7.50	1.00	☐☐☐☐☐
e.	"Parcel Post" below "US Postage"	7.50	1.00	☐☐☐☐☐
f.	"Bound Printed Matter" below "US Postage"	7.50	1.00	☐☐☐☐☐
g.	"BPM" below "US Postage"	7.50	1.00	☐☐☐☐☐
1CVP12 37c	Holly	3.00	1.50	☐☐☐☐☐
a.	"First Class" below "US Postage".	2.00	1.00	☐☐☐☐☐
b.	"Priority" below "US Postage"	8.00	1.00	☐☐☐☐☐
c.	"Express" below "US Postage"	25.00	3.00	☐☐☐☐☐
d.	"Media Mail" below "US Postage"	7.50	1.00	☐☐☐☐☐
e.	"Parcel Post" below "US Postage"	7.50	1.00	☐☐☐☐☐
f.	"Bound Printed Matter" below "US Postage"	7.50	1.00	☐☐☐☐☐
g.	"BPM" below "US Postage"	7.50	1.00	☐☐☐☐☐
1CVP13 37c	Dove	3.00	1.50	☐☐☐☐☐
a.	"First Class" below "US Postage".	2.00	1.00	☐☐☐☐☐
b.	"Priority" below "US Postage"	8.00	1.00	☐☐☐☐☐
c.	"Express" below "US Postage"	25.00	3.00	☐☐☐☐☐
d.	"Media Mail" below "US Postage"	7.50	1.00	☐☐☐☐☐
e.	"Parcel Post" below "US Postage"	7.50	1.00	☐☐☐☐☐
f.	"Bound Printed Matter" below "US Postage"	7.50	1.00	☐☐☐☐☐
g.	"BPM" below "US Postage"	7.50	1.00	☐☐☐☐☐
1CVP14 37c	Gingerbread Man and Candy	3.00	1.50	☐☐☐☐☐
a.	"First Class" below "US Postage".	2.00	1.00	☐☐☐☐☐
b.	"Priority" below "US Postage"	8.00	1.00	☐☐☐☐☐
c.	"Express" below "US Postage"	25.00	3.00	☐☐☐☐☐
d.	"Media Mail" below "US Postage"	7.50	1.00	☐☐☐☐☐
e.	"Parcel Post" below "US Postage"	7.50	1.00	☐☐☐☐☐
f.	"Bound Printed Matter" below "US Postage"	7.50	1.00	☐☐☐☐☐
g.	"BPM" below "US Postage"	7.50	1.00	☐☐☐☐☐
h.	Strip of 5, #1CVP10-1CVP14	12.50		☐☐☐☐☐

2004, Mar., Stamps.com

Scott No.	Description	Unused Value	Used Value	/ / / / / /
1CVP15 37c	Mailbox	25.00	15.00	☐☐☐☐☐
a.	"First Class" below "US Postage".	25.00	15.00	☐☐☐☐☐
b.	"Priority" below "US Postage"	—	—	☐☐☐☐☐
c.	"Express" below "US Postage"	—	—	☐☐☐☐☐
d.	"Media Mail" below "US Postage"	—	—	☐☐☐☐☐
e.	"Parcel Post" below "US Postage"	—	—	☐☐☐☐☐
f.	"Bound Printed Matter" below "US Postage"	—	—	☐☐☐☐☐
g.	"BPM" below "US Postage"	—	—	☐☐☐☐☐

Scott No.	Description	Unused Value	Used Value	/ / / / / /
2004, Apr., Stamps.com				
1CVP16 37c	George Washington	2.00	1.00	☐☐☐☐☐
a.	"First Class" below "US Postage".	1.10	.75	☐☐☐☐☐
b.	"Priority" below "US Postage"	5.00	2.50	☐☐☐☐☐
c.	"Express" below "US Postage"	20.00	5.00	☐☐☐☐☐
d.	"Media Mail" below "US Postage"	5.00	2.50	☐☐☐☐☐
e.	"Parcel Post" below "US Postage"	5.00	2.50	☐☐☐☐☐
f.	"Bound Printed Matter" below "US Postage"	5.00	2.50	☐☐☐☐☐
g.	"BPM" below "US Postage"	5.00	2.50	☐☐☐☐☐
1CVP17 37c	Thomas Jefferson	2.00	1.00	☐☐☐☐☐
a.	"First Class" below "US Postage".	1.10	.75	☐☐☐☐☐
b.	"Priority" below "US Postage"	5.00	2.50	☐☐☐☐☐
c.	"Express" below "US Postage"	20.00	5.00	☐☐☐☐☐
d.	"Media Mail" below "US Postage"	5.00	2.50	☐☐☐☐☐
e.	"Parcel Post" below "US Postage"	5.00	2.50	☐☐☐☐☐
f.	"Bound Printed Matter" below "US Postage"	5.00	2.50	☐☐☐☐☐
g.	"BPM" below "US Postage"	5.00	2.50	☐☐☐☐☐
1CVP18 37c	Abraham Lincoln	2.00	1.00	☐☐☐☐☐
a.	"First Class" below "US Postage".	1.10	.75	☐☐☐☐☐
b.	"Priority" below "US Postage"	5.00	2.50	☐☐☐☐☐
c.	"Express" below "US Postage"	20.00	5.00	☐☐☐☐☐
d.	"Media Mail" below "US Postage"	5.00	2.50	☐☐☐☐☐
e.	"Parcel Post" below "US Postage"	5.00	2.50	☐☐☐☐☐
f.	"Bound Printed Matter" below "US Postage"	5.00	2.50	☐☐☐☐☐
g.	"BPM" below "US Postage"	5.50	2.50	☐☐☐☐☐
1CVP19 37c	Theodore Roosevelt	2.00	1.00	☐☐☐☐☐
a.	"First Class" below "US Postage".	1.10	.75	☐☐☐☐☐
b.	"Priority" below "US Postage"	5.00	2.50	☐☐☐☐☐
c.	"Express" below "US Postage"	20.00	5.00	☐☐☐☐☐
d.	"Media Mail" below "US Postage"	5.00	2.50	☐☐☐☐☐
e.	"Parcel Post" below "US Postage"	5.00	2.50	☐☐☐☐☐
f.	"Bound Printed Matter" below "US Postage"	5.00	2.50	☐☐☐☐☐
g.	"BPM" below "US Postage"	5.00	2.50	☐☐☐☐☐
1CVP20 37c	John F. Kennedy	2.00	1.00	☐☐☐☐☐
a.	"First Class" below "US Postage".	1.10	.75	☐☐☐☐☐
b.	"Priority" below "US Postage"	5.00	2.50	☐☐☐☐☐
c.	"Express" below "US Postage"	20.00	5.00	☐☐☐☐☐
d.	"Media Mail" below "US Postage"	5.00	2.50	☐☐☐☐☐
e.	"Parcel Post" below "US Postage"	5.00	2.50	☐☐☐☐☐
f.	"Bound Printed Matter" below "US Postage"	5.00	2.50	☐☐☐☐☐
g.	"BPM" below "US Postage"	5.00	2.50	☐☐☐☐☐
h.	Strip of 5, #1CVP16-1CVP20	10.00		☐☐☐☐☐

Scott No.	Description	Unused Value	Used Value	/ / / / / /
1CVP21 37c	Flag and Star Type of 2002 (1CVP1) Redrawn with Orange Stars and Text at Left, "Stamps.com" in upper case letters	2.00	1.00	☐☐☐☐☐
a.	"First Class" below "US Postage".	1.35	.75	☐☐☐☐☐
b.	"Priority" below "US Postage"	6.00	2.50	☐☐☐☐☐
c.	"Express" below "US Postage"	22.50	5.00	☐☐☐☐☐
d.	"Media Mail" below "US Postage"	6.00	2.50	☐☐☐☐☐
e.	"Parcel Post" below "US Postage"	6.00	2.50	☐☐☐☐☐
f.	"Bound Printed Matter" below "US Postage"	6.00	2.50	☐☐☐☐☐
g.	"BPM" below "US Postage"	6.00	2.50	☐☐☐☐☐
1CVP22 37c	Bicycling	3.00	2.00	☐☐☐☐☐
a.	"First Class" below "US Postage".	2.50	1.50	☐☐☐☐☐
b.	"Priority" below "US Postage"	8.00	1.00	☐☐☐☐☐
c.	"Express" below "US Postage"	25.00	3.00	☐☐☐☐☐
d.	"Media Mail" below "US Postage"	7.50	1.00	☐☐☐☐☐
e.	"Parcel Post" below "US Postage"	7.50	1.00	☐☐☐☐☐
f.	"Bound Printed Matter" below "US Postage"	7.50	1.00	☐☐☐☐☐
g.	"BPM" below "US Postage"	7.50	1.00	☐☐☐☐☐
1CVP23 37c	Running	3.00	2.00	☐☐☐☐☐
a.	"First Class" below "US Postage".	2.50	1.50	☐☐☐☐☐
b.	"Priority" below "US Postage"	8.00	1.00	☐☐☐☐☐
c.	"Express" below "US Postage"	25.00	3.00	☐☐☐☐☐
d.	"Media Mail" below "US Postage"	7.50	1.00	☐☐☐☐☐
e.	"Parcel Post" below "US Postage"	7.50	1.00	☐☐☐☐☐
f.	"Bound Printed Matter" below "US Postage"	7.50	1.00	☐☐☐☐☐
g.	"BPM" below "US Postage"	7.50	1.00	☐☐☐☐☐
1CVP24 37c	Swimming	3.00	2.00	☐☐☐☐☐
a.	"First Class" below "US Postage".	2.50	1.50	☐☐☐☐☐
b.	"Priority" below "US Postage"	8.00	1.00	☐☐☐☐☐
c.	"Express" below "US Postage"	25.00	3.00	☐☐☐☐☐
d.	"Media Mail" below "US Postage"	7.50	1.00	☐☐☐☐☐
e.	"Parcel Post" below "US Postage"	7.50	1.00	☐☐☐☐☐
f.	"Bound Printed Matter" below "US Postage"	7.50	1.00	☐☐☐☐☐
g.	"BPM" below "US Postage"	7.50	1.00	☐☐☐☐☐
1CVP25 37c	Boxing	3.00	2.00	☐☐☐☐☐
a.	"First Class" below "US Postage".	2.50	1.50	☐☐☐☐☐
b.	"Priority" below "US Postage"	8.00	1.00	☐☐☐☐☐
c.	"Express" below "US Postage"	25.00	3.00	☐☐☐☐☐
d.	"Media Mail" below "US Postage"	7.50	1.00	☐☐☐☐☐
e.	"Parcel Post" below "US Postage"	7.50	1.00	☐☐☐☐☐
f.	"Bound Printed Matter" below "US Postage"	7.50	1.00	☐☐☐☐☐
g.	"BPM" below "US Postage"	7.50	1.00	☐☐☐☐☐

Scott No.	Description	Unused Value	Used Value	/ / / / / /
1CVP26 37c	Equestrian	3.00	2.00	☐☐☐☐☐
a.	"First Class" below "US Postage".	2.50	1.50	☐☐☐☐☐
b.	"Priority" below "US Postage"	8.00	1.00	☐☐☐☐☐
c.	"Express" below "US Postage"	25.00	3.00	☐☐☐☐☐
d.	"Media Mail" below "US Postage"	7.50	1.00	☐☐☐☐☐
e.	"Parcel Post" below "US Postage"	7.50	1.00	☐☐☐☐☐
f.	"Bound Printed Matter" below "US Postage"	7.50	1.00	☐☐☐☐☐
g.	"BPM" below "US Postage"	7.50	1.00	☐☐☐☐☐
1CVP27 37c	Basketball	3.00	2.00	☐☐☐☐☐
a.	"First Class" below "US Postage".	2.50	1.50	☐☐☐☐☐
b.	"Priority" below "US Postage"	8.00	1.00	☐☐☐☐☐
c.	"Express" below "US Postage"	25.00	3.00	☐☐☐☐☐
d.	"Media Mail" below "US Postage"	7.50	1.00	☐☐☐☐☐
e.	"Parcel Post" below "US Postage"	7.50	1.00	☐☐☐☐☐
f.	"Bound Printed Matter" below "US Postage"	7.50	1.00	☐☐☐☐☐
g.	"BPM" below "US Postage"	7.50	1.00	☐☐☐☐☐
1CVP28 37c	Judo	3.00	2.00	☐☐☐☐☐
a.	"First Class" below "US Postage".	2.50	1.50	☐☐☐☐☐
b.	"Priority" below "US Postage"	8.00	1.00	☐☐☐☐☐
c.	"Express" below "US Postage"	25.00	3.00	☐☐☐☐☐
d.	"Media Mail" below "US Postage"	7.50	1.00	☐☐☐☐☐
e.	"Parcel Post" below "US Postage"	7.50	1.00	☐☐☐☐☐
f.	"Bound Printed Matter" below "US Postage"	7.50	1.00	☐☐☐☐☐
g.	"BPM" below "US Postage"	7.50	1.00	☐☐☐☐☐
1CVP29 37c	Soccer	3.00	2.00	☐☐☐☐☐
a.	"First Class" below "US Postage".	2.50	1.50	☐☐☐☐☐
b.	"Priority" below "US Postage"	8.00	1.00	☐☐☐☐☐
c.	"Express" below "US Postage"	25.00	3.00	☐☐☐☐☐
d.	"Media Mail" below "US Postage"	7.50	1.00	☐☐☐☐☐
e.	"Parcel Post" below "US Postage"	7.50	1.00	☐☐☐☐☐
f.	"Bound Printed Matter" below "US Postage"	7.50	1.00	☐☐☐☐☐
g.	"BPM" below "US Postage"	7.50	1.00	☐☐☐☐☐
1CVP30 37c	Gymnastics	3.00	2.00	☐☐☐☐☐
a.	"First Class" below "US Postage".	2.50	1.50	☐☐☐☐☐
b.	"Priority" below "US Postage"	8.00	1.00	☐☐☐☐☐
c.	"Express" below "US Postage"	25.00	3.00	☐☐☐☐☐
d.	"Media Mail" below "US Postage"	7.50	1.00	☐☐☐☐☐
e.	"Parcel Post" below "US Postage"	7.50	1.00	☐☐☐☐☐
f.	"Bound Printed Matter" below "US Postage"	7.50	1.00	☐☐☐☐☐
g.	"BPM" below "US Postage"	7.50	1.00	☐☐☐☐☐
1CVP31 37c	Tennis	3.00	2.00	☐☐☐☐☐
a.	"First Class" below "US Postage".	2.50	1.50	☐☐☐☐☐
b.	"Priority" below "US Postage"	8.00	1.00	☐☐☐☐☐

Scott No.		Description	Unused Value	Used Value
c.		"Express" below "US Postage".....	25.00	3.00
d.		"Media Mail" below "US Postage"	7.50	1.00
e.		"Parcel Post" below "US Postage"	7.50	1.00
f.		"Bound Printed Matter" below "US Postage".............................	7.50	1.00
g.		"BPM" below "US Postage".........	7.50	1.00
h.		Block of 10, #1CVP22-1CVP31...	15.00	

2004, July, Stamps.com

Scott No.		Description	Unused Value	Used Value
1CVP32	37c	Leaning Tower of Pisa..................	3.00	2.00
a.		"First Class" below "US Postage".	2.30	1.50
b.		"Priority" below "US Postage".....	8.00	1.00
c.		"Express" below "US Postage".....	25.00	3.00
d.		"Media Mail" below "US Postage"	7.50	1.00
e.		"Parcel Post" below "US Postage"	7.50	1.00
f.		"Bound Printed Matter" below "US Postage".............................	7.50	1.00
g.		"BPM" below "US Postage".........	7.50	1.00
1CVP33	37c	Sphinx and Pyramids....................	3.00	2.00
a.		"First Class" below "US Postage".	2.30	1.50
b.		"Priority" below "US Postage".....	8.00	1.00
c.		"Express" below "US Postage".....	25.00	3.00
d.		"Media Mail" below "US Postage"	7.50	1.00
e.		"Parcel Post" below "US Postage"	7.50	1.00
f.		"Bound Printed Matter" below "US Postage".............................	7.50	1.00
g.		"BPM" below "US Postage".........	7.50	1.00
1CVP34	37c	Sydney Opera House....................	3.00	2.00
a.		"First Class" below "US Postage".	2.30	1.50
b.		"Priority" below "US Postage".....	8.00	1.00
c.		"Express" below "US Postage".....	25.00	3.00
d.		"Media Mail" below "US Postage"	7.50	1.00
e.		"Parcel Post" below "US Postage"	7.50	1.00
f.		"Bound Printed Matter" below "US Postage".............................	7.50	1.00
g.		"BPM" below "US Postage".........	7.50	1.00
1CVP35	37c	Mayan Pyramid...........................	3.00	2.00
a.		"First Class" below "US Postage".	2.30	1.50
b.		"Priority" below "US Postage".....	8.00	1.00
c.		"Express" below "US Postage".....	25.00	3.00
d.		"Media Mail" below "US Postage"	7.50	1.00
e.		"Parcel Post" below "US Postage"	7.50	1.00
f.		"Bound Printed Matter" below "US Postage".............................	7.50	1.00
g.		"BPM" below "US Postage".........	7.50	1.00
1CVP36	37c	Asian Temple...............................	3.00	2.00
a.		"First Class" below "US Postage".	2.30	1.50
b.		"Priority" below "US Postage".....	8.00	1.00
c.		"Express" below "US Postage".....	25.00	3.00

Scott No.	Description	Unused Value	Used Value	/ / / / / /
d.	"Media Mail" below "US Postage"	7.50	1.00	□□□□□
e.	"Parcel Post" below "US Postage"	7.50	1.00	□□□□□
f.	"Bound Printed Matter" below "US Postage"...............................	7.50	1.00	□□□□□
g.	"BPM" below "US Postage".........	7.50	1.00	□□□□□
h.	Strip of 5, #1CVP32-1CVP36.......	15.00		□□□□□

2005, Mar., Stamps.com

Scott No.	Description	Unused Value	Used Value	/ / / / / /
1CVP37 37c	Computer and Letters....................	25.00	15.00	□□□□□
a.	"First Class" below "US Postage".	25.00	15.00	□□□□□
b.	"Priority" below "US Postage".....	—	—	□□□□□
c.	"Express" below "US Postage".....	—	—	□□□□□
d.	"Media Mail" below "US Postage"	—	—	□□□□□
e.	"Parcel Post" below "US Postage"	—	—	□□□□□
f.	"Bound Printed Matter" below "US Postage"...............................	—	—	□□□□□
g.	"BPM" below "US Postage".........	—	—	□□□□□

2005, Aug., Stamps.com

Scott No.	Description	Unused Value	Used Value	/ / / / / /
1CVP38 37c	Logo...	1.00	.30	□□□□□
a.	"Priority" below "US Postage"......	8.00	1.00	□□□□□
b.	"Express" below "US Postage"......	25.00	3.00	□□□□□
c.	"Media Mail" below "US Postage"	7.50	1.00	□□□□□
d.	"Parcel Post" below "US Postage".	7.50	1.00	□□□□□
e.	"BPM" below "US Postage"..........	7.50	1.00	□□□□□
f.	"Aerogramme" below "US Postage"	1.40	1.00	□□□□□
g.	"Intl Air Letter" below "US Postage"	1.25	1.00	□□□□□
h.	"Intl Eco Letter" (Economy Letter Mail) below "US Postage".....................	5.50	1.00	□□□□□
i.	"GXG" (Global Express Guaranteed) below "US Postage".....................	50.00	6.00	□□□□□
j.	"EMS" (Global Express Mail) below "US Postage"...............................	32.50	4.00	□□□□□
k.	"GPM" (Global Priority Mail) below "US Postage"...............................	8.00	1.00	□□□□□
l.	"Intl Air Parcel" (Air Parcel Post) below "US Postage".....................	26.00	3.00	□□□□□
m.	"Intl Eco Parcel" (Economy Parcel Post) below "US Postage"............	32.50	4.00	□□□□□
n.	"M-Bag (Air)" below "US Postage"	35.00	5.00	□□□□□
o.	"M-Bag (Economy)" below "US Postage".......................................	18.00	3.00	□□□□□
p.	"Mat for Blind" below "US Postage"	.20	—	□□□□□

2005, Nov., Stamps.com

Scott No.	Description	Unused Value	Used Value	/ / / / / /
1CVP39 37c	Snowman..	1.60	.20	□□□□□
a.	"Priority" below "US Postage"......	8.00	1.00	□□□□□
b.	"Express" below "US Postage"......	25.00	3.00	□□□□□
c.	"Media Mail" below "US Postage"	7.50	1.00	□□□□□

Scott No.	Description	Unused Value	Used Value	/ / / / / /
d.	"Parcel Post" below "US Postage".	7.50	1.00	□□□□□
e.	"BPM" below "US Postage"..........	7.50	1.00	□□□□□
f.	"Aerogramme" below "US Postage"	1.40	1.00	□□□□□
g.	"Intl Air Letter" below "US Postage"	1.25	1.00	□□□□□
h.	"Intl Eco Letter" (Economy Letter Mail) below "US Postage"...........	5.50	1.00	□□□□□
i.	"GXG" (Global Express Guaranteed) below "US Postage".....................	50.00	6.00	□□□□□
j.	"EMS" (Global Express Mail) below "US Postage"..............................	32.50	4.00	□□□□□
k.	"GPM" (Global Priority Mail) below "US Postage"..............................	8.00	1.00	□□□□□
l.	"Intl Air Parcel" (Air Parcel Post) below "US Postage".....................	26.00	3.00	□□□□□
m.	"Intl Eco Parcel" (Economy Parcel Post) below "US Postage"...........	32.50	4.00	□□□□□
n.	"M-Bag (Air)" below "US Postage"	35.00	5.00	□□□□□
o.	"M-Bag (Economy)" below "US Postage".......................................	18.00	3.00	□□□□□
p.	"Mat for Blind" below "US Postage"	.20	—	□□□□□
1CVP40 37c	Candy Cane...................................	1.60	.20	□□□□□
a.	"Priority" below "US Postage"......	8.00	1.00	□□□□□
b.	"Express" below "US Postage"......	25.00	3.00	□□□□□
c.	"Media Mail" below "US Postage"	7.50	1.00	□□□□□
d.	"Parcel Post" below "US Postage".	7.50	1.00	□□□□□
e.	"BPM" below "US Postage"..........	7.50	1.00	□□□□□
f.	"Aerogramme" below "US Postage"	1.40	1.00	□□□□□
g.	"Intl Air Letter" below "US Postage"	1.25	1.00	□□□□□
h.	"Intl Eco Letter" (Economy Letter Mail) below "US Postage"...........	5.50	1.00	□□□□□
i.	"GXG" (Global Express Guaranteed) below "US Postage".....................	50.00	6.00	□□□□□
j.	"EMS" (Global Express Mail) below "US Postage"..............................	32.50	4.00	□□□□□
k.	"GPM" (Global Priority Mail) below "US Postage"..............................	8.00	1.00	□□□□□
l.	"Intl Air Parcel" (Air Parcel Post) below "US Postage".....................	26.00	3.00	□□□□□
m.	"Intl Eco Parcel" (Economy Parcel Post) below "US Postage"...........	32.50	4.00	□□□□□
n.	"M-Bag (Air)" below "US Postage"	35.00	5.00	□□□□□
o.	"M-Bag (Economy)" below "US Postage".......................................	18.00	3.00	□□□□□
p.	"Mat for Blind" below "US Postage"	.20	—	
1CVP41 37c	Dove...	1.60	.20	□□□□□
a.	"Priority" below "US Postage"......	8.00	1.00	□□□□□
b.	"Express" below "US Postage"......	25.00	3.00	□□□□□
c.	"Media Mail" below "US Postage"	7.50	1.00	□□□□□

Scott No.	Description	Unused Value	Used Value
d.	"Parcel Post" below "US Postage".	7.50	1.00
e.	"BPM" below "US Postage"..........	7.50	1.00
f.	"Aerogramme" below "US Postage"	1.40	1.00
g.	"Intl Air Letter" below "US Postage"	1.25	1.00
h.	"Letter Mail (Economy)" below "US Postage"................................	5.50	1.00
i.	"Global Express Guaranteed" below "US Postage"................................	50.00	6.00
j.	"Global Express Mail" below "US Postage".......................................	32.50	4.00
k.	"Global Priority Mail" below "US Postage".......................................	8.00	1.00
l.	"Pacel Post (Air)" below "US Postage".......................................	26.00	3.00
m.	"Parcel Post (Economy)" below "US Postage"................................	32.50	4.00
n.	"M-Bag (Air)" below "US Postage"	35.00	5.00
o.	"M-Bag (Economy)" below "US Postage".......................................	18.00	3.00
p.	"Mat for Blind" below "US Postage"	.20	—
1CVP42 37c	Stylized Christmas Tree and Window	1.60	.20
a.	"Priority" below "US Postage"......	8.00	1.00
b.	"Express" below "US Postage"......	25.00	3.00
c.	"Media Mail" below "US Postage"	7.50	1.00
d.	"Parcel Post" below "US Postage".	7.50	1.00
e.	"BPM" below "US Postage"..........	7.50	1.00
f.	"Aerogramme" below "US Postage"	1.40	1.00
g.	"Intl Air Letter" below "US Postage"	1.25	1.00
h.	"Letter Mail (Economy)" below "US Postage".......................................	5.50	1.00
i.	"Global Express Guaranteed" below "US Postage"................................	50.00	6.00
j.	"Global Express Mail" below "US Postage".......................................	32.50	4.00
k.	"Global Priority Mail" below "US Postage".......................................	8.00	1.00
l.	"Pacel Post (Air)" below "US Postage".......................................	26.00	3.00
m.	"Parcel Post (Economy)" below "US Postage"................................	32.50	4.00
n.	"M-Bag (Air)" below "US Postage"	35.00	5.00
o.	"M-Bag (Economy)" below "US Postage".......................................	18.00	3.00
p.	"Mat for Blind" below "US Postage"	.20	—
q.	Vert. Strip, 2 each #CVP39-1CVP42	6.00	

2005-6, Endicia.com

Scott No.	Description	Unused Value	Used Value
1CVP43 24c	"Postcard" under "US Postage".....	10.00	4.00

Scott No.		Description	Unused Value	Used Value	/ / / / / /
a.	39c	"First Class" under "US Postage"..	2.00	.50	□□□□□
b.	63c	"Intl. Mail" under "US Postage"....	3.25	2.50	□□□□□
c.	4.05	"Priority Mail." under "US Postage"	12.00	2.50	□□□□□
1CVP44	24c	"Postcard" under "US Postage," coil stamp, perf. 10½ x 10¼ on 2 sides	11.00	4.00	□□□□□
a.	39c	"First Class" under "US Postage," coil stamp, perf. 10½ x 10¼ on 2 sides	2.25	.50	□□□□□
b.	63c	"Intl. Mail." under "US Postage," coil stamp, perf. 10½ x 10¼ on 2 sides	3.50	2.50	□□□□□
c.	$4.05	"Priority Mail" under "US Postage," coil stamp, perf. 10½ x 10¼ on 2 sides	12.50	2.50	□□□□□

2006, Mar., Stamps.com

1CVP51	39c	Flag and Mount Rushmore..........	.80	.20	□□□□□
1CVP52	39c	Flag and Eagle..........	.80	.20	□□□□□
1CVP53	39c	Flag and Statue of Liberty..........	.80	.20	□□□□□
1CVP54	39c	Flag and Liberty Bell..........	.80	.20	□□□□□
a.		Vert. Strip of 8, 2 each #1CVP51-1CVP54..........	8.00		□□□□□

2006, Stamps.com

1CVP55	39c	Leaning Tower of Pisa..........	.80	.20	□□□□□
1CVP56	39c	Taj Mahal..........	.80	.20	□□□□□
1CVP57	39c	Eiffel Tower..........	.80	.20	□□□□□
1CVP58	39c	Parthenon..........	.80	.20	□□□□□
a.		Vert. Strip, 2 each #1CVP55-1CVP58	8.00		□□□□□

2006 Pitney Bowes Stamp Expressions

1CVP59	39c	Any label picture (or without)........	1.35	.80	□□□□□

2006, Stamps.com, Personalized Images

1CVP60	39c	Any label picture..........	1.50	.95	□□□□□
1CVP61	39c	Any label picture..........	1.50	.95	□□□□□
1CVP62	39c	Autumn Leaves..........	1.25	.20	□□□□□
1CVP63	39c	Pumpkins..........	1.25	.20	□□□□□
1CVP64	39c	Basket of Apples, Sheaf of Wheat, Falling Leaves and Pumpkins......	1.25	.20	□□□□□
1CVP65	39c	Leaves and Carved Pumpkin..........	1.25	.20	□□□□□
a.		Vert. Strip, 2 each #1CVP62-1CVP65	10.00		□□□□□
1CVP66	39c	Season's Greetings..........	1.25	.20	□□□□□
1CVP67	39c	Christmas Trees..........	1.25	.20	□□□□□
1CVP68	39c	Snowman..........	1.25	.20	□□□□□
1CVP69	39c	Dove..........	1.25	.20	□□□□□
a.		Vert. Strip, 2 each #1CVP66-1CVP69	10.00		□□□□□
					□□□□□

Scott No.	Description	Unused Value	Used Value

NON-PERSONALIZABLE POSTAGE

3CVP1

3CVP2

These stamps, approved by the USPS, were non-personalizable stamps that could be purchased directly from private manufacturers, which shipped them to the customer. Other non-personalizable stamps have been created by a variety of companies, all sold at excessive amounts over face value as "collectibles." Such items are not listed here. Most items created that sold for excessive amounts over face value have vignettes that are licensed images, usually depicting sport team emblems or other sports-related themes, or celebrities.

Personalized postage stamps, first available in 2004, created by a variety of different companies, and heretofore listed with Scott numbers having a "2CVP" prefix, are no longer listed. Personalized stamps, though valid for postage, are not sold at any U.S. Postal Service post office. They are available only by on-line ordering through the company's website. Stamps are only available from the companies in full panes of 20. Each pane is sold at a significant premium above the stated face value to cover the costs of personalization, shipping and handling.

In recent years, there has been a steadily increasing number of private companies, either directly licensed by the USPS or created as spinoff companies of these licensees, creating distinctly different personalized stamps. None of the companies has issued fewer than seven stamps for each rate change, with one issuing as many as 42 different stamps. Because mailing rates set by the USPS are expected to change yearly, the collective output of distinctly different, rate-based stamps from these various companies likely will increase. There are no restrictions in place to prevent more firms from bringing personalized stamps to the marketplace, or to keep stamp producers from offering even more customer options. Some personalized stamps do not differ in any appreciable manner from some of the non-personalizable stamps sold as collectibles and not listed here.

Stamps.com

2007, May, Die Cut

3CVP1 2c	Black & gray	.20	.20
a.	Inscribed "US Postag"	—	—

Die Cut Perf. 5¼ at Right

3CVP2 2c	"Your Photo Here" Ad at Left	.20	.20
a.	Tagged	1.40	1.40

2008

3CVP3 1c	Type of 2007 (3CVP1)	0.20	0.20

LO1

LO2

1LB1

1LB6

1LB8

3LB1

3LB2

4LB1

4LB3

4LB5

4LB8

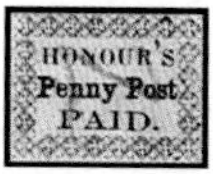

4LB11

4LB13

4LB14

4LB15

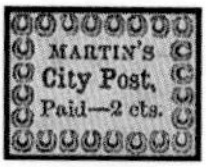

4LB16

4LB18

4LB19

9LB1

10LB1

10LB2

Scott No.		Description	Unused Value	Used Value
CARRIER'S STAMPS				
OFFICIAL ISSUES				
1851				
LO1	(1c)	Franklin, dull blue on *rose*	*6,500.*	*7,500.*
LO2	1c	Eagle, blue, imperf	50.00	*80.00*
1875 REPRINTS, No gum				
LO3	(1c)	Franklin (LO1), blue on *rose*, imperf.	50.00	
LO4	(1c)	Franklin (LO1), blue, perf. 12	*16,000.*	
LO5	1c	Eagle (LO2), blue, imperf.	25.00	
LO6	1c	Eagle (LO2), blue, perf. 12	175.00	
SEMI-OFFICIAL ISSUES				
1850-55, Imperf.				
1LB1	1c	Post Office Despatch, red on *bluish*.	180.00	160.00
1LB2	1c	Post Office Despatch, blue on *bluish*	200.00	150.00
a.		Bluish laid paper	—	—
1LB3	1c	Post Office Despatch, blue	160.00	100.00
a.		Laid paper	200.00	150.00
b.		Block of 14 containing three tete-beche pairs	*6,000.*	
1LB4	1c	Post Office Despatch, green	—	1.000.
1LB5	1c	Post Office Despatch, red	2,250.	1,750.
1856				
1LB6	1c	Carriers Dispatch, blue	130.00	90.00
1LB7	1c	Carriers Dispatch (1LB6), red	130.00	90.00
1857				
1LB8	1c	Horse & Rider, black	65.00	50.00
a.		SENT	100.00	75.00
b.		Short rays	100.00	75.00
1LB9	1c	Horse & Rider (1LB8), red	100.00	90.00
a.		SENT	140.00	110.00
b.		Short rays	140.00	110.00
c.		As "b," double impression		*800.00*
1849-50				
3LB1	1c	"Penny Post.," blue	375.00	180.00
a.		Wrong ornament at left, on cover (not tied)		*400.00*
1851				
3LB2	1c	"Penny Post. Paid," blue (shades) on *slate*	190.00	100.00
1849				
4LB1	2c	Honour's City Express, black on *brown rose*	*10,000.*	

5LB1

5LB2

6LB1

6LB2

6LB7

6LB9

7LB1

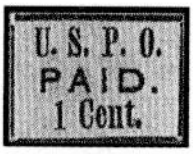

7LB6

7LB11

7LB14

7LB18

8LB1

8LB2

8LB3

HOW TO USE THIS BOOK

The number in the first column is its Scott number or identifying number. Following that is the denomination of the stamp and its color or description. Finally, the values, unused and used, are shown.

Scott No.		Description	Unused Value	Used Value	/ / / / / /
4LB2	2c	Honour's City Express (4LB1), black on *yellow,* cut to shape	—		□□□□□
4LB2A	2c	Honour's City Express (4LB1), black on *bluish gray,* on cover, cut to shape		—	□□□□□
1854					
4LB3	2c	City Post, black		*1,500.*	□□□□□
1849-50					
4LB5	2c	Honour's City Post, black on *bluish,* pelure paper	*750.00*	*500.00*	□□□□□
a.		"Ceuts"	*5,750.*		□□□□□
4LB7	2c	Honour's City Post (4LB5) , black on *yellow*	*750.00*	*1,000.*	□□□□□
a.		"Ccnts"		*14,500.*	□□□□□
1851-58					
4LB8	2c	Paid, Honour's City Post, black on *bluish*	350.00	175.00	□□□□□
a.		Period after Paid	500.00	250.00	□□□□□
b.		Cens	700.00	*900.00*	□□□□□
c.		Conours and Bents		—	□□□□□
4LB9	2c	Paid, Honour's City Post (4LB8), black on *bluish,* pelure paper	*850.00*	*950.00*	□□□□□
4LB10	2c	Paid, Honour's City Post, black on *pink,* pelure paper, on cover	—	*7,000.*	□□□□□
4LB11	(2c)	Honour's Penny Post Paid, black on *bluish*	—	*375.00*	□□□□□
4LB12	(2c)	Honour's Penny Post Paid (4LB11), black on *bluish,* pelure paper	—	—	□□□□□
4LB13	(2c)	Honour's City Post Paid, black on *bluish*	750.00	400.00	□□□□□
a.		Comma after PAID	1,100.		□□□□□
b.		No period after Post	1,400.		□□□□□
1851(?)-58(?)					
4LB14	2c	Kingsman's City Post Paid, black on *bluish*	*1,400.*	*900.00*	□□□□□
a.		"Kingman's" erased		*5,000.*	□□□□□
4LB15	2c	Paid, Kingsman's City Post, black on *bluish*	*800.00*	*800.00*	□□□□□
a.		"Kingman's" erased on cover with 3c #11, tied by pen cancel (unique)		*4,500.*	□□□□□
1858					
4LB16	2c	Martin's City Post, black on *bluish*	*8,000.*		□□□□□
1860					
4LB17	2c	Beckman's City Post (4LB18), black		—	□□□□□
1859					
4LB18	2c	Circle Frame, Steinmeyer's, black on *bluish*	*21,000.*		□□□□□

Scott No.		Description	Unused Value	Used Value
4LB19	2c	Steinmeyer's, Rods & Circles Frame, black on *bluish*	*4,500.*	—
4LB20	2c	Steinmeyer's, Rods & Circles (4LB19), black on *pink*	*200.00*	—
4LB21	2c	Steinmeyer's, Rods & Circles (4LB19), black on *yellow*	200.00	
1854				
9LB1	2c	Williams' City Post, brown	—	*4,000.*
1854				
10LB1		Bishop's, nondenominated, blue	*5,000.*	*4,000.*
10LB2	2c	Bishop's, black on *bluish*	*7,000.*	*7,000.*
1857				
5LB1	(2c)	Wharton's, bluish green	125.00	
1858				
5LB2	(2c)	Brown & McGill's, blue	250.00	*750.00*
5LB3	(2c)	Brown & McGill's (5LB2), black	*4,500.*	*15,000.*
1842				
6LB1	3c	City Despatch Post, black on *grayish*		*2,000.*
1842-45				
6LB2	3c	United States City Despatch Post black on *rosy buff*	*2,500.*	
6LB3	3c	United States City Despatch Post (6LB2) black on *light blue*	*550.00*	500.00
6LB4	3c	United States City Despatch Post (6LB2) black on *green*	*11,500.*	
6LB5	3c	United States City Despatch Post (6LB2) black on *blue green (shades)*	200.00	175.00
a.		Double impression		1,*500.*
b.	3c	black on *blue*	650.00	*250.00*
c.		As "b.," double impression		*850.00*
d.	3c	black on *green*	1,000.	*900.00*
e.		As "d.," double impression	—	
6LB6	3c	black on *pink*		*14,500.*
1846				
6LB7		No. 6LB5 surcharged "2" in red		*70,000.*
1849				
6LB9	1c	U.S. Mail, black on *rose*	100.00	100.00
1849-50				
6LB10	1c	U.S. Mail (6LB9), black on *yellow*	100.00	100.00
6LB11	1c	U.S. Mail (6LB9), black on *buff*	100.00	100.00
a.		Pair, one stamp sideways	*2,850.*	

Scott No.		Description	Unused Value	Used Value
1849-50				
7LB1	1c	U.S.P.O., black on *rose* (with letters L.P.)	450.00	
7LB2	1c	U.S.P.O. (7LB1), black on *rose* (with letter S)	*3,000.*	
7LB3	1c	U.S.P.O. (7LB1), black on *rose* (with letter H)	275.00	
7LB4	1c	U.S.P.O. (7LB1), black on *rose* (with letters L.S.)	400.00	*500.00*
7LB5	1c	U.S.P.O. (7LB1), black on *rose* (with letters J.J.)		*7,500.*
7LB6	1c	U.S.P.O. , no letters, black on *rose*	300.00	250.00
7LB7	1c	U.S.P.O. (7LB6), black on *blue*, glazed	*1,000.*	
7LB8	1c	U.S.P.O. (7LB6), black on *vermilion*, glazed	*700.00*	
7LB9	1c	U.S.P.O. (7LB6), black on *yellow*, glazed	*2,750.*	*2,250.*
1850-52				
7LB11	1c	U.S.P.O., fancy frame, gold on *black*, glazed	175.00	110.00
7LB12	1c	U.S.P.O. (7LB11), fancy frame, blue	400.00	275.00
7LB13	1c	U.S.P.O. (7LB11), fancy frame, black	750.00	*550.00*
7LB14	1c	Eagle above oval, blue on *buff*	3,250.	
1855(?)				
7LB16	1c	Eagle above oval (7LB14), black		*5,000.*
1856(?)				
7LB18	1c	Oval, black	*1,250.*	*2,000.*
1849				
8LB1	2c	U.S. Penny Post, Numeral, black, type 1	*7,000.*	*3,000.*
8LB2	2c	U.S. Penny Post, Numeral, black, type 2	*6,000.*	—
1857				
8LB3	2c	U.S. Penny Post, Star, blue		*22,500.*

RW1

RW6

RW16

RW26

RW27

RW36

RW45

RW58

RW64

RW65

RW67

RW68

RW69

RW70

RW71

RW72

RW73

RW74

RW75

RW76

Scott No.	Description	Unused Value	Used Value	/ / / / / /
HUNTING PERMIT STAMPS				
1934				
RW1	$1 *Mallards Alighting*	800.00	150.00	□□□□□
a.	Imperf., pair	—		□□□□□
b.	Vert. pair, imperf. horiz.	—		□□□□□
1935				
RW2	$1 *Canvasback Ducks Taking to Flight*	800.00	160.00	□□□□□
1936				
RW3	$1 *Canada Geese in Flight*	350.00	75.00	□□□□□
1937				
RW4	$1 *Scaup Ducks Taking to Flight*	400.00	60.00	□□□□□
1938				
RW5	$1 *Pintail Drake and Duck Alighting*	475.00	60.00	□□□□□
1939				
RW6	$1 *Green-Winged Teal*	275.00	45.00	□□□□□
1940				
RW7	$1 *Black Mallards*	250.00	45.00	□□□□□
1941				
RW8	$1 *Family of Ruddy Ducks*	250.00	45.00	□□□□□
1942				
RW9	$1 *Baldpates*	250.00	45.00	□□□□□
1943				
RW10	$1 *Wood Ducks*	125.00	35.00	□□□□□
1944				
RW11	$1 *White-fronted Geese*	135.00	45.00	□□□□□
1945				
RW12	$1 *Shoveller Ducks in Flight*	110.00	25.00	□□□□□
1946				
RW13	$1 *Redhead Ducks*, red brown	55.00	16.00	□□□□□
a.	$1 bright rose pink	*35,000.*		□□□□□
1947				
RW14	$1 *Snow Geese*	57.50	17.50	□□□□□
1948				
RW15	$1 *Bufflehead Ducks in Flight*	60.00	16.00	□□□□□
1949				
RW16	$2 *Greeneye Ducks*	70.00	15.00	□□□□□
1950				
RW17	$2 *Trumpeter Swans in Flight*	95.00	12.00	□□□□□
1951				
RW18	$2 *Gadwall Ducks*	95.00	12.00	□□□□□

Scott No.		Description	Unused Value	Used Value
1952				
RW19	$2	*Harlequin Ducks*	95.00	12.00
1953				
RW20	$2	*Blue-winged Teal*	95.00	12.00
1954				
RW21	$2	*Ring-necked Ducks*	85.00	10.50
1955				
RW22	$2	*Blue Geese*	85.00	10.50
a.		Back inscription inverted	*5,500.*	*4,500.*
1956				
RW23	$2	*American Merganser*	85.00	10.50
1957				
RW24	$2	*American Eider*	85.00	10.50
a.		Back inscription inverted	*5,000.*	
1958				
RW25	$2	*Canada Geese*	85.00	10.50
a.		Back inscription inverted	—	
1959				
RW26	$3	*Labrador Retriever carrying Mallard Drake*	125.00	11.00
a.		Back inscription inverted	*27,500.*	—
1960				
RW27	$3	*Redhead Ducks*	95.00	10.50
1961				
RW28	$3	*Mallard Hen and Ducklings*	110.00	10.50
1962				
RW29	$3	*Pintail Drakes Landing*	125.00	12.50
a.		Back inscription omitted	—	
1963				
RW30	$3	*Pair of Brant Landing*	120.00	12.50
1964				
RW31	$3	*Hawaiian Nene Geese*	110.00	12.50
1965				
RW32	$3	*Three Canvasback Drakes*	110.00	12.50
1966				
RW33	$3	*Whistling Swans*	110.00	12.50
1967				
RW34	$3	*Old Squaw Ducks*	125.00	12.50
1968				
RW35	$3	*Hooded Mergansers*	70.00	10.50

Scott No.	Description	Unused Value	Used Value	/ / / / / /
1969				
RW36	$3 *White-winged Scoters*	70.00	8.00	☐☐☐☐☐
1970				
RW37	$3 *Ross's Geese*	70.00	8.00	☐☐☐☐☐
1971				
RW38	$3 *Three Cinnamon Teal*	45.00	7.75	☐☐☐☐☐
1972				
RW39	$5 *Emperor Geese*	25.00	7.00	☐☐☐☐☐
1973				
RW40	$5 *Stellers Eiders*	20.00	7.00	☐☐☐☐☐
1974				
RW41	$5 *Wood Ducks*	18.00	6.00	☐☐☐☐☐
a.	Back inscription missing, but printed vertically on face of stamp and selvage, from foldover	—		☐☐☐☐☐
1975				
RW42	$5 *Canvasback Decoy and three flying Canvasbacks*	17.50	6.00	☐☐☐☐☐
1976				
RW43	$5 *Family of Canada Geese*	17.50	6.00	☐☐☐☐☐
1977				
RW44	$5 *Pair of Ross's Geese*	17.50	6.00	☐☐☐☐☐
1978				
RW45	$5 *Hooded Merganser Drake*	15.00	6.00	☐☐☐☐☐
1979				
RW46	$7.50 *Green-winged teal*	17.50	7.00	☐☐☐☐☐
1980				
RW47	$7.50 *Mallards*	17.50	7.00	☐☐☐☐☐
1981				
RW48	$7.50 *Ruddy Ducks*	17.50	7.00	☐☐☐☐☐
1982				
RW49	$7.50 *Canvasbacks*	17.50	7.00	☐☐☐☐☐
a.	Orange and violet omitted	*10,000.*		☐☐☐☐☐
1983				
RW50	$7.50 *Pintails*	17.50	7.00	☐☐☐☐☐
1984				
RW51	$7.50 *Widgeon*	17.50	7.00	☐☐☐☐☐
1985				
RW52	$7.50 *Cinnamon Teal*	17.50	8.00	☐☐☐☐☐
a.	Light blue (litho.) omitted	*22,500*		☐☐☐☐☐

Scott No.	Description	Unused Value	Used Value	/ / / / / /
1986				
RW53	$7.50 *Fulvous Whistling Duck*	17.50	7.00	□□□□□
a.	Black omitted	*3,000.*		□□□□□
1987				
RW54	$10 *Redheads*	17.50	9.50	□□□□□
1988				
RW55	$10 *Snow Goose*	17.50	10.00	□□□□□
1989				
RW56	$12.50 *Lesser Scaups*	20.00	10.00	□□□□□
1990				
RW57	$12.50 *Black Bellied Whistling Duck*	20.00	10.00	□□□□□
a.	Back inscription omitted	*375.00*		□□□□□
b.	Black inscription printed on the stamp paper rather than the gum		*3,500.*	□□□□□
1991				
RW58	$15 *King Eiders*	30.00	11.00	□□□□□
a.	Black (engr.) omitted	*20,000.*		□□□□□
1992				
RW59	$15 *Spectacled Eider*	30.00	11.00	□□□□□
1993				
RW60	$15 *Canvasbacks*	27.50	11.00	□□□□□
a.	Black (engr.) omitted	*3,000.*		□□□□□
1994				
RW61	$15 *Red-breasted Mergansers*	30.00	11.00	□□□□□
1995				
RW62	$15 *Mallards*	30.00	11.00	□□□□□
1996				
RW63	$15 *Surf Scoters*	30.00	11.00	□□□□□
1997				
RW64	$15 *Canada Goose*	30.00	11.00	□□□□□
1998				
RW65	$15 *Barrow's Goldeneye*	45.00	20.00	□□□□□
RW65A	$15 *Barrow's Goldeneye* self-adhesive (RW65)	25.00	15.00	□□□□□
1999				
RW66	$15 *Greater Scaup*	40.00	15.00	□□□□□
RW66A	$15 *Greater Scaup*, self-adhesive (RW66)	25.00	12.00	□□□□□
2000				
RW67	$15 *Mottled Duck*	30.00	14.00	□□□□□
RW67A	$15 *Mottled Duck*, self-adhesive (RW67)	22.50	14.00	□□□□□

Scott No.	Description	Unused Value	Used Value
2001			
RW68	$15 *Northern Pintail*..............................	27.50	15.00
RW68A	$15 *Northern Pintail*, self-adhesive (RW68)	25.00	10.00
2002			
RW69	$15 *Black Scoters*	27.50	15.00
RW69A	$15 *Black Scoters*, self-adhesive (RW69)	25.00	10.00
2003			
RW70	$15 *Snow Geese*	27.50	15.00
b.	Imperf, pair	*7,500.*	
c.	Back inscription omitted.................	*4,500.*	
RW70A	$15 *Snow Geese* self-adhesive (RW70)	25.00	10.00
2004			
RW71	$15 *Redheads*	27.50	11.00
RW71A	$15 *Redheads*, ... self-adhesive (RW71)	25.00	10.00
2005			
RW72	$15 *Hooded Mergansers*, type I (no outer framelines).................................	22.50	11.00
b.	Souvenir sheet of 1	*2,000.*	
c.	Type II (black frameline at top, right and bottom).........................	22.50	11.00
RW72A	$15 *Hooded Mergansers*, self-adhesive (RW72).......................................	22.50	11.00
2006			
RW73	$15 *Ross's Goose*	22.50	11.00
b.	Souvenir sheet of 1..........................	*160.00*	
c.	As "b," without artist's signature (error)	*3,000.*	
RW73A	$15 *Ross's Goose,* self-adhesive (RW73)	22.50	11.00
2007			
RW74	$15 *Ring-necked Ducks*..........................	22.50	11.00
b.	Souvenir sheet of 1..........................	*140.00*	
c.	As "b," without artist's signature (error)	*2,250.*	
RW74A	$15 *Ring-necked Ducks,* self-adhesive (RW74)...	22.50	11.00
2008			
RW75	$15 *Northern Pintails*............................	22.50	11.00
b.	Souvenir sheet of 1..........................	75.00	
RW75A	$15 *Northern Pintails,* self-adhesive (RW75)	22.50	11.00
RW76	$15 *Long-tailed Duck and Decoy*...........	22.50	11.00
b.	Souvenir sheet of 1	75.00	
RW76A	$15 *Long-tailed Duck and Decoy,* self-adhesive (RW76)....................	22.50	11.00